Moral Regulation and
Governance in Canada

Moral Regulation and
Governance in Canada
History, Context, and Critical Issues

Canadian Scholars' Press Inc.

Toronto

Moral Regulation and Governance in Canada: History, Context, and Critical Issues
edited by Amanda Glasbeek

First published in 2006 by
Canadian Scholars' Press Inc.
180 Bloor Street West, Suite 801
Toronto, Ontario
M5S 2V6

www.cspi.org

Canadian Scholars' Press gratefully acknowledges financial support for our publishing activities from the Government of Canada through the Book Publishing Industry Development Program (BPIDP) and the Government of Ontario through the Ontario Book Publishing Tax Credit Program.

Library and Archives Canada Cataloguing in Publication

Glasbeek, Amanda, 1967-
    Moral regulation and governance in Canada : history, context and critical issues / Amanda Glasbeek.

 Includes bibliographical references.
ISBN 1-55130-302-7

    1. Deviant behavior--Canada--History. 2. Social legislation--Canada--History. 3. Canada--Moral conditions.
I. Title.

KE417.M67G58 2006   340'.112'0971   C2006-900056-5
KF345.G58 2006

06   07   08   09   10   5   4   3   2   1

Printed and bound in Canada by Marquis Book Printing Inc.

Canadä

Table of Contents

Preface vii
Introduction 1

Part I: Moral Regulation: Genealogy of a Concept 9

    Chapter 1: Social Control: Analytical Tool or Analytical Quagmire?,
    Dorothy E. Chunn and Shelley A.M. Gavigan 11
    Chapter 2: Introduction to Regulating Girls and Women,
    Joan Sangster 31
    Chapter 3: On Moral Regulation: Some Preliminary Remarks,
    Philip Corrigan 57
    Chapter 4: The Struggles of the Immoral: Preliminary Remarks on Moral
    Regulation, Mariana Valverde and Lorna Weir 75
    Chapter 5: The Creation of Homosexuality as a "Social Problem,"
    Gary Kinsman 85
    Chapter 6: Introduction to the Age of Light, Soap, and Water,
    Mariana Valverde 117

Part II: Studying Moral Regulation: Putting a Concept to Work . . 143

    Chapter 7: Regulating the "Respectable" Classes: Venereal Disease, Gender, and
    Public Health Initiatives in Canada, 1914–35, Renisa Mawani . 145
    Chapter 8: Recipes for Democracy? Gender, Family, and Making Female Citizens
    in Cold War Canada, Franca Iacovetta 169
    Chapter 9: Incarcerating "Bad Girls": The Regulation of Sexuality through the
    Female Refuges Act in Ontario, 1920–1945, Joan Sangster . . . 189
    Chapter 10: "Manhunts and Bingo Blabs": The Moral Regulation of Ontario
    Single Mothers, Margaret Hillyard Little 217
    Chapter 11: Almost Anything Can Happen: A Search for Sexual Discourse in the
    Urban Spaces of 1940s Toronto, Mary Louise Adams 233
    Chapter 12: The Space of Africville: Creating, Regulating, and Remembering the
    Urban "Slum," Jennifer J. Nelson 251

Part III: The Limits of Moral Regulation and Beyond 275

Chapter 13: "A Social Structure of Many Souls": Moral Regulation, Government, and Self-Formation, Mitchell Dean. 277

Chapter 14: The Power of Powerlessness: Alcoholics Anonymous's Techniques for Governing the Self, Mariana Valverde. 299

Chapter 15: Welfare Law, Welfare Fraud, and the Moral Regulation of the "Never Deserving" Poor, Dorothy E. Chunn and Shelley A.M. Gavigan . . 327

Chapter 16: "Governmentality" and the Problem of Crime: Foucault, Criminology, Sociology, David Garland. 357

PREFACE

This text emerged out of an upper-year course I teach on moral regulation. I wanted to pull together readings that demonstrated the history of the concept and its evolution in practice, while also pointing to the particularly Canadian and feminist influences in the scholarship. But I also wanted to bypass any definitive claim on what moral regulation means. Instead, it is my hope that this reader demonstrates that sociological work is alive with debates and critical engagements through which scholars present, re-work, and re-think ideas in the ongoing and cumulative project of academic production.

■ A NOTE FROM THE PUBLISHER

Thank you for selecting *Moral Regulation and Governance in Canada: History, Context, and Critical Issues,* edited by Amanda Glasbeek. The editor and publisher have devoted considerable time and careful development (including meticulous peer reviews) to this book. We appreciate your recognition of this effort and accomplishment.

Teaching Features

This volume distinguishes itself on the market in many ways. One key feature is the book's well-written and comprehensive part openers, which help to make the readings more accessible to undergraduate students. The part openers add cohesion to the section and to the whole book. The themes of the book are very clearly presented in these section openers.

The general editor, Amanda Glasbeek, has also greatly enhanced the book by adding pedagogy to close and complete each section. Each part ends with critical thinking questions pertaining to each reading and detailed annotated recommended readings.

INTRODUCTION

[T]he "moral terrain" is difficult if not impossible to map, among other reasons because ... it is not so much a distinct realm but a mode of regulation.

Mariana Valverde and Lorna Weir, 1988:33

■ MORAL REGULATION: THE EVOLUTION OF THE CONCEPT

Moral regulation is hard to pin down. It is a seemingly obvious yet, at the same time, theoretically complex concept. The concept of moral regulation began as a method for understanding the state, and especially the development of the capitalist state. Philip Corrigan initially insisted that "we can only understand moral regulation in terms of state formation, agencies and policies" (1981:323).

Later moral regulation scholars offer a different interpretation. In their 1997 publication, *Making Good: Law and Moral Regulation in Canada, 1867-1939*, Carolyn Strange and Tina Loo identify the ways in which "various branches of law ... are meant to govern our moral conduct" (p. 3). In this approach, moral regulation is the regulation of that which is constituted as moral.

Thus, moral regulation can refer both to a way of doing sociology and to practices which social scientists can study. It has been identified as a method for studying certain processes, such as state-formation and nation-building. It has also been identified as a description of how some behaviours (e.g., alcohol consumption and sexual activity) and subjectivities (e.g., the "bad girl" and welfare mother) get constituted, resisted, and regulated. In part, it is this shifting, enigmatic quality of moral regulation that makes it such an interesting concept to study.

This volume examines the development of moral regulation as a concept, its application to a variety of topics, and the critiques of moral regulation as a method of inquiry. Two interrelated tensions frame the text: (1) the role of the state, and especially the law, as a site of, or mechanism of, moral regulation; and (2) the influences of materialism and post-structuralism on the development of moral regulation.

■ WHAT IS MORAL REGULATION?

> Like some ancient "fear of God," moral regulation works within us so that we become part of the working of the state.
>
> Mary Louise Adams, 1993:119

Mary Louise Adams's above quotation suggests that moral regulation is the modern, secular equivalent of religious fervour in maintaining social order. But the relationship between morality, order, and regulation is more complex than it appears.

Moral regulation offers a series of theoretical, as well as historical, challenges to previous literatures on the complex processes of governing. Moral regulation scholarship has developed in opposition to theories of social control, and in the context of Michel Foucault's insights on power, knowledge, and discourse. Moral regulation scholarship has challenged the "general dichotomization between coercion (associated with the state) and consensus (associated with acculturation and value-systems)" (Corrigan 1981:325) in favour of theories of multi-directional processes of governance. In all, moral regulation is a complex field of scholarship that has had significant implications for both "the moral" and the politics of regulation.

■ WHAT DO WE MEAN BY "MORAL"?

Moral regulation scholars are clearly not the first to study the relationship between morality and political order. But one of the most important contributions that this scholarship has made has been in transforming a politics of "the moral" into a central category of analysis, rather than a descriptive term that typically signifies a politics of (conservative) consciousness. Prior to the development of moral regulation scholarship, analyses of moral reform movements saw such politics as distinct from state development. Often, such analyses treated "the moral" as a religious, sometimes conservative, and typically unstable form of politics. Conversely, the state was presented as the product of a rational, progressive, and inventive evolution, responding to inexorable developments in the social and economic landscape. Moral reformers thus appeared as outside observers of political processes. From this perspective, the increasingly secularized state renders anachronistic the moral reformers of an older age (see, for example, Allen 1971; Cook 1985).

Sometimes, the moral has been presented as a dangerously "backwards" ideology. One example is John McLaren's (1986) otherwise excellent study of the evolution of Canadian prostitution laws. McLaren focuses primarily on how "moral concern and the assumptions on which it proceeds have influenced the development of the criminal law in the area of conduct branded as sexually aberrant" (p. 125). He demonstrates that despite the concerted efforts of moral reformers to find a regulatory resolution to the "social evil," there never was any solid evidence that a crisis existed in the first place. Ultimately, McLaren argues, the "claims of moral zealots" had the ironic effect of making prostitutes *more* vulnerable to abuse and exploitation. McLaren attributes this paradox to the "excessive moral fervour" of the reformers themselves. At the heart of the problem, he writes, was "rhetoric and its capacity for obfuscating the issues" (p. 155). Thus, while acknowledging the importance of morality in the development of criminal law provisions, McLaren presents this relationship as suspect: "If there is a lesson in all of this, it is that those responsible for social policy formulation have to be continually vigilant against being influenced by these features of the crusading mentality" (p. 155).

In stark contrast to these studies of morality is the moral regulation approach. This approach sees morality as a comprehensive politics that cannot be treated as "vacuous rhetorical flourishes" (Valverde 1991:28). Instead of viewing moral politics as an attempt to impose a particular (bourgeois) morality on others, moral regulation scholars treat moral reformers as "concerned with self-transformation"(Hunt 1999:190). Instead of asking how "moral concerns" affected the regulation of sexually problematic behaviours, moral regulation scholars ask why sexuality—an ostensibly private concern—has become important enough to warrant public intervention and action. Finally, rather than treating morality and politics as separate, moral regulation scholars argue that political developments are always conjoined with moral imperatives.

The term "moral regulation" was originally coined by Philip Corrigan (1981) and elaborated by Corrigan and Derek Sayer (1985).[1] In *The Great Arch* (1985:4), Corrigan and Sayer define moral regulation as a project of normalizing, rendering natural, taken for granted, in a word "obvious" what are in fact ontological and epistemological premises of a particular and historical form of social order. Moral regulation is coextensive with state formation, and state forms are always animated and legitimated by a particular moral ethos. Centrally, state agencies attempt to give unitary and unifying expression to what are in reality multifaceted and differential historical experiences to groups within society, denying their particularity.

In this paradigm, the state appears not simply as a mechanism of repression, but also as a means by which subjectivities are constituted. Moral regulation here refers to a mode of sociological inquiry pertaining to the state.

■ THE FEMINIST CONTRIBUTION

In the hands of feminist scholars, moral regulation has undergone several transformations. Feminist scholars have challenged the emphasis on the state as the exclusive site of political developments, while still upholding the central insight that moral regulation involves "forms and norms" (Corrigan 1981:321) that encourage some subjectivities and suppress others.

Feminist moral regulation studies also emphasize that sexuality is essential to the development of moral subjects. These studies link moral regulation to the formation and regulation of sexual subjectivities. In this view, the state is conceptualized as more than a collection of economic interests, and regulation is seen as an activity that occurs beyond the boundaries of the state. Importantly, in this formulation, moral regulation refers not only to a method of inquiry, but also to the regulation of moral categories or conduct in particular historical periods.

■ WHAT DO WE MEAN BY "REGULATION"?

Moral regulation scholarship has also forced a reconsideration of the concept of regulation. Most significantly, the concept of moral regulation has been embraced as an alternative to the social control model. While social control theorists often see the state as a "hammer" exercising total control over passive subjects (Chunn and Gavigan 1988), moral regulation theorists argue that agency plays a role: "A central issue of all processes of governing and regulating [is] agency. Who is it that attempts to govern whom and how those targetted respond should be central questions" (Hunt 1999:19). Thus, the term "regulation" is preferred to "control" in large part because it can better allow for issues of agency and resistance.

This important distinction between "control" and "regulation" also owes much to the influence of Michel Foucault's "simple inversion of commonplace assumptions" about power (Lazarus-Black and Hirsch 1994:3). Foucault argued that power is neither wholly monopolized by the state nor exclusively repressive. Instead, Foucault claimed that power is also productive, constitutive, and exercised through the diffuse construction of knowledges.

In addition to challenging traditional ideas about power, Foucault's work reminds us of the significance of discourse and sexuality to modern life. In the first volume of *History of Sexuality* (1980), Foucault transferred the point of analysis away from the negative content of the Victorian discourses about sex to the "veritable discursive explosion" about sex that occurred in the 19th century. In addition to giving sex and sexuality a history, this approach allows for a consideration of sexual discourses as productive of subjectivities, rather than as prohibitive forces. In other words, messages (or discourses) about sex, even negative ones (such as "sex is dirty"), have a positive or regulatory effect by constructing an environment in which people conduct themselves and assess the conduct of others. These insights on power, knowledge, discourse, and sexuality have been highly influential in the development of moral regulation scholarship.

■ DEBATES AND TENSIONS

As a result of these varying influences in the development of the scholarship, there are substantial debates over the significance of material and discursive forces in the creation and regulation of moral categories. A clear tension runs through moral regulation scholarship. The roles of the state, of control, of repression, and of coercion are consistently counter-posed against the roles of the community, of knowledge, of constitutive powers, and of discipline. This tension follows the more broad split between socialist and post-structuralist scholars.

An example of a post-structuralist scholar, Mariana Valverde has argued that the key to understanding moral reform in turn-of-the-century English Canada is a Foucault-inspired focus on the discursive formations of moral politics. In her analysis, what is significant is the moral reformers' "vision [that] I will here call 'positive' not because it was necessarily good but to distinguish it from negativity, from mere prohibition" (1991:23). Similarly, Mary Louise Adams (1993:118) concludes that "moral regulation helps us to remember that state concerns encompass far more than the traditionally defined realms of economics and politics." These scholars decentre the state and emphasize the productive powers of discourse and extra-legal forms of regulation as key to the larger project of moral regulation.

Yet, for other moral regulation scholars, such as Joan Sangster, focussing too much on the discursive aspects of moral regulation threatens to overshadow the fact that some populations, constituted as in need of moral correction, "experienced a more *repressive* version of regulation" (2001:3, emphasis original). More recently, Dorothy Chunn and Shelley Gavigan, also interested in the coercive power of the state, argue that "the state never ceases to be a player" and that moral regulation "need not be considered as an alternative or necessarily superior concept [to social control]"(2004:223).

For these socialist scholars there are dangers inherent in underestimating the power of the state in controlling "problem" populations. They also argue that it is unwise to conflate all forms of regulation together. Rather, legal mechanisms are seen to operate differently from extra-legal forms of regulation, and to have different effects on those targetted by such exercises of power. As this reader demonstrates, this substantive difference within the moral regulation literature ultimately results in two different lines of inquiry: (1) governmentality, with its emphasis on diffuse, non-state forms of regulation, and (2) a return to theories of the state, control, and coercion.

■ WHY STUDY MORAL REGULATION?

Moral regulation scholars have altered the shape of sociology, largely by transforming the terrain of "the moral" into a central political category that is intimately linked to processes of state- and nation-building enterprises. This area of study is also a uniquely feminist and multi-disciplinary brand of scholarship. Like few other areas of study, it brings together sociologists, historians, criminologists, and political theorists in the collective project of analyzing the contingent, historical, and political processes whereby the categories of "normal" and "deviant" are constituted, contested, resisted, changed, and reconstituted in Canadian society.

Moral regulation is also significant to those sociologists who work outside the field of deviance. Debates and tensions evident in the literature—debates surrounding the nature of power, control, regulation, discourse, and the state—mirror the tensions that have charged sociological enquiry more broadly. In particular, the impact of feminism, sexuality studies, Foucault, historical sociology, criminology, and materialism are rendered visible in the moral regulation literature. In this way, moral regulation stands as an emblematic study of Canadian sociological inquiry at the turn of this century.

■ OVERVIEW OF THIS READER

As noted earlier, this volume examines the development of moral regulation, its application to a variety of topics, and the critiques of moral regulation. Two interrelated tensions frame the text: (1) the role of the state in moral regulation, and (2) the influences of materialism and post-structuralism on the development of moral regulation.

This volume unites the key readings in Canadian moral regulation scholarship. It tracks the evolution of the concept, from theories of social control, to moral regulation, to governmentality, to a return to theories of control.

While the text is largely chronological, each section highlights debates, tensions, and theoretical reconfigurations. The last section demonstrates the links between the predominantly historical-sociological moral regulation scholarship and the history-of-the-present governmentality literatures. It also traces the ways in which moral regulation literature has helped to shape contemporary sociological inquiries.

■ NOTES

1. Stuart Hall also used the term "moral regulation," in a 1980 essay, to refer to the "permissive period" in Britain. Hall's usage, however, does not form an explicit part of the historiography of moral regulation scholarship. For a discussion of Hall's definition of moral regulation, see Dorothy Chunn and Shelley Gavigan's 2004 essay, in this volume.

■ REFERENCES

Adams, Mary-Louise. "In Sickness and in Health: State Formation, Moral Regulation, and Early VD Initiatives in Ontario." *Journal of Canadian Studies* 28, 4 (1993):117-130.

Allen, Richard. *The Social Passion: Religion and Social Reform in Canada, 1914-1928.* Toronto: University of Toronto Press, 1971.

Chunn, Dorothy and Shelley Gavigan. "Welfare Law, Welfare Fraud, and the Moral Regulation of the 'Never Deserving' Poor." *Social and Legal Studies* 13, 2 (2004):219-243.

———. "Social Control: Analytic Tool or Analytic Quagmire?" *Contemporary Crises* 12 (1988):107-124.

Cook, Ramsay. *The Regenerators: Social Criticism in Late Victorian English Canada.* Toronto: University of Toronto Press, 1985.

Corrigan, Philip. "On Moral Regulation: Some Preliminary Remarks." *Sociologial Review* 29, 2 (1981):313-338.

Corrigan, Philip and Derek Sayer. *The Great Arch: English State Formation as Cultural Revolution.* London: Basil Blackwell, 1985.

Foucault, Michel. *The History of Sexuality, Volume I: An Introduction.* Trans. Robert Hurley. New York: Vintage Books, 1980.

Hall, Stuart. "Reformism and the Legislation of Consent." In National Deviancy Conference, eds., *Permissiveness and Control: The Fate of the Sixties Legislation.* London: MacMillan, 1980:1-43.

Hunt, Alan. *Governing Morals: A Social History of Moral Regulation.* Cambridge: Cambridge University Press, 1999.

Lazarus-Black, Mindie and Susan Hirsch. "Introduction." In Lazarus-Black and Hirsch, eds. *Contested States: Law, Hegemony, and Resistance* (New York: Routledge, 1994).

McLaren, John. "Chasing the Social Evil: Moral Fervour and the Evolution of Canada's Prostitution Laws, 1867-1917." *Canadian Journal of Law and Society* 1 (1986):125-165.

Sangster, Joan. *Regulating Girls and Women: Sexuality, Family, and the Law in Ontario, 1920-1960.* Toronto: Oxford, 2001.

Strange, Carolyn and Tina Loo. *Making Good: Law and Moral Regulation in Canada, 1867-1939.* Toronto: University of Toronto Press, 1997.

Valverde, Mariana. *The Age of Light, Soap, and Water: Moral Reform in English Canada, 1885-1925.* Toronto: University of Toronto Press, 1991.

——— and Lorna Weir. "The Struggles of the Immoral: Preliminary Remarks on Moral Regulation." *Resources for Feminist Research* 17, 3 (1988):31-34.

PART I

MORAL REGULATION:
GENEALOGY OF A CONCEPT

This section includes some of the key readings in the evolution of moral regulation. It introduces the central themes of this volume—namely, the tensions between Marxist and post-structuralist theories of deviance, power and the state; and the debates surrounding the role of the state, and of coercive mechanisms specifically, in the regulation of deviance and normality.

The term "genealogy" is borrowed from Michel Foucault. It is used deliberately in this section to underscore both the significance of Foucauldian analyses to the development of moral regulation and to alert the reader to the fact that the readings are not meant to provide a "scientific" or complete history of moral regulation. Instead, these readings are intended to introduce some of the key writings in the field of moral regulation. The readings in this volume are also intended to introduce students to the debates that have marked moral regulation scholarship from the start.

Dorothy Chunn and Shelley Gavigan outline the dissatisfaction with, or limitations of, the theory of social control, the model that precedes moral regulation. As they show, the term "social control" has been used so much that it no longer holds analytic power. In addition, the term is not very useful, either to a critical appraisal of the state or to feminist categories of inquiry. It is these kinds of insights that will lead to moral regulation scholarship.

Joan Sangster's insightful overview of Foucault's major contributions raises similar issues. She critically assesses Foucauldian scholarship in terms of how it affects our ability to think about power, regulation, and the state. She also assesses the relevance of Foucault to the specific concerns of feminist scholars, and especially to those studying female crime and deviance.

The readings then turn to moral regulation itself. Admittedly a difficult read, Philip Corrigan's "Preliminary Remarks" are indispensable as the initial, classic offerings on moral regulation. Corrigan presents moral regulation as a theory of the state. His aim is to find a middle ground between Emile Durkheim's notions of a moral consensus and Marxist theories of conflict, especially with respect to the capitalist state and emerging notions of regulation.

Readers should note the fundamental difference between Corrigan's "preliminary remarks" and those of Mariana Valverde and Lorna Weir. As the concept of moral regulation began to draw more heavily on Foucauldian analysis, and was adapted both to the Canadian context and to feminist categories of analysis, the concept underwent a near revolution in meaning. Rather than a theory of the state, moral regulation is, for Valverde and Weir, a specific type of regulation located in "the nation." This type of regulation is largely concerned with the production of what they call "ethical subjectivity." Arguably, it is Valverde and Weir's definition of moral regulation that more dramatically shapes the evolution of the concept in Canadian sociology.

This expanding definition of moral regulation is evident as moral regulation "comes of age." Gary Kinsman's essay offers an early example of moral regulation theory in action. He takes the theoretical formulations of Corrigan (and Corrigan and Sayer) and applies them to the Canadian history of sexuality. Kinsman argues that moral regulation is important for elaborating the relationship between the state and sexual regulation.

Mariana Valverde's book on moral regulation in English Canada was a groundbreaking study. In this excerpt, Valverde outlines the varying influences of Foucault, materialist analysis, feminism, sexuality studies, race, and moral tropes. She does this in order to understand the historical constructions of "ethical subjectivity" in Canada.

CHAPTER I

SOCIAL CONTROL:
ANALYTICAL TOOL OR ANALYTICAL QUAGMIRE?

Dorothy E. Chunn and Shelley A.M. Gavigan

I find Social Control a key that unlocks many doors.

E.A. Ross

The term "social control" has lately become something of a Mickey Mouse concept.

S. Cohen

There is probably no concept which is used more widely and with less precision than that of "social control."[1] Given the lack of agreement about what "social control" is, researchers usually employ the term in one of two ways. Either they assume that its meaning is obvious and requires no clarification, or they begin with a perfunctory acknowledgment of the definitional problems associated with the concept and proceed to use it anyway. The eclecticism of the latter approach has stimulated attempts over the years to produce a universally applicable definition of "social control" that could be employed both systematically and scientifically in research (Clark and Gibbs 1965, Gibbs 1977, Janowitz 1978, Mayer 1983). While these efforts are commendable and may ultimately prove fruitful, the ongoing elusiveness of such a formulation has led us in a different direction. We have concluded that the concept of "social control" incorporates ambiguities which severely undermine its effectiveness as an analytical tool. The argument is developed in two stages: first, by tracing the historical evolution of the concept to illustrate the problematic nature of a "social control" model; and second, by demonstrating, through an assessment of the "women, law and social control" literature, its inadequacy as an analytical construct.[2]

■ "SOCIAL CONTROL" AND AMERICAN SOCIOLOGY; ONE MODEL FITS ALL

To understand the limitations of the concept of "social control" requires a brief discussion of its historical origins and subsequent elaboration. Janowitz (1975: 82, see also 1976; 1978) points out that the term was first used by the classical 19th-century European theorists to draw a link between sociology and social philosophy. However, there seems to be express agreement that the self-conscious formulation of "social control" as an analytical concept and its utilization in sociological research were the accomplishments of American academics (Schwendinger and Schwendinger 1974: 198–221, Janowitz 1975: 87, 1978: 33, Brown 1978: n.l, Hunt 1978: 19–20, Gibbons 1979, Adlam and Rose 1981, Cohen and Scull 1983: 5–7). Since the 1890s, American sociologists have formulated two definitions of "social control" which, although seemingly contradictory, share a common focus; namely, the question of how social order is maintained in pluralist democracies, specifically the United States. One definition is premised on the assumption that societal integration is achieved through the operation of numerous non-coercive social control processes; the other on the belief that coercive state control mechanisms, particularly law, play the most crucial role in reproducing the status quo (Janowitz 1975, 1978; Rothman 1981; Cohen 1985).

Both versions of "social control" have been products of the functionalist and interactionist strands within American sociology. What might be called the benign formulation originated in the work of E.A. Ross during his tenure at Stanford University (Ross 1969: xv; see also Geis 1964, Schwendinger and Schwendinger 1974); wound its way via the pages of the *American Journal of Sociology* into the writings of various Chicago School members (Cooley 1966, Park and Burgess 1969: c.1, c.12); and from there into the thought and publications of Talcott Parsons (1951). The basic concern of all these men was to explain how "fundamental harmony" and "cooperation" were being achieved in America without frequent recourse to or reliance on "coercion or external discipline" (Rothman 1981: 11). What they concluded was that informal, non-institutionalized mechanisms of social control, "located in primary social activities," were the key to the maintenance of social order (Hunt 1978: 147). Thus, social control was viewed primarily "in terms of the socialisation process operating through the internalization of values" (*ibid*). It is this conception of "social control" which has surfaced in the work of some contemporary control theorists (Reckless 1961, Hirschi 1969, Downes and Rock 1982, c.9).[3]

The conception of social control as organized repression emerged in the 1960s and 1970s and owed an intellectual debt to the observations of Tannenbaum (1938) and Lemert (1951, 1967) about the deleterious effects of official stigmatization. The idea that the social control exercised by state agents produced and reinforced deviance was extensively elaborated and refined by the neo-Chicagoan labelling theorists of the 1960s and 1970s. During the same period, radical deviancy theorists (Quinney 1974, Spitzer 1975, Chambliss 1976, Platt 1977) developed macro analyses of the functions served by the *essentially* undemocratic and coercive character of the institutions used by "top dogs" or ruling classes to impose their will on the exploited underclasses in American society (Rothman 1981, Cohen 1985). Premised on notions of coercion and cooptation, the "new" version of "social control" constituted an apparently severe critique of the existing capitalist social order in the United States. The concept of "social control" as "doing good" had become the concept of "social control" as "doing bad."

It is important to emphasize how tremendously influential the concept of social control has been among Anglo-American sociologists of deviance throughout the 20th century. Researchers applied the concept in one sphere after another until it was eventually "taken for granted" that weak or strong, informal or formal controls were "manifest in every single phase of social life" (Schwendinger and Schwendinger 1974: 203; see also Janowitz 1975, 1978: 39–44). Moreover, both the benign and coercive definitions of social control have been widely adopted by academics in other disciplines such as law (Pound 1930, 1942) and history (Stedman Jones 1977, Pisciotta 1981, Mayer 1983). Thus, to a great extent, the discourse of North American sociology and of related disciplines in the 20th century has been, and is, the discourse of social control. Functionalists and interactionists, Marxists and non-Marxists all employ the concept, many uncritically, assuming that its meaning is one of the two previously outlined.

But, from the late 1970s, the recognition has spread that "social control" is an extremely problematic term. Brown (1978: 126; see also Hay 1978: 107) describes it as "an ambiguous concept" which is difficult to use in research because definitions vary and the range of phenomena to which "social control" is applied varies as well. However, despite these acknowledgments, many academics argue that it would be exceedingly difficult to coin a superior concept "to describe the processes by which society is preserved from disruption"; they express optimism that the problems associated with the term "social control" can be eliminated through "clear definition and consistent use of the concept" (Hay 1978: 108; see also Janowitz 1978, Mayer 1983). Indeed, a number of sociologists are presently engaged in attempts to formulate systematic theories of social control (Davis 1980, Anderson and Davis 1983, Melossi 1985).

However, the hegemony of the concept is not absolute. On the contrary, some trenchant criticisms of the term have appeared in recent years (Muraskin 1976, Schwendinger and Schwendinger 1974, Stedman Jones 1977, Hall et al. 1978, Corrigan and Sayer 1981, Hall and Scraton 1981, Rothman 1981). Despite the faith of its adherents, therefore, critics have maintained that the concept of "social control" suffers from some very serious flaws which stunt its efficacy as an analytical tool, and provide good reason for its abandonment by critical academics. On the one hand, they argue that, as an American "invention" and export, the term is characterized by a certain ethnocentricity and is thus unavoidably encumbered with the ideological baggage of liberalism. On the other, they point to the fact that, whether we are speaking about the benign or coercive formulation of "social control," researchers use the concept as if it is a universally applicable one.

What this means, then, is that a "social control" model is essentially ahistorical and determinist. These criticisms are elaborated by Hall et al. (1978: 195) in a short, but damning, comment which indicts what they call the contemporary "control-culture" approach for its lack of focus on historically specific types of state or political regime. Thus, the "social control" model fails to distinguish not only between different kinds of social formations but also between social formations of the same general type (for example, market societies). Rather, it suggests either the natural evolution of informal/formal social controls or the arbitrary imposition of controls by state agents and agencies. Moreover, although inextricably tied to the liberal democratic, capitalist social formations of the 20th century, the concept of social control as employed by researchers frequently becomes a determinist one because it is devoid of any theorization of the state. The latter, then, remains an undifferentiated entity in both the benign and coercive formulations of "social control." In the former, it either assumes the role of neutral arbiter or acts as an advocate of the "best interests" of citizens (Ross 1969). In the latter, it is reified as an omnipotent, essentially malevolent Leviathan (Matza 1969). These monolithic formulations leave little room for resistance or self-determination—collective or individual—on the part of those who are controlled.

We agree with the critics about the ahistorical, determinist character of the "social control" model. Indeed, when placed in context, both the benign and coercive definitions of social control are clearly linked to specific configurations of social conditions that promoted their ascendancy at particular points in time. Thus, Ross's concept of social control was the result of his attempts to confront and explain the extensive social change that was sweeping the United States and other Western market societies in the late 19th century. A coalescence of political, economic and demographic lines of development—namely, urbanization, industrialization and universal suffrage—during the period from the 1880s to the 1930s created the foundations of the welfare state

(Garland 1981, 1985, Hall 1984). In America, the upheaval wrought by these changes was exacerbated by the influx of numerous ethnic, religious and national groups from Europe as well as massive internal migration from farms to cities.

While Durkheim was describing the movement from mechanical to organic solidarity, then, Ross (1969) was simultaneously discussing the shift from natural, undifferentiated societies to composite or differentiated ones. This evolutionary process, he argued, was characterized by the emergence of private property and free enterprise; the growth of impersonal and transient urban relationships; and a high degree of occupational mobility, deterioration of marriage, kinship and religious traditions and technological change (Ross 1969; see also Schwendinger and Schwendinger 1974: 204–211). "Social control" emerged as the pivotal concept in a reformulation of liberalism which accompanied the ideological shift from an emphasis on individualism and the minimal state characteristic of the classical *laissez-faire* state to a focus on individualization and the interventionist state characteristic of the social welfare state (Garland 1985). Ross perceived the United States in ideal-type terms as a "classless" or "democratic" form of society where "social control" would ultimately replace class conflict and class control (Ross 1969: 376–395).

As a quintessential Progressive, Ross did not believe that capitalism and social classes could or should be eliminated, but he was convinced that the rough edges could be smoothed off and disruptive conflicts between individuals and groups eliminated. In addition to the state functioning as the institutional arena for conflict resolution, Ross also envisaged other kinds of relationships which would prevent selfish interest groups from dominating differentiated societies (*ibid*). Thus, although capitalists were strong, countervailing forces of "public opinion," tradition and enlightened politicians (for example, Theodore Roosevelt) would maintain a balance. Ross and his "progressive" successors, then, formulated a concept of "social control" premised on assumptions about harmony, cooperation and progress. As the benign concept of "social control" worked its way into the work of the pre-WWII functionalists and from there into modern American sociological thought (Hunt 1978: 19), it increasingly came to mean the "scientific management" of people by technocrats and experts. Confident of their ability to "do good," psychologists, social workers and other professionals provided assistance in the mobilization of various resources for the production of conformity.

However, the coercive version of "social control," which made its debut in the 1960s and was refined during the 1970s, strongly challenged the conventional assumption that informal social controls were the fundamental basis, or *essence* of social order. Like its benign counterpart, the repressive model of "social control" emerged within the context of particular historical conditions. Some contemporary analysts (Scull 1977, Cohen 1985) argue that another fundamental restructuring of Western market societies is in progress. While this has not yet been demonstrated unequivocally, it can definitely be established that a widespread perception of "crisis"—fiscal, political, legal—in liberal democracies formed the backdrop for the reconceptualization of "social control" (Unger 1976, Scull 1977, Hall et al. 1978, Janowitz 1978). Indeed, radical criminologists, sociologists and historians not only brought "control," in the sense of repressive state control, to centre stage but also called for forms of political practice linked to such a conception (Garland and Young 1983: 6).

Unfortunately, the radical promise of these "social control" theorists has not been realized. Their critique remains underdeveloped; in radical analyses, "control" remains a "vague force" and revolutionary politics have been confined almost exclusively "to the written page or conducted in abstract" (*ibid*). In some ways, then, the coercive formulation of "social control" does not represent an advance over the traditional theorizing about it. As Garland has suggested in another context, "A *philosophical* inversion is not in itself a *theoretical* advance" (1983: 50). Thus, the presumed critical function of the coercive model of "social control" can be seriously questioned.

At the same time, although no systematic accounts of "control" have been produced, radical theorists tend to assume that any "control" is in and of itself bad or unjust. Such an assumption has led to what Adlam and Rose (1981) call the "tedious repetition" of "unmaskings" of the social control functions of psychiatry, medicine, social policy and the welfare state, as well as the criminal law. This denunciation of the state and all its works is not radical, however, because everything and therefore nothing can count as an instance of repressive social control (*ibid*). The controlled, then, are passive robots at the mercy of a carceral apparatus which expands almost daily. But to what extent do people voluntarily participate in their own subjugation? To what degree do they receive genuine assistance from the people who presumably control them? To what extent do individuals and groups resist efforts to repress them? These are questions which we believe cannot be addressed within the constraints of a "social control" model.

■ LAW AS SOCIAL CONTROL: OBVIOUS OR OBFUSCATION?

The limitations of the "social control" model become more apparent when the implications of its coupling with law are examined. Yet, despite (or perhaps because of) the frequent use in the literature of the law and social control couplet, which is enjoying a certain renaissance in both criminology and sociology of law, in literature of both critical (see for e.g., Greenaway and Brickey 1978, Hamner 1981, Scull and Cohen 1983, Ratner and McMullen 1985, Snider 1985, Boyd 1986) and non-critical literature alike (see, e.g., Black 1978, Hagan et al. 1979, Vago 1981, Gibbs 1982), what is curious is the absence of any serious interrogation of this pairing. It seems that the social reality of law, its *raison d'être*, is pure, simple and obvious: it is an instrument of (social) control. And yet, its appeal is precisely the trap: because of its "somewhat self-evident character there has been insufficient attention to the implications that flow from the 'law as social control' perspective" (Hunt 1978: 146).

In the non-critical socio-legal literature, resort to the formal social control of law is said to be had when informal methods of control are no longer available or capable of producing acquiescence. The formal shores up or enforces the values of the informal. The baldest (if admittedly least critical) restatement of law as social control is found in the work of Donald Black (1976, 1978). Social control is the "normative aspect of social life ... which defines and responds to deviant behaviour" (1978: 105); Black defines (rather than locates) law as "governmental social control" (1978: 2). He eschews a jurisprudential approach to the sociology of law: law is simply "behaviour," a quantifiable, measurable variable:

> The quantity of law varies in time and space. It varies across centuries, decades and years, months and days, even the hours of the day. It varies across societies, regions, communities, neighborhoods, families, and relationships of every kind. It varies across the world and its history, the settings of a society or community, the cases in a court, the daily round of a policeman (1978: 3–4).

Black's conception of law as social control is not particularly innovative and can be characterized as an updated restatement of Durkheim (Menzies 1983); however, it is important because of its influence in sociology of law and in criminology. But beyond that, Black's work both exemplifies and illustrates the weakness of the perspective: law is exclusively bound up with the notion of sanctioning "deviant behaviour" and it explicitly *denies* the importance of historical specificity. In his sociology of law, the formal social control of law is a natural and inevitable consequence of social life:

> The constraint of society over its members is thus the constraint that flows naturally from the primary constituents of social life itself. The constraint that is exercised through the informal mechanisms of social control is seen as being essentially a process of self-regulation endemic in the postulation of social life itself. Now, if law is regarded as one of the forms of social control there is implied a view that they form a continuum ranged along a scale from informal means to the more institutionalised forms of which law is regarded as the most specialised form (Hunt 1976: 27–28).

This notion of a continuum between informal and formal is not confined to the non-critical literature in the sociology of law. Indeed, the radical social control literature evinces the same commitment, although the formal enforcement of informal relations is given a coercive edge. However, within this literature, even the apparent retreat from formality is seen to be a trick, or as Maureen Cain has observed, "a disguised form of state expansion" (1985: 339).

The commitment of radical social theorists to a conception of social control is puzzling. As we have argued above, one is bound to ask what is *social* about the control of law and how are we to identify its manifestations? Is *all* law committed to social control? What is the role of the state? Of ideology? Admittedly these are questions not even posed by the mainstream writers. However, if the answers to these questions seem obvious to some, it is, we would argue, because critical scholars have not been inclined to seriously interrogate the social reality of law in different historical contexts, but rather have been content to apply *a priori* theories to the place of law.

Despite its powerful challenge to the hegemony of jurisprudence in the sociology of law (see Hunt 1976, 1978), one must query the analytical utility of conceptualizing law as simply a form of "social control," with or without a coercive edge. How, if at all, can it facilitate our understanding of resistance, struggle and social change? Can it help us understand the nature and significance in shifts in both the position and the role, as well as the content, of law in different historical contexts (see Hall et al. 1978, Hall 1980, Smart 1984)? As Gareth Stedman Jones has argued:

> There is no political or ideological institution which could not in some way be interpreted as an agency of social control. There is no indication in the phrase of who the agents or instigators of social control may be: no indication of any common mechanism whereby social control is enforced: no constant criterion whereby we may judge whether social control has broken down ... (1977: 164).

In its narrow emphasis on the sanctioning of deviance by the imposition of controls, the possibility of understanding *whole* social formations and *whole* legal systems—the totality rather than a segment—is neglected (Sugarman 1983: 214). This then highlights yet another problematic aspect of the "law as social control" perspective: the focus is invariably upon criminal law, penal law, and forms of administrative law such as welfare and mental health law, and the emphasis is upon the manipulative, "containing" aspects of that law. Just as Hunt (1982) has criticized the coercion-consent dichotomy within sociology of law, so too it is clear that within both the "benign" and "critical" social control perspectives the dichotomy is reinforced with different emphasis: the law either controls or coerces—the result is the same: the targeting of a problem population for control.

As we have suggested above, the concept has been employed in radical critiques of law to attempt to expose and demystify liberal and legislative reforms and policies (of which there are fewer and fewer in the current context). As a result, the work of critical "social control" theorists must be located at the "instrumentalist" level of Marxist theorizing on law (see Hunt 1981a), adopting (albeitly implicitly) a rejection of law as a (useful) site of struggle, coupled with a desire to unmask the dark side of the legal reform. Hunt himself does not address the "critical" social control literature; however, we would argue that it finds its place in his conceptualization of "instrumentalist" theorizing on law. This is important, because although Hunt cogently argues that within the "law as social control" perspective there is a tendency to neglect the coercive character of law (1976: 28, 1978: 147, 1981a: 96), it is clear that within the radical/critical social control literature there is identified a thinly masked coercive edge to the thrust of "legal control."

■ FORMAL AND INFORMAL CONTROL

Within the "law as social control perspective," there is identified a particular relationship with "informal" control. The formal control of law is juxtaposed with informal social controls and the relationship is unequivocal: law varies inversely with other social controls (Black 1978, Hagan et al. 1979). The position advanced is that men are controlled by formal controls and women are controlled by informal controls (specifically the "informal control process of childcare": Hagan et al. 1979: 27)—the model presents "functional alternatives" and purports to explain the apparently differential sanctioning of conduct of men and women (see Barrett 1980: 236). And although the "invisibility" of men and women in the private and public realms respectively is acknowledged (Hagan et al. 1979: 27), the ideological dimensions of this neat, static bifurcation of the world, and its coercive implications, are not interrogated.

This emphasis on formal and informal neither apprehends nor addresses the ideological character of the processes of the state and the law. It reproduces an image of society in which there is both a simple bifurcation between formal and informal and an implied continuum between the two (Hunt 1976, 1978): a reinforcement of the informal by the formal. To divide society unproblematically into two realms—the formal and informal (or the public and the private)—is to neglect the ideological nature of these two "discrete" realms and to ignore the *nature* of the relationship between the two. Indeed, insofar as it contributes to the notion that the "formal" law either does not or ought not intrude into the ordinary and everyday workings of a smoothly running informal sphere, it distorts (and directs attention away from) the nature of the law's contribution to the construction of the "public" and "private" spheres. To put it at its simplest, one cannot opt out of the law and seek refuge in the invisibility and sanctuary of the "informal" realm: as Julia Brophy and Carol Smart have argued, "the law still has something [indeed much] to say about our domestic lives and intimate relations and we cannot assert its irrelevance by ignoring it" (1985: 1). The nature and social significance of "informal" relationships may change; indeed, legislative initiatives of the 1970s in Canadian family law and the amended, expanded definitions of "spouse" for the purpose of maintenance and child support, but significantly not property, bestowed a legal status upon previously "subterranean" relationships.[4] The "family" is still defined by law, and notwithstanding gender-neutral references to "spouses" and "parent," it is still taken to mean male adult, female adult, and their biological or adopted children.

Feminists have identified the importance of the "private sphere" and, at the same time, the essentially ideological nature of a reified split between the public and the private. For instance, while Tove Stang Dahl and Annika Snare (1978) identify the importance of the "informal" control of women, in particular the male-dominated family household, their analysis expressly addresses the coercive nature of the "informal" or "private" sphere, with conflicting interests between wife and husband, and the "status quo" effect of its invisibility (1978: 22). Further, they explicitly identify the role of the *state* in *constructing* and supporting the home as a private prison for women. As Michèle Barrett has observed, "This argument relies on a recognition of the role of the state in maintaining the myth of a separation of the public from the private sphere, according to which women are held to occupy a privileged (albeit at the same time restricted) place in the private arena" (1980: 239–40). Gender becomes not simply a variable in "sexual stratification": gender relations are social relations that are socially constructed, the subject and site of struggle, and in most social contexts the locus of the oppression of women.

■ LAW AND THE SOCIAL CONTROL OF WOMEN

Renée Kasinsky's (1978) analysis of rape and the social control of women is illustrative of the instrumental and coercive emphasis of the critical social control perspective, as applied to women:

> In addition to controlling and psychologically assaulting the rape victim, the law and legal practices also exert social control over the entire female population through the wide fear of rape. The law and court processes help legitimize the assailants' actions through the lack of prosecution. Women soon learn that they cannot rely upon the authority of the State, controlled by male interests, to protect themselves from rape (1978: 63).

In feminist accounts of social control, the "social" is really "male" and the "control" emanates from the law, legal practices, the state—all controlled by "male interests" (see also Hanmer 1981). The "social control" of women is thus achieved by the direct and instrumental manipulation of the law and the state by male interests (see also MacKinnon 1983).

As others have argued (see e.g., Petchesky 1984, Brophy and Smart 1985), there are both theoretical and practical limitations to this approach to law. In arguing that the law and the state represent the interests of men as a group, one is hard pressed to offer a coherent explanation for changes in the law which have not resulted from "male" pressure nor witnessed benefits for "men" as a whole (for example, the repeal of spousal immunity in sexual assault legislation in Canada). Implicit as well in this position is the notion that "male interests" may be understood to be unproblematically mono-lithic (Smart 1984)—a position which is rich in polemics but will not withstand serious scrutiny, particularly if class, race and ethnicity are considered.

An insistence on both historical specificity and the importance of the role of law in "organizing" consent is a recent theme in socio-legal research (see, e.g., Hay 1975, Thompson 1975, Hall et al. 1978, Hall 1980). These issues are no less important for an understanding of the nature of the law's contribution to the oppression of women. And while the gaze must be broad, the focus must be precise. For instance, the reformist legislation of two periods of the postwar British state in the area of morality has been carefully analyzed. These legislative initiatives, which crossed the civil/criminal boundaries of legal classification, dealt, *inter alia*, with prostitution, suicide, obscen-ity in the first period (1950s) and with abortion, contraception, homosexuality and divorce in the later period (1960s) (Hall 1980). The thrust of the legislative reforms has often been characterized as one of liberalization and permissiveness (cf. Greenwood and Young 1980), although as Hall illustrates, the core of the tendency of the legis-lation was increased state regulation coupled with selective privatization (1980: 18). Although he examines the limited nature of some of the reforms, he cautions against posing the issue in "too simple and binary a form"—that is, viewing them as a tight-ening of control under the veneer of reform (1980: 18). The message of the legislation was directed toward the regulation of morality: "that is, inevitably it was about sexual practice" (1980: 20). The target of the "message" was not simply the "problem" popu-lation directly affected by the legislation (for example, homosexual men, consumers of sexual services, obscene literature and so on); rather, Hall argues, the principal object/subject of the legislation was the position of women—a reshaping of the field of female sexual conduct (see also Smart 1981). Rather than identifying simply the limits of reform, Hall insists that the issue must be approached with a more theoretically informed perspective:

This attempt to reshape the field of female sexual conduct must be set in the context of other practices and discourses concerning women in the period, and against the material conditions affecting their position (1980: 21).

The two periods witnessed somewhat different thrusts, the legislation of the 1950s being involved in the more general ideological campaign—characterized by the "reconstruction of femininity" (1980: 21)—to return women to the home, marriage and family. The economic policy and planning of the British state promoted, and was thought to depend upon, consumption within the "private and familial sphere" and "women had to be located at the heart and centre of the principal unit of consumption, the family" (1980: 23). In the 1960s, the combined effect of the growing women's movement and wider access to abortion and contraception facilitated the "partial break" with the domestic ideal of the 1950s.

If one is committed to developing a coherent explanation of the impact and significance of this constellation of legislation which attempted to reconstruct sexual practices, it is clear that the "law as social control" couplet is too blunt and imprecise an analytical instrument to detail the full social significance thereof. It can be argued, for instance, that the "named" targets of individual pieces of legislation were not necessarily those most affected; nor is it tenable to argue that the net effect of the "restructuring" of the field of female sexual practice was simply the widening of the net of control over women's sexuality (although a strong argument can be made with respect to the punitive control of prostitutes—see Smart 1981), because some of the legislation gave women some room to manoeuvre, either directly as in abortion law reform (cf. Mackinnon 1983) or indirectly as in the case of divorce law reform. The sustained support of the British state in the postwar period for a particular model of family household and familial ideology (through social policy and legislative initiatives) was far more problematic for women (see McIntosh 1978, Barrett 1980, Taylor 1981).

When applied to women, then, the "law as social control" perspective neglects this important insight that the position and importance of law shifts in different historical contexts (Hall 1980). These shifts are neither simply nor easily imposed from "above" but may be forced from "below" through resistance, opposition and struggle (see, for example, Linebaugh 1975). This is as true of women's struggles and resistance as it is for other social groups. To understand the significance of different forms of struggle, one requires, as Stuart Hall and his colleagues have argued, a "more differentiated historically located analysis":

In such a perspective, it is precisely the whole repertoire of struggle—strategies, positions, solutions—which must inform the analysis, and which throws a revealing light back onto those sections of the [working] class taking or driven along the specific path of "criminalisation" (1978: 188).

Changes in legal definitions and categories of crime, or indeed in legal reforms generally, must be understood within the context of struggle not simply as concessions granted voluntarily, benevolently or with "manipulation aforethought." This is as important for an understanding of the nature of and significance of class struggle historically as it is for an understanding the historical contexts of women's struggles for equality at law.

In 19th- and early 20th-century England, the development of the notion of the importance of mothers to young children, and indeed the ideology of motherhood (see Davin 1978), was inextricably bound up with a long struggle by women to challenge the bald patriarchal principles of the English law of husband and wife (see Brophy and Smart 1981), which had long held that the children of a marriage were the children of the father. In this century, the ideology of "motherhood" has reinforced the notion that woman's proper place is in the home and that her secondary position is in the work force. Still, some ground in real terms was gained by women within the family by virtue of the "privileging" of women's/mothers' importance to children (in the best interests of the children). Similarly, Smart's (1984) analysis illuminates the shifting terrain of law, and shows that in different social contexts, the meaning and impact of the same piece of legislation may be profoundly contradictory—as in the case of matrimonial property law in the late 19th century, when legislation for the first time provided for the ownership of separate property by married women, to the 1950s, when courts interpreted the right to own separate property to mean an ability to make equal contributions to acquisition of property. Thus the principle of formal equality enshrined in the 19th-century legislation was used by 20th-century courts against married women unable to demonstrate any real (financial) contribution to the family home.

Clearly, the social position of women is intimately connected with regulation by the state: even pregnancy and childbirth are closely regulated, as demonstrated by the struggle around midwifery and homebirths. To ignore the "formal" or to too narrowly define it is to miss completely the myriad complex and contradictory ways in which the state ensures and reproduces women's subordination. However, as Mary McIntosh (1981) reminds us, in the current context neither socialists nor feminists can afford "the luxury of a purely critical stance" vis-à-vis the state. This is particularly appropriate in the context of conservative governments' targeting such parts of the "control apparatus" as welfare, education and health care—all of which have been key arenas for women's employment since the Second World War (see Armstrong 1984). Women have much to lose when the "control apparatus" is attacked. Indeed, as Rosalind Petchesky has argued, "the 'gatekeepers' to reproductive services are more often *women*, who as counselors, nurses, physicians, and agency bureaucrats mediate state reproductive policies—sometimes progressively" (emphasis in original) (1984: 67). Clearly the locus—if one can be identified—of the "control" of women is neither primarily "informal" nor totally determined by a monolithic (male or capitalist) state.

■ CONCLUSION

In this paper we have undertaken what we regard as a preliminary critique of the concept of "social control" and its utility for a critical criminology in Canada. In tracing its emergence and historical development as a key concept in American sociology, we have illustrated that its ascendancy represented a victory for liberal sociology. The recent attempts by critical criminologists and sociologists to rehabilitate the concept of "social control" by insisting upon the essentially coercive nature of control have not resulted in an advance over traditional theorizing.

By examining the "women, law and social control" literature, in particular the use of the "formal/informal" dichotomy, we have attempted to illustrate the limited utility of the concept for developing an historically and theoretically informed understanding of the complex and contradictory relationship of women to the state and law. The concept of "social control" is ahistorical: when coupled with law, moreover, it lends itself to instrumentalism. It is our view that the concept of "social control" ought to be abandoned by critical scholars in favour of one attentive to the dynamic complexity of history, struggle and change.

■ ACKNOWLEDGEMENTS

We wish to thank Judy Deverell for her assistance in the preparation of this paper, and Stan Cohen and Ian Taylor for their valuable comments.

■ NOTES

*Paper presented at the Annual Meeting of the Canadian Association of Sociology and Anthropology, 4–7 June 1986, Winnipeg. Manitoba. Equal authorship.

1.   See, for example, how the concept of social control is employed in Greenaway and Brickey (1978), Hanmer (1981), Cohen and Scull (1983), Anderson and Davis (1983), Schur (1984), Boyd (1986), Menzies, Lowman and Palys (1987).

2. The concept of "social control" is, of course, inextricably bound up with the equally problematic concept of "deviance" (Sumner 1983).

3. Although we are concerned with sociological conceptions of "social control," it should be noted that non-sociological formulations have also been extremely influential, both in the past and at the present point in time (Zimring and Hawkins 1973).

4. *The Family Relations Act*, R.S.B.C. 1979, c. 121, s. 1. defines spouse as a wife or a husband and includes

(c) except under Part 3, a man or woman not married to each other, who lived as husband and wife for a period of not less than 2 years, where an application under this Act is made by one of them against the other not more than one year after the date they ceased living together as husband and wife.

This expanded definition of spouse is excepted under the important Part 3 of the legislation which pertains to family property and assets: for the purpose of property ownership, the spouse must be a "legal" spouse.

The Ontario legislation is similar; however, "spouse" is more narrowly defined in the definition section to mean either of a man and woman who "are married to each other" or "who have entered into a marriage that is voidable or void in good faith on the part of the person asserting a right under this Act" (Family Law Act, S.O., 1986. c. 4, as amended by 1986, c. 5, s. 1 (1)). The expanded definition of "spouse" is contained only in the part of the Act which relates specifically to support obligations; s. 29 defines a spouse as follows:

29. In this Part, "spouse" means a spouse as defined in subsection 1(1), and in addition includes either of a man and woman not being married to each other and have cohabited,
(a) continuously for a period of not less than three years, or
(b) in a relationship of some permanence if they are the natural or adoptive parents of a child.

■ REFERENCES

Adlam, D. and N. Rose. "The Politics of Psychiatry." *Politics and Power* 4 (1981): 165–202.
Anderson, B. and N.J. Davis. *Social Control*. New York: Irvington Publishers, 1983.

Armstrong, P. *Labour Pains*. Toronto: Women's Press, 1985.

Barrett, M. *Women's Oppression Today: Problems in Marxist Feminist Analysis*. London: Verso, 1980.

Barrett, M. and M. McIntosh. *The Anti-Social Family*. London: Verso, 1982.

Black, D.J. *The Behavior of Law*. New York: Academic Press, 1976.

Black, D.J. "The Boundaries of Legal Sociology." In *The Sociology of Law*, edited by C.E. Reasons and R.M. Rich, 97–113. Toronto: Butterworths, 1978.

Boyd, N., ed. *The Social Dimensions of Law*. Scarborough: Prentice-Hall, 1986.

Brophy, J. and C. Smart. "From Disregard to Disrepute: The Position of Women in Family Law." *Feminist Revue* 9 (1981): 3–16.

Brophy, J. and C. Smart, eds. *Women in Law: Explorations in Law, Family and Sexuality*. London: Routledge and Kegan Paul, 1985.

Brown, J. (1978). "Social Control and the Modernization of Social Policy, 1890–1929." In *The Origins of British Social Policy*, edited by P. Thane, pp. 126–146. London: Croom Helm.

Cain, M. "Beyond Informal Justice." *Contemporary Crises* 9 (1985): 335–373.

Chambliss, W.J. and M. Mankoff, eds. *Whose Law? What Order?* New York: Wiley, 1976.

Clark, A.L. and J.P. Gibbs. "Social Control: A Reformulation." *Social Problems* 12 (1965): 398–415.

Cohen, S. "The Punitive City: Notes on the Dispersal of Social Control." *Contemporary Crises* 3(4) (1979): 339–363.

Cohen, S. "Social Control Talk: Telling Stories About Correctional Change." In *The Power to Punish*, edited by D. Garland and P. Young, 101–129. London: Heinemann, 1983.

Cohen, S. *Visions of Social Control*. Cambridge: Polity Press, 1985.

Cohen, S. and A. Scull. "Introduction: Social Control in History and Sociology." In *Social Control and the State*, edited by S. Cohen and A. Scull, 1–14. Oxford: Martin Robertson, 1983.

Cooley, C.H. *Social Process*. Carbondale: Southern Illinois University Press, 1966.

Corrigan, P. and D. Sayer. "How the Law Rules: Variations on Some Themes in Karl Marx." In *Law, State and Society*, edited by B. Fryer et al., 21–53. London: Croom Helm, 1980.

Coward, R. "Sexual Violence and Sexuality." *Feminist Revue* 11(1982): 9–22.

Davin, A. "Imperialism and Motherhood." *History Workshop* (5, Spring, 1978): 9–65.

Davis, N.J. *Sociological Constructions of Deviance*. Dubuque, Iowa: Wm. C. Brown, 1980.

Downes, D. and P. Rock. *Understanding Deviance*. Oxford: Clarendon Press, 1982.

Garland, D. "The Birth of the Welfare Sanction." *British Journal of Law and Society* 8 (1981): 29–45.

Garland, D. "Durkheim's Theory of Punishment: A Critique." In *The Power to Punish*, edited by D. Garland and P. Young, 37–61. London: Heinemann, 1983.

Garland, D. *Punishment and Welfare*. Brookfield, Vt.: Gower, 1985.

Garland, D. and P. Young. "Toward a Social Analysis of Penality." In *The Power to Punish,* edited by D. Garland and P. Young, 1–36. London: Heinemann, 1983.

Garland, D. and P. Young, eds. *The Power to Punish.* London: Heinemann, 1983.

Geis, G. "Sociology and Sociological Jurisprudence: Admixture of Lore and Law." *Kentucky Law Journal* 52(1964): 267–293.

Gibbons, D.C. *The Criminological Enterprise.* Englewood Cliffs, N.J.: Prentice-Hall, 1979.

Gibbs, J.P. "Social Control, Deterrence and Perspectives in Social Order." *Social Forces* 56(2) (1977): 408–423.

Gibbs, J.P. "Law as a Means of Social Control." In *Social Control: Views from the Social Sciences,* edited by J.P. Gibbs, 83–113. Beverly Hills, CA: Sage, 1982.

Gouldner, A.W. *The Coming Crisis of Western Sociology.* London: Heinemann, 1970.

Greenaway, W. and S. Brickey. *Law and Social Control in Canada.* Scarborough: Prentice-Hall, 1978.

Hagan, J., J.H. Simpson and A.R. Gillis. "The Sexual Stratification of Social Control: A Gender-Based Perspective on Crime and Delinquency." *British Journal of Sociology* 30(1) (1979): 25–38.

Hall, S. "Reformism and the Legislation of Consent." In *Permissiveness and Control: The Fate of the Sixties Legislation,* edited by National Deviancy Conference, 1–43. London: MacMillan, 1980.

Hall, S. "The Rise of the Representative Interventionist State 1880s–1920s." In *State and Society in Contemporary Britain,* edited by G. McLennan et al., 7–49. Cambridge: Polity Press, 1984.

Hall, S. et al. *Policing the Crisis.* London: Macmillan, 1978.

Hanmer, J. "Male Violence and the Social Control of Women." In *No Turning Back,* edited by Feminist Anthology Collective, 190–195. London: Women's Press, 1981.

Hay, D. "Property, Authority and the Criminal Law." In *Albion's Fatal Tree: Crime and Society in Eighteenth Century England,* by D. Hay et al., 17–63. New York: Pantheon, 1975.

Hay, J. "Employers' Attitudes to Social Policy and the Concept of 'Social Control,' 1900–1920." In *The Origins of British Social Policy,* edited by P. Thane, 107–125. London: Croom Helm, 1978.

Hirschi, T. *Causes of Delinquency.* Los Angeles: University of California Press, 1969.

Hunt, A. "Perspectives in the Sociology of Law." In *The Sociology of Law,* edited by P. Carlen, 22–44. Keele: University of Keele (Sociological Monograph #23), 1976.

Hunt, A. *The Sociological Movement in Law.* Philadelphia: Temple University Press, 1978.

Hunt, A. "Marxism and the Analysis of Law." In *Sociological Approaches to Law,* edited by A. Podgórecki and C.J. Whelan, 91–110. London: Croom Helm, 1981a.

Hunt, A. "The Politics of Justice." *Politics and Power* 4 (1981b): 3–26.

Hunt, A. "Dichotomy and Contradiction in the Sociology of Law." In *Marxism and Law*, edited by P. Beirne and R. Quinney, 74–97. New York: John Wiley & Sons, 1982.

Janowitz, M. "Sociological Theory and Social Control." *American Journal of Sociology* 81(1) (1975): 82–108.

Janowitz, M. *Social Control of the Welfare State*. New York: Elsevier, 1976.

Janowitz, M. *The Last Half Century*. Chicago: University of Chicago Press, 1978.

Kasinsky, R. "Rape: The Social Control of Women." In *Law and Social Control in Canada*, edited by W.K. Greenaway and S.L. Brickey, 59–69. Scarborough: Prentice-Hall, 1978.

Kingdom, E. "Legal Recognition of a Woman's Right to Choose." In *Women in Law: Explorations in Law, Family and Sociology*, edited by J. Brophy and C. Smart, 143–161. London: Routledge and Kegan Paul, 1985.

Lemert, E.M. *Social Pathology*. New York: McGraw-Hill, 1951.

Lemert, E.M. *Human Deviance, Social Problems and Social Control*. Englewood Cliffs, N.J.: Prentice-Hall, 1967.

Linebaugh, P. "The Tyburn Riot Against the Surgeons." In *Albion's Fatal Tree*, by D. Hay et al., 65–117. New York: Pantheon, 1975.

MacKinnon, C.A. "Feminism, Marxism, Method and the State: Toward a Feminist Jurisprudence." *Signs* 8(4) (1983): 635–658.

McIntosh, M. "The State and the Oppression of Women." In *Feminism and Materialism*, edited by A. Kuhn and A.M. Wolpe, 254–289. London: Routledge and Kegan Paul, 1978.

McIntosh, M. "Feminism and Social Policy." *Critical Social Policy* 1(1) (1981): 32–42.

Matza, D. *Becoming Deviant*. Englewood Cliffs, N.J.: Prentice-Hall, 1969.

Mayer, J.A. "Notes Toward a Working Definition of Social Control in Historical Analysis." In *Social Control and the State*, edited by S. Cohen and A. Scull, 17–38. Oxford: Martin Robertson, 1983.

Melossi, D. "Overcoming the Crisis in Critical Criminology: Toward a Grounded Labeling Theory." *Criminology* 23(2) (1985): 193–208.

Menzies, R.J. "A Farewell to Norms: Black's Theory of Law Revisited." In *Deviant Designations: Crime, Law and Deviance in Canada*, edited by T. Fleming and L. Visano, 433–449. Toronto: Butterworths, 1983.

Menzies, R.J., J. Lowman and T. Palys, eds. *Transcarceration: Essays in the Sociology of Social Control*. Aldershot: Gower, 1987.

Muraskin, W.A. "The Social-Control Theory in American History: A Critique." *Journal of Social History* 10 (1976): 559–569.

Park, R.E. and E.W. Burgess. *Introduction to the Science of Sociology*. 3rd ed. Chicago: University of Chicago Press, 1969.

Parsons, T. *The Social System*. Glencoe, Ill.: The Free Press, 1951.

Pashukanis, E.B. *Law and Marxism*. Introduction by C. Arthur. London: Ink Links, 1978.

Petchesky. R. "Abortion as 'Violence Against Women': A Feminist Critique." *Radical America* 18 (1984): 64–68.

Pisciotta, A. "Corrections, Society and Social Control in America: A Metahistorical Review of the Literature." *Criminal Justice Review* 2 (1981): 109–130.

Platt, A. *The Child-Savers.* Rev. ed. Chicago: University. of Chicago Press, 1977.

Pound, R. (1930). *Criminal Justice in America.* Reprint. New York: DaCapo Press, 1972.

Pound, R. *Social Control Through Law.* New Haven: Yale University Press, 1942.

Pound, R. "Sociology of Law and Sociological Jurisprudence." *University of Toronto Law Journal* 5(1) (1943): 1–20.

Quinney, R. *Critique of Legal Order.* Boston: Little, Brown, 1974.

Ratner, R.S. and J.L. McMullen. "Social Control and the Rise of the 'Exceptional State' in Britain, the United States, and Canada." In *The New Criminologies in Canada: State, Crime and Control,* edited by T. Fleming, 85–205. Toronto: Oxford University Press, 1985.

Reckless, W. "A New Theory of Delinquency and Crime." *Federal Probation* 25 (Dec. 1961): 42–46.

Ross, E.A. *Social Control.* Cleveland: Case Western Reserve University Press, 1969.

Rothman, D.J. *Conscience and Convenience.* Boston: Little, Brown, 1980.

Rothman, D.J. "Social Control: The Uses and Abuses of the Concept in the History of Incarceration." *Rice University Studies* 67(1) (1981): 9–20.

Rowbotham, S. "The Trouble with 'Patriarchy.'" In *People's History and Socialist Theory,* edited by R. Samuel, 364–369. London: Routledge and Kegan Paul, 1981.

Schwendinger, H. and J. Schwendinger. *The Sociologists of the Chair.* New York: Basic Books, 1974.

Schur, E.J. *Labelling Women Deviant: Gender, Stigma and Social Control.* New York: Random House, 1984.

Scull, A. *Decarceration.* Englewood Cliffs, N.J.: Prentice-Hall, 1977.

Scull, A. "Progressive Dreams, Progressive Nightmares: Social Control in 20th Century America." *Stanford Law Revue* 33 (1981): 575–590.

Scull, A. "Community Corrections: Panacea, Progress or Pretence?" In *The Power to Punish,* edited by D. Garland and P. Young, 146–165. London: Heinemann, 1983.

Scull, A. and S. Cohen, eds. *Social Control and the State: Historical and Comparative Essays.* Oxford: Martin Robertson, 1983.

Smart, C. "Law and the Control of Women's Sexuality—The Case of the 1950s." In *Controlling Women: The Normal and the Deviant,* edited by B. Hutter and G. Williams, 40–60. London: Croom Helm, 1981.

Smart, C. *The Ties That Bind: Law, Marriage and the Reproduction of Patriarchal Relations.* London: Routledge and Kegan Paul, 1984.

Smart, C. "Legal Subjects and Sexual Objects: Ideology, Law and Female Sexuality." In *Women in Law*, edited by J. Brophy and C. Smart, 50–70. London: Routledge and Kegan Paul, 1985.

Spitzer, S. (1975). Toward a Marxian Theory of Deviance. Social Problems 22(5): 638–651.

Stang Dahl, T. and A. Snare. "The Coercion of Privacy: A Feminist Perspective." In *Women, Sexuality and Social Control*, edited by C. Smart and B. Smart, 8–26. London: Routledge and Kegan Paul, 1978.

Stedman Jones, G. "Class Expression versus Social Control? A Critique of Recent Trends in the Social History of 'Leisure.'" *History Workshop* (4, Autumn, 1977): 162–170.

Sugarman, D. "Law, Economy and the State in England, 1750–1914: Some Major Issues." In *Legality, Ideology and the State*, edited by D. Sugarman, 213–266. London: Academic Press, 1983.

Sumner, C. "Rethinking Deviance: Toward a Sociology of Censures." *Research in Law, Deviance and Social Control* 5 (1983): 187–204.

Tannenbaum, F. *Crime and the Community*. New York: Columbia University Press, 1938.

Thompson, E.P. *Whigs and Hunters*. Middlesex: Penguin, 1975.

Taylor, I. *Law and Order: Arguments for Socialism*. London: Macmillan, 1981.

Taylor, I. *Crime, Capitalism and Community: Three Essays in Socialist Criminology*. Toronto: Butterworths, 1983.

Unger, R. *Law in Modern Society*. New York: Free Press, 1976.

Vago, S. *Law and Society*. Englewood Cliffs, N.J.: Prentice-Hall, 1981.

Young, J. "Left Idealism, Reformism and Beyond: From New Criminology to Marxism." In *Capitalism and the Rule of Law*, edited by B. Fine et al., 11–28. London: Hutchinson, 1979.

Zimring, F.E. and G.J. Hawkins. *Deterrence: The Legal Threat in Crime Control*. Chicago: University of Chicago Press, 1973.

CHAPTER 2

INTRODUCTION TO REGULATING GIRLS AND WOMEN

Joan Sangster

In a rare public disavowal of the courts, Alberta police and child welfare workers recently decried a judicial decision declaring as unconstitutional a law that allows police to seize and isolate minor prostitutes in "safe houses" for three days. In the war of words between zealous police and the constitutionally cautious courts, those advocating forced removal of prostitutes from the streets claim the law should be used as a protective measure to forestall the sexual exploitation of young girls.[1] Forty years ago the courts may well have concurred, reflecting the prevailing belief that the law should intervene to protect and reform sexually precocious young females.

To historians, on the other hand, the word "protection" sets off unsettling alarm bells. Sexual protection applied to girls under the previous Juvenile Delinquents Act (1908–84) often slid into coercive surveillance, even stigmatizing incarceration. The protective impulse, no matter how well intentioned, could not effectively counter the abuse or alienation leading many girls to the streets. Moreover, protection was differentially applied according to social class and it might take on the character of racist paternalism when directed at Aboriginal girls. Protection, then, has a troubled history.

As with many current issues relating to youth crime, however, social and political commentators are unlikely to call on history and more likely to situate their discussion within acutely polarized debates over whether youth crime is escalating, why, and what the response should be: "boot camps or therapy."[2] While history does not offer pat solutions to present dilemmas, it may stimulate some sobering second thoughts on current debates—by dissecting the changing definitions of criminality and the process by which law constituted gender, race, and class relations; by mounting a critique of past reform efforts; and, importantly, by suggesting how the law affected the lives of girls and women who came into conflict with it.

Like politicians, historians have recently expressed new interest in the law and criminalization. Working-class history, for instance, has redefined its reach, including more discussion of the so-called "underclass" that often fell through the cracks of wage work and organized labour. Questions of sexuality and sexual orientation, the regulation and practices of working-class eroticism, have also become more central to its agenda. The discursive construction of both criminality and sexuality (and their connections) and the techniques of disciplinary and penal power are being explored through records of the courts, asylums, prisons, expert discourse on crime, and media accounts of criminal trials.[3]

This shift in historical interest—from earning to stealing, from modes of production to modes of pleasure—is comprehensible in the current political context, not only because of the heightened politicization of sexuality and discussion of the underclass metaphor,[4] but also because the theoretical and political tenor of our times has shifted from Marxist debates to post-structuralist and deconstructionist ones. The latter perspectives may not automatically lead to an emphasis on sexuality, law-breaking, and "deviance." Yet, as Terry Eagleton suggests, they redirected our gaze to these issues with Foucauldian eyes focused on the "margins" and on the construction of sexual subjectivity—or, as Marxist critic Teresa Ebert claims, they have cast our eyes away from the very real issues of racism, "exploitation, labor and production."[5]

These debates were an important stimulus to the subject of this book, the sexual and familial regulation of women through the law, with the law representing not one monolithic text but a complex of institutions, codes, practices, and personnel designed to govern, control, and aid women. Admittedly, theft, murder, and other crimes against property and persons are not uncomplicated issues. But the sexual regulation of girls and women is intertwined with so many other histories—of the family, medical and social work practice, working-class culture—as well as with debates about the role of the state, courts, and the law in shaping belief and subjectivity, that it is necessarily highly charged and interpretively contested terrain.

Rather than providing a comprehensive history of all familial and sexual regulation, I concentrate on some key issues that drew women into the courts, as plaintiffs or defendants, exploring how women attempted—not always successfully—to use the law (or defy it) to define their own sexual and family lives, as well as the way some women were classified as deviant or criminal by the law, courts, and helping professions. I draw on

North American sources to frame my discussion, but have intensively used primary sources from Ontario; my conclusions are thus shaped by this regional context but should still have some broader resonance with women's experiences in other Canadian jurisdictions. Many North American histories of moral regulation have focused on the Progressive period of reform, especially with reference to prostitution,[6] while criminologists tend to concentrate on the contemporary era. I have attempted to join these two together, examining the interwar, war, and postwar period, ending at the beginning of the 1960s when shifts in social theory and politics resulted in significant changes in law and criminology. Although this is not a study of incarceration, I have used penal records, as the histories of crime and punishment are intertwined, often implicating their mutual explanations for criminality. Finally, while conceding that the legal regulation of male and of female sexuality is intimately connected, my focus, due to feminist proclivities, is on the gender-specific supervision of girls and women, who I would argue—contra Foucault's aversion to the word—experienced a more *repressive* version of regulation.

Only a small percentage of the female population came before the courts, and women less often than men, yet the suppositions of the law, as well as women's reactions to their legal ordeals, reveal a broad gamut of social relations based on class, gender, and race. Indeed, the legal treatment accorded a small number of women reveals a much broader web of regulation shaping the proper definitions of sexuality, the family, and gender roles for *all* women. Examining the changing contexts framing women's conflicts with the law, and the strategies women employed to deal with these conflicts, also speaks directly to differences between women and to the importance of class and race in women's criminalization. The links between colonialism and criminalization are especially important because this period saw the alarming increase of the incarceration of Native women in training schools and reformatories, a "tragedy of recent vintage"[7] that has become more pronounced in recent years. Finally, women's confrontations with the law also shed light on whether, and how, legal reforms facilitated or hindered women's ability to confront oppression, thus addressing issues of public power and the state, as well as private lives and subjectivity.

In the ongoing social and legal struggles to define women's sexuality and family life, there were recurring tensions between domination and defiance, official legalities and practised illegalities.[8] How these tensions worked themselves out is one question addressed in this book. How did the law, in contributing to moral regulation, reinforce but sometimes contest authority? How did the law construct an ideology of proper versus deviant womanhood, but also become the focus for conflicts over these polarized definitions? My emphasis, however, rests decidedly on the side of regulation rather than resistance, in part because of the law's successes in inducing consent, but also because the historical sources I have used—including the records of reformatories and training schools, courts, Crown attorneys, professionals, and reform groups—were constructed primarily by those in positions of authority.

The records of women before the court, or of those who were incarcerated, are especially problematic, highly mediated sources. Women's voices come to us through the enigmatic, sometimes contradictory narratives they and their regulators have left for us; these records are often biased by the recorder's views and incomplete, and may encompass justifications, fabrications, or supplications on the part of an expert, a state official, or the defendant herself.[9] While recognizing these limitations and silences, I believe that alternative stories and subjugated knowledges are perceptible in these records. However mediated, the responses of women, their families, and their communities to crime and punishment suggest that if "the face of the law was domination, it was not complete."[10]

■ THEORETICAL IMPASSES AND ADVANCES

Since the 1960s an explosion of feminist research in history, law, and criminology has sensitized us to the inequalities that women as defendants and as victims face in the courtroom, and to how the very definitions of crime are shaped within discourses mirroring unequal power relations of class, race, and gender.[11] Ranging in method from quantitative to deconstructive analyses, this new research agenda marked a decisive break with the past. At the end of the historical period covered in this book—the 1950s—criminology had very little to say about women's experiences, or as Colin Sumner puts it, "nothing much of value."[12] Those who did address women and crime often assumed that females were subject to more effective informal controls in the family (an idea resurrected more recently in a new guise),[13] that their crime was more hidden and devious, and especially that their transgressions emerged from arrested or thwarted individual psychological development.[14] While biological explanations of women's lawlessness (still lingering in the interwar period) had faded by the post-World War II period, "psychogenic"[15] or psychological theories were in full flower.

Staking out different territory, feminist, Marxist, and social control perspectives of the 1960s and 1970s stressed structural and social—rather than familial and pathological—interpretations of crime and criminality. The former may have been implied earlier in some labelling, cultural, or anomie theories of criminology, but new consideration was given to the way the law mediated class relations, conveyed and embodied domination, and reproduced gender hierarchies. Attempting to root the law and crime firmly in economic and social relations, new frameworks and questions centred on how the law constituted, explained, and reproduced forms of domination and, importantly, how this might be changed.[16]

Some emerging Marxist analyses, influenced by a New Left anti-statism and suspicion of policing, initially veered towards the one-dimensional and instrumental, suggesting that crime and policing were used by the bourgeoisie and the state to create a disciplined working class.[17] More often, Marxist analyses rejected the concept that law was simply the "epiphenomena of the economic system";[18] they attempted to map out the law as a set of social relations and practices that reflected objective social, economic, and political circumstances but was also constructed in the realm of language, culture, and consciousness.[19] The ideological construction and mystification of the law and justice, the creation of "willing subjects" to the law in democratic capitalist societies, and the way in which the working class might themselves use the law to claim legal redress were all explored by Marxist historians, often under the influence of Gramsci's writings.[20] Similar tools were applied in anti-colonial explorations of the law as a tool of conquest, a "reflection" of racist tenets "universalized" in Western legal discourse as "natural" and just.[21]

Feminists also explored the reflection and reproduction of ideology and social power in the law, though often with reference to the patriarchal or masculinist assumptions underlying it, especially with relation to sexuality and the family. Women's law-breaking, feminists argued, was shaped and interpreted within a different political, economic, and ideological context from men's. Courtroom mercy, for instance, was measured out according to one's adherence to appropriate gender roles, and for women this necessitated an embrace of "femininity, domesticity and pathology."[22] While forensic psychiatry depicted women as less rational and balanced than men, often at the mercy of internal emotions,[23] feminist criminologists countered that criminalized women were responding understandably and logically to the difficult social, economic, and familial inequalities shaping their lives.[24] Indeed, the belief in a locatable social reality was a cardinal assumption in much early feminist writing on crime, with the corollary that class was an important structural category of analysis—titles such as *Women, Crime and Poverty* spoke to this assumption.

Some historical work was also influenced by conceptions of social control, a sociological concept defined in so many different ways over the century that, as Pat Carlen noted, it could become "vacuous."[25] By the 1970s the concept was often employed as a means of explaining the regulation and control, by informal or formal means, of groups such as the dispossessed or working classes by those with more economic, professional, and social power, as well as by the state. Early anti-delinquency efforts, for example, were linked to middle-class reformers' desire to control the unruly aspects of working-class life as much as to philanthropic concern.[26] In the hands of Nicole

Hann Rafter, social control was used to expose the ideology of domesticity and purity underlying early penal reform for women, but also to suggest how criminalized women responded to the social agenda imposed on them by women from different racial and class backgrounds.[27] Similarly, the attempts to control French-Canadian women who "broke the rules" of legal and social conformity were contrasted by Quebec historian Andrée Lévesque to women's attempts to flout the Church and state, making their own rules.[28]

By the late 1980s the whole terminology of social control was under intense critique. Marxist-inspired studies of the law were faulted both for ignoring gender and for slighting the subtle forms of non-legal and non-state regulation that shape everyday life. Social control theories in general were considered too all-encompassing, deterministic, and top-down in their approach, too much like Marxist instrumentalism in their actual use.[29] Social control became a synonym for mechanistic models that failed to differentiate the shifting historical uses of social/legal regulation, ignored human struggle, contest, and resistance to the law, and assumed a one-way street from formal (state) to informal (familial) control.[30]

Feminist versions of social control, which argued that women's experiences were structured by a patriarchal legal and welfare system, contended other critics, veered towards essentialism and ignored contradiction, negotiation, struggle, and complexity in the making of the law and social policy.[31] In early juvenile courts, for example, the judges and social workers were never the sole authorities shaping the fate of working-class girls and women. Women's interests were fractured by age, class, and race as well as gender, and the efforts of reformers were sometimes embraced by working-class families, or alternatively misappropriated by the state, with unintended, contradictory effects.[32]

The charge that social control theories were used like a "hammer" is not without justification.[33] Nonetheless, though now scorned as passé in comparison to post-structuralist insights, such theories did spark novel efforts to ask how "conformity was induced, even assented to, among the less powerful."[34] They encouraged useful revisions of uncritical histories of reformers, reformatories, and asylums, as well as critiques of the supposedly neutral, benevolent welfare state; indeed, they brought the state "back in" to challenge pluralistic, consensual views of law and social change. As Adrian Howe notes, the "politicality"[35] of these works in revisionist criminology and social history was significant for the time. Spurning liberal and administrative approaches, and often critical of punishment in its many guises, this writing attempted to pinpoint the oppressive consequences of social control, implicitly positing an alternative vision of justice and equality.

Although social control terminology is now seldom employed in historical explorations of crime, Marxist or materialist critiques of law and society have not been totally abandoned. Economic determination, state power, and ideology remain important themes, or at least questions, in some historical analyses. Works detailing the creation of a "moral culture" in the context of bourgeois economic relations, or the class distinctions inherent in the law's operation,[36] articulate concerns that remain compatible with theories of legal pluralism. While many materialists have been influenced by Foucault's emphasis on the dispersed operation of power, they maintain a critical interest in the linkages between calls "little powers" and "big powers, assuming that the 'local effects of power are made possible or facilitated' by the condensation of power and its proximity to the coercive capacity of the state."[37]

Also influenced by Foucault, some feminist scholars turned their attention to how legal discourses define immorality and how "expert" knowledge normalizes and pathologizes, producing disciplinary powers that cross the boundaries of state and civil society. By the late 1980s, postmodern analyses also questioned the value of grand, overarching theories exploring the structures of class or patriarchal oppression inherent in the law.[38] One work on the history of female delinquency, for example, maintains that feminist indictments of girls' "sexualization" by a patriarchal criminal justice system were reductionist and "essentialist"; rather, one should explore the "multiplicity of discourses, norms and practices invoked to regulate" girls.[39]

Following on this trajectory, earlier feminist and Marxist analyses of the "anti-social" family, as a site of oppression shaped by capitalist, heterosexist, and patriarchal social relations sustained in law by ideological consecration of a "public/private" split, were rejected for their *a priori* doctrinaire assumptions. Challenging such feminist theories, Nikolas Rose presents the family as a "complex grid of power relations" reflecting "new forms of political rationality ... and transformations in subjective realities," none of which were "orchestrated by groups imposing the interest of one class or gender upon another."[40] Though on the surface a more elastic, non-partisan perspective, his analysis is nonetheless also implicitly political in its very antithesis to notions of structure and oppression.[41]

Rose's antipathy to Marxist-feminist formulations reflects the immense influence of Foucault on contemporary social theory. No one writing on either criminality or sexuality today can avoid Foucault's power—myself included. This study has benefited from his appraisal of the law as an expression of power and politics, from his writing on biopower, the body, and sexuality, and from the impetus in Foucauldian theory to extend our gaze beyond the state, dissecting power as a multi-dimensional, complex process and analyzing the disciplinary practices, discourses, and self-governance associated with expert knowledges. His trilogy of "power/knowledge/body" has tested and enriched feminist theory, though even the converted sardonically concede that the "Foucauldian industry" of replications and dissections of "the grand master of penality" now approaches a "religion."[42]

By the 1980s, Foucauldian influence was articulated through the concept of moral regulation, that is, the "discursive and political practices" whereby some behaviours, ideals, and values were marginalized and proscribed while others were legitimized and naturalized.[43] In understanding the regulation of sex especially, Foucauldian insights on the "power/knowledge nexus" have been valuable, illuminating how medical, social science, and legal discourses defined normality and abnormality, setting out boundaries within which "populations and bodies" were encouraged to act.[44] Medical and social work experts, as this study shows, produced "classifications and typologies" of girls' delinquency, "constituted individuals as cases"[45] to be investigated, and explored their actions as overt signs of covert feelings that could best be detected by their investigation and analysis. Foucault thus refocused attention on the operation of power at its micro level through the family, school, church, philanthropy, professions, sciences, and community—forms of regulation not apparently "reducible to capitalism" or the state.[46] Challenging and even inverting Marxist theories (though often oversimplifying them), Foucault saw power as productive, not repressive, moving "from bottom to top as well as top to bottom in socio-economic hierarchies of society,"[47] dispersed, localized, "never in anyone's hands."[48]

By taking up questions relating to how bodies are constituted by and become invested with power relations, Foucault also posed a question already on the agenda for feminists.[49] Portraying sexuality as a social and historical construction, a "dispersed system of morals, techniques of power, discourses and procedures designed to mould sexual practices to certain strategic ends," he inspired insightful feminist critiques of the female body as a "strategic site of power."[50] Women's bodies, Foucault also emphasized, though culturally constructed, may become "saturated with sex" and thus "the objects of discipline,"[51] an observation that applies strikingly to the legal handling of prostitutes and "promiscuous" women described in this book. Moreover, the dominant understanding of normal sexuality, circulating through the law and its apparatus, pervaded wider social groups, directing all women's self-governance. As Carolyn Strange and Margaret Little argue in their studies of moral regulation, the benevolent institutions and welfare policies established for young working women and single mothers were designed to chastise and isolate women heedlessly embracing extramarital sex. If only a minority of women were apprehended by the law or cut off welfare, their fate was not lost on the wider community of women.[52]

Finally, and crucially for this study, Foucault's influence has led to proliferating claims that, in the modern period, the law has increasingly been "absorbed" by the norm.[53] The sovereign power of the law—direct, centralized, held and expressed through the state and its formal codes—was now permeated by non-legal forms of ex-

pertise and knowledge such as the medical and social sciences. In the case of delinquency, for example, emphasis was placed not on legal infractions as much as on the
child's moral or psychological deviance and the need to reconstruct her conscience.
"The Juvenile Court," wrote Jacques Donzelot in a famous Foucauldian history of the
modern family, "does not really pronounce judgment on crimes; it examines individuals."[54] Donzelot's work showed how familial regulation emanated not only from the
state but from self-justifying centres of professional power or expertise. These experts
created an important space in between the state and the individual, which he termed
"the social," a concept employed by subsequent historians of criminality, though with
more critical attention to contest and conflict within this sphere.[55]

The time period covered by this study was supposedly characterized by the increasing regulation of daily life by the authority of such experts, including the "long arms"
of psychology, psychiatry, and social work, and some Foucauldian writing suggests
that the law literally came to function *as* the norm. "The operation of discipline," Foucault himself wrote, "is not ensured by right but by technique, not by the law but by
normalization."[56] Yet the contention that the law has been displaced or "invaded" by
the norm[57] may be overstated, a linear interpretation of history that ignores the persisting plurality of forms of law. This results, as Alan Hunt contends, in the wrongful
"expulsion of law" from modernity.[58] Indeed, even some scholars sympathetic to Foucault are wary of this argument, reminding us that "juridical power" remains "formi-
dable"[59] in our time; others, seeking to avoid a polarized depiction of sovereign law versus disciplinary power, have explored how "social law was welded to the power of the
norm." [60] Rather than presuming the ascendency of discipline over the law, of the norm
over sovereignty, I have found it more useful to ask how the law and the professions
interacted and combined to regulate women. How, and why, did they produce a system
that institutionalized relatively more girls than boys, failed to aid battered wives, and
masked the sexual abuse of children? Moreover, were there changing stresses and fis-
sures in this interaction? Why did certain disciplinary discourses come to dominate
the legal agenda?

Emanating from his repudiation of the idea of a centralized state and the power of
juridical law was Foucault's emerging emphasis on governmentality, that is, the regulatory strategies and techniques operating from and within many discourses, institutions, and practices that shape and guide the conduct of groups and individuals: the
"conduct of conduct," to use Colin Gordon's abbreviation.[61] This idea of "government
at a distance" allows us to see regulation not simply as coercive or objectifying, but as
a process involving the "cultivation of subjectivity," for as active agents, individuals
come to make choices embracing regulatory aims, techniques, and strategies.[62] In the
Family Court, for instance, women were not simply pressured to take back abusive

husbands; they embraced the experts' version of the intact family and the forgiving wife as the best family form for themselves and their children.

Of course, the context that shaped their choices (which were hardly free)[63] is an issue evaded by theorists disinterested in historical determination or causation. Whether self-governance is itself a radically new idea has also been questioned.[64] Our preoccupation with governmentality may reflect the current transition from a "welfarist" to a neo-liberal society, resonating also with the political moment of "anti-modernity, anti-authoritarianism and a distrust of an increasingly regulatory society."[65] Governmentality theorists argue persuasively that we are presently witnessing a heightened "de-governmentalization of the state," as individuals are persuaded by a diverse array of interests and techniques to become privatized, self-regulating "experts of themselves."[66] However, this theory has been criticized by Marxists for its totalizing tendencies, implicit functionalism, and uncritical acceptance of neo-liberalism.[67] Most important for historians, caution needs to be exercised against the embrace of an "iron rule" of intensifying de-governmentalization of the state over time. The period covered in this study was still characterized by substantial state control over—and by broadening definitions of "delinquent" and "deviant"—women but this pattern, like the current impetus towards governmentality, was never an inevitable, inexorable process.

Foucault's power over contemporary social theory has also been challenged on other grounds. Claims that power is diffuse, decentralized, and dispersed, suggest some feminists, mask the recognition that certain "headquarters" of power do exist, with these interests reflecting and reproducing structural, social oppressions based on class, gender, and race.[68] Focusing on the operation but never the origins of power, on "the techniques, but never the distributive consequences of rule," has the effect of obscuring discussion of capital accumulation and implies the *raison d'être* of regulation is simply more regulation—offering a grim picture of inescapable domination.[69] Indeed, some Foucauldian literature offers a more profoundly depressing view of "top inward" regulation/governance than social control paradigms ever did.[70]

For those critical of this anti-foundationalist project, political pessimism, a brake on Utopian thinking, and the paralysis of skepticism are the outcomes of some Foucauldian analyses. One recurring critique of more relativist versions of post-structuralism is their rejection of any normative commitments or "truth" claims on which to base appeals for justice and freedom—since those concepts themselves are "invented" and discredited Enlightenment concepts.[71] Even Carol Smart concedes that such a postmodernist deconstruction of sexuality and the law sits uncomfortably with a politics of feminist action around violence, for the former so completely destabilizes the values and claims upon which feminist critiques of violence have been based.[72] Furthermore, even though Foucault pointed to subjugated, alternative discourses that challenge domination, resistance remains inadequately understood or theorized because it persists as a mere reflex reaction, never the product of conscious reflective agency or an awareness of differential access to power.[73] Finally, the calls of postmodern feminists to "decentre the law," thus avoiding "general theories" of women's oppression,[74] are a troubling prescription for feminists who see the connections between empirical research and the construction of metatheory as a valuable feminist project. This is especially so for those committed to a materialist analysis of exploitation and a deconstructive *critique* of the state, who believe that the law "and its application are [still] about the centralization of power,"[75] often administered to the detriment of marginalized women.

The concept of social censure, developed by Colin Sumner and others, was one alternative means of analyzing legal regulation, merging insights from Foucault with a commitment to a "socialist criminology."[76] Censuring processes of demarcating the good/bad, holy/demonic, they argue, are intrinsic in all knowledges, and these processes order social relations with political and moral judgments that simultaneously enforce power relations structured upon "hegemonic masculinity" as well as race and class power.[77] "Censures, as categories of denunciation," are "lodged within historically specific moral debates and practical conflicts" that are ideological in nature, and are connected to the dynamics of class as well as gender and race relations.[78] Though drawing heavily on notions of normalization and the power/knowledge alliance, this approach emphasizes that the designation of particular behaviour as "criminal, wicked, dangerous" is a contested realm of economic, political, and ideological constitution.

■ REGULATION AND RESISTANCE

The semantics of naming regulation may be less important than understanding its operation, contradictions, and *raison d'être*. Without imposing a Foucauldian template on women's lives, it is important to explore the specific, local, mundane, lived encounters of women with the law to discover how power, domination, and resistance operated through and against the law. These confrontations must then be situated within a broader historical and theoretical framework: to understand women's criminality it is important to survey the material and social circumstances of women's lives, as well as expert discourses on the family and sexual morality, exploring their mutual imbrication.

In this regard, a materialist and feminist framework[79] allows us to draw on insights about discourse, power, and subjectivity while still allowing for a measure of structural determination; historical materialism makes intelligible how material life shapes the possibilities of discourse and social practice, how the materiality of discourse mediates social practices.[80] However important the discourse of sexualization was for delinquent girls, for example, we must ask why those sentenced to correctional institutions were overwhelmingly poor, working-class, and Native girls. Many women in this study came before the lower courts and were given the "cheap" or "low" justice reserved for the working classes, which offered them little in the way of majesty, mercy, or equality.[81] Their misdemeanours and difficulties were often construed by the courts as problems of "therapy or morality,"[82] but this discursive construction was inevitably conditioned by social relations based on class, race, and the sexual double standard.

Moreover, suggestions that we analyze forms of regulation expressed through the law need not lead to an avoidance or downgrading of the state. Rather, the pressure points between women, families, expert discourses, legal institutions, and the state can be examined with an eye to locating patterns and concentrations of power, to identifying how women used the law as a resource for redress while also suffering under its most punitive supervision. In the last resort, the law was an important means of conveying the authority of the state through arrests, fines, imprisonment, or even the refusal to act in women's interest. However important experts and families were to the process of familial and sexual regulation, juridical power offered the final, most coercive answer to women's immorality: incarceration. In some instances, such as with the creation and operation of state-run training schools, the state not only kept a close watch on disciplinary regulation in this period, but actually extended its political ambitions and administrative rule.

We should also be cautious of fully embracing Foucault's overly decentred power, totally subjected subjectivity, and completely governmentalized souls. Feminists and materialists need to engage with Foucault without embracing a universalizing reading of his oeuvre, remaining wary of a preconceived assumption of an ever-increasing, irrational urge to disciplinary power that avoids the central questions of who the agents and benefactors of power are, how social, racial, and economic relations of privilege reproduce that power, and whether resistance to the *unequal* access to power can be mobilized. Questions of privileged interests and strategies of control are critical to the history of women's criminalization, for we need to know which social groups or institutions promoted, used, and endorsed legal regulation, why, and how consent to this rule, including self-governance, was accomplished.

Moreover, interpreting normalization only as a "libertarian negative,"[83] misconstrues women's complex relationship to legal institutions, as well as our own ethical, interpretive responsibilities. Depending on how (and in whose interests) power was exercised, normalization might refer to the sexual restraint of so-called promiscuous women; it might also refer to the application of laws prohibiting incestuous assaults on children. To assume that we must limit ourselves to endlessly tracking the operation of power and normalization, while never distinguishing, ethically, between certain regimes of power, is not acceptable.

Uncovering or at least suggesting "how it really was" for women in conflict with the law also remains one goal of this study. Some feminists perceive similar, contemporary questions to be potential minefields of essentialism and naïveté, a reflection of the completely compromised enterprise of positivist criminology.[84] Though this goal may be considered impossible (or perhaps unimportant)[85] in the current theoretical moment, I draw instead on older theoretical traditions of socialist humanism, feminist engagement, and even the traditional historical tenets of causation, explication, and empirical inquiry.[86] Indeed, some dissenting criminologists also continue to claim the possibilities of a "transgressive" feminist scholarship that embraces political, humanist motives.[87]

I would concede that locating women's experience and understandings and assessing their resistance to the law remain deeply problematic, perhaps especially so for historians using closed rather than open-ended sources, which were usually created by the regulators, not criminalized women themselves. This may be even more difficult for those of us like myself whose privileged lives in the present mark our distance from criminalized women of the past. However, historians have long interrogated their sources critically and skeptically, "working with their limitations,"[88] reading them against the grain. Some also advocate attempting to write across boundaries of difference, avoiding a rigid insider/outsider stance on historical reconstruction.[89] Similarly, I believe women's responses and resistance may have been indirect, involving the smallest queries, verbal protests, or acts of non-compliance, but they can be uncovered and assessed. A focus on the coercive side of regulation need not lead to the presumption that all responses to authority-makers are merely knee-jerk reactions to the points of power, never "active" or transformative in nature.[90]

As a process producing values, beliefs, and symbols and encompassing lived practices, the law worked as ideology, and its claim to truth and fairness offered it immense ideological power, often the invisible, naturalizing hegemony identified by Gramsci. Crime could thus be construed as immorality, in the process transforming other structures of being—poverty, violence, alienation—into narrowly legal issues and obscuring their social nature. Deeply "embedded both materially and symbolically in the legal process,"[91] power was often expressed through regulation, enforcement, or coercion, but it might also manifest itself through contentions and skirmishes over the law's meaning and application. As those contests unfolded, however, they bore the unmistakable markings of hierarchies of race, class, and gender.

The social relations of race and racism encoded in the law were inevitably intertwined with the ongoing project of the Canadian state to colonize and assimilate First Nations peoples. Even if "race" as a legal category was not articulated in Canadian statutes, racist ideology and relations resonated through the operation of the law.[92]

By the 1930s, 19th-century biological theories of race were in question, but racism in society and law was simply rearticulated in new forms with reference to culture and environment.[93] Moreover, these notions of racial difference were intertwined with gender and sexuality; though the Female Refuges Act described in Chapter 4 never mentioned race, its actual workings punished white women involved with men of colour and assumed the immoral and promiscuous criminality of First Nations women.[94] Creating and sustaining "ideal" families through law and bureaucratic policy had long been an enduring ingredient of the state's nation-building project.[95] As a result, the regulation of white working-class and Native women's sexuality sometimes overlapped in intent and strategy, with monogamous marriages, patriarchal and nuclear families, female purity, and domesticity advanced as projects of legal and social "reform." But regulation—and by consequence resistance too—also differed in significant ways, as both the image of Native peoples' moral codes and the legal regime they faced were quite distinct.[96]

In an analysis of colonial and race relations embedded in the law, the linkage between law and ideology remains significant. Though it has embraced a postmodern skepticism with the natural classification of race, critical race theory often presupposes a legitimizing, mystifying, and falsifying role of the law in maintaining racial categories and racism. Granting the historical instability and social construction of "race" does not negate the very real effects of racism. Often clothed in the legitimating language of necessity as well as justice, the law both confirmed popular beliefs concerning racial difference and defined racist boundaries, with whiteness invariably naturalized as superior, non-whiteness as different, inferior.[97] As a means of producing social knowledge, the law played a crucial role in encouraging legal actors and the wider community to perceive, and accept, the world through the racial categories and judgments it sanctified.[98] Moreover, as some critical race theorists have suggested, the law was based not just on consent but also on coercion, with the latter operating more decisively for the non-white and the dispossessed, in part due to "their material oppression."[99] The persistence of racism, Kimberlé Crenshaw argues, is produced both by coercion and by ideological consent, but for blacks, whose daily experiences continually contradict the dominant ideology of race equality and "fairness," coercion is more central. "Ideology," as she notes succinctly, "convinces one group that coercion of the other is acceptable."[100]

Her hypothesis aptly captures the legal regulation of First Nations women described in this study, who were subject, beyond the normal legal regulation of the courts, to an extra layer of state-orchestrated surveillance through the Indian Act. The Indian Act, like other forms of legal regulation explored here, must be interrogated both ethically and politically. More than the infinitesimal operation of power, more than an effect of racialized discourse, more than a normalizing strategy, the Act was grounded in the material and social foundations of colonialism and provided rationales, systems, means, and agents of oppression for generations of Native women. We should not, therefore, abandon as misguided and Utopian the search for other forms of justice for First Nations peoples or for women, even if the current constructions of justice leave much to be desired.

While embracing the "invigorating skepticism" and deconstructive method of post-structuralism, then, this study remains committed to theoretical traditions of materialism and feminism, to the assumption that historical research can contribute to the construction of theories that analyze and critique exploitation and subordination. To cut ourselves off from these theoretical anchors means the perilous abandonment of a critique of the *systems* of social and gender inequality so clearly entrenched in the criminal justice system. The need to develop an "emancipatory critical knowledge"[101] concerning women and the law is essential if we are to prevent ourselves from slipping into infinite deconstructions of criminality. The project, instead, is to direct our thoughts to the transformation of those oppressive social relations that sustain criminality.

■ NOTES

1. Alexandra Highcrest, "When protection is punishment," *Globe and Mail*, 14 Aug. 2000.

2. Such rhetoric may not actually reflect public opinion. Anthony Doob, "Transforming the Punishment Environment: Understanding Public Views of What Should Be Accomplished at Sentencing," *Canadian Journal of Criminology* 42, 3 (2000): 323–40.

3. Early works in criminal justice history often employed quantitative methods or drew on social control and class analyses. See, for example, Harvey Graff, "Pauperism, Misery and Vice: Illiteracy and Criminality in the Nineteenth Century," *Journal of Social History* 11 (1977): 245–68; Elizabeth Langdon, "Female Crime in Calgary, 1914–40", in L. Knafla, ed., *Law and Justice in a New Land: Essays in Western Canadian Legal History* (Toronto, 1986). Some works accept the dominant definitions of criminality. For example, see D. Owen Carrigan, *Crime and Punishment in Canada* (Toronto, 1991); Peter Oliver, "To Govern with Kindness: The First Two Decades of the Mercer Reformatory for Women," in Jim Phillips, Tina Loo, and Susan Lewthwaite, eds., *Essays in the History of Canadian Law* (Toronto, 1994), 516–71. Others are more critical (though not Marxist), such as John Weaver, *Crimes, Constables, Courts* (Montreal, 1996). Research has often taken a "law and society" focus: see the volumes of *Essays in the History of Canadian Law* published by University of Toronto Press. Feminist studies

have been numerous, including excellent overviews of women and the law, such as Constance Backhouse, *Petticoats and Prejudice: Women and Law in Nineteenth Century Canada* (Toronto, 1991), and thematic explorations, such as Karen Dubinsky's analysis of women and violence: *Improper Advances: Rape and Heterosexual Conflict in Ontario, 1880–1929* (Chicago, 1993) and Carolyn Strange's study of incarceration, "The Velvet Glove: Maternalistic Reform at the Andrew Mercer Ontario Reformatory for Females, 1874–1927," MA thesis (University of Ottawa, 1983). Only a few (usually 19th-century) studies examine the criminal "underclass" with gender as a focus. See, e.g., Judith Fingard, *The Dark Side of Victorian Halifax* (Porters Lake, 1989); Mary Anne Poutanen, "The Homeless, the Whore, the Drunkard and the Disorderly: Contours of Female Vagrancy in the Montreal Courts, 1810–42," in K. McPherson et al., eds., *Gendered Pasts: Historical Essays in Femininity and Masculinity in Canada* (Toronto, 1999), 29–47. Recent studies are more likely to embrace discourse analysis and/or draw on Foucauldian ideas: see, e.g., Carolyn Strange, *Toronto's Girl Problem: The Perils and Pleasures of the City 1880–1920* (Toronto, 1995). Other authors are exploring the intersection of working-class culture and homosexuality. Steven Maynard, "Through the Lavatory Wall: Homosexual Subcultures, Police Surveillance and the Dialectics of Discovery, Toronto, 1890–1930," *Journal of the History of Sexuality* 5 (1994).

4.   The "underclass" is used as a metaphor for social transformation and reflects ongoing constructions of the "deserving" and "undeserving" poor. See Michael Katz, *The Underclass Debate: Views from History* (Princeton, NJ, 1993), 3–26.

5.   Terry Eagleton, *The Illusions of Postmodernism* (Oxford, 1996), 69; Teresa L. Ebert, *Ludic Feminism and After: Postmodernism, Desire and Labor in Late Capitalism* (Ann Arbor, Mich., 1996), 23.

6.   Many excellent studies end by the 1920s. See, e.g., Ruth Rosen, *The Lost Sisterhood: Prostitution in America, 1900–1918* (Baltimore, 1982); Barbara Hobson, *Uneasy Virtue: The Politics of Prostitution and the American Reform Tradition* (New York, 1987); Timothy Gilfoyle, *City of Eros: New York City, Prostitution and the Commercialization of Sex* (New York, 1992); D. Nilsen, "The Social Evil: Prostitution in Vancouver, 1900–20," in Barbara Latham and Cathy Kess, eds., *In Her Own Right: Selected Essays on Women's History in B.C.* (Victoria, 1984); Constance Backhouse, "Nineteenth Century Prostitution Laws: Reflection of a Discriminatory Society," *Histoire sociale/Social History* 18 (1985): 387–423; Lori Rotenberg, "The Wayward Worker: Toronto's Prostitute at the Turn of the Century," in Janice Acton et al., eds., *Women at Work: Ontario* (Toronto, 1974), 33–70.

7.   Bradford Morse, "Aboriginal Peoples, the Law and Justice," in Robert Silverman and Marianne Nielsen, eds., *Aboriginal Peoples and Canadian Criminal Justice* (Toronto, 1992), 56.

8. This term from Susan Hirsch and Mindie Lazarus-Black, eds., *Contested States: Law, Hegemony and Resistance* (New York, 1994). On this issue I have also been influenced by John Comaroff and Jean Comaroff, *Ethnography and the Historical Imagination* (Boulder, Colo., 1992); Sally Merry Engle, *Getting Justice and Getting Even: Legal Consciousness among Working-Class Americans* (Chicago, 1990).

9. For discussion of such case files, see Linda Gordon, *Heroes of Their Own Lives: The Politics and History of Family Violence* (Boston, 1988), 13–17; Steven Noll, "Patient Records as Historical Stories: The Case of the Caswell Training School," *Bulletin of the History of Medicine* 69 (1994): 411–28; Regina Kunzel, *Fallen Women, Problem Girls: Unmarried Mothers and the Professionalization of Social Work, 1890–1945* (New Haven, 1993), 5–6. For the argument that they can help uncover client views, see Lykke de la Cour and Geoffrey Reaume, "Patient Perspectives in Psychiatric Case Files," in Franca Iacovetta and Wendy Mitchinson, eds., *On the Case: Explorations in Social History* (Toronto, 1998), 242–65. On women's use of narrative in the courtroom, see Joan Sangster, "Pardon Tales from Magistrates Court: Women, Crime and the Courts in Peterborough County, 1920–60," *Canadian Historical Review* 74 (June 1993): 161–97.

10. Engle, *Getting Justice and Getting Even*, 180.

11. The literature on criminology and women is vast. For a few different examples, see Carol Smart, *Women, Crime and Criminology: A Feminist Critique* (London, 1976); Smart, *Feminism and the Power of the Law* (London, 1989); Pat Carlen, *Women, Crime and Poverty* (Philadelphia, 1988); Lorraine Geisthorpe and Allison Morris, eds., *Feminist Perspectives in Criminology* (Philadelphia, 1990). For Canadian examples, see Ellen Adelberg and Claudia Currie, eds., *Too Few to Count: Canadian Women in Conflict with the Law* (Vancouver, 1987); Karlene Faith, *Unruly Women: The Politics of Confinement and Resistance* (Vancouver, 1993). For a review essay, see Dorothy Chunn and Shelley Gavigan, "Women, Crime and Criminal Justice in Canada," in Margaret Jackson and Curt Griffiths, eds., *Canadian Criminology: Perspectives on Crime and Criminality* (Toronto, 1995), 141–84. Historical studies examined the nature of women's crime, how women's crime was perceived by society, and women's treatment by the courts and correctional institutions. See note 3.

12. Colin Sumner, *The Sociology of Deviance: An Obituary* (New York, 1994), 288.

13. J. Hagan, J. Simpson, and A.R. Gillis, "The Sexual Stratification of Social Control," *British Journal of Sociology* 30 (1979): 25–38; J. Hagan, "Class in the Household: A Power-Control Theory of Gender and Delinquency," *American Journal of Sociology* 92, 4 (Jan. 1987): 788–816.

14. On the latter two approaches, see Otto Pollock, *The Criminality of Women* (Philadelphia, 1961); Otto Pollock and A. Friedman, eds., *Family Dynamics and Female Sexual Delinquency* (Palo Alto, Calif., 1969).

15. Albert Cohen, *Delinquent Boys* (New York, 1955), 14. In the Ontario Training School for Girls, for example, an EEG study looking for abnormal brain waves in the girls was conducted alongside the more dominant approach, psychotherapeutic interviews concerning girls' family history and personality.

16. Alan Hunt, *Explorations in Law and Society: Toward a Constitutive Theory of Law* (New York, 1993), 253.

17. One example was Sidney Harring, *Policing a Class Society: The Experience of American Cities, 1865–1915* (New Brunswick, NJ, 1983). The recent suggestion that a "conspiratorial" analysis is all the Marxist perspective amounted to is simply untrue. For this characterization, see D. Owen Carrigan, *Juvenile Delinquency: A History* (Toronto, 1998), 144.

18. Colin Sumner, *Reading Ideologies: An Investigation into the Marxist Theory of Ideology and Law* (London, 1979), 247–48.

19. Hunt, *Explorations in Law and Society*, 252.

20. Poulantzas quoted in Sumner, *Reading Ideologies*, 262. Douglas Hay, ed., *Albion's Fatal Tree: Crime and Society in Eighteenth Century England* (London, 1974); E.P. Thompson, *Whigs and Hunters* (New York, 1975). For comment on the Marxist tradition in regard to women, see Shelley Gavigan, "Marxist Theories of the Law: A Survey, with Some Thoughts on Women and the Law," *Criminology Forum* 4, 1 (1983): 755–90. For a review of Canadian works, see Brian Young, "Law in the 'Round,'" *Acadiensis* 16 (Autumn 1986): 155–64. For a comparative view of Marxist and Foucauldian interpretations of punishment, see David Garland, *Punishment and Modern Society: A Study in Social Theory* (Chicago, 1990).

21. Robert Williams, *The American Indian in Western Legal Thought: The Discourses of Conquest* (New York, 1990). Despite the emphasis on discourse, the notion of ideology is employed: "The Doctrine of Discovery [in law] was nothing more than the reflection of a set of Eurocentric racist beliefs" (326). See also Ron Bourgeault, "The Struggle for Class and Nation: The Origin of the Metis in Canada and the National Question," in Bourgeault et al., eds., *1492–1992: Five Centuries of Imperialism and Resistance* (Halifax, 1992), 153–89. See below for a discussion of critical race theory.

22. Pat Carlen and Anne Worrall, eds., "Introduction," *Gender, Crime and Justice* (Philadelphia, 1987). See also Mary Eaton, *Justice for Women?* (Philadelphia, 1986).

23. Hilary Allen, *Justice Unbalanced: Gender, Psychiatry and Judicial Decisions* (Philadelphia, 1987).

24. Faith, *Unruly Women*; Pat Carlen, *Women, Crime and Poverty* (Philadelphia, 1988); Pat Carlen, "Out of Custody, into Care: Dimensions and Deconstructions of the State's Regulation of Twenty-Two Young Working-Class Women," in Carlen and Worrall, eds., *Gender, Crime and Justice*; Dawn Currie, "Feminist Encounters with Postmodern-

ism: Exploring the Impasse of Debates on Patriarchy and Law," *Canadian Journal of Women and the Law* 5, 1 (1992): 63–86.

25. Pat Carlen, "Virginia, Criminology and the Antisocial Control of Women," in Thomas Blomberg and Stanley Cohen, eds., *Punishment and Social Control: Essays in Honour of Sheldon Messinger* (New York, 1995), 213.

26. For some examples, see Anthony Platt, *The Child Savers: The Invention of Delinquency* (Chicago, 1977); Eric Schneider, *In the Web of Class: Delinquency and Reformers in Boston, 1810s–1930s* (New York, 1992); Susan Houston, "The 'Waifs and Strays' of a Late Victorian City: Juvenile Delinquents in Toronto," in Joy Parr, ed., *Childhood and Family in Canadian History* (Toronto, 1982), 129–42.

27. Nicole Hahn Rafter, *Partial Justice: Women in State Prisons, 1800–1935* (Chicago, 1985).

28. Andrée Lévesque, *Making and Breaking the Rules: Women in Quebec, 1919–1939* (Toronto, 1994). These examples of how social control was actually employed by historians indicate a variety of applications and research conclusions. Some historians who offer critiques of social control add important qualifications, but then circle back to similar arguments. For example, see David Bright, "Loafers Are Not Going to Subsist Upon Public Credulence: Vagrancy and the Law in Calgary, 1900–14," *Labour/Le Travail* 36 (1995): 37–58. Social theory critics tend to overgeneralize about historical works using social control terminology. Allan Hunt, for example, claims it always ignores "human agency." Hunt, *Governing Morals: A Social History of Moral Regulation* (Cambridge, 1999), 18–19.

29. For the definition of critical (or revisionist) social control theory, see Stanley Cohen, "The Critical Discourse on 'Social Control': Notes on the Concept as a Hammer," *International Journal of the Sociology of Law* 17 (1989): 347–57. See also essays critical of social control in Stanley Cohen and Andrew Scull, eds., *Social Control and the State: Historical and Comparative Essays* (Oxford, 1983).

30. For an excellent feminist critique of social control, see Dorothy Chunn and Shelley Gavigan, "Social Control: Analytical Tool or Analytical Quagmire?," *Contemporary Crises* 12 (1988): 107–24.

31. *Ibid.* See also Linda Gordon, "Family Violence, Feminism and Social Control," *Feminist Studies* 12, 3 (Fall 1986): 453–78.

32. Mary Odem, *Delinquent Daughters: Protecting and Policing Adolescent Female Sexuality in the United States, 1885–1920* (Chapel Hill, NC, 1995).

33. See Cohen, "The Critical Discourse."

34. Rafter, *Partial Justice*, 157.

35. Adrian Howe, *Punish and Critique: Towards a Feminist Analysis of Penality* (London, 1994), 64.

36. Philip Corrigan and Derek Sayer, *The Great Arch: English State Formation as Cultural Revolution* (Oxford, 1985); Douglas Hay, "Time, Inequality and Law's Violence," in Austin Sarat and Thomas Kearns, eds., *Law's Violence* (Ann Arbor, Mich., 1992), 141–73. For sociological examples, see Stephen Brickey and Elizabeth Comack, eds., *The Social Basis of Law: Critical Readings in the Sociology of Law* (Toronto, 1986).

37. Hunt, *Explorations in Law and Society*, 276, 253.

38. The best-known work was Smart, *Feminism and the Power of the Law.*

39. Kerry Carrington, *Offending Girls: Sex, Youth and Justice* (Sydney, 1993), 107, 88. For the earlier views on sexualization she is criticizing, see Meda Chesney-Lind, "Girl's Crime and Woman's Place: Toward a Feminist Model of Female Delinquency," *Crime and Delinquency* 35, 1 (Jan. 1989): 5–29; Steven Schlossman and Stephanie Wallach, "The Crime of Precocious Sexuality: Female Juvenile Delinquency in the Progressive Era," *Harvard Educational Review* 48 (1978): 65; Gloria Geller, "Young Women in Conflict with the Law," in Adelberg and Currie, eds., *Too Few to Count*; Indiana Matters, "Sinners or Sinned Against?: Historical Aspects of Female Juvenile Delinquency in British Columbia," in Barbara Latham and Roberta Pazdro, eds., *Not Just Pin Money: Selected Essays on the History of Women's Work in British Columbia* (Victoria, 1984).

40. Nikolas Rose, "Beyond the Public/Private Division: Law, Power and the Family," in Peter Fitzpatrick and Alan Hunt, eds., *Critical Legal Studies* (Oxford, 1987), 66, 73–74. For another attempt to develop a "feminist-pluralist" analysis, in contrast to the so-called "ideological indoctrination" of Marxist-feminist analyses, see Faith Robertson Elliot, "The Family: Private Arena or Adjunct of the State," *Journal of Law and Society* 16, 4 (1989): 443–63.

41. Rose and others claim that feminist theories rest on notions of false consciousness, but this has been answered by those who point out that materialist and feminist works attempted to understand "multi-faceted ways in which power was manifested, while never ignoring the 'centrality' of state formations." Susan Boyd, "(Re)Placing the State: Family, Law and Oppression," *Canadian Journal of Women and the Law* 9, 1 (1994): 47.

42. Howe, *Punish and Critique*, 83. This is all the more ironic since Foucault is reported to have noted that "they [his commentators] don't understand what I am saying." Quoted *ibid.*

43. This definition draws on Hunt, *Governing Morals*, ix; also Mariana Valverde, "Introduction," in Valverde, ed., *Studies in Moral Regulation* (Toronto, 1994), v. There are still important differences between authors claiming to use Foucault. An early British contribution, R. Dobash, R. Dobash, and S. Gutteridge, *The Imprisonment of Women* (Oxford, 1986), draws on Foucault but still uses the idea of social control.

44. Michel Foucault, *Discipline and Punish: The Birth of a Prison* (New York, 1977), 177; Foucault, *History of Sexuality*, vol. 1 (New York, 1980), 144. For some feminist reinterpretations of Foucault, see Sandra Lee Bartky, *Femininity and Domination* (London, 1990); Susan Bordo, "Feminism, Foucault and the Politics of the Body," in Caroline Ramazanoglu, ed., *Up Against Foucault: Explorations of Some Tensions between Foucault and Feminism* (London, 1993), 179; Irene Diamond and Lee Quinby, eds., *Feminism and Foucault: Reflections on Resistance* (Boston, 1988); Jana Sawicki, *Disciplining Foucault: Feminism, Power and the Body* (London, 1991); Carol Smart, "Disruptive Bodies and Unruly Sex: Historical Essays on Marriage, Motherhood and Sexuality," in Smart, ed., *Regulating Womanhood: Historical Essays on Marriage, Motherhood and Sexuality* (London, 1992); Mary Louise Adams, *The Trouble with Normal: Post-War Youth and the Making of Heterosexuality* (Toronto, 1998).

45. Nancy Fraser, "Michel Foucault: 'A Young Conservative'?," in Susan J. Hekman, ed., *Feminist Interpretations of Michel Foucault* (University Park, Penn., 1996), 26.

46. Alan Hunt and Gary Wickam, *Foucault and Law* (London, 1994).

47. Quoted in Linda Alcoff, "Feminist Politics and Foucault: The Limits to Collaboration," in Arleen Dallery et al., eds. *Contemporary Crises in Continental Philosophy* (Albany, NY, 1990), 75.

48. Michel Foucault, in Colin Gordon, ed., *Power/Knowledge: Selected Interviews, 1972–77* (New York, 1980), 98. See also Ladelle McWhorter, "Foucault's Analysis of Power," in Callery et al., eds. *Contemporary Crises in Continental Philosophy*, 119–26.

49. Kate Soper, "Productive Contradictions," in Ramazanoglu, ed., *Up Against Foucault*, 31; Bordo, "Feminism, Foucault, and the Politics of the Body," 179–202.

50. Karlene Faith, "Resistance: Lessons from Foucault and Feminism," in H. Lorraine Radtke and H. Stam, eds., *Power/Gender: Social Relations in Theory and Practice* (London, 1994), 55. At the same time, this emphasis on the body risks "retaining the emphasis on female corporeality that has been so prevalent in patriarchal culture." Soper, "Productive Contradictions," 35.

51. Foucault, *History of Sexuality*, 45.

52. Strange, *Toronto's Girl Problem*; Margaret Little, *"No Car, No Radio, No Liquor Permit": The Moral Regulation of Single Mothers in Ontario, 1920–97* (Toronto, 1998).

53. Foucault, *Discipline and Punish*, 22, 170, 222–23. Allan Hunt and Gary Wickam note that Foucault explores the interdependence of the law and the disciplines, but there is still a tendency for the disciplines to dominate the law. See Hunt and Wickam, *Foucault and Law* (London, 1994), 47, 49.

54. Jacques Donzelot, *The Policing of Families* (New York, 1979), 110.

55. Linda Mahood, *Policing Gender, Class and Family: Britain, 1850–1940* (London, 1995); Dorothy Chunn, *From Punishment to Doing Good: Family Courts and Socialized Justice in Ontario, 1880–1940* (Toronto, 1992).

56. Foucault, *The History of Sexuality*, 89.

57. Foucault, *Discipline and Punish*, 170.

58. Hunt, *Explorations*, ch. 12.

59. Smart, *Feminism and the Power of the Law*, 4.

60. Nikolas Rose and Mariana Valverde, "Governed by Law?," *Social and Legal Studies* 7, 4 (1998): 542.

61. Graham Burchell and Colin Gordon, eds., *The Foucault Effect: Studies in Governmentality* (London, 1991), 2–3, 102–03.

62. David Garland, "Governmentality and the Problem of Crime: Foucault, Criminology, Sociology," *Theoretical Criminology* 1, 2 (1997): 182.

63. As David Garland observes, governmentality theorists often conflate "agency" with "freedom"—two very different things. *Ibid.*, 197.

64. *Ibid.*, 204–05.

65. Hunt, *Explorations*, 288.

66. Nikolas Rose, "Governing 'Advanced' Liberal Democracies," in Andrew Barry, Thomas Osborne, and Nikolas Rose, eds., *Foucault and Political Reason* (Chicago, 1996), 42, 56, 60.

67. Boris Frankel criticizes the failure to discuss the role of globalized capitalist market values of individualism, competition, and consumerism in this turn of events. See Frankel, "Confronting Neo-liberal Regimes: The Post-Marxist Embrace of Populism and Realpolitik," *New Left Review* 226 (1997): 57–92.

68. Nancy Hartstock, "Foucault on Power: A Theory for Women?," in Linda Nicholson, ed., *Feminism/Postmodernism* (New York, 1990), 157–75; Hartstock, *The Feminist Standpoint Revisited* (Boulder, Colo., 1998), 205–27. See also Faith, "Resistance: Lessons from Foucault and Feminism," 36–66.

69. Frankel, "Confronting Neo-Liberal Regimes," 83–84.

70. For example, Nikolas Rose, *Governing the Soul: The Shaping of the Private Self* (New York, 1990).

71. Ebert, *Ludic Feminism and After*. Although some claim Foucault's projects are implicitly grounded in truth claims, they are not explicitly so. For the former, see Nancy Cook, "The Thin within the Thick: Social History, Postmodern Ethnography and Textual Practice," *Histoire sociale/Social History* 63 (May 1999): 98.

72. As Smart points out, "work like [Judith] Butler's, should it be used in the legal forum, would almost certainly be treated as incomprehensible." Carol Smart, "Law, Feminism and Sexuality: From Essence to Ethics?," *Canadian Journal of Law and Society* 9, 1 (1994): 26.

73. Alcoff, "Feminist Politics and Foucault": "Since subjectivity is nothing but the product of discourses, there can be no autonomous agent who rebels against regulation or oppression."

74. Smart, *Feminism and the Power of the Law*, 163–64.

75. Currie, "Feminist Encounters with Postmodernism," 76, 82.

76. Colin Sumner, "Introduction: Contemporary Socialist Criminology," in Gelsthorpe and Morris, eds., *Feminist Perspectives in Criminology*, 1–11.

77. Colin Sumner, "Re-thinking Deviance: Towards a Sociology of Censure," in Gelsthorpe and Morris, eds., *Feminist Perspectives in Criminology*, 15–40. See also Sumner, "Foucault, Gender and the Censure of Deviance," *ibid.*; Paul Roberts, "Social Control and the Censure(s) of Sex," *Crime, Law and Social Change* 19 (1993): 171–86.

78. Sumner, "Re-thinking Deviance," 28–29.

79. For a discussion of the evolution of materialist feminism, see Rosemary Hennessy and Chris Ingraham, "Introduction: Reclaiming Anticapitalist Feminism," in Hennessy and Ingraham, eds., *Materialist Feminism: A Reader in Class, Difference and Women's Lives* (New York, 1997).

80. What Foucault thought about the "extra-discursive" is open to contention. For one view, see Maureen Cain, "Foucault, Feminism and Feeling: What Foucault Can and Cannot Contribute to Feminist Epistemology," in Ramazanoglu, ed., *Up Against Foucault*, 73–96.

81. Hay, "Law's Violence."

82. Engle, *Getting Justice and Getting Even*, 10, 180.

83. Eagleton, *The Illusions of Postmodernism*, 56.

84. Smart, "Feminist Approaches to Criminology," 70.

85. Nikolas Rose and Peter Miller, "Political Power Beyond the State: Problematics of Government," *British Journal of Sociology* 43, 2 (1992): 177: "Our studies of government eschew sociological realism and its burdens of explanation and causation. We do not try to characterize how social life really was." For a defence of sociological "realism," see Garland, "Governmentality."

86. Empirical inquiry can be differentiated from much maligned "empiricism," or the idea there is a recoverable, exact truth. As Richard Price argues, the historical method, especially in social history, inevitably rubs up against some post-structuralist writing. See Price, "Postmodernism as Theory and History," in John Belcham and Neville Kirk, eds., *Languages of Labour* (Aldershot, 1997), 11–43. For other materialist critiques, see Bryan Palmer, *Descent into Discourse: The Reification of Language and the Writing of Social History* (Philadelphia, 1990); Alex Callinicos, *Theories and Narratives: Reflections on the Philosophy of History* (Durham, NC, 1995); Neville Kirk, "History, Language, Ideas and Postmodernism: A Materialist View," in Keith Jenkins, ed., *The Postmodern History Reader* (London, 1997). Feminist theorists have also argued for the radical potential of empiricism, as well as the continuing relevance of standpoint theory. See Hartstock, *The Feminist Standpoint Revisited*;

Dorothy E. Smith, *Writing the Social: Critique, Theory and Investigations* (Toronto, 1989); Maureen Cain, "Realism, Feminism, Methodology and Law," *International Journal of the Sociology of Law* 14 (1986).

87. Maureen Cain, "Towards Transgression: New Directions in Feminist Criminology," *International Journal of the Sociology of Law* 18, 1 (1990): 1–18.

88. Richard Evans, *In Defence of History* (London, 1997), 98.

89. This issue is discussed in Ruth Roach Pierson, "Experience, Difference, Dominance and Voice in Writing of Canadian Women's History," in Karen Offen, Ruth Pierson, and Jane Rendall, eds., *Writing Women's History: International Perspectives* (Bloomington, Ind., 1991), 79–106; Radha Jhappan, "Post-Modern Race and Gender Essentialism or a Post-Mortem of Scholarship," *Studies in Political Economy* 51 (1996): 15–63.

90. I am not sure we need to make the polar distinctions that Tina Loo suggests: "focusing on coercion can reduce subjects of regulation to objects or victims who possess little agency .... what little they do have is limited to ... reacting to the actions and agenda of the powerful." Loo, "Dan Cranmer's Potlach: Law as Coercion, Symbol and Rhetoric in British Columbia, 1884–1951," *Canadian Historical Review* 73, 2 (1992): 125–65.

91. Susan F. Hirsch and Mindie Lazarus-Black, "Performance and Paradox: Exploring Law's Role in Hegemony and Resistance," in Hirsch and Lazarus-Black, eds., *Contested States*, 1.

92. Walter Tarnopolsky, *Discrimination and the Law in Canada* (Toronto, 1982); James W. St. G. Walker, *"Race" Rights and the Law in the Supreme Court of Canada* (Toronto, 1997), 12–50: Constance Backhouse, *Colour Coded: A Legal History of Racism in Canada 1900–50* (Toronto, 1999); Constance Backhouse, "White Female Help and Chinese Canadian Employers: Race, Class, Gender and Law in the Case of Yee Clung, 1924," *Canadian Ethnic Studies* 26, 3 (1994): 34–52; James W.St. G. Walker, "The Quong Wing Files," in Iacovetta and Mitchinson, eds., *On the Case*, 204–23. Sexuality and race also converged in eugenic discourse and legislation. See Angus McLaren, *Our Own Master Race: Eugenics in Canada, 1885–1945* (Toronto, 1990).

93. Peggy Pascoe, "Miscegenation Law, Court Cases, and Ideologies of 'Race' in Twentieth Century America," in Martha Hodes, ed., *Sex, Love, Race: Crossing Boundaries in North American History* (New York, 1999), 464–90.

94. On feminist critical race theory, see Sharene Razack, *Looking White People in the Eye: Gender, Race and Culture in Classrooms and Courtrooms* (Toronto, 1998); F. Anthais and N. Yuval-Davis, eds., *Racialized Boundaries: Race, Nation, Gender and Colour and Class and the Anti-Racist Struggle* (London, 1992); Rose Brewer, "Theorizing Race, Class and Gender," in Stanlie James and A. Busia, eds., *Theorizing Black Feminisms: The Visionary Pragmatism of Black Women* (New York, 1993); Adrian K. Wing, ed., *Critical Race Feminism: A Reader* (New York, 1997).

95. Enakshi Dua, "Beyond Diversity: Exploring the Ways in Which the Discourse of Race Has Shaped the Institution of the Nuclear Family," in Dua and A. Robertson, eds., *Scratching the Surface: Canadian Anti-Racist Feminist Thought* (Toronto, 1999), 237–60.

96. Winona Stevenson, "Colonialism and First Nations Women in Canada," in Dua and Robertson, eds., *Scratching the Surface*, 49–82.

97. For specific explications relating to women, see, e.g., Marlee Kline, "Complicating the Ideology of Motherhood: Child Welfare Law and First Nation Women," in Martha A. Fineman and Isabel Karpin, eds., *Mothers in Law: Feminist Theory and the Legal Regulation of Motherhood* (New York, 1995), 118–41; Razack, *Looking White People in the Eye*.

98. Ian F. Haney Lopez, *White by Law: The Legal Construction of Race* (New York, 1996), 144.

99. *Ibid.*

100. Kimberlé Williams Crenshaw, "Race, Reform and Retrenchment: Transformation and Legitimation in Antidiscrimination Law," *Harvard Law Review* 101 (1988): 1358.

101. Hennessy and Ingraham, "Introduction," 4.

CHAPTER 3

ON MORAL REGULATION:
SOME PRELIMINARY REMARKS*

Philip Corrigan

■ I: DURKHEIM AND BERNSTEIN

In his lectures on "Civic Morals," Durkheim argues against Spencer:

> There is an inward activity that is neither economic nor commercial and this
> is moral activity. Those forces that turn from the outward to the inward are
> not simply used to produce as much as possible and to add to creature comfort,
> but to organize and raise the moral level of society, to uphold this moral struc-
> ture and to see that it goes on developing. It is not merely a matter of increas-
> ing the exchanges of goods and services, but of seeing that they are done by
> rules that are more just; it is not simply that everyone should have access to
> rich supplies of food and drink. Rather, it is that each one should be treated as
> he deserves, each be freed from an unjust and humiliating tutelage, and that,
> in holding to his fellows and his group, a man should not sacrifice his individu-
> ality. And the agency on which this special responsibility lies is the State. So
> the State does not inevitably become either simply a spectator of social life (as
> the economists would have it), in which it intervenes only in a negative way,
> or (as the socialists would have it) simply a cog in the economic machine. It
> is above all, supremely the organ of moral discipline. It plays this part at the

present time as it did formerly, although the discipline has changed. (Here we see the error of the socialists.)[1]

[...]

All I intend by these preliminary remarks is a reflection upon these views. [...] I seek to emphasize their strengths (usefulness, coherence, exciting qualities) and indicate their limits (evasions, self-defeating contradictions, reproduction of subordination). In this way I hope to illuminate the contours, context and some of the content of the *concept* moral regulation which I have been attempting to elaborate for several years.[2]

[...]

Durkheim from his earliest work through until the last is concerned to try to avoid two elemental "superstitions": the "naturalness" of society assembled by *a priori* (social) individuals,[3] and the equally false conflation or dichotomization of "individual" and "society."[4] This last may seem an odd quality to draw from Durkheim, as he was considered for many years an exponent of the "group mind" thesis, but a quotation from his 1898 lecture "Individual and collective representations" will indicate what I am trying to show:

> We can see here how it is that society does not depend on the nature of the individual personality. In the fusion from which it results all the individual characteristics, by definition divergent, have neutralised each other. Only those more general properties of human nature survive, and precisely because of their extreme generality they cannot account for the specialized and complex forms which characterise collective facts. This is not to say that they count for nothing in the resultant, but they are only its mediate conditions. Without them it could not emerge, but they do not determine it.[5]

But Durkheim's work is structured around a number of absences which have effects upon the coherence and usefulness of his explorations. There is first the almost total representation of the social world as exclusively male (and I suspect French)—as examples quoted above indicate. This is part of a general weakness which follows from the very strength of the focus upon "the social": the odd part that "secondary groups" play in Durkheim's schema.[6] There are two other "generalizations" in his work which have serious consequences. There is a slippage between the categories "moral" and "social," and between

"State" and "Society"; taken together, these result in systematically suppressing the con-strained-*but-constructed* features of human sociation in favour of their naturalization as normalized states of human life (*any* human life). [...]

Nevertheless, to conclude this brief overview of Durkheim's work, I think his utility is to be found in three emphases: his representation of the State (of regulation and dis-cipline) is far superior to that of any Marxist account at the time (although not to that of Marx's own work *now available to us*). It is possible to draw from some of his shorter pieces a quite outstandingly advanced understanding of the means through which bi-ological persons have to be distinguished from their social individuality, which results from their construction, under highly constraining circumstances and with already meaningful signs and symbols, of various possible and passable identities responding to the social classifications "at play" *and* "in contradiction" (the latter concept is one which Durkheim rarely articulates). Thirdly, in his sustained reflection on the generic modes of making sense Durkheim suggests just how much *Society is like a Language;* although this, being metaphorical, is not without risks.

Basil Bernstein shares some of Durkheim's emphases very directly. In a characteris-tic passage in 1975 he admits to "the difficulty I have in separating very general ques-tions of control from specific class related forms."[7] Nevertheless by 1973 (in the "Post-cript" to the Paladin edition of Volume I) Bernstein was focusing quite directly and coherently upon class (rather than social) controls:

> The class structure distributes power unequally; it distributes access to, control
> over, and facility to exploit property, whether this property is physical or symbolic.
> It does this through its penetration into educational arrangements and processes
> and through its penetration into primary socialization within the family, in such
> a way that a vicious self-perpetuating circle is often set up between home, school
> and work. Any analysis of how class structures repeat themselves in the process of
> socialization must necessarily show the class realizations in the family and school
> and work.[8]

[...]

Two years later, in 1977, Bernstein states similarly:

> The ruling class—that is, those who dominate production by deciding its means,
> contexts and possibilities—have necessarily a direct relation to production but an
> *indirect* relation to education, in particular, and cultural reproduction in general.[9]

Later, on the same page, he argues:

> That is we have distinguished between those who are categories of the social divi-
> sion of labour of production and those who are categories of the social division of
> labour of symbolic control. Now it follows that the latter fraction has a *direct* rela-
> tion to cultural reproduction but an *indirect* relation to production.

I think one way of understanding a central difficulty in the work of Bernstein [...]—
which also represents a problem for Durkheim's project—is to focus upon the distinction between *constituting* and *regulating*. On the one hand it is implied that individuals
are *constituted* through the relations depicted—and, relatedly, that categories create
relations.[10] On the other, in two distinct senses, it is revealed that relations create/sus-
tain categories through which individuals are *regulated*.

[...]

We can pose this contrast quite sharply, in a return to my main concerns here: *what*
(and to some extent, materially, *how*) do codes *code*. Are they the resultant of categories
which compel a certain appropriation of the flux of experience somewhat one-sidedly?
Or are they—as I believe them to be—the-never-to-be-fully-visible structural relations which enable us to understand how particular forms and relations around, for
example, production of material goods share a certain patterning with the forms and
relations of politics or culture? [...]

■ II: MORAL REGULATION: A FIRST APPROXIMATION (CODES CONSTRAIN)

Durkheim (and those who have followed his lead) can be understood, at a high level
of generality, as offering an interpretation of social formations as morally regulated.
This contrasts with other interpretations, at the same level of generality, such as Weber's stress upon cognitive calculation and the consequence of beliefs for conduct, in
a word, rationality; or that of a relatively mechanical marxism which holds to some
understandable realm in-and-of-itself called "the economic" (technology and the laws
of political economy) which is a fetishized myth. Moral regulation [...] concerns forms
and contexts, determining thus the realization of utterance, display, gesture, indication, action—in a phrase, *proper forms of expression* which are always-ever far more
than lingual. It is not simply that meanings are context-linked but that the structured

means of expression are already "valued," providing not simply (in Austin's terms) the illocutionary along with the locutionary but a variety of other indicators. These moral repertoires are what establish social identity, or rather, (an important qualification, as I shall argue) *identities*. Although the phenomenal form of the moral constraints which identify us to ourselves (and for others) may well be conceptual and categorial we should not slip into the error of seeing these as determining alone. On the contrary, they determine because of what they repeat, and represent: structured relations resulting from power and control. In this mode of proceeding the originating social self must be seen as a combination (a contradictory combination, as I shall argue) of both the "space" (how and where you look when you look for someone) and the *possibility* of coherence (the sentencing "I" which nonetheless will always leave much unsaid).[11]

The problem with the Durkheimian project, in the above perspective, is *not* that we are enjoined to consider social facts as things, as (a) external and (b) constraining, but that he insufficiently allows for the multiple constitution and understanding of such facts. This follows from his provision but insufficient elaboration of the distinctions nature/society as realized in biological (and, perhaps, after Chomsky and Levi-Strauss, we should add or stress *logical*) persons and social individuals. Although the variety of structural deviances he discusses (such as anomie and alienation in *Suicide*) stress the space (and indicate the operations of) moral regulation, this remains a relatively crude conceptualization in his work. That project, however, remains the basis for all (and any) sociology. Responding to critics in a footnote to *The Elementary Forms*, Durkheim wrote

> Since we have made constraint the *outward sign* by which social facts can be most easily recognized and distinguished from the facts of individual psychology, it has been assumed that according to our opinion, physical constraint is the essential thing for social life. As a matter of fact, we have never considered it more than the material and apparent expression of an interior and profound fact which is wholly ideal: this is *moral authority*. The problem of sociology—if we can speak of *a* sociological problem—consists in seeking, among the different forms of external constraint, the different sorts of moral authority corresponding to them and discovering the causes which have determined these latter.[12]

In *Suicide* Durkheim argues that moral

> maxims are actual living sentiments ... If, then we ascribe a kind of reality to them, we do not dream of supposing them to be the whole moral reality. That would be to take the sign for the thing signified.[13]

That is precisely what moral regulation accomplishes; through its reproduction of particular (proper, permitted, encouraged) forms of expression it fixes (or tries to fix) particular signs, genres, repertoires, codes, as normal representations of "standard" experiences which represent human beings as far more standardly "equal" than they in fact *can* be. If we follow Volosinov (which I shall, but in a qualified way indicated below)

> there is no such thing as experience (intentions, ambitions and the like) outside its embodiments in signs ... It is not experience that organises expression, but the other way round—expression organises experience. Expression is what first gives experience its form.[14]

It is clear that what I shall call expressive forms and norms are the means of moral regulation. But we need to qualify Volosinov in recognizing both a variety of possible forms (to distinguish our position from the discourse theorists who *fix* the subject in a far too singular and once-and-for-all manner) and the consistent generation of certain experiences which are only represented by distortion in the obvious forms of expression. In ways of representation which, significantly, will win not so much what Gramsci calls "active consent" but a kind of grudging, often bewildered approval or, better, acceptance, indicated by the term "Seems so!" Or by the weak affirmation, "I suppose so ...", both denied by gesture, tone, facial expression and frequently verbally denied in other contexts.[15]

■ III: THE SIGNIFICANCE OF HISTORY (CODES CONSTRUCT)

In his 1974 London lecture, Thomas Luckmann made a number of points congruent with my analysis thus far, drawing attention to "corporeality" (specifically human body) and "sociability" (specifically human association), *and* "that the juncture of two of the elementary structures of the human condition ... is the presupposition of the third, i.e., historicity."[16] But, he continues in the same paragraph,

> here we must note a peculiar dialectics. It follows from the very nature of historicity as a general structure of human existence that both corporeality and sociability are *historical* structures of the forms of human life.

This reminds us that history is not external to "corporeality" (the meaning and naming of the body in history) or "sociability." The moral forms of expression have origins and lineages, ruptures and reconstructions, which can be *traced* (here I differ radically from most structuralists) in the contemporary structured relations through which we live. As I have remarked previously, we do not have structural conflict and class struggle *there* (in The Origins) and technically adjusted forms *here* (in the Present). No forms of expression can be understood without their history—back to and including their originating contexts. History is, quite literally and materially, the internal texture of these forms.

[...]

Without both a theoretical understanding of the pervasiveness of moral regulation and the historical construction of the present forms of that regulation we constantly run the danger of seeing "anomie" or "ascription" to be temporary phases in an otherwise improving progress toward consensus and achievement.[17] Relations understood only through power and control are insufficient to explain the internal quality of the "moral authority" which Durkheim investigated all his life, that alone ensures some qualities of Gramsci's "active consent" or Weber's (and others') emphasis upon *legitimacy*. Providing we do not understand surface features of individual behaviour (or answers to certain forms of survey questions) as rendering total accounts of the biography or commitment of the social individuals concerned. As I have often remarked role-performance must not be read off as (total) role-commitment or rule-internalization.

I think we can only understand moral regulation in terms of State formation, agencies and policies and I shall attend to that in my final section below. It is necessary, first, however, to return to some implications of my critical remarks thus far. So long as we expect to find unitary (or potentially unitary) social individuals *constituted* around particular identities we shall not be able to understand the fragility, permeability, difficulty, agony and yet poetic energy of most human lives which result from attempting to live with and through the contradictory combination of a variety of possible social classifications, possible identities. Whilst there are central signs realized and shared in being a wife, mother, lover, worker and other classifications, there are also violent antagonisms involved. Brecht remarked of the distantiation effect in everyday life that was needed "for a man to see his mother as the wife of another man; it occurs, for instance, when he suddenly finds he has a stepfather."[18] In other words we are (and find other) social individuals multiply *regulated* morally in exactly the way that a language imprisons and relates us in terms of its structures of operations and our abilities to understand its rules. For all the risks involved, we can agree to begin to (re)think social relations through the metaphor that Society is constraining-constructing like a Language. But the ways of speaking/listening ("making public") are various, that for fathers may be different to that for husbands which is different in turn for lovers, workers, voters, patients, witnesses, clients and other classifications.

There are two related points. First, and the obvious *is* here worth stating, languages (in utterance) conceal as much as reveal, or, better, they handle and represent in particular ways. [...] Secondly, whilst I remain unhappy about the unitariness implied (preferring to understand the accomplishment of an individual constitution as a curiously collective and certainly fully conscious, or increasingly conscious, active struggle-in-permanence), Basil Bernstein *has* drawn attention to the differential operation of what I am calling moral regulation. In a footnote to his 1977 paper he adds:

> It is possible that education is relatively more successful in the *constituting* of specific personalities only in the case of high-level agents of reproduction, whereas for manual workers it is rather more *regulative* of the expression of, than constituting, the personality.[19]

To be fair, we must note how he sees strong disciplinary insulation making

> it extraordinarily difficult to grasp how contradictions, cleavages, ambiguities and dilemmas are constituted in the individual.[20]

■ IV: STATE FORMATION AND MORAL REGULATION[21]

In a recent contribution,[22] not uncongenial to my own argument, Nicholas Abercrombie and Bryan S. Turner significantly almost entirely avoid any mention of the State in their discussion of the nature and changes within the "dominant ideology" in early, mature and late capitalism. This is fairly common and is a feature of a more general dichotomization between coercion (associated with the State, "bodies of armed men" and so on) and consensus (associated with acculturation, value-systems and so on). Althusser, notoriously, tried to solve this dichotomy, at a stroke, with the conception of "Ideological State Apparatuses" (although there is much more to be gained from other parts of his work, including Part II of that essay).[23] It seems that theorizing about the social cannot escape *either* separation and dichotomy *or* identity and conflation. I shall argue here that we have to understand the regularity and reliability of social relations, despite the contradictory features of both structured inequality and antagonistic social identities coercively "on offer," through Erastian agencies of regulation. Sociologists in general, and Marxists in particular, frequently ignore a central stage in theorizing the social world, *the return to phenomenal forms* to explain how/what it is that their inferential logic of a structured set of relations operating in specific ways *explains*. More narrowly, the State is often discussed both ahistorically and without any attention to the textured forms of agencies and apparatuses without which any policy, function, operation remains purely rhetorical. The forms of State (and recalling that we are dealing always with State *formation* not stasis) have themselves to be sensitively situated in the contexts of operation since it is these forms which are, in lived relations, how/what the State is known as.

How am I suggesting, then, the State formation and moral regulation can be understood? Abercrombie and Turner are quite right to stress the way in which the "dominant ideology" operates as one of the means to unify the bourgeoisie. I think it highly important to keep some space between the categories "bourgeoisie" as owners of profitable property and "ruling class" since the latter must, whilst the former much more diffusedly may, operate definitively through the State apparatuses, at least in a strategic sense. But they could more powerfully have drawn from Weber and Marx the way in which the coherence of the bourgeoisie is accomplished as a *feature of State formation*, the other side of which (as a very significant form of the dominant ideology) is nationalism. Whilst they are also correct to emphasize the moral features of the dominant ideology, they do not sufficiently understand that its main dominance, and here *across* the social formation, is exercised through the preferred forms and modes of social relations and practices. The famous quotation from Marx and Engels's *German Ideology* (which they provide in part) should always be read and thought through *to the end*:

> The ideas of the ruling class are in every epoch the ruling ideas: i.e., the class which is the ruling *material* force of society is at the same time its ruling *intellectual* force. The class which has the means of material production at its disposal, consequently also controls the means of mental production, so that the ideas of those who lack the means of mental production are on the whole subject to it. The ruling ideas are nothing more than the ideal expression of the dominant material relations, the dominant material relations grasped as ideas; hence of the relations which make the one class the ruling one, therefore, the ideas of its dominance.[24]

It is equally important to stress how Marx overcomes the force/will (coercion/consensus) images of "how society is possible":

> In actual history, those theoreticians who regarded *might* as the basis of right were in direct contradiction to those who looked on *will* as the basis of right ... If power is taken as the basis of right, as Hobbes, etc., do, then right, law, etc. are merely the symptom, the expression of *other* relations upon which state power rests. The material life of individuals, which by no means depends merely on their "will,"

their mode of production and form of intercourse, which mutually determine each other—this is the real basis of the state and remains so at all the stages to which division of labour and private property are still necessary, quite independently of the *will* of individuals. These actual relations are in no way created by the state power; on the contrary they are the power creating it. The individuals who rule in these conditions—leaving aside the fact that their power must assume the form of the *state*—have to give their will, which is determined by these definite conditions, a universal expression as the will of the state, as law, an expression whose content is always determined by the relations of this class, as the civil and criminal law demonstrates in the clearest possible way.[25]

As Marx once wrote in a draft, "every *social* form of property has 'morals' of its own ..."[26] by which I take him to mean material outcomes and cultural consequences. Christopher Hill and Edward Thompson[27] have marked stages in the long maturation of capitalism as *modes of social discipline* which cannot be thought separately from changes in State formation and agencies. Both in the general regulation of moral relations, including the various approved forms for the institutional expression ("making public") of moral solidarity and, crucially, in attending to the style and settings of legitimacy, State activity in England was and remains dominant. The English Reformation, as Christopher Hill pointed out almost 40 years ago, was after all an act of State, accompanied by early forms of that range of controls and routines which we so much take for granted as to see as merely technical or administrative solutions to social (i.e., neutral) problems—such as the registration of births and deaths, the authorization of certain areas of expression (official publications, legalized theatres), and those characteristic features of English State regulation, licensing and encouraging of approved forms and marginalization (up to and including coercive prohibition) of other forms.

This is not to collapse or conflate together State formation and its orchestration and articulation of *some* features and forms of moral regulation, with the total sum of repertoires of moral relations. The latter—cognitively and normatively—define human sociation as such, representing the evaluative side of how sense is made. But that latter is never entirely accomplished from "within" as it always is marked by the resistance of the raw materials employed, the relations of production of sense, *and* the proper and obvious ways of accepting sense made by others. Nevertheless State agencies play a strong definite part in establishing the range of what are proper ways of public performance; which has implications for notions of competence since it can deride or even deny qualities of competence which do not relate to the narrow approved performance forms.

I am therefore suggesting that it is *not* necessary for a dominant group to accomplish total belief and commitment amongst the dominated, but that the world of "public"

evaluations and judgments should be such that rituals (including, importantly, ritual-
ized forms of humour and challenge) confirm the correctness, truth and validity of the
Obvious. This might be, for example, that without profits there can be no production
(an odd judgment on the history of human beings) or it might be an aggressive asser-
tion of "equality of opportunity," producing, as Basil Bernstein has noted in several
places, both the personalization of *failure* (rather than a shared class perspective on
educational *exclusion*) and the ideology of education compensating for society. What
the State regulates are thus moral features of the social environment, above all the
encouraged/discouraged forms of expression, depressing, repressing and suppressing
alternative forms which portray contrasting moralities. It is in this way which we need
to see the modern democratic nation State in England as the *theatre of educative tendencies*. In 1860, writing of "Social Education," James Hole argued

> There are some agencies which, though they cannot be classed as schools, have
> an educational influence of the most powerful kind. That view of education which
> limits it to mere scholastic instruction, is narrow and incomplete. Let any one
> analyse the influences that have formed his own character ... Just so with any
> community, whether comprising a nation or a town. Whatever tends to render
> the conditions of social existence more favourable—physically, intellectually, or
> morally—has an *educative tendency*.[28]

[...]

It is worth repeating an earlier stress if I am not to be misunderstood. Nothing said
here should be read as implying incorporation or consensus—the singular male stress
(itself concealing the quite different life-situations of Irish, Welsh, Scots males, as well
as those differentiated by education, occupation, location, religion and—latterly—
race) should be sufficient reminder of the ways in which this ideology of improvement,
civility, and reasonableness concealed half the population. But it remains nonetheless
the dominant orchestration of moral authority. From the 1880s onwards as much if not
more is achieved through the increasing spread of the commodity-form as the normal
mode of provision as the "good life" becomes increasingly identified with the purchase
of consumption goods. This initial phase by the State [...] persists in its effects, providing a crucial institutional network of regulation which "broadcasts" back the defining
social relations of capitalist production, exchange and consumption, through the unitary categories of individualism: voter, witness, client, subject, and citizen. Large-scale
advertising is a product of this phase from the 1880s (although some national brand-

names were established by then) and the moral qualities displayed there remind us that much can be said in forms other than words; we should take that insight back to the "social architecture" of the earlier phases, to that civic righteousness and national authority embodied in those major buildings of the era which also "reflected" back the obvious powerfulness and legitimacy of the powerful.

■ CONCLUSION

We live in worlds which are as much moral as material; indeed there is no way of appropriating and handling the material which does not involve forms of expression some of which carry a higher evaluation than others. Impurity, as Mary Douglas has argued, is "matter out of place"; so too is improperness; behaviour and moral beliefs which are "out of place." Education in moral correctness is far wider than formal education, all social relations have an "educative tendency." The State acts formally and informally to establish and encourage some forms of expression as against others in recognition of the multiple meanings associated with the "morals" of social forms of property and property-like relations (e.g., marriage, child-parent links). The conveying of moral values is as much accomplished by style and context as it is by content, there are not only hidden curricula but hidden messages: the unsaid policing as much as the said[29] and the technical and routine operating as effectively as the political and public ritual.

Against the regulation by the morals that are signified in those expressive forms shaped and focused by the "ideal expression of the dominant material relations," which stress as obvious and normal the attainment of a constituted unitary individualism; differentially and multiply comprehended relations of difference (class, gender, race, location, religion, occupation and grading) generate personal troubles and private pains which lack (most of the time) any approved, legitimate, acceptable ways of their being made public, at least in forms which are given equivalent status to the expressive forms of the dominant ideology. Nevertheless, expressed or not, there *are* cultural forms of resistance which signify (for their participants and for those they oppose) as collective languages prefiguring alternative social arrangements which would celebrate difference(s) and make possible the *conscious* constitution of human beings as the general rule.

Much sociology ignores that the achievement of singular unitary individualism is permitted only a tiny minority of (male) members of the dominant classes, whilst for the rest they have to contend with the antagonistic contradictions of the different social discourses (which index difference as disadvantage) which allow, at best, a lopsided development itself displayed through consumption goods. It means, in terms of methodology, the impossibility of single methods garnering more than (however useful) surface details. Sustained ethnography, coupled with historicizing the contexts of examination and theorizing the utterances and actions thus constructed, for example, has again and again shown the limits of the "sociological glance." It also means that the sociology of culture (and the minuscule attention to so-called non-rational, non-verbal actions and significations) becomes a far more central area as technical or policy matters are seen to have cultural consequences (i.e., educative tendencies) whether the forms of wage payment[30] (or more widely labour regimes, e.g., casualization versus non-casualization) or the nature of habitation relations.[31]

Whilst the State does not inculcate in any deep sense dominant values within the dominated, it does act (systematically) as part of a moral project to provide the conditions for the reproduction of manners, rituals and moral relations as much as legal, technical and economic relations narrowly considered. The links between different moments of State formation (as between different moral contexts) is not to be taken as implying any essentialist notion, nor yet a simple linear continuity; rather they are linked by "family resemblances" sharing features resulting from the reproduction of certain relations of production. Moral-relations-in-general is as useful (and limited) as Marx's conception of production-in-general, that is "this *general* category, this common element sifted out by comparison, is itself segmented many times over and splits into different determinations. Some determinations belong to all epochs, others only to a few."[32]

The purpose of these preliminary remarks is no more than exploratory. They have attempted to show the material outcomes which follow from certain obvious routines, manners, evaluations of some means and forms as proper and expected. The contrast is drawn with those who argue that the material outcomes are to be explained by the internalization (acceptance) of certain values and/or by the outcome of certain uniform normal mental processes (rationality). But, as militantly, I am offering a provisional critique of those who consider people fixed and held-in-place either by the coercion of "bodies of armed men" etc. (which is not to deny the ready availability of such men, machine guns and tanks when ordinary social order is effectively challenged) or by the operations of language-in-general, discourses, or other micro-physics of power. The emphasis here, as in my other work, is on *forms* (of relations and of thought), on ways, on the manner through which ... and so on. It is also on complexity: that the textured modes of moral regulation are complex practices which are combined, aligned, inflected, orchestrated in modern social formations by secular State agencies. But these latter are not the authors of their effects, they represent and reproduce dominant material powers. Nevertheless, moral regulation-in-general, and State formation and discipline in particular, sustain the links between the powerful and the controllers, determine the legitimacy of the mode and means that the codes of power classify and the codes of control frame. It is the most general (and yet most nationally distinctive) way in which (publicly denied and yet officially administered) "class regulates the elaborated codes of education and in the family" and at work and more generally in the home.[33]

We have to seek, as Durkheim said, "among the different forms of external constraint, the different sorts of moral authority corresponding to them" and discover "the causes which have determined these latter."[34] That is *the* problem of sociology.[35]

—December, 1980

■ NOTES

*This paper should be seen as an extended and somewhat belated footnote to my earlier "Dichotomy is contradiction," *Sociological Review*, Vol. 23, 1975. I am grateful to Basil Bernstein for a number of extended conversations on these matters over the last few years. The final realization remains, of course, my own.

1. These are the manuscripts which Professor H.N. Kubali discovered to be held by Marcel Mauss in 1934. Durkheim gave the lectures both at Bordeaux between 1890–1900 and at the Sorbonne in 1904, 1912 and later years. They were translated into English by Cornelia Brookfield as *Professional Ethics and Civic Morals*, London, Routledge and Kegan Paul, 1957. This quotation is drawn from pp. 71–72, but the whole of Chapters 4–9 are central to my discussion.

2. For example my doctoral thesis "State Formation and Moral Regulation in Nineteenth-Century Britain: Sociological Investigations," University of Durham 1977; my work with Derek Sayer, "Class struggle, political economy, moral relations," *Radical Philosophy*, no. 12, 1975 and "How the law rules," paper to the B.S.A. 1979 conference, in B. Fryer (ed.): Law, State, Society, Croom Helm, London, 1981; and with Val Corrigan, "State formation and social policy before 1971" in N. Parry and others (eds.): *Social Work, Welfare and the State*, Edward Arnold, Leeds, 1979.

3. See, for example, the chapter "Origins of society" in Durkheim: *Rousseau's "Social Contract"* in Durkheim: *Montesquieu and Rousseau*, University of Michigan Press, Ann Arbor, 1970; the critique of sociocentrism in Durkheim and M. Mauss: *Primitive Classification*, Cohen and West, London, 1963, pp. 86–87 and the "Conclusion" to Durkheim: *Elementary Forms of the Religious Life*, Allen and Unwin, London, 1915, amongst many other places.

4. Apart from the references in n. 3 above, see, for example Durkheim: *Moral Education ...*, Free Press, New York, 1973, pp. 67, 277; "Preface to the second edition" of Durkheim:

Rules of Sociological Method, Free Press, New York, 1966; and "The dualism of human nature and its social conditions," a 1914 essay in K.H. Wolff (ed.): *Essays on Sociology and Philosophy*, Harper, New York, 1964.

5. "Individual and Collective Representations" in Durkheim: *Sociology and Philosophy*, Cohen & West, London, 1965, p. 26. The essays in this volume along with those in K. H. Wolff's volume already cited are a major resource for me.

6. For example in *Professional Ethics, op. cit.*, n. 1 above, pp. 62–64 but the feature is quite general. One partial exception to my criticisms is to be found in Durkheim: *Socialism*, ed. A. Gouldner, Collier Books, New York, 1962, but see the important letter by S. Wolin in *New York Review of Books*, 30 October 1974.

7. "Introduction" to volume III, p. 21. This text, along with the "Introduction" and "Postcript" to the Paladin ed. of Volume I are very important explorations of many of the themes I am discussing. I would put them on the same level as the chapters they comment upon. Bernstein revealed earlier "it took me a little time to free myself of the standard U.S.A. work on socialization," volume I, p. 272.

8. Volume I, p. 265. Of course, the whole of Bernstein's work turns on the centrality of difference, particularly that of class. An employment of penetration occurs in the work of Paul Willis: *Learning to Labour*, Saxon House, London, 1977, as discussed, for example, in P. Woods (ed.): *Teaching Strategies*, Croom Helm, London, 1980 or extended by M. MacDonald: "Cultural Reproduction: The Pedagogy of Sexuality," *Screen Education*, nos. 32/33, 1980.

9. Volume III, p. 191.

10. For example, in Volume III, the 1977 paper, pp. 175, 177, 179.

11. I am drawing here from Philip Corrigan and Paul Willis: "Cultural forms and class mediations," *Media, Culture and Society*, 2, 1980, 297–312 and Paul Willis and Philip Corrigan: "The Orders of Experience," *Social Text*, 1981, forthcoming.

12. *Elementary Forms, op. cit.*, n. 3 above, p. 208, n. 4.

13. *Suicide* ..., Routledge and Kegan Paul, London, 1952, p. 35.

14. V.N. Volosinov: *Marxism and the Philosophy of Language*, Seminar Press, New York, p. 85. Cf. R. Rossi-Landi: *Ideologies of linguistic relativity*, Hague, Mouton, 1973.

15. Cf. R. Reynolds and B.T. Wolley: *Seems so! A Working Class View of Politics*, Macmillan, London, 1911; S. Yeo: "Working class association ..." in N. Parry and others (eds.): *Social Work, Welfare and the State*, Arnold, Leeds, 1979; J. Seabrook: *What Went Wrong*, Gollancz, London, 1978.

16. T. Luckmann: "On the rationality of institutions in modern life," *Archives européennes de sociologie*, vol. 16, 1975, p. 10.

17. I tried to question these assumptions in P. Corrigan: "Feudal relics or capitalist monuments?," *Sociology*, vol. II, 1977.

18. Bertold Brecht: "The E-effect," *Gemini*, Autumn, 1959, p. 40.

19. Volume III, 1977 paper, p. 199, n. 5.

20. Volume III, original "Introduction," p. 23.

21. My understanding of materiality owes much to the later Poulantzas, especially Part I of his *State, Power, Socialism*, New Left Books, London, 1978. My understanding of the State as a series of moral regimes would have been impossible without the work of Michel Foucault; for an admirable introduction to the latter's work see A. Sheridan: *Michel Foucault ...*, Tavistock, London, 1980.

22. N. Abercrombie and B.S. Turner: "The Dominant Ideology Thesis," *British Journal of Sociology*, vol. 29, 1978.

23. L. Althusser: "Ideology and Ideological State Apparatuses" in *Lenin and Philosophy*, New Left Books, London, 1971.

24. K. Marx and F. Engels: *Collected Works*, Progress, Moscow, volume 5, p. 59. Abercrombie and Turner quote the first sentence only in their article, *op. cit.*, n. 22, p. 151.

25. Marx and Engels, *op. cit.*, n. 24 above, p. 329. This is clearly expressed in Marx's "Moralising Criticism and Critical Morality" (Collected works, vol. 6, e.g., pp. 319f) of 1847 and in *Capital, IV: Theories of Surplus Value*, I, Progress, Moscow, 1963, e.g., pp. 359–360, of 1863.

26. K. Marx: *Civil War in France*, draft version, Foreign Languages Press, Peking, 1971, p. 191.

27. Cf. Christopher Hill: "Discipline" in his *Society and Pluralism in Pre-Revolutionary England*, Panther, London, 1969; "The dialectic of discipline and liberty" in his *Milton*, Faber, London, 1977; E.P. Thompson: "Time, work-discipline and industrial capitalism," *Past and Present*, no. 38, 1967. Cf. L.B. Wright: *Religion and Empire*, University of North Carolina Press, Chapel Hill, N.C., 1943; D.W.R. Bahlman: *The Moral Revolution of 1688*, Yale University Press, 1957, New Haven; E.F. Paul: *Moral Revolution and Economic Science*, Greenwood Press, Westport, Conn., 1979; P. Corrigan (ed.): *Capitalism, State Formation and Marxist Theory*, Quartet, London, 1980; P. Corrigan: *State Formation and Moral Regulation in England*, Macmillan, London, 1981.

28. James Hole: *Light, more light ...*, Longman, Brown, London, 1860, p. 106. On the educative tendency of political rituals and categories consider Miall's *The Franchise as the means of a people's training*, 1851 and Monckton Milnes's "On the Admission of the Working Classes as Part of our Social System," the third of the *Essays on Reform*, Macmillan, London, 1867.

29. Diana Geddes: "'You do not exist' is the hidden message many coloured children receive," *Times*, 26 November 1979, reports Brian Jackson's analysis of 7,767 greetings and anniversary cards; 3,384 drawings in comics, and 996 images in books, posters and so on.

30. Cf. J. Ditton: "Moral Horror versus Folk Terror: output restriction, class and the social organisation of exploitation," *Sociological Review* vol. 24, 1976 and P. Willis: "Shop-floor culture ..." in J. Clarke and others (eds.): *Working Class Culture*, Hutchinson, London, 1979.

31. For example the general moral consequences (and educative tendencies) that are argued to flow from becoming "A Nation of Home Owners" (*Times* editorial, 21 December 1979) which will, it seems, result in "a major shift of economic power into the hands of the individual, *with all that means* in terms of self-respect, freedom and mobility" (my emphasis).

32. Karl Marx: "Introduction" (1857) in *Grundrisse*, Penguin, Harmondsworth, 1973, p. 85 explicated by Derek Sayer: *Marx's Method*, Harvester Press, Brighton, 1979, pp. 78f.

33. This draws upon Bernstein's 1977 paper, the quotation comes from Note (a) p. 196 of Volume III.

34. Durkheim: *Elementary Forms*, quoted fully in section II of this article, "Moral regulation: a first approximation (codes constrain)."

35. For some further documentation and argument see P. Corrigan: "Curiouser and Curiouser ... ," *British Journal of Sociology*, vol. 31, no. 2, 1980; *On celebrating difference(s)*, Paper to the 1981 B.S.A. Conference, University College of Wales, Aberystwyth; (with Derek Sayer) "On the real peculiarities of the English" (forthcoming); (with Harvie Ramsay and Derek Sayer) "Bolshevism and the Soviet Union," *New Left Review*, no. 125, 1981, especially the last section.

CHAPTER 4

THE STRUGGLES OF THE IMMORAL:
PRELIMINARY REMARKS ON MORAL REGULATION

Mariana Valverde and Lorna Weir

The control and construction of morality and sexuality have been theorized from various social scientific perspectives. Socialization theory has understood morality and sexuality as learned processes involving the "internalization" of "norms" in and from primary (familial) and secondary (educational and other extra-familial) social institutions. On its part, the "dominant ideology" thesis problematizes norms but mainly in terms of their relation to class: systems of values and beliefs are envisaged as "reflections" of more fundamental class interests, determined in production relations. Much feminist social theory has used either or both of these approaches, concentrating on the socialization of women and/or the male vested interests supposedly "reflected" in norms.[1] In some feminist work the class reductionism of Marxist theory of ideology has been quietly transformed into an equally totalizing gender reductionism which sees all moral and sexual regulation as explainable by reference to "male interests."[2] It has certainly been important to document masculine dominance; nonetheless, contemporary feminist theory might benefit from a critical analysis of non-feminist frameworks that have been uncritically incorporated into feminist analyses.

Socialization theory and the dominant ideology thesis both suffer from a common failure to account for the processes through which "norms" are produced and for the linked, multiple sites across which they are implemented. Moreover, both theories have been rightly criticized for attributing a non-conflictual homogeneity to regulatory practices.

Philip Corrigan's article "On Moral Regulation: Some Preliminary Remarks"[3] departed

75

in fundamental ways from the liberalism of socialization theory and the economism of the dominant ideology thesis. Drawing on Durkheim's view of the state as ethical educa-tor, and on the writings of social linguists, particularly Basil Bernstein, on social class, Corrigan analyzed moral regulation as the privileging of certain forms of expression. "The establishment of proper ways of public performance," results in the subordina-tion of other expressive behaviours, and, Corrigan emphasizes, controls the forms of self-identification and social recognition. He is particularly concerned to understand moral regulation in relation to the formation of subjectivity, and that subjectivity as post-structuralist—multiple and contradictory. From a feminist perspective, Corrigan's work is very valuable, not least because it provides us with ways of overcoming the legacy of both socialization theory and the dominant ideology thesis.

Distinguishing his theory from the dominant ideology thesis which demonstrates little concern for the systems of social practices connecting ideology with capital, Corrigan locates moral regulation on a terrain of preferred forms, social relations and practices continuously specified as an integral part of state formation. In short, Corrigan elaborates the concept of moral regulation to mean official disciplinary re-gimes with complex class articulation. Although he himself did not stress the point, Corrigan's formulation of moral regulation represents a great leap forward from both neo-Marxist theories of ideology and simplistic notions of "social control" used in radical sociology.[4]

In the course of our separate research projects,[5] both of us have met with difficulties in using the term "moral regulation." The meaning of "moral" has proved elusive; in the 19th century this term included what we would now call the social/psychological. Since the contemporary common usage of "moral" conveys a more restricted range of meanings, it is clear that there is a potential for ambiguity in the term. With respect to "regulation," Corrigan tends to assume that the state is *the* agency of moral regula-tion, thus obscuring the complex relationships among state and non-state institutions involved in developing and reproducing codes of moral regulation. For these and oth-er reasons, it is difficult to determine what practices, social relations and institutions might be termed "moral" or "regulatory."

This article does not present any general theory of moral regulation, even if this were possible or desirable. We are only making certain suggestions which may be of help to feminists and others engaged in researching regulatory practices and discourses. In this spirit we will first make some observations regarding the positioning of moral regu-lation within 19th-century economic and political regulation. Secondly, we suggest that greater attention be given to methods and procedures of regulation. Thirdly, we empha-size the systematic importance of extra-state regulatory agencies in liberal-democratic state systems, concluding with ruminations on the struggles of the immoral.

◼ FINDING MORAL REGULATION

The regulatory projects of 19th-century ruling blocs in countries such as Britain and Canada included the following:

a) The formation of an economic subjectivity among both the bourgeoisie and the proletariat in which thrift was an absolute moral value as well as an instrumental good.

b) The formation of a political subjectivity that would support and be congruent with the emerging state forms.[6]

c) The formation of a moral subjectivity that would not only be congruent with but also would provide the psychological basis for what was known as nation-building. Purity education at the turn of the century, as carried out in schools, churches, rescue homes and missions, was based on the premise that "we want to build a nation, not gather together a mob" (as a Presbyterian minister put it in 1908). We suggest that nation-building was not synonymous or even coterminous with state formation: while the state needed citizens, the nation needed moral subjects, subjects with "character." The difference between the mob and the nation was precisely character, and, conversely, an individual without character was a miniature mob. Sexual regulation formed a crucial part of the larger project of the production of moral subjects through religious training, health education, and patriotism, and although gender organization was not its only principle or aim, sexual regulation helped to shape gender discourses and practices.

The moral and the sexual were not sets of social practices independent of economic and political regulation. The sexual in particular was not an autonomous regulatory site subject to the jurisdiction of distinct institutions: there never have been ministries of sexuality.[7] Rather, sexual and moral regulation have frequently been constructed and inscribed within other institutional locations: ministries of revenue and finance, and of citizenship and culture, have exercised moral regulation. All departments of the state, including the military, have at times been, and potentially always are, sites of moral regulation. For the purposes of socialist and feminist research, the beginning point for an analysis of moral regulation will be determined from the perspective of those who are regulated. This perspective becomes knowable, through social movement organizations, to the researcher, who is then led to examine particular state institutions.

Protective legislation is a good example of an economic practice which involves the moral regulation of women and children. For instance, when Mackenzie King (then Deputy Minister of Labour) found in 1907 that the female workers at Bell Canada were being cruelly exploited, he justified reform measures not in terms of the need to regulate capital but by reference to the state's interest in "regulating the health of young women."[8] Thus, moral regulation crosscuts many of the organizing categories of social scientific and Marxian analysis, including "the economic" and "the political." Concrete analysis of different regulatory practices is required to uncover instances of moral regulation which may not be immediately apparent.

■ METHODS OF REGULATION

The social organization of regulatory discourses and practices has often been superficially investigated. We would like to suggest that approaching the question of moral regulation from the perspective of its methods will lead to much closer descriptions of connections between regulatory discourses and the work practices through which they are formed.

The 18th-century British state, for instance, developed certain methods for quantifying the social which served to legitimize new forms of social regulation. Without the invention of "social facts," social policies would have been seen as political decisions dictated by factional interests. The novel features of the new "facticity" cannot be explored here, but they include an emphasis on continuous record-keeping over time, the compilation of information in numerical form, and the publication of the resulting "facts." This new approach to the social was not exclusive to state institutions; many extra-state organizations and private individuals were leaders in this field (e.g., settlement houses, charity hospitals, and life insurance companies). Social investigation, then, was a crucial new method in the constitution and regulation of that equally new regulatory field, "the social." Since in many ways the allegedly scientific methods of investigative work shape not only the factual results but also the impact these results will eventually have on the people being regulated, any full analysis of social regulation requires that regulatory discourses be analyzed from the perspective of their production and circulation. The ways in which facts were constituted, collected and publicized (the text-as-process) is as important as the content (the text-as-product).

■ MORAL REGULATION AND LIBERAL DEMOCRATIC STATES

We earlier referred to the danger of assuming that state systems are the main, if not sole, agencies of regulation. This assumption is particularly problematic in the context of analyzing *moral* regulation in liberal democratic states. Such states are characterized by the establishment of legal, social and economic boundaries between "the public" and "the private." As both Marxist and feminist theorists have shown, these boundaries are state-defined and state-manipulated; it is also true that there is no single, fixed boundary between public and private, but rather there are variable and multiple boundaries. This does not mean, however, that the public/private distinction is a mere illusion: it is in fact a crucial principle separating the state from civil society and from "the individual." These are central categories in the political organization of liberal democratic societies, and arguments about where exactly to draw the line (e.g., in debates about whether the police ought to break up "domestic disputes") do not threaten the separation. This separation is not dichotomous, however: the sites of privacy are various and continually renegotiated. The privacies of sexuality, the family, domestic labour and capital are regulated through different bodies of law and interact with one another as well as with "the public." The public/private distinction operates as a complex regulatory strategy organizing multiple "realms" which in practice do not remain separate.

Thus, it is dangerous to conceptualize women's oppression as due to the confinement of femininity within "the private" (identified in turn with "the family"). The official distinction between public and private does not only organize familial relations; it regulates many kinds of social relations. There is no single paradigmatic instance of privacy, but rather coexisting and shifting boundaries between public and private: the relation between public and private enterprise, for instance, is not equivalent to that between public and private sex. Further, the sphere of the private is not completely female, and neither is the public inherently or completely male. It might be better to look at the ways in which a specific public-private distinction came to be gendered than to make generalizations about women's confinement to "privacy."

The right to privacy may of course be illusory, especially for women, the mentally or criminally "deviant," sexual minorities and other oppressed groups. Nevertheless, the existence of a structural commitment to a private sphere within which religious, political, racial and sexual opinions can exist free of state control means that it is not an easy matter for liberal democratic states to control the ethical subjectivity of their populations directly. Fascist states, by contrast, which do not claim to respect the private but rather make a point of subordinating all life to the state, can undertake vast projects for the re-shaping of racial, gender and moral subjectivity without falling into contradiction.

A liberal democratic state will always face certain difficulties if official policies to reshape the racial, gender and moral character of "the public" are seen as desirable, insofar as the whole legal and political apparatus officially claims to treat people as abstract "citizens" with individual rights such as freedom of thought and expression.

This internal contradiction within the state sheds some light on the tortuous (and necessary) relations between official and non-official organizations in the moral domain.
In this domain the Canadian state has, for instance, an interest in the "rehabilitation"
of offenders, but the explicitly moral aspects of reshaping the subjectivity of "offenders" have in large part been left to such bodies as the Salvation Army (which even
today administers Community Service Orders on behalf of the state).[9] One might also
argue that in the absence of the churches and the Right to Life movement, liberal states
would find it very difficult to legitimize restrictive abortion legislation.

There is, in other words, not only a pragmatic but also a structural reason why voluntary organizations are essential to moral reform campaigns of whatever political
stripe. These organizations cannot be seen as mere pawns of the state engaged in doing
its dirty ideological work in puppet-like fashion; voluntary organizations usually have
their own agendas and are in some ways in opposition to the state even when they receive most of their funding from it. The interaction between state and extra-state agencies of moral regulation must be concretely analyzed in order to reveal both the ways in
which they reinforce each other and the ways in which they come into conflict.

Many of the extra-state agencies of moral regulation or moral reform are composed
of, or led by, licenced professionals (doctors, clergymen, social workers). The historical
development of each group of experts, their internal contradictions and their points
of interaction with different state agencies all need to be researched if we are to avoid
abstract generalizations and conspiracy theories. Even when the state leads the way
in setting up regulations, for instance in new laws, the actual administration of the
regulations is often left to self-regulating professions.

The current Canadian debate on abortion regulation, to give a timely example, has
to take into account that self-regulating professions, such as doctors, have interests
which are not necessarily coterminous with the interests of the state. Furthermore,
it is in any case impossible to determine unequivocally what the interests of the state
system are, for it is readily apparent that it is not monolithically unified. One part of the
state may have an interest in promoting both abortion and sterilization among some
groups of women; another state body may be attempting to curb the power of doctors;
yet another arm of the state may be seeking to increase the birth rate with a view to
restricting immigration.

Women's bodies are rarely directly regulated, but are rather caught up in a complex
constellation of regulatory practices which are not necessarily in harmony with one
another.[10] Abortion laws and administrative regulations are not merely gender regulations: family, reproduction, medical practice, sexuality, population, and women (and
sometimes race and class) are all directly administered under the heading of "abortion." Since a single regulation (e.g., a law on abortion) has so many different levels of

operation, involving very different social groups, it cannot be assumed to have a single target or a single meaning. All of which demonstrates the need to transcend explanations of women's oppression that rely either on the single category of "male interests," or on the assumption of a cohesive set of "norms."

No 1 "AS IT WAS." No 2 "AS IT IS."

■ MOBILIZING AGAINST MORAL REGULATION: THE STRUGGLE OF THE IMMORAL?

Economic regulations are subject to struggle within both civil society and the state; these struggles are generally based on classes or class fractions. In general, each mode of regulation could be seen as occupying a distinct terrain and mobilizing obvious contenders to fight for or against particular regulatory practices. But the "moral terrain" is difficult if not impossible to map, among other reasons because, as we have argued here, it is not so much a distinct realm but a *mode* of regulation. One can differentiate between "sexual rule" and oppositional "sexual politics,"[11] but what might "moral politics" mean?

If we define our subject matter as moral—not just sexual—regulation, dilemmas quickly arise which are political as well as conceptual. One can find many instances of moral rule both inside and outside the state, but can one speak of movements of resistance based on moral politics? If so, would one include only movements that provide an alternative moral system, such as feminism, or would one have to include the amorphous amoral resistance to moral rule of gamblers, drinkers, and thieves?

It may perhaps be premature to speculate on possible theories of moral politics, given the absence of consensus on the meaning and scope of "moral regulation." Nevertheless, we along with many others involved in researching popular movements have to keep in mind the dialectical interplay between rulers and ruled, regulation and resistance, and the internal contradictions within both rulers and ruled. We have shown that the character or meaning of regulation is not always immediately obvious, partly because of the complex nature of ruling practices but also because discourses which appear to address a single social relation often have other underlying meanings and effects. An example of this overdetermination of regulatory discourses is the recently repealed Canadian abortion law, which if textually analyzed would seem to be "about" the division of powers between medicine and criminal law, but is with good reason popularly interpreted to be "about" sexuality, gender, life in general, religion, and population. If ruling is complex and internally contradictory, resistance is also far from monolithic or univocal. The pro-choice struggle, for instance, presents the peculiar situation of support for choice being given by liberal or libertarian men who are by no means feminists.

We would like to suggest that by focusing on the *relationship* between rule and resistance in particular struggles, one can use analyses of regulation to shed light on resistance movements, and vice versa. For instance, the lesbian/gay movement is partly shaped by legal definitions and restrictions, but it is not totally defined by that which it opposes; it has sometimes questioned the assumptions underlying regulation (for instance, by questioning medico-legal definitions of who is or is not gay). Attempts to redefine problems and to change the agenda of "public" discussion in turn affect the agencies of regulation, which might select some of the issues or concepts and give them back to "the public" in a sanitized form—as has happened to the very term "feminism," which developed among the oppressed as a self-definition but is now in danger of being defined by academic, media and state institutions.

This dialectical approach might help to guide concrete analyses which avoid making assumptions about the "essence" or "intent" of either particular regulations or resistance movements, and which concentrate on following the methods and processes of regulation and resistance through this complex interactive formation. Theory generated in this way can then be measured against concrete analysis developed from the standpoint of resistance, in order to be refined and put to work in further concrete analysis.

■ NOTES

1. An approach to feminist social theory which implicitly criticizes these two approaches and replaces them with a framework which has been very influential for us here is D.E. Smith, *The Everyday World as Problematic: A Feminist Sociology* (Toronto: Univ. of Toronto Press, 1987).

2. A recent example is Catharine MacKinnon, *Feminism Unmodified* (Harvard Univ. Press, 1986). See Mariana Valverde, "Beyond Gender Dangers and Private Pleasures: Theory and Ethics in the Sex Debates," forthcoming in *Feminist Studies*, for further comments on gender reductionism. The conceptualization of interests as pre-existing social and political relations has been criticized among socialists: see Chantal Mouffe, "Working Class Hegemony and the Struggle for Socialism," *Studies in Political Economy* 12 (1983), pp. 7–26, and Anthony Culter et al., *Marx's Capital and Capitalism Today* (London: Routledge and Kegan Paul, 1977), vol. I, esp. part III.

3. P. Corrigan, "On Moral Regulation: Some Preliminary Remarks," *Sociological Review* 29, 2 (1981), pp. 313–337.

4. The "social control" model of radical sociology (which is but a version of the "dominant ideology" thesis) has impoverished feminist accounts of social and moral regulation, as pointed out in Linda Gordon, *Heroes of Their Own Lives: The politics and history of family violence* (New York: Viking, 1988), pp. 289–300.

5. Mariana Valverde is writing a book on social purity and philanthropy in turn-of-the-century Canada; Lorna Weir is writing about Anne Green, an English servant hanged in 1650 for infanticide.

6. This is explored for English Canada by Bruce Curtis, "Preconditions of the Canadian State," in A. Moscovitch and J. Albert, eds., *The Benevolent State: The Growth of Welfare in Canada* (Toronto: Garamond, 1987), pp. 47–67. See also Philip Corrigan, "State Formation and Moral Regulation in Nineteenth-Century Britain," (Ph.D. thesis, Durham University); P. Corrigan and D. Sayer, *The Great Arch* (Oxford: Blackwell, 1986); P. Corrigan, ed., *Capitalism, State Formation and Marxist Theory* (London: Quartet, 1980).

7. We have not as yet elaborated a clear distinction between what is moral regulation and what is specifically sexual. Nevertheless, it is clear that Sunday blue-laws or temperance efforts are instances of moral regulation that are not sexual, and hence one must distinguish between the formation of ethical subjectivity (the field of moral regulation) and the formation of sexual subjectivity—although the two are obviously intertwined.

8. See the report of the Royal Commission [on Bell Canada], 1907. Mackenzie King called 20 women strikers to testify, but their experiences were interpreted through the lens provided by the 26 male doctors.

9. This complex relationship between religious/philanthropic bodies and the criminal justice system is explored by David Garland, *Punishment and Welfare: A History of Penal Strategies* (London: Gower, 1985). One reason, which Garland does not discuss, for the usefulness of religious bodies to the state is the enthusiasm with which such bodies can undertake the gender reform of convicts (for instance, women in prisons have traditionally been subjected to domestic science classes and various other gender moral regulatory processes).

10. The mediated and historically specific character of the processes affecting and controlling women's bodies is emphasized by Rosalind Petchesky, "Foetal Images: The Power of Visual Culture in the Politics of Reproduction," in Michelle Stanworth, ed., *Reproductive Technologies* (Minneapolis: Univ. of Minnesota Press, 1987). She points out that in much feminist writing in this area, "the specific forms taken by male strategies of reproductive control ... are reduced to a pervasive, transhistorical 'need'" (p. 72).

11. Lorna Weir, "Sexual Rule, Sexual Politics: Studies in the Medicalization of Sexual Danger, 1820-1920" (Ph.D. thesis, York University, 1986).

CHAPTER 5

THE CREATION OF HOMOSEXUALITY AS A "SOCIAL PROBLEM"

Gary Kinsman

■ WHY HISTORICAL MATERIALISM?

My method of exploration is a historical materialist one: that is, a perspective that views historical transformation as central to understanding our lives and that sees social relations and practices, rather than ideas or discourse separate from these,[1] as the primary elements in social change. Discourse both organizes and is organized through social relations. I am using "materialism" here in a broad sense, including eroticism and sexualities, as sensuous human practices. I do not view class as separate from other social relations and struggles, or as simply "economic" in character. Rather than displacing class relations and struggles, we need new ways of viewing class—not as a reified concept, but as lived historical, social experience and practice.[2] Sexual relations have been an important part of the formation of class relations and struggles; and class relations have shaped sexual relations and struggles.[3]

We can learn a great deal from the method of historical materialism. But to do this, we cannot read historical materialism—as a critical method of analysis—as a form of economic determinism in which "the economy" determines everything. This is unfortunately the main reading in current postmodernism and queer theory.[4] This is also a major problem with the "political economy" tradition that has been the hegemonic intellectual interpretation of Marxism in Canada until recently and that has not engaged seriously with critical work on gender, and especially with sexual regulation.[5] Unfortunately, it is this very reading of Marxism that has provided part of the basis for the growth of a "queer theory" divorced from and often antagonistic to the insights of historical materialism.

While Marx's and Engels's public and private writings on sex, and same-gender sex in particular, are an instance of "unthinking sex," as Andrew Parker[6] suggests, this was in part because in the context of the times in which they lived and of their own gender and sexual practices they were unable to apply their revolutionary method to this arena. Their critical social method that contested naturalism in other spheres of social life accepted a form of sexual naturalism. The "founding fathers" of Marxism relegated sex and eroticism to a historically insignificant terrain. Marx remained a prisoner of hegemonic social ideologies and practices, taking for granted the hegemonic forms of sexuality (and to some extent gender and race) he lived and found around himself as "natural." At the same time his critical method can be extended to these areas if it is taken up and transformed from the standpoints of women, gays, people of colour and others who face oppression and marginalization.

Marx's critique of capitalist political economy shattered the "natural" and ahistorical character of capitalist social relations and provided a way of moving beyond the appearance of "fair" exchange between capitalist and worker to disclose the underlying relations of exploitation upon which this rested. He was able to go beyond the equal and ahistorical appearance of the exchange between capitalist and worker to reveal the underlying appropriation of surplus value by the capitalist, which defined the exploitation of the worker during the process of production; yet he proved unable to move beyond the "natural" appearance of the existing and developing heterosexual social forms of sexual life to reveal how these, too, were historical and social creations. In the sphere of commodity production, exchange, and circulation, Marx and Engels were able to analyze commodity fetishism as the mystified surface appearance of capitalist social relations in which social relationships appear to be relations between products.[7] They could therefore reveal in the realm of commodities the relation between this phenomenal form, or the ways in which the everyday accepted phenomena of the world present themselves, and the underlying social relations organizing this experience.[8] Marx and Engels could not, however, go beyond the surface appearance of sexual relations to reveal the process of fetishism which obscures the social relations in which our sexuality is made. Insofar as they considered the matter, they were prisoners of a naturalist and essentialist view.

Marx focused on the social character of the processes of production and capitalist relations and did not produce a narrow "economic" theory. He was able to disclose the ideological practices through which bourgeois political economy separated its concepts from the social practices and relations through which they were produced.[9]

In stressing the insights of historical materialism, I am focusing on the revolutionary aspects of Marx's method: the historical character of social processes, the importance of social practices and relations, and his vital critique of ideological practices. People's social worlds are made through the practices and activities of people themselves. I emphasize the need for a central critique of "naturalism," of "surface appearances," and of the phenomenal forms through which social processes often get presented to us. This centrally includes a critique of the ideological practices that produce forms of knowledge separated from the social practices that produce them, resulting in forms of knowledge that are removed from experience and that attend to ruling and managing people's lives.[10] I am also pointing to Marx's crucial critique of reification—his opposition to converting social relations between people into relations between things.[11] Above all, this liberatory approach emphasizes that what is socially made can be socially transformed.

Rather than dismissing the insights of a non-reductionist historical materialism, we need to reclaim and transform them *for* queers in our struggles for liberation. It will be through various subordinated, marginalized and exploited groups taking up critical historical materialist work from their own standpoints that the resources for new transformative socialist theoretical and activist movements will be made.

Historical materialism *for* queers, as I develop it here, shatters the natural and ahistorical character of heterosexual hegemony, discloses the oppressions lying beneath the "natural" appearance of this hegemony, points to the socially and historically made character of sexualities, and puts heterosexual hegemony in question. It directs our attention to the ideological practices through which heterosexual hegemonic relations are constructed. This points toward the possibilities of overturning heterosexual hegemony and transforming erotic relations, and would link this to the transformation of State, class, gender, and race relations. Marx's work and method still have a lot to tell us about the dynamics of capitalist social relations and how these shape the lives of lesbians and gay men as well as others. This approach also sharpens our focus of attention on class relations and struggles within gay, lesbian, and other communities.

History, in this sense, belongs not only to the past. It participates in forming what Jeffrey Weeks calls the "historical present."[12] Examining historical experiences and practices can help us understand from where lesbian and gay oppression and, more generally, oppressive sexual regulation has come, where it may be going, and the possibilities for transformation. The concepts necessary for an understanding of sexual rule and resistance exist only in initial form at present. One way of proceeding is by studying our past to develop the historically rooted categories necessary for this exploration. This approach explores how people's experiences are socially organized and how they change over time.[13] When examining official government documents or police records, we must immediately place them in the context of people's lives. The emergence of "lesbianism" and "homosexuality," and that of lesbian, homosexual, and heterosexual categories in official discourse, were part of broader shifts in class, gender, and social organization. Same-gender sex was relegated to a subordinate position through relations of sex and gender regulation that established a particular form of heterosexuality as the social norm.

If analysis can be rooted in the social relations that have organized these experiences, then a much better understanding of how sexuality has been defined, organized, and regulated in capitalist and patriarchal societies will be possible. Capitalism is a dynamic social system that is constantly "transforming the 'ground' on which we stand so that we are always ... experiencing changing historical process."[14] History does not stand still, and it is this very undermining of previous forms of sex and gender regulations that has created the basis for gay liberation and feminist movements.

These needed historical investigations do not replace the need for critical social analysis of the contemporary forms of social organization of our oppression, including studies of policing, AIDS, family and social policies, violence against lesbians and gay men, problems facing lesbian and gay youth, and others.[15] At the same time, this critical historical work can help to develop the concepts needed for critical analysis of the present and future possibilities.

In undertaking these historical materialist journeys, I have drawn on a number of sources. These are the historical and social organization of sexuality perspective; the perspective of taking up the standpoint of the oppressed, and the social organization of knowledge approach of Marxist-feminist Dorothy E. Smith; and various Marxist-inspired approaches to State formation, moral and cultural regulation, historical sociology, and the social organization of hegemony.

■ SEXUALITY, HISTORY, AND SOCIAL ORGANIZATION

Contrary to "common sense," sexuality is not natural nor innate. Cross-cultural and historical studies have unearthed the diverse ways in which eroticism has been organized in various social settings. Sexuality is not simply biologically defined; it is socially created, building on physiological potentialities.

> Biological sexuality is the necessary precondition for human sexuality. But biological sexuality is only a set of potentialities, which is never unmediated by human reality, and which becomes transformed in qualitatively new ways in human society.[16]

The various possible erotic zones of the human body provide the preconditions for the social and cultural forms of activity and meaning that come to compose human sexual practices. It is in this transition from "biological"[17] to historical and social that the definitions and regulations of sexuality have emerged. Physiological capacities are transformed to create sexuality as a social need, and, in turn, to produce new erotic needs.

Our various forms of sexuality and the social identities built around them are organized through the sex and gender relations that have existed in different societies.[18] Sex is fundamentally a social activity. A history of sexuality *is* a history of social relations. Human sexual practice is composed of thoughts (eroticized images, socially learned courses of action, or "sexual scripts"[19]) and physical/sensual activities themselves. The way in which our erotic capacities come together with mental constructs, language, and symbolic systems and images is a social process. For instance, in our everyday lives we are able to differentiate between the touch of a doctor on our genitals as part of a medical examination and the caress of a lover in a more intimate setting. Our lover's touch will be responded to erotically through the enactment of a "sexual script" even though the touch of the doctor could have been the same physical touch as that of a lover. Together, thought and activity form human praxis that provides the basis for a historical materialist view of sexual relations.[20]

In making sense of sexuality as a social practice, a historical materialist method is very useful. At the most general level, erotic activity, In all its diversity and meanings, can be seen as a human universal similar to the way in which Marx saw human production. Sexual activity, like production in general, has existed in all human societies.[21] However, what can be said about sexual practice in this general sense is extremely limited. It provides us with no basis from which to explore sexuality in the historical sense. What organizes and comprises sexual relations in each period is therefore a historical and empirical question—a topic for exploration.[22] We need historically rooted concepts, and we must reject transhistorical categorizations—for instance, the notion that the homosexual, the lesbian, or the heterosexual has been around for all time (or, for some, since Sodom and Gomorrah). Both same-sex and different-sex sexual practices have existed throughout human history, but they have differed radically in their social organization.

But it is even more complex than this when we enter the social construction of gender into the picture since there have also been same-gender and different-gender erotic practices. For instance, in some aboriginal cultures in North America, there were same-sex erotic relations between what might be described as "regular" men and "berdache" (biological males who were members of a "third" gender that combined masculine/feminine characteristics). This would have been seen culturally as different-gender eroticism since there were more than two gender groupings in these societies.

Contemporary "heterosexuality" and "homosexuality" are historically and socially specific organizations of different-gender and same-gender desires and pleasures. For instance, male same-gender erotic activities have ranged from structured "educational" relationships between men and boys in particular class, family, and State relations, to acts surrounding puberty or masculinity rituals, to cross-dressing and gender activity reversals.[23] These had different social meanings in different social/cultural contexts and were different social practices. Among the Sambia of Papua, for instance, same-gender sex for males between seven and nineteen was mandatory. Boys fellated men on a daily basis, so that they would grow into masculine adults. According to this culture males cannot produce sperm on their own; they can only recycle it from one generation to another. In their adult lives, these males engage in sex with women.[24] Our contemporary notions of the heterosexual/homosexual dichotomy make no sense in a culture like this. It is impossible to hold onto any transhistorical notion of homosexuality or homosexual behaviour—or transhistorical heterosexuality, for that matter—in the face of these diverse practices and social meanings.

Much critical understanding of the social organization of sexuality comes from how we see the social organization of gender. Sexuality, like gender, is a product of social interaction—a continuous social accomplishment.[25] Gender is assigned in our society at birth by doctors and nurses based on apparent genital features. It then takes on many social features that have nothing to do with physiology, even though biological determinist approaches argue that biology determines gender, whether it be through genes or hormones.[26] Tied in with this social organization of gender is an associated sexuality and sexual "identity." Through this social process a "natural" attitude toward sexuality and gender is created.[27]

In patriarchal and capitalist societies, sexuality and sexual identities connect a number of needs—emotional contact, friendship, sensual closeness, bodily pleasure, and genital sex—with notions of biology, gender, and reproductive capacity. This formation of sexuality implants naturalized constructs of masculinity and femininity within our very social and sexual beings, making it very difficult to disentangle our various needs grouped together as sexuality from biology, reproduction, and gender. Sexuality can be seen as a collecting category that groups together diverse needs, capacities, and desires.[28] Our sexuality has come to be defined by naturalist notions to such a degree that the process of social organization is rendered invisible (or unconscious).[29] We tend to "reify sex as a thing-in-itself."[30] We see our sexualities as a personal essence defining who we are, rather than as constituted through the social practices that we ourselves have been active in through which our sexualities have been made. To critically investigate sexuality, we must put in question this "natural attitude" to recover the social practices and relations through which sexualities are made.

The human and social praxis involved in the formation of sexualities is obscured by the relations in which this process takes place. In a similar but different fashion to Marx's analysis of commodity fetishism, sexuality has come to be fetishized as something individual, "natural," and essential in which social relations and practices disappear. It should be clear, however, that the social relations organizing commodity fetishism and sexual fetishism are not the same and need their own historical investigation.[31] Ideologies of naturalism and an essential sexual nature are tied to the appearance of sexual fetishism. It must be stressed that powerful State and social policies lie behind the "naturalness" of heterosexuality in this society.

Sexual practice and "identity" is formed through a process of social interaction and encounters with social discourse, significant others, and bodily-based pleasures.[32] There is no "natural" or "unitary" sexuality. No situation is inherently sexual, but many situations are capable of being eroticized. Sexuality is subject to "socio-cultural moulding to a degree surpassed by few other forms of human behaviour."[33] Sexuality is not simply individual or "private," and the individual is only an individual in a social context. Social individuals come to take part in and take up particular sexual practices and identities. "Proper" gender is associated with "normal" sexuality, since gender shapes sexual conduct. Part of this process of normalization "derives from organs being placed in legitimate orifices."[34] "Identities" such as heterosexual, homosexual, lesbian, and bisexual are socially created.

While heterosexuality in contemporary societies is established as "natural," some of us do come to realize that we are erotically "different." Masculinity, femininity, heterosexuality, and family life itself are contradictory. Subversive readings of dominant erotic images, along with the experiences of bodily pleasures and erotic play, are the initial bases for our queer desires. We may see ourselves as "outsiders" or as "different" as we grow up or at a later stage of development. This is a dialectic of broader social and self-definition. We may eventually encounter homosexual, lesbian, bisexual, or "queer" labelling and discover other lesbian and gay individuals and cultures that have managed to seize social spaces from the dominant order.[35]

Mary Douglas, in her anthropological work, explores one bridge between the individual and broader social worlds; how social and moral notions of purity, pollution, and taboo have been built on the social relations of biological reproduction and sexuality. These symbols play an important role in organizing social boundaries and in providing a sense of social and moral order in a chaotic world.

> Ideas about separating, purifying, demarcating and punishing transgressions have as their main function to impose system on an inherently untidy experience. It is only by exaggerating the difference between within and without, above and below, male and female, that a semblance of order is created.[36]

As Douglas writes, "nothing is more essentially transmitted by a social process of learning than sexual behaviour and this of course is closely related to morality."[37] Reproductive and sexual norms and taboos produce a "natural" order around which life comes to be organized. This natural order depends on boundaries separating the normal from the ambiguous. Any challenge to these boundaries by anomalous behaviour leads to the mobilization of fear and anxiety. This moral order therefore depends on the marginalization of anomalies and firm social boundaries demarcated by "natural" markers that are rigorously policed: heterosexuality, in contemporary Western society, is associated with the natural, the normal, the clean, the healthy, and the pure; homosexuality, with the dangerous, the impure, the unnatural, the sick, and the abnormal.[38]

Frank Pearce used Douglas's perspective in an analysis of the presentation of gay men in the media. Homosexuals are viewed as anomalies since they violate and defy the natural boundaries of sex and gender behaviour. Homosexuals, according to Pearce,

> Fracture the coherence of the core gender identities thought to be necessarily associated with male and female biological equipment. These men finding other men attractive are anomalies, and "anomalies," as Mary Douglas points out, endanger the natural moral order of this society.[39]

We therefore mobilize anxiety, fear, and hatred. Pearce describes four main strategies whereby the threat to heterosexuality is deflected: ignoring or condemning homosexuality; providing easy definitions such as gender "inversion" to explain it away and reduce ambiguity; using homosexuals as a negative reference point; and labelling us as dangerous, even inciting violence against us.[40]

■ THE SOCIAL ORGANIZATION OF SEXUAL KNOWLEDGE

This book proposes a shift of focus in the study of same-gender and different-gender desire and pleasure and sexual regulation: a shift away from homosexuality and lesbianism as a "problem" and toward a historical and social account of the emergence of sexual life, including heterosexuality. The "traditions" of religion, psychology, medicine, criminology, sexology, history, sociology, and anthropology have created the "problem," defining us as sick, deviant, abnormal—even criminal—and defining heterosexuality as "normal." These socially organized forms of knowledge have been crucial to the construction of heterosexual hegemony. In these forms of knowledge production that have also been forms of social power (what Foucault describes as "power/knowledge"[41]), lesbians and gay men have been treated as objects of study to be researched. It has always been homosexuality and lesbianism and not heterosexuality that stands in need of explanation. The "problematization" of homosexuality has been a crucial part of the normalization[42] of heterosexuality. Four examples help clarify this social process.

Anthropology in the 18th and 19th centuries was engaged in setting sexual and social norms. Classification of the races was a main preoccupation,[43] integral to which was the classification of sexual behaviour. "Savages" came to be defined as more primitive with regard to sexual behaviour than "civilized" peoples, although sometimes the savages were romanticized as acting more "naturally." Anthropologists carried their own cultural values with them, displaying an acute ethnocentric and Eurocentric[44] bias but, at the same time supplying much of the data upon which the work of the sex psychologists and sexologists in the metropolitan countries relied.[45] Anthropology as a profession was very much involved in the organization of colonial, class, racial, gender, and sexual relations.

Perhaps this process can best be seen through an examination of Bronislaw Malinowski's classic study of the Trobriand Islanders. The villagers described their villages from ground view as a number of bumps. Malinowski saw them as a series of concentric circles, describing them from above using a mapping representation. This disparity in descriptions was socially rooted. Malinowski came from a vigorously class-divided society, and he was a member of the academic discipline of anthropology. His account was addressed to a specialized intelligentsia in the metropolitan countries. There was no position within Trobriand culture from which their villages could be seen thus, but Malinowski, located as he was outside and "above" their society, could so describe them. Malinowski's anthropological work embodied the developing social relations of imperialism.[46]

Malinowski's work also embodied a developing heterosexual hegemony. Among the Trobriand Islanders, they did not see different-gender sexual intercourse and reproduction as linked. In one book, Malinowski included homosexuality, masturbation, and fellatio in a section entitled "The Censure of Sexual Aberrations."[47] Despite accounts of widespread same-gender sex in Melanesian societies, he argued that homosexuality was not prevalent and that it was treated with contempt and derision.[48] His work embodied the imposition of sexual norms on indigenous populations. Malinowski saw things from the standpoint of the missionaries, the administrators, and a developing heterosexual hegemony. In the next chapter, I again touch on the links between imperialism and heterosexual hegemony.

The work of 19th-century forensic psychiatrists and sex psychologists—who classified and categorized sexualities and sexual practices—also reveals the social relations that their work embodied and helped organize. Dr. Richard Von Krafft-Ebing, the fore-most forensic psychiatrist of the last century who addressed sexual pathologies (and the "grand-daddy" of sexology), felt that sexual relations outside heterosexual mar-riage represented not only a degeneration to an earlier, lower stage of evolution, but that they threatened Western civilization itself. For example:

> Every expression of the sex-drive ... which does not comply with the goals of na-ture, i.e., procreation, must be declared perverse ... Episodes of moral decline in the life of peoples fall regularly together with times of effeminacy, voluptuousness, and luxury ... Rapidly growing nervousness results in an increase in sensuality and by leading to the dissipation among the masses of people, undermines the pillars of society: morality and purity of family life. If this is undermined through dissipation, adultery and luxury, then the fall of the state is inevitable.[49]

Krafft-Ebing's work expresses not only the standpoint of State agencies, but also mid-dle-class assumptions about the class character of sexual morality.

Mainstream psychiatry and psychology in the 20th century have generally viewed ho-mosexuality as a symptom of "infantile regression" or some other pathological disorder, and have developed various strategies to cure, regulate, or adjust patients to the hetero-sexual norm.[50] This has included various forms of aversion therapy, as well as partial lobotomies. Psychiatrists and psychologists rarely treated lesbians and gay men as in-dividuals with our own unique biographies and experiences. Instead we are slotted into clinical and abstract categories of "homosexuality" and produced as "cases." We were already cut out of "normal" social interaction by this diagnosis.[51] Before we even enter a psychiatrist's or a psychologist's office, a homosexual or lesbian "typology" has often already defined us as "deviant," laying out a particular course of "treatment."

Homosexual "deviance" is investigated with the aim of our elimination, containment, or control. Knowledge has been produced so that ruling institutions can formulate legal codes, policing policies, and social policies. According to Magnus Hirschfeld, an early sex psychologist and homosexual-rights reformer, most of the thousand or so works on homosexuality that appeared between 1898 and 1908 were addressed to the legal pro-fession.[52] Many early works by medical and legal experts "were chiefly concerned with whether the disgusting breed of perverts could be physically identified for the courts, and whether they should be held legally responsible for their acts."[53] The men and women engaged in same-gender love have thus been labelled "deviants," "perverts," "gender inverts," "gender non-conformists," "sexual psychopaths," "dangerous sex offenders," "promiscuous," guilty of committing "gross indecency," engaging in "anonymous" sex, and have been the subjects of the distinction between "public" and "private" sex.

Official knowledge about homosexuals and lesbians came chiefly from studies of imprisoned or "psychologically disturbed" homosexuals.[54] Much of this work relies on data such as the legal codification of offences, court and police records, and sexological, medical and psychological discourse,[55] and often incorporates features of the power relations of the legal and prison systems and the psychiatric and medical professions. A great deal of official knowledge about homosexuality and lesbianism has been produced so that social agencies can "understand," classify, police, and regulate our sexual lives.

This knowledge has in turn shaped popular cultures and "common-sense" notions of how society is organized, through the mass media, the schools, government policies, the Criminal Code, police action, and the social organization of intended "moral panics"[56] on sexual questions.

During the last part of the 19th century, homosexuality was often seen by the scientific disciplines as a form of congenital inversion rooted in biological degeneration or anomaly. These approaches reduced homosexuality to a biological cause. More recently, given the challenge presented by lesbian and gay liberation to psychological theories of homosexuality and lesbianism as a mental illness, there has been a certain return to these types of approaches by some researchers. Initial results of some of this research have been magnified and intensified by mass-media coverage. The research usually starts off by assuming the "normality" of heterosexuality and that it is (usually male) homosexuality that stands in need of explanation. It assumes that there are only two rigidly dichotomous sexualities (heterosexuality and homosexuality), and these are based in biological difference. Men and women who are interested in both men and women undermine the basis of this research.

Ignoring the rich work done on the historical and social construction of sexuality, this research is directed at finding the biological cause or causes of homosexuality. This reduces the complex social and cultural process through which sexuality is formed to biological causes, whether they be located in a different structure in the hypothalamus, or genetic or elements—there is even one theory suggesting that stress for the mother during pregnancy produces homosexuality in the male fetus.[57] Liberal proponents of this more recent research argue that the establishment of homosexual difference as biological in character will lead to greater social acceptance, as homosexuality will now be "natural" for a minority of the population. This does not address how the acceptance of "race" as biological in character has done nothing to eliminate racism against people of colour. Appeals to "nature" do not get rid of discrimination and oppression. And the response of some to reports that there may be a "gay gene" is to try to eliminate this gene in order to eliminate homosexuality. Again the problem to be explained is "homosexuality," while the "naturalness" of heterosexual hegemony is just accepted.[58]

The resurgence of biological determinist explanations of homosexuality is occurring in the context of a new popularity for biological explanations of human behaviours and differences. This is also related to a resurgence of biological explanations of gender and gender inequality and in some circles of race and racial inequality.[59] For instance, some researchers now suggest that women's math and spatial skills really are biologically inferior to men's. Therefore, the social equality that feminism has demanded is seen to go against "nature."[60] This is part of a broader social organization of a "backlash" to feminism, and not the first time biological explanations have been used to buttress social inequality. "Biology" has long been invoked to justify the social subordination of blacks, women and lesbians, and gay men.

Heterosexist ideas about the naturalness of heterosexuality and the sickness of homosexuality are not simply backward individual ideas; they are organized through the social relations and practices of heterosexual hegemony. This points to one of the problems with the use by gay, lesbian, queer, and other activists of the concept of "homophobia"—the "dread of being in close quarters with homosexuals."[61] This term quite accurately describes the panic some heterosexuals feel when confronted by visible lesbians and gays. It has also been used to explain homosexual oppression in general, however, and as such tends to simply reverse existing psychological definitions of homosexuality as mental illness, turning them back onto heterosexuals who have difficulty dealing with "queers." "Homophobia" does not seriously dispute these psychological definitions; it individualizes and privatizes gay and lesbian oppression and obscures the social relations that organize it. It reduces homophobia to a mental illness, detaching it from its social contexts and reproducing all the problems of psychological definitions.[62] Unfortunately, "homophobia" has also been the main way in which other movements and groups of people beyond the feminist movement have taken up our oppression, and this leads them to misunderstand the roots of our oppression.[63]

"Homophobia" also continues to be used as a major way of accounting for our oppression even in the new forms of queer activism that emerged in the late 1980s and early 1990s. "Queer Nation" groups with their "in your face" politics took "anti-homophobic" politics to their most militant expression. At times it seemed as if militant confrontations with individual homophobes would lead to the ending of our oppression, which has not allowed this queer activism to get at the social roots of queer oppression. "Homophobia" is continued as a central concept even in much of the new "queer theory" that emerged in the late 1980s and early 1990s in the U.S. In Eve Kosofsky Sedgwick's influential book *The Epistemology of the Closet*, for instance, her taking up of an antihomophobic position has allowed her to separate sexual oppression from gender oppression, and has allowed her to focus on literary and cultural re-readings of texts to discern homophobic assumptions.[64] Such a focus on homophobia often operates to obscure the social relations and practices that shape lesbian and gay oppression.

I therefore prefer to use the term "heterosexism," relating the practices of heterosexual hegemony to institutional and social settings and to sex and gender relations without reducing gay and lesbian oppression to an "effect" of gender. In this context, homophobia can be seen as a particularly virulent personal response organized by heterosexist discourse and practice.

Until recently, heterosexuals rarely encountered visible gays, lesbians, or bisexuals. Most images were those projected by the mass media and those circulating in popular cultures, which generally came from psychology, sexology, the churches, and the courts and police. Dorothy E. Smith describes the "ideological circle" through which the world is interpreted by the media and other agencies;[65] this is one of the ways heterosexual hegemony operates. The world is interpreted through the schemas of "expert sources" (police, policy analysts, government bureaucrats) and hegemonic cultural narratives to confirm the dominant interpretation of same-gender sexuality. "Scientific" theories of homosexual deviance, criminality, or sickness thereby enter public discussion.

■ SHIFTING STANDPOINTS

In suggesting that the basis of sexual inquiry be reoriented, I draw upon what can be called a standpoint approach, which, as formulated by Dorothy E. Smith, calls for a change in vantage point from that of hegemonic ruling relations to that of women and other oppressed groups.[66] Ruling relations and regimes are the agencies involved in the management of contemporary capitalist patriarchal societies. Ruling relations are broader than those of State agencies, and include the mass media, various professional groups, and the forms of bureaucracy that have emerged over the last century.[67]

In "A Sociology for Women," Smith analyzes how ruling relations produce knowledge from the standpoint of a male-dominated ruling class.[68] A sociology *for* women entails a reorientation of inquiry starting from the social experiences of individual women or groups of women. Smith's analysis provides insights into how ruling knowledge is produced and how it rules—bringing into view the social relations through which women are subordinated.

> As we explored the world from this place in it, we became aware that this rupture in experiences and between experience and the social forms of its expression, was located in a relation of power between women and men, in which men dominated over women.[69]

Inquiry, then, begins with questions about everyday experiences and the social practices we engage in on a day-to-day basis. It proceeds to render the everyday world "problematic" by investigating the social relations in which women's experiences (or the experiences of other groups) are located.[70] For this perspective, the notion of social relation is key, being the process by which our own activities participate in but are also shaped, constrained, and regulated by broader social forces. The notion of a social relation links together social practices in different local sites in a combined and inter-linked social process. While we participate in producing these social relations, we also, as individuals and as groups, tend to lose control over them, and they come to stand over and against our everyday lives. While social relations develop historically, in con-temporary societies, they render the world in which we live natural and ahistorical. This provides a social basis for the ideologies and discourses of naturalism that we find around us.

The social world is, however, composed of people's own activities articulated through these social relations. We daily engage in practices that produce relations of class, gen-der, race and sexuality. Social "structures" cannot be seen as separate from human ac-tivity; they are organized by, and, at the same time, organize social interaction. Social relations are actual practices, not merely concepts or structures. They are produced by people but they are not constituted by individual actors alone, as they are sequences of actions and relationships that no single individual can complete.

The social relations that organize women's experiences in this society are capital-ist, patriarchal, racist, and heterosexist. An example from the work of Marx may help clarify this: a commodity (a product made to be exchanged) as a social object is real-ized—made socially real as a commodity—only through exchange in a market. If the commodity is not exchanged, its value cannot be realized. If it does not enter into a series of social relationships between different individuals composing a social relation, it cannot be realized as a commodity. As Marx also argued, through this process of exchange the commodity comes to appear as though it has intrinsic value as a thing. Exchange therefore comes to be seen as a relation between different commodities (be-tween things) rather than a social relationship between producers, buyers, and sellers. This is what Marx called the fetishism of commodities,[71] and can also be seen as a form of reification (or "thingification").

Similarly, although differently, women's experiences are organized through a series of social practices that define and regulate sex and gender and in which women are themselves active. This web of relations shapes gender identifications, gender dichoto-mies, sexualities, and patriarchal social organization.[72]

Making the everyday world problematic moves analysis from "experience" itself to the specific social relations that organize it. This helps to make people's social practices visible. There is no pure unmediated "telling of experience," as this is always affected by social discourse, but starting with the experiences of the oppressed and marginalized and then making them problematic locates our investigation in a very different place, at least partially outside of or in rupture with ruling regimes and discourse. This allows us to see the workings of ruling relations from the standpoint of the oppressed. As Smith notes:

> It is not individual social behaviour which is our interest but the social determinations of our everyday experience. The object of inquiry is the historical processes and development of social relations which organize, shape and determine our directly experienced worlds.[73]

In this book I apply this method of inquiry to the historical and social situations of lesbians and gay men. A history and sociology for lesbians and gay men involves both a critique of official knowledge (which I begin in this chapter) and a reorientation of inquiry to begin from the experiences of those who have engaged in same-gender sex and others who have been oppressed by ruling sexual regulation (which I begin in the historical sections). The purpose is not to interrogate the experiences of lesbians and gay men but instead to learn from their experiences about the social organization of heterosexual hegemony and oppressive sexual regulation so that these ruling practices can be interrogated and transformed.[74]

The contemporary lesbian and gay experience of a rupture between our lives as "deviants" or outsiders and the heterosexual norm serves as the beginning of inquiry. This rupture is lived differently by people on the basis of class, race, and gender. How this tension has come about is one of the key questions to be explored. By making our everyday experiences problematic and locating them in emerging social relations, we can reveal aspects of our oppression and of heterosexual hegemony that are not visible from the vantage point of ruling relations. This process exposes not only the work of the agencies who have labelled us "perverts" and "criminals," but also the activities of those engaged in same-gender sex ourselves. We have been able to construct a certain "naturalness" and "normalness" for ourselves in opposition to heterosexual hegemony. If we start from here —the experiences of lesbians, gays, and others who engage in queer sex of the ruptures we feel between hegemonic heterosexuality and the actualities of our lives—then the problem is no longer homosexuality, but rather heterosexual hegemony and sexual rule more generally.

From this socially and historically grounded standpoint, the absolute distinction between homosexuality and heterosexuality is rooted in the work of the ruling regime and relations. This distinction is not as clearly expressed in our individual erotic lives, however. The actual relationship between social categories, identity construction and formation, and sexual activity is not as clear-cut as official discourse contends.

Sexual preferences and "identities" are not fixed in stone. They develop unevenly, are often contradictory, and are potentially fluid. Kinsey's statistics suggested that a majority of men involved in reported homosexual acts did not see their experiences as defining them as homosexual.[75] Many are able to engage in occasional erotic delights with males while maintaining a heterosexual and masculine gender "identity." Prison inmates and hustlers often managed their identities so that they were not tainted by the stigma of homosexuality. For instance, in prison, the "masculine" man who plays the "active" role in anal intercourse but never plays the "passive" position in anal intercourse and who gets his penis fellated but never sucks another penis, may be able to escape the label of "queer" and preserve his "heterosexual" identity. Some hustlers manage their identities by claiming they have sex only for the money, or that they engage only in acts that don't define them as homosexual. John Rechy in *City of Night* quotes Pete, a hustler:

> Whatever a guy does with other guys, if he does it for money that don't make him queer. You're still straight. It's when you start doing it for free, with other young guys, that you start growing wings.[76]

George Chauncey, in an illuminating historical analysis, shows us that, in the early twentieth century in the U.S. among working class and other cultures, there was often a distinction made between "queer" men who were associated with effeminacy and full-time participation in same-gender sexual activities and those men who occasionally would allow these "queers" to have sex with them. This latter group of men would not be tainted with "queerness."[77] And in the Canadian Navy in the 1950s, some doctors felt that only "effeminate" men were real homosexuals while men who were more "masculine" and only occasionally engaged in sex with other men when women were not available were basically "normal" (see chapter 7). Men who are married and have children may feel that their sexual adventures in tea rooms (washrooms), steam baths, or parks do not define them as homosexual.[78]

Ruling discourse rigorously associates sexual acts with gender and sexual identity (or else views homosexual activity as merely a brief "phase" one is passing through). In real life, however, it is not that neat. A sexual act may not be immediately associated with a particular sexuality or sexual identity. There is also the experience of bisexuality that undermines the dominant sexual dichotomy and that allows some people to combine same- and different-gender erotic desires. While bisexuality is not the only "natural" sexuality, as some bisexual liberationists argue, given it is as socially constructed as other sexualities, it does destabilize the heterosexual/homosexual polarity in a powerful way.[79]

At the same time, the historical and social accounts presented in this book demonstrate that contemporary lesbian and gay experiences are very real social and experiential realities that cannot be dismissed as simply the imposition of ruling sexual classifications. Lesbians and gay men have participated in the creation of our own cultures and networks.

Ruling concepts cannot simply be stretched to cover our experiences. We must step outside ruling discourses—as we must as women, people of colour, and other oppressed groups—if we are to create knowledge to help us in our struggles.[80]

This perspective starts from our own experiences and practices.[81] We must become the subjects of our work rather than its objects. We must move beyond this starting point, however, to view everyday life as problematic; to see the struggles between ruling institutions and lesbians and gays over the meanings, images, and definitions of sexual regulation. We must move beyond our immediate experiences and the assumed "naturalness" of our existence by uncovering the social relations in which homosexuality and heterosexuality have emerged historically.

■ HEGEMONY, STATE FORMATION, AND CULTURAL REVOLUTION

My analysis also draws upon a number of recent developments within Marxism and historical materialist approaches.[82] Recent historical and sociological explorations of capitalist or bourgeois State formation have illuminated how crucial to the formation of the contemporary State has been what can be called a "bourgeois cultural revolution."[83]

Building on earlier State forms, the capitalist class made itself the ruling class and forged contemporary State relations by attempting to remake society in its own image. Crucial to this process was the creation of approved or respectable social identities, which necessarily meant the denial of alternatives. State formation is therefore always an active process, always contested and resisted, and riveted with contradictions. Heterosexual hegemony, as a part of this process, was constructed at the expense of other social and sexual possibilities, such as emerging homosexual and lesbian cultures. Heterosexuality was established as "normal." Homosexuality and lesbianism were disadvantaged as perverted, sick, and criminal.[84]

This approach stresses the importance to capitalist and patriarchal rule of the cultural and moral regulation of social identities and practices. The oppressive regulation of social life establishes some forms of activity as acceptable, respectable, responsible, normal and natural; some ways of life are empowered, others are devalued. This approach refuses to reduce capitalism to its economic dimensions alone. State forma-tion is seen as central to capitalist development. Class relations include struggles over cultural norms, social identities, and sexualities. Non-economic relations are thereby crucial to class relations.[85] Within historical materialism using these insights, the re-lationship of class, State formation, and sexual rule can be explored. This perspective on State formation will be particularly useful when we examine the making of the Canadian State and its relation to English and U.S. State formation.

A crucial aspect of this State formation and cultural revolution has been the estab-lishment of social, cultural, and political forms of hegemony. "Hegemony," as I use the term, derives from the writings of the Italian Marxist Antonio Gramsci in the 1920s and 1930s.[86] Hegemony unites the process of coercion and consent, viewing the two as often taking place through the same social practices. Hegemony occurs through the normalization or naturalization of existing relations and is achieved when one class can exert social authority and leadership over others. This includes the power to

> frame alternatives and contain communities, to win and shape consent so that the granting of legitimacy to the dominant classes appears not only "spontane-ous" but natural and "normal."[87]

Hegemony is, however, not simply imposed by State agencies and the ruling class. It must be continually reestablished. It is therefore never total or exclusive.

> [Hegemony] is not self-securing, it is constructed, sustained, reconstructed, by particular agents and agencies, in part by violence.[88]

When successfully established, hegemony shapes, redefines, and incorporates the needs and concerns of the subordinated groups so that they conform to the interests of ruling groups.[89]

The development, transformation, and struggle over cultural and social definitions, boundaries, acceptable knowledge, identities, and norms are a key terrain for the con-tinuous organization and reorganization of hegemonic relations.

> The dominant culture represents itself as the culture. It tries to define and contain all other cultures within its most inclusive range. Its views of the world, unless challenged, will stand as the most natural, all-embracing culture.[90]

Hegemonic approaches therefore allow for a combination in historical explorations of people as active participants in the making of their worlds with the social constraints that limit their activities. Unfortunately, until recently, most attempts to use hegemony to explore the process of ruling have confined it to a rather narrow economic realm, or to narrow, economically defined notions of class relations, and have remained male, white, and heterosexually defined.[91]

I use a hegemonic approach to examine Canadian struggles over sexual definitions and regulations. Hegemony must therefore be freed from its narrower meanings and made relevant to sexual and other political movements so that the organization of racial, patriarchal, and heterosexual hegemonies can be explored and challenged. While these forms of hegemony have their own features, they are part of a larger social and historical organization of class and State rule.

Hegemonic approaches can be used to explore lesbian and gay oppression and resistance. Heterosexual hegemony came about with the emergence of distinct heterosexual and homosexual/lesbian identities and cultures over the last two centuries. Its bases are the relations of ruling class morality, sex and gender, the gender division of labour, family and kinship relations, State policies, and sexual policing, and it relies not only on consent, legitimation, and "common sense," but also on moments of denial, silencing, and coercion. Heterosexuality is "freely compelled" for many in this society. Coercive laws, police practices, "queer-bashing," and limited social options all attempt to make heterosexuality compulsory (or compulsive).[92] At the same time, there is an active social construction of "consent" to heterosexual desire through strategies of the naturalization and normalization of heterosexuality and the construction of heterosexual cultures.

Heterosexual hegemony is produced on many fronts—from family relations that often marginalize and sometimes exclude gays and lesbians,[93] to the violence we face on city streets, to State policies, to the medical profession, to sociology, sexology, and psychiatry, to the church, the school system, and the media. These forms of sexual regulation (which do not develop in a linear fashion)[94] interact with the social relations we live to produce heterosexist "common sense." There exist also conflicts between and within various agencies over definitions of homosexuality and jurisdictional disputes over who can best deal with the sexual deviant.

The entry of heterosexual hegemony into public "common sense" involves many variants of heterosexist discourse, each of which merits its own analysis (which I explore in later chapters). These include homosexuality as a sin (in religious discourse); as unnatural (in both religious and secular discourse); as an illness (in medicine and psychiatry and, in a new sense, with the current AIDS crisis); as a congenital disorder or inversion (in sex psychology and sexology); as deviance (in some sociological theory); homosexuals as child molesters, seducers, and corruptors (in certain sexological studies, the law, and the media); as a symptom of social or national degeneration (in

Social Darwinist and eugenic discourse); homosexuals as communists, "pinkos," and a national security risk because of the potential for blackmail (rooted in McCarthyism, military organization, the Cold War and 1950s/1960s security regime practices); as tolerated only when practised between consenting adults in "private" (the Wolfenden strategy of privatization); and as a criminal offence or a social menace (in police campaigns, "moral panics," and the media).

How these various forms of heterosexism interact, and how they are based in social practices and relations, is a question for social and historical investigation. It is sufficient to note here that all these ideas can be found in contemporary discourse. There is a continuing resiliency for anti-gay/anti-lesbian discourses formed in previous historical periods that can still be remobilized against us. In certain periods, some regulatory strategies and discourses achieve a degree of cogency for maintaining and reconstructing heterosexual hegemony.[95] Given the various social processes at play, heterosexual common sense clearly suffers from many internal contradictions.

My historical investigation involves an analysis of the social relations that have organized heterosexual hegemony. Heterosexual hegemony and contemporary lesbian and gay cultures are two sides of the same relational social process. Heterosexual hegemony necessarily involves lesbian and gay subordination. As Rachel Harrison and Frank Mort note, "[t]he 'deviant' subject is not absent from the discourse but she/he is only permitted to speak from a subordinate position: as patient, as 'pervert,' etc."[96] Heterosexual hegemony, and oppressive sexual regulation more generally, are an integral aspect of the organization of class, State, gender, and race relations. Let us now turn to look at how this has historically come about, first in England and the United States, and then in Canada.

■ NOTES

1. This can be a danger in "queer" and much discourse-driven theory.
2. See Dorothy E. Smith, *The Everyday World as Problematic* (Toronto: University of Toronto Press, 1987), pp. 128-135; 223-224.
3. See Michel Foucault, *The History of Sexuality. V. 1, An Introduction* (New York Vintage, 1980), pp. 116-127.
4. See my unpublished paper "'Queer Theory' versus Heterosexual Hegemony: Towards a Historical Materialism for Gay Men and Lesbians," presented at the "Queer Sites" lesbian and gay studies conference, Toronto, May 14, 1993.
5. See Dorothy E. Smith, "Feminist Reflections on Political Economy" in *Studies in Political Economy*, No. 30, Autumn 1989, pp. 37-59, and Lorna Weir, "Socialist Feminism

and the Politics of Sexuality" in Heather Jon Maroney and Meg Luxton, eds., *Feminism and Political Economy* (Toronto: Methuen, 1987), pp. 69-83.

6.   See Andrew Parker, "Unthinking Sex: Marx, Engels and the Scene of Writing" in Michael Warner, ed., *Fear of a Queer Planet: Queer Politics and Social Theory* (Minneapolis: University of Minnesota Press, 1995), pp. 19-41. Unfortunately, Parker does not focus on how lesbians and gay men can use the method of historical materialism, and also seems unable to view sex and sexuality as forms of human practice/production.

7.   Fetishism "is a definite social relation between men (sic) that assumes, in their eyes, the fantastic form of a relationship between things." Karl Marx, *Capital: A Critique of Political Economy*. V. 1 (New York: International Publishers, 1967), p. 72.

8.   See Sayer, *Marx's Method* (Sussex and New Jersey: Harvester/Humanities, 1983) pp. 8-9.

9.   Dorothy E. Smith, *The Conceptual Practices of Power* (Toronto: University of Toronto Press, 1990), pp. 31-57; Dorothy E. Smith, *Texts, Facts and Femininity* (London and New York: Routledge, 1990), pp. 86-119.

10.   See D.E. Smith, *The Conceptual Practices of Power, op. cit.*, pp. 31-57; Himani Bannerji, "Writing 'India,' Doing Ideology" in *Left History*, V. 2, No. 2, Fall 1994, pp. 5-17.

11.   On this type of approach to Marxist method, see, among others, Derek Sayer in *Marx's Method* (Sussex and New Jersey: Harvester/Humanities, 1983) and *The Violence of Abstraction* (Oxford and New York: Basil Blackwell, 1987); Roslyn Wallach Bologh, *Dialectical Phenomenology: Marx's Method* (London: Routledge and Kegan Paul, 1979); I.I. Rubin, for his emphasis on social forms and social relations in his *Essays on Marx's Theory of Value* (Montreal: Black Rose Books, 1982); Frigga Haug's comments on Marxism, especially in her *Beyond Female Masochism: Memory-Work and Politics* (London, New York: Verso, 1992); and the work of Dorothy E. Smith.

12.   Jeffrey Weeks, *Sexuality and Its Discontents* (London, Melbourne and Henley: Routledge and Kegan Paul, 1985), pp. 5-10, and Roslyn Wallach Bologh, *Dialectical Phenomenology: Marx's Method* (Boston, London and Henley: Routledge and Kegan Paul, 1979), p. 241. My use of "historical present" differs from that of Weeks in that my usage is not that of a history of relatively ungrounded discourses of sexuality, but rather a history of official discourses as actively organizing practices and relations that to some extent still participate in the organizing of the present. My use of historical data is also non-ideological in character in always being grounded in forms of social life. I use the notion of "historical present" to focus on how sexual regulations were socially put in place and not to deny differences in time, place and historical context.

13.   This can be seen as an attempt to use Dorothy E. Smith's sociological perspective of starting from people's social experiences to develop a critical and grounded analysis of social organization in a more historical context. See Dorothy E. Smith, *The Everyday*

World as Problematic: A Feminist Sociology, op. cit.; The Conceptual Practices of Power: A Feminist Sociology of Knowledge (Toronto: University of Toronto Press, 1990); and Texts, Facts and Femininity: Exploring the Relations of Ruling (London and New York: Routledge, 1990) and the other references to her work later in this chapter. Also see my Ph.D. thesis, "Official Discourse as Sexual Regulation" and my "The Textual Practices of Sexual Rule: Sexual Policing and Gay Men" in Marie Campbell and Ann Manicom, eds., Knowledge, Experience and Ruling Relations: Studies in the Social Organization of Knowledge (Toronto: University of Toronto Press, 1995), pp. 80-95.

14. Dorothy E. Smith, "Women, Class and Family" in Socialist Register 1983 (London: The Merlin Press, 1983), p. 7.

15. There has been some important progress on these fronts. See George Smith, "Policing the Gay Community: An Inquiry into Textually-Mediated Social Relations" in International Journal of the Sociology of Law, V. 16, 1988, pp. 163-183, and his "Political Activist as Ethnographer" in Social Problems, V. 57, No. 4, pp. 629-648; Madiha Didi Khayatt, Lesbian Teachers, an Invisible Presence (Albany: State University of New York Press, 1992) and her "Compulsory Heterosexuality: Schools and Lesbian Students" in Marie Campbell and Ann Manicom, eds., Knowledge, Experience and Ruling Relations: Studies in the Social Organization of Knowledge (Toronto: University of Toronto Press, 1995); Carol-Anne O'Brien and Lorna Weir, "Lesbians and Gay Men Inside and Outside Families" in Nancy Mandell and Anne Duffy, eds., Canadian Families: Diversity, Conflict and Change (Toronto: Harcourt Brace Canada, 1995); Carol-Anne O'Brien, "The Social Organization of the Treatment of Lesbian, Gay and Bisexual Youth in Group Homes and Youth Shelters" in Canadian Review of Social Policies, No. 54, Winter 1994, pp. 37-57; and Carol-Anne O'Brien, Robb Travers, and Laurie Bell, "No Safe Bed: Lesbian, Gay and Bisexual Youth in Residential Services" (Toronto: Central Toronto Youth Services, 1993).

16. Robert A. Padgug, "Sexual Matters: On Conceptualizing Sexuality in History" in Radical History Review, No. 20, Spring/Summer, 1979, p. 9. Also in other collections including Passion and Power and Hidden from History.

17. It is also to be remembered that all biological knowledge, like all other forms of knowledge, is socially constructed. See Suzanne J. Kessler and Wendy McKenna, Gender: An Ethnomethodological Approach (Chicago and London: The University of Chicago Press, 1978), especially pp. 42-80 and Donna Haraway, Simians, Cyborgs, and Women (New York: Routledge, 1991), especially pp. 7-68, among others.

18. This perspective draws some of its insights from Gayle Rubin's "The Traffic in Women" in Rayna R. Reiter, ed., Toward an Anthropology of Women (New York: Monthly Review Press, 1975), and her notion of a "sex/gender" system. I do not use sex/gender system because it tends to conflate questions of sexuality and gender, and also because it sug-

gests that sex/gender relations are some sort of system separate from other social relations rather than an integral aspect of them. It also suggests that this system has been static throughout history rather than historically transformed. In my view, sex and gender relations vary historically and always exist in articulation with class, race, and other social relations. They are therefore part of class relations in a broad sense. Rubin herself has now rejected her earlier approach. In "Thinking Sex: Notes for a Radical Theory of the Politics of Sexuality" in Vance, ed., *Pleasure and Danger: Exploring Female Sexuality* (Boston and London: Routledge and Kegan Paul, 1984), pp. 307-309, she rejects this category, but in a pre-feminist regression asserts that sex and gender are two completely autonomous and separate systems. This later position of Rubin's continues to shape recent "queer theory," including the influential work of Eve Kosofsky Sedgwick who, in her *The Epistemology of the Closet* (Berkeley and Los Angeles: University of California Press, 1990), uses Rubin's later work to argue for the need to separate gender and sexual analysis.

19. On "sexual scripts," see the work of symbolic interactionists, such as J.H. Gagnon and William Simon, *Sexual Conduct* (Chicago: Aldine, 1973) and Kenneth Plummer, *Sexual Stigma* (London: Routledge and Kegan Paul, 1975).

20. Padgug, *op. cit.*

21. As Marx states: "all epochs of production have certain common traits, common characteristics. Production in general is an abstraction, but a rational abstraction insofar as it really brings out and fixes the common element ... Still this general category, this common element sifted out by comparison, is itself segmented many times over and splits into different determinations. Some determinations belong to all epochs, some only to a few." Karl Marx, *Grundrisse* (Harmondsworth: Penguin, 1973), p. 85.

22. See Derek Sayer, *op. cit.*, for this type of view in relation to production. Also see Roslyn Wallach Bologh, *Dialectical Phenomenology: Marx's Method, op. cit.*

23. See K.J. Dover, *Greek Homosexuality* (New York: Vintage, 1980); Michel Foucault, *The Use of Pleasure. V. 2, History of Sexuality* (New York: Pantheon, 1985); David Halperin, *One Hundred Years of Homosexuality* (New York and London: Routledge, 1990); Ford and Beach, *Patterns of Sexual Behavior* (New York: Harper Colophon, 1972), p. 132; Vern Bullough, *Sexual Variance in Society and History* (Chicago and London: The University of Chicago Press, 1976), pp. 32-34.

24. On the Sambia see sources cited in Joseph Harry, *Gay Children Grown Up: Gender Culture and Gender Deviance* (New York: Praeger, 1982), p. 3.

25. See S.J. Kessler and W. McKenna, *Gender: An Ethnomethodological Approach, op. cit.* Despite its date of publication, this is still one of the best books on the social making of gender. In many ways, it provides a much better socially grounded account of gender than that which is common in post-structuralist or postmodernist theory, includ-

ing within queer theory. Judith Butler's *Gender Trouble, Feminism and the Subversion of Identity* (New York and London: Routledge, 1990) is often cited within queer theory regarding gender. Despite Butler's use of the term "performativity," she does not focus on gender as actual social performance or accomplishment, but instead on the performative effects of discourse. I would argue quite strongly that gender is not simply a discursive effect.

26. For a critique of these biological reductionist approaches, see Nelly Oudshoorn, *Beyond the Natural Body: An Archeology of Sex Hormones* (London and New York: Routledge, 1994), and Gail Vines, *Raging Hormones: Do They Rule Our Lives?* (Berkeley and Los Angeles: University of California Press, 1994).

27. On the "natural attitude" toward gender, see Harold Garfinkel, *Studies in Ethnomethodology* (Englewood Cliffs, NJ: Prentice-Hall, 1967) and Kessler and McKenna, *Gender: An Ethnomethodological Approach, op. cit.*

28. On collecting categories and devices that bring together a range of different activities, practices, or groups under common administrative classifications so they can be dealt with by ruling agencies, see Philip Corrigan, "On Moral Regulation" in *Sociological Review*, V. 29. 1981, pp. 313-316.

29. See the very interesting account developed by the Red Collective, who describe the "givenness" of our sexuality and feelings that prevents analysis and change. *The Politics of Sexuality in Capitalism* (London: Red Collective and Publications Distributors Cooperative, 1978).

30. Ellen Ross and Rayna Rapp, "Sex and Society: A Research Note from Social History and Anthropology" in *Comparative Studies in Society and History*, V. 23 (1981), p. 71; also in Snitow, et al., *Powers of Desire*, (New York: Monthly Review, 1985).

31. On commodity fetishism see Marx, *Capital*, V. 1 (New York: International, 1975), pp. 71-83.

32. J.H. Gagnon and William Simon, *Sexual Conduct* (Chicago: Aldine, 1975).

33. *Ibid.*, p. 26.

34. *Ibid.*, p. 5.

35. See Kenneth Plummer, *Sexual Stigma* (London: Routledge and Kegan Paul, 1975). Plummer applies a social interactionist perspective to gay men. However, his perspective is severely limited because it is based on an isolated individual abstracted from social relations. He thereby neglects the questions of cultural and historical investigation that are necessary to explore these relations. To further clarify these points, a historically grounded social interactionist account that is able to investigate how sexuality is organized through broader social relations would be necessary.

36. Mary Douglas, *Purity and Danger* (London: Routledge and Kegan Paul, 1979), p. 4.

37. Mary Douglas, *Natural Symbols* (New York: Penguin, 1973), p. 93.

38. For some similar analysis, see Gayle Rubin's "Thinking Sex: Notes for Radical Theory of the Politics of Sexuality" in Carole S. Vance, ed., *Pleasure and Danger: Exploring Female Sexuality* (Boston, London: Routledge and Kegan Paul, 1984), pp. 280-283.

39. Frank Pearce, "How to Be Immoral and Ill, Pathetic and Dangerous, All at the Same Time: Mass Media and the Homosexual" in Cohen and Young, eds., *The Manufacture of News: Deviance, Social Problems and the Mass Media* (London: Constable, 1973), pp. 284-301.

40. *Ibid.*, pp. 287-288.

41. Unfortunately, valuable insights in Foucault's work, such as "power/knowledge," are limited by his lack of attention to social standpoint and the deletion of active subjects from his discourse analysis. Foucauldian-derived notions of "power/knowledge" often tend to be relatively ungrounded from the social practices that produce them. Sometimes "power/knowledge" almost seems to be self-generating and not produced through social practices. For some useful critical analysis of this, see Dorothy E. Smith, "The Social Organization of Textual Reality" in *The Conceptual Practices of Power, op. cit.*, pp. 70, 79-80.

42. On normalization as a strategy of power, see Michel Foucault, *Discipline and Punish* (New York: Vintage, 1995).

43. George L. Mosse, *Toward the Final Solution: A History of European Racism* (New York: Harper Colophen, 1978), pp. 16-17 and *Nationalism and Sexuality* (New York: Howard Fertig, 1985).

44. On Eurocentrism see Samir Amin, *Eurocentrism* (New York: Monthly Review Press, 1989) and Edward W. Said, *Orientalism* (New York: Vintage, 1979).

45. Jeffrey Weeks, "Discourse, Desire and Sexual Deviance" in Plummer, ed., *The Making of the Modern Homosexual* (London, Hutchinson, 1981), p. 77.

46. This point comes from a lecture by Dorothy E. Smith in the Social Organization of Knowledge course, Sociology Dept., Ontario Institute for Studies in Education, Fall 1980.

47. Bronislaw Malinowski, *The Sexual Life of Savages in North-Western Melanesia: An Ethnographic Account of Courtship, Marriage, and Family Life Among the Natives of the Trobriand Islands, British New Guinea* (London: Routledge and Kegan Paul, 1968), pp. 395-402.

48. See Randolph Trumbach, "London's Sodomites: Homosexual Behaviour and Western Culture in the Eighteenth Century" in *Journal of Social History*, V. 2, No. 1 Fall 1977, note 11, p. 26.

49. Isabel J. Hull, "The Bourgeoisie and Its Discontents: Reflections on Nationalism and Respectability" in *Journal of Contemporary History*, V. 17, No. 2, April 1982, p. 258. Also see Krafft-Ebing, *Psychopathia Sexualis* (New York: C.P. Putnam's Sons, 1965), and Lorna Weir, "Studies in the Medicalization of Sexual Danger," Ph.D. thesis, Dept. of Social and Political Thought, York University, Toronto, 1986, chapter on sex psychology.

50. Freud's psychoanalytical work was simultaneously a recognition of how sexual desire was organized in a particular class, patriarchal, racial and historical setting, and a universalization of this experience, which made it ahistorical, thereby articulating new oppressive regulations of erotic life. Freud's work has been transformed and integrated into the strategies of heterosexual hegemony and sexual rule. While there is much to be learned from Freud's work, Freudian psychoanalysis has been incorporated into the present practices that define sex and normalize only a particular form of male-dominated heterosexuality. Also see Jennifer Terry's "Theorizing Deviant Historiography" in *differences*, V. 3, No. 2, Summer 1991, pp. 55-74. For one lesbian's struggle with the psychiatric system, see Persimmon Blackbridge and Sheila Gilhooly, *Still Sane* (Vancouver: Press Gang, 1985). Also see "Mad, Angry, Gay and Proud: A Lesbian and Gay Supplement" in *Phoenix Rising*, V. 8, No. 3/4, July 1990.

51. On "cutting out" operations, see Dorothy E. Smith's "K Is Mentally Ill" in her *Texts, Facts, and Femininity: Exploring the Relations of Ruling* (London and New York: Routledge, 1990), pp. 12-51.

52. Lon G. Nungessar, *Homosexual Acts, Actors and Identities* (New York: Praegar, 1983), p. 55.

53. Arno Karlen, *Sexuality and Homosexuality* (New York: W.W. Norton, 1971), p. 185.

54. Diane Richardson, "Theoretical Perspectives on Homosexuality" in John Hart and Diane Richardson, eds., *The Theory and Practice of Homosexuality* (London: Routledge and Kegan Paul, 1981), p. 34. The major exceptions were the Kinsey Studies and the psychological work of Evelyn Hooker, which was directed at uprooting the construct that gay men were mentally ill.

55. See George Smith's "Overturning State's Evidence: From Social Constructionism to Historical Materialism," unpublished paper given at the "Sex and the State Lesbian/Gay History Conference" in Toronto, July 1985; "Policing the Gay Community: An Inquiry into Textually-Mediated Social Relations" in *International Journal of the Sociology of Law*, 1988, 16, pp. 163-183; and his "Political Activist as Ethnographer" in *Social Problems*, V. 37, No. 4, Nov. 1990, pp. 629-648.

56. "Moral Panics" are defined by Stan Cohen:

> A condition, episode, person or group of persons emerges to become defined as a threat to societal values and interests; its nature is presented in a stylized and stereotyped fashion by the mass media; the moral barricades are manned by editors, bishops, and politicians and other right-thinking people; socially accredited experts pronounce their diagnoses and solutions; ways of coping are evolved, or (more often) resorted to; the condition then disappears, submerges or deteriorates ... Sometimes the panic is passed over and forgotten, but at other times it has more serious and long-term repercussions and it might produce changes in legal and social policy or even in the way in which societies conceive themselves.

Stan Cohen, *Folk Devils and Moral Panics* (London: MacGibbon and Kee, 1972), p. 9.

Unfortunately, "moral panic" tends to get so overused in the literature that it almost seems to be self-generating. I try to specifically locate and ground the notion of moral panic in social and institutional relations and practices actively constructed between the media, the police, the courts, "citizens' groups," professional experts, and State agencies. These relations combine in different ways in different "panics." They are an active process of social organization. I do not see "moral panics" as an explanation of a social process, rather as pointing toward an investigation of social relations.

57. The theory that stress during pregnancy can lead to homosexuality is put forward in "Brain Sex," which was shown on *Witness*, CBC TV, 1992. Also see Simon LeVay, *The Sexual Brain* (Cambridge, Massachusetts: The MIT Press, 1994). For more critical commentary, see Kay Diaz, "Are Gay Men Born That Way?" in *Z Magazine*, V. 5, No. 12, Dec. 1992, pp. 42-46; Gail Vines, *Raging Hormones: Do They Rule Our Lives?* (Berkeley, Los Angeles: University of California Press, 1994), especially pp. 85-123; Sarah Schulman, "Biological Determinism, Uncontrollable Instincts—'He's Gotta Have It'" in *Rouge*, No. 20, 1995, pp. 20-21; and also see Gary Kinsman, "Not in Our Genes: Against Biological and Genetic Determinism," *Sociologists' Lesbian and Gay Caucus Newsletter*, Issue No. 76. Fall 1993 Newsletter, pp. 4-6.

58. Also see Gary Kinsman, "Queerness Is Not in Our Genes: Against Biological Determinism—For Social Liberation," *Border/Lines*, No. 33, 1994, pp. 27-30.

59. See Richard J. Herrnstein and Charles Murray, *The Bell Curve: Intelligence and Class Structure in American Life* (New York: Free Press, 1994) and the controversies surrounding it. See Steven Fraser, *The Bell Curve Wars* (New York: Basic Books, 1995).

60. See "Brain Sex," *op. cit.*

61. George Weinberg, *Society and the Healthy Homosexual* (New York: Anchor Books, 1973).

62. See Kenneth Plummer, "Homosexual Problems: Some Research Problems in the Labelling Perspective of Homosexuality" in Plummer, ed., *The Making of the Modern Homosexual* (London: Hutchinson, 1981), pp. 53-75.

63. See Gary Kinsman, "'Inverts,' 'Psychopaths,' and 'Normal' Men: Historical Sociological Perspectives on Gay and Heterosexual Masculinities" in Tony Haddad, ed., *Men and Masculinities: A Critical Anthology* (Toronto: Canadian Scholars' Press, 1993), pp. 7-8.

64. Sedgwick, *Epistemology of the Closet, op. cit.*

65. See Dorothy E. Smith, "No One Commits Suicide: Textual Analysis of Ideological Practices" (particularly the diagram on p. 14), unpublished paper, Feb. 1980. Also see Smith's "The Social Construction of Documentary Reality" in *Sociological Inquiry*, 44:4, 1974, pp. 257-268. Revised versions of these articles appear in *The Conceptual Practices of Power, op. cit.*

66. This is not the same as what is referred to as feminist-standpoint theory, which implies that women have a common standpoint and perspective. Instead, Dorothy E. Smith's work argues for a shift in where we begin our inquiry to take up a particular social standpoint in exploring social relations. Standpoint is then a place from which to explore social relations and practice. The standpoints of oppressed groups allow us to see aspects of ruling relations not visible from within ruling institutions.

67. Dorothy E. Smith, "Women, Class and Family," *op. cit*, p. 12.

68. Dorothy E. Smith, "A Sociology for Women" in Sherman and Back, eds., *The Prism of Sex: Essays in the Sociology of Knowledge* (Madison: University of Wisconsin Press, 1979), p. 135-187. A revised version of this article appears in *The Everyday World as Problematic, op. cit.*

69. *Ibid.*, p. 137 in *The Everyday World as Problematic*, p. 51.

70. Dorothy E. Smith, "The Experienced World as Problematic: A Feminist Method," The Twelfth Annual Soroken Lecture. University of Saskatchewan, Saskatoon, Jan. 28, 1981, p. 23. A revised version of this article appears in *The Everyday World as Problematic, op. cit.*

71. Karl Marx, *Capital* V. 1 (New York: Vintage, 1977), pp. 163-177.

72. Also see Dorothy E. Smith, "Femininity As Discourse" in *Texts, Facts and Femininity: Exploring the Relations of Ruling, op. cit.*, pp. 159-208 and "Women, Class and Family" in *The Socialist Register* (London: Merlin Press, 1983), pp. 1-44.

73. Dorothy E. Smith, "The Experienced World as Problematic," *op. cit.*, p. 17, also in *The Everyday World as Problematic*.

74. For important contributions, see George Smith's "Policing the Gay Community: An Inquiry into Textually-Mediated Social Relations" in *International Journal of the Sociology of Law, op. cit.*; his "Political Activist as Ethnographer" in *Social Problems, op. cit.* and his "The Ideology of 'Fag': The School Experience of Gay Students," unpublished paper, Ontario Institute for Studies in Education; and Madiha Didi Khayatt, *Lesbian Teachers, an Invisible Presence, op. cit.* and her "Compulsory Heterosexuality: Schools and Lesbian Students," *op. cit.*

75. See Mary McIntosh, "The Homosexual Role," originally in *Social Problems*, V. 16, No. 2 (Fall 1968), reprinted with a postscript in Plummer, ed., *The Making of the Modern Homosexual, op. cit.*, pp. 38-43; and Kinsey, Gebhard, Pomeroy, and Martin, *Sexual Behavior in the Human Male* (Philadelphia: W.B. Saunders, 1953).

76. John Rechy, *City of Night* (New York: Grove Press, 1963), p. 40. This expression is also used by the character played by Keanu Reeves in the film *My Own Private Idaho*.

77. George Chauncey, Jr., "Christian Brotherhood or Sexual Perversion? Homosexual Identities and the Construction of Sexual Boundaries in the World War I Era" in *Journal of Social History* (1985), pp. 189-212, and in Duberman, Vicinus, and Chauncey, eds., *Hidden from History* (New York: Meridian, 1990), pp. 294-317; also see his *Gay New York* (New York: Basic Books, 1994).

78. See Laud Humphreys, *Tea Room Trade* (Chicago: Aldine, 1975).

79. On bisexuality see Mariana Valverde, *Sex, Power and Pleasure* (Toronto: Women's Press, 1985), especially "Bisexuality: Coping with Sexual Boundaries," pp. 109-120; L. Kaahumanu and L. Hutchins, *Bi Any Other Name: Bisexual People Speak Out* (Boston: Alyson, 1991); Clare Hemmings, "Resituating the Bisexual Body: From Identity to Difference" in J. Bristow and A. Wilson, eds., *Activating Theory: Lesbian, Gay and Bisexual Politics* (London: Lawrence and Wishart, 1993); and Clare Hemmings, "Locating Bisexual Identities: Discourses of Bisexuality and Contemporary Feminist Theory" in David Bell and Gill Valentine, eds., *Mapping Desire: Geographies of Sexualities* (London and New York: Routledge, 1995), pp. 41-55.

80. See Dorothy E. Smith, "A Sociology for Women," *op. cit.*

81. Some inkling of this shifting in vantage point from "outsider" to "insider" can be seen in Joseph Styles, "Outside/Insider Researching Gay Baths" in *Urban Life*, V. 8. No. 2, July 1979, pp. 135-152. Styles describes how an insider vantage point let him see things in a way that the outsider perspective obscured. On an insider's sociology, also see the work of Dorothy E. Smith, especially *The Everyday World as Problematic.*

82. Also offering important insights is recent work on governmentality influenced by the work of Michel Foucault. Among others, see Graham Burchell, Colin Gordon, and Peter Miller, eds., *The Foucault Effect, Studies in Governmentality* (Chicago: The University of Chicago Press, 1991) and Mike Gane and Terry Johnson, eds., *Foucault's New Domains* (London and New York: Routledge, 1993).

83. In particular, see Philip Corrigan and Derek Sayer, *The Great Arch: English State Formation as Cultural Revolution* (Oxford: Basil Blackwell, 1985).

84. See Philip Corrigan, "Towards a Celebration of Difference(s): Notes for a Sociology of a Possible Everyday Future" in D. Robbins, ed., *Rethinking Social Inequality* (London: Gower, 1982).

85. See the work of the late E.P. Thompson, particularly *The Making of the English Working Class* (Harmondsworth: Penguin, 1968), and Dorothy E. Smith, "Women, Class and Family," *op. cit.*, for an account of women's activity in the organization of this broader notion of class relations.

86. See Antonio Gramsci, *Selections from the Prison Notebooks* (New York: International Publishers, 1971); Carl Boggs, *Gramsci's Marxism* (London: Pluto Press, 1976); Perry Anderson, "The Antimonies of Antonio Gramsci" in *New Left Review*, No. 100, Nov. 1976–Jan. 1977, pp. 5-78; Chantal Mouffe, ed., *Gramsci and Marxist Theory* (London: Routledge and Kegan Paul, 1979); and Ernesto Laclau and Chantal Mouffe, *Hegemony and Socialist Strategy: Towards a Radical Democratic Politics* (London: Verso, 1985). Unfortunately, while Laclau and Mouffe trace some of the genealogy of the concept

of hegemony, they treat hegemony as only a discursive concept, separating it from social practices and severing it from its historical, social, and organizational contexts. They also completely sever hegemony from class relations and class struggles in their latest work. There are difficulties with notions of "hegemony," especially if hegemony is construed as an explanatory category in and of itself. But it points us toward the relational and social character of social regulation in a clearer fashion than do terms like dominant culture or notions of domination. Unlike social or ideological reproduction, it suggests that social regulation is actively accomplished by individuals in diverse institutional sites and is always "problematic." It points us toward the social organization of ruling relations while including within it the activities and resistances of the subordinated. It is never total, never exclusive, and there is always the possibility of subversion and transformation. It is these opportunities we have to seize.

87. John Clarke, Stuart Hall, Tony Jefferson, and Brian Roberts, "Subcultures, Cultures and Class: A Theoretical Overview" in Hall and Jefferson, eds., *Resistance through Rituals* (London: Hutchinson, 1976), p. 38.

88. Corrigan and Sayer, *The Great Arch, op. cit.*, p. 142.

89. See Gary Kinsman, "Managing AIDS Organizing: 'Consultation,' 'Partnership,' and the National AIDS Strategy" in William K. Carrol, ed., *Organizing Dissent: Contemporary Social Movements in Theory and Practice* (Toronto: Garamond, 1992), pp. 215-231.

90. Clarke, et al., *op. cit.*, p. 12.

91. See Mary O'Brien, "The Comatization of Women: Patriarchal Fetishism in the Sociology of Education," paper presented to the British Sociological Association Conference, Manchester, 1982.

92. See Adrienne Rich, "Compulsory Heterosexuality and Lesbian Existence" in *Signs*, V. 5, No. 4 (Summer 1980), pp. 631-660. Despite the many insights of this article, her suggestion that heterosexuality is simply "compulsory" for women is rather one-sided. It does not adequately take into account that "consent" to heterosexuality is also actively constructed through practices of normalization and naturalization. This is why I prefer heterosexual hegemony to compulsory heterosexuality since it includes these moments of coercion and consent.

93. See Carol-Anne O'Brien and Lorna Weir, "Lesbians and Gay Men Inside and Outside Families" in Nancy Mandell and Anne Duffy, eds., *Canadian Families: Diversity, Conflict and Change, op. cit.*

94. See Frank Mort, "Sexuality Regulation and Contestation" in Gay Left, ed., *Homosexuality: Power and Politics, op. cit.*, pp. 41-42.

95. See Gary Kinsman, "The Textual Practices of Sexual Rule: Sexual Policing and Gay Men" in Marie Campbell and Ann Manicom, eds., *Knowledge, Experience and Ruling*

Relations: Studies in the Social Organization of Knowledge (Toronto: University of Toronto Press, 1995), pp. 80-95.

96. Rachel Harrison and Frank Mort, "Patriarchal Aspects of Nineteenth-Century State Formation: Property Relations, Marriage and Divorce and Sexuality" in Philip Corrigan, ed., *Capitalism, State Formation and Marxist Theory* (London: Quartet, 1980), p. 106.

CHAPTER 6

INTRODUCTION TO THE AGE OF LIGHT, SOAP, AND WATER

Mariana Valverde

ractically all historians claim that the period of their particular interest is "a transitional age" witnessing profound changes in economy and society. At the risk of appearing both trite and self-serving, it can nevertheless be claimed that the decades from the 1880s to World War One saw major changes in Canadian society, many of which have had a lasting influence. It can also be claimed with some plausibility that these were in fact transitional decades: in the 1870s Canada was a very sparsely populated, barely post-colonial state where farming and staples production predominated; by the 1920s the Native populations had been firmly marginalized, the weight of the economy had shifted toward industry and finance, and urban living had become the rule rather than the exception. By the 1920s the Canadian state had developed, at least in embryonic form, most of the institutions it has today, and in English Canada a certain cultural consensus, based to a large extent on American and British influence but incorporating a new nationalism, had emerged and was being consolidated.

There were many different elements in this consolidation of a nation (an English Canada centred on and dominated by the Toronto-Ottawa axis) and a corresponding state:[1] this book is largely concerned with certain social and cultural aspects of this consolidation. The practices and discourses described herein were largely aspects of the class relations of the emerging urban and capitalist social formation.

As historians have pointed out, one important aspect of the growth of modern Canada was the development of an urban-industrial working class.[2] The correlate of that was the development of an urban bourgeoisie, certain sectors of which initiated a philanthropic project to reform or "regenerate" Canadian society. One strand of this book's argument is that the social reform movements of the turn of the century helped to shape the bourgeoisie, which led the movements, as well as the working class, toward which they were generally aimed. Although there is very little secondary literature on the constitution of the English-Canadian bourgeoisie at the social and cultural levels (as opposed to the economic formations traced in business history), an attempt will be made to analyze, in however tentative a fash ion, the making of the subclass involved in social reform. This was composed mostly of professionals and charity workers, who acted partly to uphold the specific interests and perspectives of their professions but who were also connected to the larger bourgeois culture of which they formed part.

This process of fragmented, interactive, and multiple class formation was in turn always gendered and racially specific. The process through which race, gender, and class were intertwined in what was known as "nation-building" is one of the main themes of this book. It is furthermore not assumed here that "gender" is merely a euphemism for women, "race" one for people of colour, and "class" one for working-class and poor people—just as class formation takes place in the bourgeoisie as well as in the proletariat, masculinity and Anglo-Saxon whiteness are as worthy of critical analysis as femininity and racial minorities.

The economic and cultural developments that form the background to the reform movement analyzed here were not unique to Canada: similar developments in the northeastern United States and in urban Britain have been described by many historians. The ideas and practices of class formation that were popular in urban Canada were to a large extent adapted from English and American sources. The development of both unions and employers' associations, the workings of private charity and public relief, and the cultural practices of the various classes were all heavily influenced by the overall fact of Canadian dependence. In some cases, reformers imported certain ideas from abroad without reflecting on the extent to which Canadian realities made these ideas unsuitable. At other times, however, the uniqueness of Canada was highlighted by patriots who insisted that Toronto or Hamilton most definitely lacked the social evils plaguing Chicago or London.

It is very difficult if not impossible to make any general statements about the specificity of Canadian social reform movements; all that can be said is that the well-educated urban English Canadians who led these movements were definitely learning from English and, increasingly, American sources. Then as now, however, there was a constant tension between the temptation to copy or import and the equally strong temptation to claim that Canada was different—less corrupt, healthier—and that social remedies ought not to be imported for non-existent social ills. It would be impossible here to detail all the forms and channels of English and American influence on

Canadian ideas about social and moral reform. The main point is that Canadians then (as now) tended to define themselves not so much positively but by way of a differentiation—from the Mother Country, first, and, in the 20th century, from the United States. As we shall see, their self-image as healthy citizens of a new country of prairies and snowy peaks contributed both to 20th-century nationalist ideas and to the success of the purity movement, one of whose symbols was pure white snow.

As Ramsay Cook has pointed out, at the turn of the century a large number of educated Canadians were interested in reforming their society and their state, and building the foundations for what they thought could be a future of prosperity and relative equality. They envisaged this reform not as a series of small isolated measures but as a grand project to "regenerate" both society and the human soul.[3] Cook's analysis confines itself largely to theological and intellectual spheres, however, and leaves in the shadow one important component of the reform project—the effort undertaken by popular educators, temperance activists, and pamphlet writers, more than by either theologians or social theorists, to reshape the ethical subjectivity of both immigrants and native-born Canadians. They called their project "moral reform," usually linked to social concerns in the common phrase "moral and social reform."

To study moral reform at the turn of the century, it is appropriate to focus primarily on the self-styled "social purity movement," which, along with temperance and Sunday observance, helped to constitute a powerful if informal coalition for the moral regeneration of the state, civil society, the family, and the individual. The social purity movement was a loose network of organizations and individuals, mostly church people, educators, doctors, and those we would now describe as community or social workers, who engaged in a sporadic but vigorous campaign to "raise the moral tone" of Canadian society, and in particular of urban working-class communities. In 1895, a Canadian clergyman speaking at an important Purity Congress in Baltimore described "social purity work in Canada" as including the following issues: prostitution, divorce, illegitimacy, "Indians and Chinese," public education, suppression of obscene literature, prevention (of prostitution) and rescue of fallen women, and shelters for women and children.[4] These same issues were addressed from an American perspective by other speakers,[5] who all agreed that purity work was not simply a question of banning obscene books or suppressing prostitution but was rather a campaign to educate the next generation in the purity ideals fitting to "this age of light and water and soap."[6]

The image of reform as illuminating society while purifying or cleansing it was already an integral part of the temperance movement, which developed in the mid-19th century in the U.S. and Britain and was taken up in Canada by such organizations as the Woman's Christian Temperance Union and the Dominion Alliance for the Total Suppression of the Liquor Traffic.[7] Many of the organizations involved in both temperance education and lobbying for prohibition took up social purity work as part of their task. In some respects, temperance and social purity acted as a single movement. However, some people involved in social purity work (notably doctors and lay sex educators) did not necessarily support prohibition—even though they usually advocated voluntary abstinence from alcohol—and undoubtedly there were many prohibitionists who were rather single-minded and did not share some of the concerns grouped under the label of "social purity." It is thus appropriate to undertake the more limited task of describing and analyzing social purity work and ideas, remembering always its close connection to temperance—and to the other great single issue of moral reformers, Sunday observance—but without seeking to assimilate one cause into another.

Social purity was advocated by many of the same people responsible for spreading the "social gospel" in Canada; and since social gospel has been the subject of various studies[8] while social purity has been almost totally ignored by historians, a word about the relation between these two projects is in order. As defined by Allen, Cook, and others, "social gospel" refers to the attempts to humanize and/or Christianize the political economy of urban-industrial capitalism. Its prophets were generally moderately left of centre but included such mainstream figures as W.L. Mackenzie King, who collaborated with the Presbyterian Board of Social Service and Evangelism in his youth and was influenced by social gospel ideas in his popular 1919 book, *Industry and Humanity*.

There was an overlap in both personnel and ideas between social gospel and social purity, and therefore one can only offer a tentative clarification: while the focus of social gospel activity was the economy and the social relations arising from production, social purity focused on the sexual and moral aspects of social life. Prostitution in all its forms was the one "social problem" guaranteed to unify the diverse constituencies—feminists, right-wing evangelicals, doctors, social reformers—of the social purity coalition; and "sex hygiene," or purity education, was one of the main positive remedies promoted. While sexual concerns were important or even central, one must guard against seeking analytical clarity at the expense of historical accuracy: for many of the people who lived it, social purity was intertwined with socio-economic reform. Thus, the term "social purity movement" will be used sparingly; it would be misleading to imagine it as a distinct movement with its own headquarters and publications, when in fact it was in one sense an aspect of a wider movement that also included critical studies of industrial conditions and other issues not generally regarded as "moral."

■ PHILANTHROPY AND "THE SOCIAL"

Sexual morality was the main target of the social purity movement, but the purity campaign has to be understood in the context of a larger project to solve the problems of poverty, crime, and vice. This larger project was primarily the task of philanthropy, with state activity often being confined to supplementing private initiatives or acting like a philanthropy.

There are various ways of characterizing philanthropy, and perhaps it is easiest to define it by contrast with what came before, namely charity. Charity, the traditional means of relieving poverty, was largely individual and impulsive, and its purpose was to relieve the immediate need of the recipient while earning virtue points for the giver. Organized charity or philanthropy sought to eliminate both the impulsive and the individual elements of giving. The London philanthropists of the 1860s who pioneered modern methods of philanthropy and social work constantly denounced the "indiscriminate alms-giving" of charity as unscientific and backward.[9] They believed that the problem with charity was not that it was never enough but, on the contrary, that there was too much of it and that the poor were becoming "pauperized" by dependence on abundant charity. A similar campaign (perhaps on a smaller scale) was carried on in the U.S.: a pioneer of organized philanthropy stated that "next to alcohol, the most pernicious fluid is indiscriminate soup."[10]

Philanthropists hence sought to rationalize and often curtail the material aid, focusing instead on training the poor in habits of thrift, punctuality, and hygiene—an economic subjectivity suited to a capitalist society. They also sought to eliminate pity from giving while maximizing rational calculation, so that, for instance, rather than give to old people, who were favoured by traditional charity, there was a new emphasis on children and, indirectly, on women, for with them one was making an investment in the future of the nation.[11]

Another way of contrasting charity and philanthropy is to differentiate poverty—the problem addressed by charity—and pauperism. In England, there was a strict legal definition of pauperism in the Poor Law; however, there was also a broader meaning of the term, indicating a larger social process specific to capitalism and affecting the working class in general, not just legal paupers. The vicar of London's parish of Stepney put it as follows in 1904: "It is not so much poverty that is increasing in the East [end] as pauperism, the want of industry, of thrift or self-reliance."[12] The term "pauperization" indicated a loss of initiative and dignity, not just physical want or legal dependence on the parish. That pauperism was moral as well as economic is evident from the fact that drinking, irregular work habits, sexual laxity, and infrequent bathing were discussed as often if not more often than low wages and poor housing.

If pauperism was more than economic, philanthropy was not merely an economic project to soften the hard edges of industrial capitalism. Its work took place in and largely shaped what Jacques Donzelot has called "the social."[13] Characteristic of this new social philosophy was an unabashed interventionism. In a liberal state, economic policy at least has to try to respect the individual autonomy of capital owners, but social policy is characterized by the opposite movement, i.e., one of expansionism even into the private sphere of family and sexual life. There is no question of letting social forces play themselves out—in modern societies there is no invisible social hand, and so some degree of engineering by visible hands in or out of the state is necessary. David Garland describes the main British social programs of the period under study (social work, eugenics, social security, and criminology) as "extending the power of government over life."[14]

While Donzelot and Garland see "the social" as a distinct realm with fairly clear if shifting boundaries separating it from both politics and economics, I would argue that "the social" is not so much a separate sphere but a new way of conceptualizing any and all problems of the collectivity. Municipal politics and industrial policy, to give two examples, were in our period seen increasingly under the aspect of the social.[15] Industry was seen as needing some form of regulation (maximum hours and minimum wages, for instance) not because of any contradictions within the economic system itself, but rather because extreme exploitation was defined as a *social* problem, involving the creation of paupers, the breakdown of the family, and a general crisis in the cohesion of the social formation.[16] Political questions, from war to immigration, also came to be regarded as more than political. The Boer War, apart from its strictly political aspects, generated a major social panic in Great Britain (which had echoes in Canada) about the poor quality of the soldiers and of the mothers who had produced them.[17] Hence, economics and politics were increasingly socialized, while social problems were persistently seen as "moral" even by modern scientific experts outside of the social purity movement.

The term "social" was usually an adjective, and the relevant noun that came to mind most readily was "problem." In the 1820s and 1830s, both French and English sources had used the term "the social question"; after mid-century, however, "the social" became fragmented into a multitude of "problems," among other reasons because the growth of specialized professions encouraged a fragmentation of jurisdictions within the social. Whether unitary or fragmented, however, the social domain was born problematic, as Donzelot's study indicates; and throughout the 19th century and into the first two decades of the 20th, the answers to social problems were usually elaborated in the idiom of philanthropy. It thus followed that the first task of philanthropy was to enumerate and study, i.e., to know, "the social." In the last two chapters we will describe some of the methods used by the social purity and philanthropy activists to both study and solve not only particular urban problems but what they referred to as "*the* problem of *the* city." It will be seen there that the work of knowing the poor became a great deal more than a means to the end of remedying poverty: it became a science for its own sake—social science, a term that in the late 19th century included the present-day fields of sociology and social work.[18] This thirst for knowledge led social researchers to leave the library and enter into the neighbourhoods and homes of the poor (home visiting was a central practice in 19th-century philanthropy). This investigation began with the kitchens, clothes, and cupboards of the poor, but it did not end there: the prying gaze of philanthropy sought to penetrate the innermost selves of the poor, including their sexual desires, which were uniformly conceptualized as vices (incest, illegitimacy, prostitution).

Sexual desire was probed not only from the standpoint of morality but also from the standpoint, and in the context, of the new field of public health. Unlike other health matters, however, sex was difficult to quantify. This was a great disappointment to reformers like English public health pioneer James Kay, who said: "Criminal acts may be statistically classed ... but the number of those affected with the moral leprosy of vice cannot be exhibited with mathematical precision. Sensuality has no record."[19] The absence of sensual records, however, did not deter investigators such as London's Rev. Mearns, who in the mid-1880s caused a public scandal by claiming that incest was common among the poor.[20] An important wing of the purity movement devoted itself to the production of books, pamphlets, and lectures with which people could probe both their own and other people's sexual habits in order to remoralize the individual and the nation. The title of what was probably the most popular sex education book in turn-of-the-century Canada, *Light on Dark Corners: Searchlight on Health*,[21] captures the distinctive emphasis on probing and rooting out vice with the powerful light of quasi-medical knowledge.

Although there was general agreement on the need to study the poor, preferably in their own homes, there were endless arguments about how to organize philanthropy, how to choose the proper targets, and how to improve its efficiency, as well as major arguments (especially in Britain) about whether the state or the private sector should be the main organizer of philanthropy. Amidst these debates, the status of philanthropy (whether private or public) as the main answer to the problem of the social was not questioned until the development of professional social work and systems of state welfare in the 1920s and 1930s—and even then, the legacy of philanthropy weighed so heavily on the new systems of relief that one could with some justice claim that philanthropy merely disguised itself as state-funded welfare and social work.[22]

The location of philanthropy in (or arising out of) the domain of the social does not imply that it was independent of politics and of the state or that it was unconnected to class formation and class struggle. The relations of gender, class, and race that both shaped moral reform and were shaped by it are, however, too complex to be captured by resorting to the hackneyed model of one class (or one gender) unilaterally repressing its class or gender enemy with Machiavellian tactics. The processes analyzed in this book are best conceptualized under the rubric of "moral regulation."

■ NATION, STATE, AND MORALITY

Insofar as there is a popular view of the social purity movement, this view is that once upon a pre-Freudian time there was a group of repressed clergymen and church ladies who tried to make everyone stop drinking, having sex, and gambling. The movement of 1885-1920 is seen as just another chapter in the history of Puritanism, and hence as a purely negative, prohibitory project.[23]

Like all popular myths, the myth of social purity as a force of negation does have a grain of truth. Such organizations as the Lord's Day Alliance were primarily concerned with preventing certain activities on Sundays, and it was only with the passage of time that reformers began to be more concerned about providing "suitable" Sunday activities such as picnics, supervised playgrounds for children, discussion groups for young people, and other activities classified as "rational recreation" (as opposed to commercialized amusements). But even the Lord's Day Alliance, and even the temperance movement, did not intend simply to stamp out one or more vices. They had a larger vision of how people ought to pass their time, how they ought to act, speak, think, and even feel. This vision—which I will here call "positive" not because it was necessarily good but to distinguish it from negativity, from mere prohibition—was often kept in the background as they pursued their efforts to prevent or negate evil, but it was always present and it became increasingly prominent after the turn of the century.

Those intent on banning the liquor traffic looked forward to the day when Canadians would not drink alcohol, but would drink great amounts of pure milk and clear country water. American temperance leader Frances Willard stated: "when you can get men to drink milk it means well for temperance, for the home, for purity," while her Canadian counterpart poetically evoked the "aquatic tendencies" of the women's temperance movement, adding that her hometown of London, Ontario, was proud of its "abundant supply of pure, sparkling water—water that leaves no excuse for drinking anything else."[24] The beneficial social effects of pure drinks were trumpeted by experts at a Milwaukee conference attended by Canadian public health doctors, reported in the Toronto *Daily News* under the headline "Fewer Criminals with Pure Milk."[25] Toronto newspapers also featured advertisements for Purity Water, bottled water sold by appealing to consumers' wish to maximize their health. The ideal of purity was extended from liquids to solids in the following advertisement for the patriotic and pure Canada Bread:

> In kitchens flooded with pure air and sunshine, neat bakers, arrayed in clothes of immaculate white, deftly and carefully prepare the materials for the "staff of Canadian life." A visit here will show that cleanliness is indeed carried to extremes.[26]

Pure foods and drinks, most commonly embodied in milk and water, were simultaneously physically and symbolically pure. Pure milk—white like the ribbons worn by the WCTU women—and clean, clear water represented moral health, truth, and beauty, in contrast not only to alcohol but to the deceitful adulterated milk and impure water of the unsanitary cities.[27] The whiteness of milk was also sometimes linked to the snow central to Canadian mythology: Havergal principal Ellen Knox typically told her schoolgirls that Canada had "a glistening line of the future, pure and free as her own ice-clad peaks of the Rockies."[28] The combination of whiteness and coldness made snow an appropriate symbol not only of Canada but also of purity.

If even the self-described prohibition movement (which nevertheless preferred the less negative name "temperance") is at least partially an example of what theorists since Foucault are calling "the positivity of power," the social purity movement must also be interpreted as a great deal more than simply a campaign against prostitution, immoral amusements, and other public manifestations of vice. Social purity was a campaign to regulate morality, in particular sexual morality, in order to preserve and enhance a certain type of human life. It was not merely a campaign to punish and repress. This can be seen in the changing emphases of the federal government's Conservation Commission (whose journal was entitled *The Conservation of Life*). During and after the war, this Commission, which encompassed a variety of matters from the conservation of fisheries and forestry to public health, pure milk, and town planning, put more emphasis on conserving human bodies and less on trees and fur-bearing animals. Although it did not last long and the component parts were absorbed by more specialized government departments, its creation was part of an ongoing if not always successful attempt to unify all social problems into one macro-problem—conserving "life"—for which a macro-solution could be found. The Conservation Commission, dismissed by historian Paul Rutherford as "strange,"[29] can be properly understood by realizing that conservation of life was more than an attempt to unify various parts of the bureaucracy: it evoked Romantic vitalist philosophies as well as the Christian concept of "the Resurrection and the Life." These spiritual dimensions were emphasized by the ex-Minister of

Labour and future Prime Minister W.L. Mackenzie King in his optimistic manifesto for Canadian reconstruction, *Industry and Humanity*. In this book, "the conservation of health and life" is said to be one of the three principles of reconstruction (the others were peace and work). Mackenzie King used the modern phrase "conservation of human resources" to name a priority of the Ministry of Labour, but this modern phrase incorporates Christian and Romantic meanings.[30]

The Great War caused a quantum leap in the concern about conserving human life. As Toronto's public health chief, Dr. Charles Hastings, put it in October of 1914,

> National Conservation Commissions that have been engaged in the conservation of natural resources, such as forests, fisheries, mines etc., have in recent years embraced the conservation of human life and human efficiency.[31]

But as Hastings himself notes, even before the Great War caused a tangible crisis in human resources, men and women engaged in "nation-building" had stressed the need to conserve, preserve, and shape human life: to conserve its physical health, to preserve its moral purity, and to shape it according to the optimistic vision shared by all political parties of what Canada would be in the 20th century. The Methodist Church's sex educator for boys typically believed that one of Canada's untapped natural resources was its young people, and he saw his own educational work as furthering the production of "self": "Our young men themselves are producing a product, self, that will command in the market of the world a value—we are building this young manhood into some kind of product, that in later years we will have to offer in the markets of the world."[32]

This is not to say, I hasten to add, that the social purity movement was a stooge or puppet of the state; on the contrary, the various levels of government often lagged behind the initiatives of churches and professional groups. Dangerous as it always is to assume that the state is the only real agent of history, in the case of Canada at the turn of the century it would be ludicrous to assume that politicians or civil servants conspired to manipulate the powerful voluntary organizations with which this book is concerned. State officials and agencies did often work with or fund private agencies, and the phenomenon of co-optation was not unknown. One cannot assume, however, that the state was—or is at present—always the dominant partner. Indeed, there are very good reasons why liberal-democratic states, far from desiring to absorb all social policy activity, have a vested interest in fostering non-state organizations that will co-operate in certain aspects of social policy, particularly in areas such as regulating morality and gender and family relations. Except in situations such as war or internal rebellion, explicitly moral campaigns are difficult for liberal democratic states to undertake with any degree of success, since such states portray themselves as neutral arbiters of opinions circulating in civil society. Such states also have a structural commitment to non-interference in private beliefs and activities of a moral and/or cultural nature. It is far easier for the state to respond to popular outcries than it is to orchestrate such a campaign on its own—although the Canadian state at its various levels has been known to sow the seeds of popular panics in order to then cast itself in the apparently neutral role of responding to popular demands.[33]

Another related reason why the state was not, and in fact could not have been, the main protagonist in the social purity campaign is that social purity was only partially concerned with restricting behaviour. States may have a monopoly over the legitimate use of force and may therefore be in a privileged position to enforce rules about behaviour, but the state can only make its citizens *internalize* certain values if it has the full and active co-operation of the family and of voluntary organizations.[34] What we will see is that many voluntary organizations were far more concerned about nation-building and even about strengthening the state than the state itself; they often chastised it for not exercising enough power, particularly in the areas of social welfare, health, and immigration.

It may seem remarkable that private organizations had such trust in the state: the Canadian situation certainly contrasts with other more conflictive situations, such as the mutual suspicion of private charity and poor law authorities in England at this time. But, for reasons beyond the scope of the present work, by the 1880s both the federal and provincial states seem to have acquired an almost unshakeable legitimacy in the eyes of the educated Anglophone middle classes. Municipal government was often denounced as corrupt, but the higher levels were remarkably free from criticism, and even as citizens agitated for changes in the personnel of the state, the structures themselves went largely unquestioned.

One reason for this trust is that civil society was very sharply divided: the Methodists would far rather see the state take control of education than risk giving more power to their Catholic rivals, and mainstream Protestants preferred to have the provinces take over social work rather than see the Salvation Army flourish. Ethnic, religious, and class divisions were highly visible and conflictive, and in the face of this obvious disunity the state had little difficulty in portraying itself as neutral.

Furthermore, Canadian state formation (with the important exception of Quebec) has as one of its ideological pillars the establishment of Protestantism as a kind of joint-stock state religion. Bruce Curtis's perceptive analysis of the successful construction of a sense of citizenship suffused with Protestantism through Rev. Egerton Ryerson's 1840s reforms helps to explain why churches and other quasi-evangelical bodies regarded the state as a friend rather than a competitor.[35]

We see, then, that a large-scale effort to mould the moral values of the population was, given the particular character of the Canadian state, bound to rely greatly on the efforts of private or semi-public agencies, in part because whether moral reform movements are aimed at building the family, the church, or the nation, they emphasize training and even constructing the subjectivity of the members. As the Presbyterian press typically put it in 1908, "we want to build a nation, not gather together a mob."[36]

The building of a nation was rightly equated with the organization of assent, not just outward conformity to legal and administrative rules. This is one reason why the outright punishment of political or moral deviants came to be seen as a last resort and as an admission of failure. David Garland points out that the turn of the century witnessed a marked decline of eye-for-eye discourses on crime and their replacement by therapeutic and reformatory strategies.[37] While the criminal, the fallen, and the destitute were being increasingly seen as subjects of treatment, through the medicalization of crime, sexuality, and poverty,[38] non-criminal populations and in particular youth were being seen as requiring a process of character-building, the individual equivalent of the nation-building just cited. An individual without character, without the kind of self that W.L. Clark sought to build, was a miniature mob: disorganized, immoral, and unhealthy as well as an inefficient member of the collectivity. Character was not to be acquired bureaucratically, by learning information or following rules. What Clark called the production of self and others called character-building was an inner, subjective task. It involved learning to lead a morally and physically pure life, not only for the sake of individual health and salvation but for the sake of the nation. The social purity lecturer A.W. Beall was clear on this point, telling schoolchildren across Ontario that "it is up to you, to each of you, to become an A.1 father of A.1 children" and having them repeat: "Jesus Christ and Canada expect me to be an A.1 boy."[39]

As many writers have pointed out, the shaping of individual sexual morality is quite important in national and religious macro-projects.[40] This shaping of morality, in the context of a grand project that was both national and religious, is perhaps the core of the social purity movement. Placing moral reform in the specific context of nation-building and state formation at the turn of the century, we can see it as a particular national project rather than simply a manifestation of a trans-historical urge to suppress pleasure and sexuality. This national project was outlined by others from slightly different but complementary perspectives. For instance, Mackenzie King's book about industrial relations in the postwar era, which is suffused by a spiritualist optimism about the role of government in preserving the health of the national organism, echoes Clark and Beall without stressing the sexual aspect:

> Education in health and character is the best insurance against the hazards of in-
> dustrial life ... character is the determining factor in all things. An inner sustain-
> ing motive is more necessary than external support if, across the reaches of Time,
> the spirit of workers in Industry is not to flag.[41]

The "character" needed by the nation was a sexual as well as a national identity. In the
literature exemplified in Canada by the "Self and Sex" series promoted by the WCTU
and the Methodist Church, and by Beall's *The Living Temple*, clean bodies and clean
minds are not just clean in the sense of having no dirt; they are portrayed as having
been produced through the active and constant scouring that was a central metaphor
of social purity.

   That the relentless scouring of the soul and shaping of individual character would
have an immediate impact on public and national affairs, nobody doubted. The house-
cleaning metaphors utilized by maternal feminists such as Nellie McClung did not only
seek to legitimize women's entry into the public sphere by comparing politics to a house
in need of spring cleaning; they also established a parallel between what was known as
"political purity" and personal hygiene. Physical and sexual hygiene—which were to a
large extent in women's sphere—were the microcosmic foundation of the larger project
of building a "clean" nation. A speech at the National Council of Women's 1907 convention, for instance, introduced the topic of sex education as follows:

> It is with a great degree of hesitancy that I presume to introduce ... the question
> we are now about to consider, and one of so great moment in our individual, our
> social and our national life, that of Purity. A question the underlying principles
> of which are the vital principles on which depends the successful building of the
> individual's or the nation's life.[42]

On his part, MP John Charlton, who in the 1880s and 1890s spearheaded many efforts
to raise the age of consent, criminalize seduction, and promote sexual purity, introduced one of his many legislative efforts as follows: "No vice will more speedily sap the
foundations of public morality and of national strength than licentiousness ...."[43]

   The rhetoric of national decline and "weakening of the moral fiber" through excessive sexuality is so familiar (even in the present day) that few writers have taken the
time to analyze its roots. It is important, however, to treat such statements not as vacuous rhetorical flourishes but as highly meaningful indicators signalling a belief in the
nation's need for specifically *moral* subjects. The nation (as distinct from the state) is, in
the discourse of national degeneration, seen as rather fragile and as subject to a quasi-
physical process of decay that can only be halted if the individuals, the cells of the body

politic, take control over their innermost essence or self. This is assumed to be morality, which a century ago included not only "the soul" but also what we now call the emotions, and the core of that is in turn sexual morality. Sexual desire is perceived as the most dangerous of forces, the worst threat to civilization, and hence as that which most needs taming. The specific sexual activities targeted for control changed over the years: in the mid-19th century, masturbation, especially among boys, was the most talked about vice, while at the turn of the century prostitution would take the spotlight, to be replaced in the 1920s by fears about non-commoditized consensual sexual encounters among young people. But regardless of the specific sexual activity targeted, the loss of individual self-control over sexuality was perceived to have far-reaching consequences *even if nobody ever knew about it*. Again, it was not so much a matter of outward behaviour but a question of inner identity, of the subjectivity of citizens.

This subjectivity was not without content. The attempt to make young boys and girls learn self-control and develop character involved very specific ideas about the use to which such highly controlled units ought to be put, and about the class, gender, and racial composition of the nation being built.

The class basis of social purity is not a simplistic matter of middle-class reformers imposing their values on working-class communities. It is true that the vast majority of leaders of the movement were of the middle class, and in particular were members of what Robert Wiebe's classic study of progressivism in the U.S. called "the new middle classes," that is, professionals and managers (as opposed to capitalists).[44] But this sub-class, precisely because it was new, was as concerned to make itself as to make others. Thus its activities cannot be wholly explained as directed at other classes or class fractions. What has been described as imposing values on another class is simultaneously a process of creating and reaffirming one's own class. Class formation is a dialectical process; it takes place in the bourgeoisie as much as in the working class, and often through the same practices.

The doctors, clergymen, and women employers of servants did not in any case expect immigrants and prostitutes to live and think exactly like upper-class Anglo-Saxon Canadians. They did want both immigrants and social deviants to embrace the culture and values of Anglo-Saxon, Protestant, middle-class urban Canadians, but this was to ensure that the power of the WASP bourgeoisie would appear as legitimate, not to democratize society and have everyone live in Rosedale- or Westmount-style homes. Both social purity and philanthropy sought to establish a non-antagonistic capitalist class structure, not to erase class differences.[45]

The gender organization of social purity is also a complex question that cannot be summarized by saying the movement was male dominated. The movement sought to reform and organize gender, not merely utilize it. This gender reform meant that some women were given the possibility of acquiring a relatively powerful identity as rescuers, reformers, and even experts, while other women were reduced to being objects of philanthropic concern. Men were equally divided by the social construction of masculinity of the social purity movement: if many men, particularly "foreigners," were seen as the epitome of impurity, other men were provided with a potential new identity as reformed, moralized, and domesticated males.

Women were often marginalized, especially in church organizations (excepting perhaps the Salvation Army). The vision of Canadian womanhood promoted by the movement was one stressing maternal selflessness and passive purity, a vision clearly reinforcing patriarchal privilege.[46] Nevertheless, large numbers of women were active in this movement, and they cannot be dismissed by seeing them as victims of false consciousness. The "search for sexual order"[47] central to the movement was seen by women to be in women's best interests: males were viewed as the main culprits in sexual disorder (although some women blamed fallen women's wiles). Hence the protection of women against male harassment, sexual violence, and everyday disrespect was a legitimate feminist goal. Furthermore, the movement's upholding of a single standard of sexual morality ("the white life for two") did give a voice to married women's protest against philandering husbands.

The great paradox about femininity formation in/through moral reform campaigns was that certain middle-class women made careers out of studying "the problem" of the immigrant woman or the urban girl. These women doctors, social workers, deaconesses, and Salvation Army officers travelled freely around the city, protected by their uniform and their profession, and perhaps did not realize that their unprecedented freedom was built on the prior assumption that ordinary women were helpless objects in need of study and reform. The pure woman did not gain her purity exclusively through silence, chastity, and seclusion: she was partially public.

If the feminine identity established in the discourses and practices of moral reform was internally divided, this division was to some extent papered over by the traditional link between femininity and purity. This link made men's position in social purity problematic, as has been noted by social historians of evangelical Protestantism.

Ann Douglas's insightful study of changes in American Protestantism in the 19th century traces the development of a sentimental Christianity in the 1830s and 1840s that softened and feminized the face of Protestantism. Harsh Calvinist theology was displaced by an alliance between sentimental women writers (Harriet Beecher Stowe is only the best known of these) and ministers who, after church disestablishment, had to win over influential ladies to maintain their position. In the Gilded Age, mid-Victorian sentimentality began to be in turn displaced by what was known as "muscular" Christianity, a new perspective connected to social Darwinism. The scientific/muscular perspectives of the 1890s, however, supplemented rather than replaced the feminized religion constructed decades earlier.[48]

Although church organization in Canada differed considerably from that in the eastern U.S., Douglas's thesis about the feminization of theology helps to explain why Methodism lost much of its fire-and-brimstone language, embracing instead a more humanist perspective emphasizing education and nurturing. As nurturing and other domestic virtues increased in value, allowing women to serve in public roles through maternal feminism, social purity helped to reconcile the apparently passive virtue of purity with active masculinity. An effort was made by a section of the urban middle class to redefine masculinity as well as femininity as actively domestic. The challenge was to purge the new male bourgeoisie of the drinking and wenching habits of the aristocracy, while avoiding effete or ascetic disengagement from the claims of masculinity.

In the English context, Leonore Davidoff and Catherine Hall have analyzed the Romantic attachment to suburban gardening as an attempt to cleanse the masculine soul from the grime of capitalist enterprise, and thus to help males to inhabit the domestic realm meaningfully.[49] The literature of Canadian social purity corroborates this. Through active gardening, physical exercise, and strenuous soul-searching, the new bourgeois male was envisaged as becoming pure without losing face or becoming weak. The popular American sex educator Sylvanus Stall, whose books were sold in Canada through the Methodist Church, addresses "young husbands" as follows:

> In woman, the love of home is usually more dominant than in man. By cultivating this in yourself you will produce a harmony of thought and purpose which will contribute greatly to the comfort and well-being of both. Adorn your home with your own hands. Beautify the lawn, the shrubbery, and all external surroundings.[50]

If domesticity could be reconciled with masculinity through the pale imitation of farming that was gardening, purity could also be defined so that it would not appear as exclusively female. Purity was not simply the absence of lust: it was an active, aggressive process of self-mastery that could be likened to a military campaign. It was furthermore connected to the unambiguously masculine pursuit of worldly success. Sylvanus Stall explained that purity was good not only for one's family but for one's business: he admits that some irreligious men are wealthy, but on the whole, pure thoughts are positively correlated with large bank accounts. Walking through the better part of any town, is it not obvious, he asks, that "the wealth of the nation" is "largely in the hands of Christian men and Christian women? These are the people who have the best credit, who can draw checks for the largest amounts."[51] The Canadian Salvation Army often published stories about former male drunkards who, once saved from drink and sin, were able to impress bank managers enough to obtain loans with their new-found "character" as security.

Despite the obvious exaggeration in these stories, there was a grain of truth in the suggestion that male purity might reinforce the capitalist ethic, even in its apparently impure social Darwinist variety (as Paul Johnson's study of the differential fortunes of saved and non-saved male citizens of Rochester shows).[52] The discourse about the new reconstituted family, with a partially public mother and a partially domesticated father, was thus a discourse about class as much as about gender.

Finally, social purity had a clear racial and ethnic organization. The "whiteness" favoured by the movement was not merely spiritual but also designated (consciously or unconsciously) a skin colour. The racist fears about "the yellow peril" and about Anglo-Saxons being overrun by more fertile "races" (as they designated what are now called ethnic groups) pervaded Canadian politics and society throughout the period under study, and are receiving increasing attention from historians of immigration and of race relations. The specific contribution of the social purity movement to this general climate of racism is what needs to be highlighted here. This can be summarized by stating that the darker and hence lower races were assumed to be not in control of their sexual desires.[53] Lacking proper Christian and Anglo-Saxon training, they had not produced the right kind of self. "Racial purity" is a phrase that appears but seldom in the texts studied, but the concept underlies common phrases such as "national purity" or "national health." Moral reformers had a significant impact on immigration policies, both directly by lobbying for such innovations as the medical/moral inspection of all immigrants and indirectly by creating a climate of opinion in which certain groups were perceived as morally undesirable. The regulation of sexuality has always been linked to racial and population policies, and it is this link—rather than the far wider subject of racism in Canadian 20th-century society—that will be analyzed.

To conclude, then, the social purity movement was indeed concerned about urban vices, but its real aim was not so much to suppress as to re-create and re-moralize not only deviants from its norms but, increasingly, the population of Canada as a whole. This was a project the state could not possibly have carried out; voluntary organizations played the starring role in the campaign to reconstruct the inner selves, and in particular the sexual/moral identity, of Canadians. This movement is by no means explained by being labelled as an agency of social control or a Puritan effort at censorship and repression: the movement was held together not only by its attacks on vice but by a common vision of the pure life that individuals, families, and the nation would lead in the near future. Therefore, despite the obviously repressive features of this movement, it is more appropriate to see its coercion as regulation and not as suppression or censorship; the term "regulation," which connotes preserving and shaping something and not merely suppressing it, more adequately captures the aims and the modes of operation of this movement.[54]

The entities being regulated were in the first instance the characters of individuals, with particular emphasis on sexual and hygienic habits; but the nation was also seen as held together by a common subjectivity, whose constant re-creation at the individual level ensured the continued survival of the collectivity. The collectivity thus organized had very specific class, gender, and racial/ethnic characteristics, generally supporting the domination of Anglo-Saxon middle-class males over all others but allowing women of the right class and ethnicity a substantial role, as long as they participated in the construction of women in general as beings who, despite their heroic and largely unaided deeds in maternity, were dependent on male protection. What this book seeks to reveal is how the practices that organized and consolidated these complex structures of social domination (along the axes of class, race, and gender) were both constituted by, and provided the operational basis for, the discourses of social purity and philanthropy generally.

■ NOTES

Abbreviations
CTA City of Toronto Archives, Toronto
NAC National Archives of Canada, Ottawa
PAO Public Archives of Ontario, Toronto
SA Salvation Army Heritage Centre, Toronto
UCA United Church Archives, Victoria College, Toronto

■ NOTE ON ARCHIVAL SOURCES

At the time the research was conducted, two of the record collections used were in the process of being classified (records of the Woman's Christian Temperance Union, in the Public Archives of Ontario, and those of the Canadian Council of Churches, National Archives of Canada). Therefore, the box and file numbers listed in the following notes were temporary numbers and may or may not correspond to the permanent numbers assigned later by archivists.

1. H. Clare Pentland, *Labour and Capital in Canada 1650-1860* (Toronto, 1981); Allan Moscovitch and Jim Albert, eds., *The "Benevolent" State: The Growth of Welfare in Canada* (Toronto, 1987); Leo Panitch, "The role and nature of the Canadian State," and Reg Whitaker, "Images of the state in Canada," in Leo Panitch, ed., *The Canadian State* (Toronto, 1977).

2. G. Kealey, *Toronto Workers Respond to Industrial Capitalism* (Toronto, 1980); G. Kealey and B. Palmer, *Dreaming of What Might Be: The Knights of Labor in Ontario 1880-1900* (Toronto, 1987); B. Palmer, ed., *The Character of Class Struggle* (Toronto, 1986); Michael Piva, *The Condition of the Working Class in Toronto* (Ottawa,1979).

3. Ramsay Cook, *The Regenerators: Social Criticism in Late Victorian English Canada* (Toronto, 1985).

4. Rev. C.W. Watch, "Social Purity Work in Canada," in A. Powell, ed., *National Purity Congress* (Baltimore, 1895), pp. 272-77.

5. These included Dr. Elizabeth Blackwell, Anthony Comstock, and Frances Willard (president of the U.S. Woman's Christian Temperance Union and one of the foremost reformers of her time).

6. Rev. Flint, in Powell, ed., *National Purity Congress*, p. 140.

7. See for instance F.S. Spence, *The Facts of the Case: A Summary of the most Important Evidence and Argument Presented in the Report of the Royal Commission on the Liquor Traffic* (Toronto, 1896). Spence claims that the first temperance convention in Canada was held In Halifax in 1834; but the movement only began in earnest in the late 1870s, and the Dominion WCTU was not founded until 1885.

8. The main source is Richard Allen, *The Social Passion: Religion and Social Reform in Canada 1914-1928* (Toronto, 1971). See also Dennis Guest, *The Emergence of Social Security in Canada* (Vancouver, 1985), pp. 31-34; Cook, *The Regenerators*, ch. 7.

9. See Gareth Stedman Jones, *Outcast London* (London, 1971), esp. pp. 244 ff. See also Christine Stansell, *City of Women: Sex and Class in New York City 1789-1860* (New York, 1986), ch. 4; and C. Smith-Rosenberg, *Religion and the Rise of the American City: The New York City Mission Movement 1812-1870* (Ithaca, N.Y., 1971).

10. Quoted in Eli Zaretsky, "Rethinking the Welfare State," in J. Dickinson and B. Russell, eds., *Family, Economy and State* (Toronto, 1987), p. 100.

11. Jacques Donzelot summarizes this shift as follows: "In general, philanthropy differed from charity in the choice of its objects, based on this concern for pragmatism: advice instead of gifts, because it cost nothing; assistance to children rather than to old people, and to women rather than to men." *The Policing of Families* (New York, 1979), p. 66. Donzelot's analysis, based on the work of Foucault, has had a strong influence on many current analyses of 19th-century philanthropy.

12. Quoted in Stedman Jones, *Outcast London*, p. 244. See also Mariana Valverde, "French Romantic Socialism and the Critique of Political Economy" (Ph.D. thesis, York University, 1982), esp. ch. II, "The Debate on Misery and the Critique of Political Economy."

13. See Donzelot, *The Policing of Families*, for a lengthy analysis of the constitution of the social.

14. David Garland, *Punishment and Welfare: A History of Penal Strategies* (London, 1985), p. 153.

15. A well-known Canadian example of the treatment of economic questions as social questions is W.L. Mackenzie King, *Industry and Humanity* (1919). See also J.S. Woodsworth, *My Neighbor: A Study of City Conditions, A Plea for Social Service* (1911; reprinted 1972).

16. Donzelot, *The Policing of Families*, argues that poverty, the family, and population are the main three "problems" that made up the social in the early 19th century.

17. See Anna Davin, "Imperialism and Motherhood," *History Workshop*, no. 5 (1978), pp. 9-57.

18. Bryan S. Green, *Knowing the Poor: A Case-Study in Textual Reality Construction* (London, 1983).

19. James Kay, *The Moral and Physical Condition of the Working Classes* (1832), quoted in Frank Mort, *Dangerous Sexualities: Medico-Moral Politics in England since 1830* (London, 1987), p. 22.

20. See Anthony Wohl's introduction to the reprint of Mearns's pamphlet *The Bitter Cry of Outcast London* (New York, 1970). This topic will be developed in the first section of Chapter 6.

21. B.G. Jefferis and J.L. Nichols, *Light in Dark Corners: Searchlight on Health* (Naperville, Ill., various editions from 1880s on). The 1922 edition was given the more modern title of *Safe Counsel or Practical Eugenics*.

22. Dennis Guest, in *The Emergence of Social Security in Canada* (Vancouver, 1985 [2nd ed.]), has a liberal framework that presupposes that whenever state benefits were organized on a philanthropic basis, this was either a mistake or a leftover of the past. The essays in A. Moscovitch and J. Alpert's edited collection *The "Benevolent" State*, however, demonstrate that many of the great new programs of the welfare state, such as mothers' allowances, were introduced for what one could only call philanthropic reasons such as concern for the eugenic future of the Canadian "race."

23. For instance, see James H. Gray, *Red Lights on the Prairies* (Saskatoon, 1971, 1986).

24. Frances Willard, in A. Powell, ed., *National Purity Congress* (Baltimore, 1896) p. 127; president's address (to the Dominion WCTU), in *White Ribbon Bulletin*, 13 December 1913, p. 180.

25. "Fewer Criminals with Pure Milk," *Daily News*, 19 October 1911, p. 13.

26. Advertisement for Canada Bread's four Toronto bakeries, in *Daily News*, 30 September

1911, p. 18. It should be noted that good bread was then assumed to be white; the association of health with brown bread is a very recent one.

27. On the campaigns to clean up the city's water supply and ensure safe milk, see Paul A. Bator, "Saving Lives on the Wholesale Plan: Public Health Reform in the City of Toronto, 1900-1930" (Ph.D. thesis, University of Toronto, 1979). The protagonist of Bator's thesis, Dr. Charles Hastings, believed in the moralizing effects of pure milk and water.

28. E.M. Knox, *The Girl of the New Day* (Toronto, 1919), p. 5.

29. Paul Rutherford, "Tomorrow's Metropolis: The Urban Reform Movement in Canada, 1880-1920," Canadian Historical Association, *Historical Papers*, 1971, p. 215.

30. W.L. Mackenzie King, *Industry and Humanity* (Toronto, 1919), pp. 330-31. See also Chapter IX, "Principles Underlying Health," which is concerned not with the health of individual bodies but with the health of the labour force as a whole, or, as King himself put it following Comte, the health of the "social organism."

31. CTA, RG-11, Box 167, Monthly Report of the Medical Officer of Health for October, 1914, p. 235.

32. W.L. Clark, *Our Sons* (1914; 5th ed.), pp. 24-25. As we shall see below, Clark's counterpart, A.W. Beall, who lectured to schoolchildren on behalf of the Ontario WCTU, not only agreed with Clark but even calculated the value of each young Canadian person at $50,000.

33. For an elaboration of this argument, see M. Valverde and L. Weir, "The Struggles of the Immoral: More Preliminary Remarks on Moral Regulation," *Resources for Feminist Research*, 17, 3 (September, 1988), pp. 31-34.

34. This point is made, from a somewhat different perspective, in an important article by Nikolas Rose, "Beyond the Public/Private Division: Law, Power and the Family," *Journal of Law and Society*, 14, 1 (Spring, 1987), pp. 61-75. In Philip Corrigan and Derek Sayer, *The Great Arch: English State Formation as Cultural Revolution* (Oxford, 1985), the role of the state in moral regulation is highlighted, and their theorization has been influential here; but the agencies of regulation internal to civil society are obscured.

35. Bruce Curtis, "Preconditions of the Canadian State: Educational Reform and Construction of a Public in Upper Canada, 1837-1846," in A. Moscovitch and J. Alpert, eds., *The "Benevolent" State* (Toronto, 1987), pp. 47-67. Curtis's insistence that educational reform was not merely social control or suppression of the working classes parallels the claim made above that social purity was more geared to moulding the subjectivity of citizens than simply controlling their behaviour. If the public education system was assigned the task of creating rationality and political subjectivity, the social purity movement sought to create an ethical/moral subjectivity.

36. Quoted in Michael Owen. "Keeping Canada God's Country: Presbyterian Perspectives on Selected Social Issues" (Ph.D. thesis, University of Toronto, 1984), p. 46.

37. David Garland, *Punishment and Welfare: A History of Penal Strategies* (London, 1985). Garland links the "modern" penal strategies centred on treatment to social work and eugenics in an analysis that is extremely relevant to social purity even though he neglects to analyze the modernization of sexual and gender regulation. He also stresses that the liberal state, though obviously in charge of the prison system, had to leave the moral reformation of prisoners in the hands of private agencies such as the John Howard and Elizabeth Fry Societies and the Salvation Army.

38. On the medicalization of poverty in 19th-century philanthropy, see Christine Stansell, *City of Women: Sex and Class in New York 1789-1860* (New York, 1986); this idea is explored in Mariana Valverde, review-essay on Stansell's book, *Labour/Le Travail*, 22 (Fall, 1988), pp. 247-57. On the medicalization of crime, see Garland, *Punishment and Welfare*, and Michel Foucault, *Discipline and Punish* (New York, 1979). For the medicalization of sexuality, see Lorna Weir, "Sexual Rule, Sexual Politics: Studies in the Medicalization of Sexual Danger 1820-1920" (Ph.D. thesis, York University, 1986); Frank Mort, *Dangerous Sexualities: Medico-Moral Politics in England Since 1830* (London, 1987).

39. A.W. Beall, *The Living Temple: A Manual on Eugenics for Parents and Teachers* (Whitby, Ont., 1933). Although this book was not published until the 1930s it purports to collect the lectures that Beall had given to Ontario schoolchildren during the first three decades of the century.

40. Michel Foucault, *A History of Sexuality*, vol. I (New York, 1979); George Moss, *Nationalism and Sexuality* (New York, 1985); Jeffrey Weeks, *Sex, Politics and Society: The Regulation of Sexuality since 1800* (London, 1981); Gary Kinsman, *The Regulation of Desire: Sexuality in Canada* (Montreal, 1987).

41. King, *Industry and Humanity*, p. 485. King shares the concern of social purity activists (with whom he had earlier collaborated on some issues, such as suppression of the opium traffic) for regulating not only the work but also the spirit and the leisure time of young Canadians: people "require Education to teach them the right use of leisure."

42. Mrs. Spofford, in National Archives of Canada (NAC), National Council of Women of Canada (hereafter NCW), *Yearbook*, 1907, p. 85.

43. John Charlton, MP, April 10, 1899, quoted in T. Chapman. "Sex Crimes in Western Canada 1890-1920" (Ph.D. thesis, University of Alberta, 1984), p. 44.

44. Michael Owen's study of the Presbyterian wing of the movement, "Keeping Canada God's Country," bears this out. Paul Bator, "Saving Lives on the Wholesale Plan," found that all public health activists identified by him were of Anglo-Saxon origin, and the vast majority were either Methodist or Presbyterian; see also Linda Kealey, ed., *A Not Unreasonable Claim: Women and Reform in Canada 1880s-1920s* (Toronto,

1979). For the new middle class, see Robert Wiebe, *The Search for Order 1877-1920* (New York, 1967).

45. The American feminist, urban reformer, and social theorist Jane Addams did seek to homogenize American urban society through cultural means; but even she, who was more radical in class, gender, and racial terms than the leading social purity activists in Canada, did not envision abolishing the economic basis of bourgeois class formation. This will be explored in Chapter 6.

46. The goals of the social purity in terms of gender organization are captured in the statement made by the Methodist Board of Temperance and Social Reform in the context of the white slavery panic; the clergymen vowed not to cease in their struggle against white slavery until "[we can] restore the victim to her home and to a life of honor, purity, and helpfulness." UCA, Methodist DESS, Annual Report, 1911, p. 33.

47. Carolyn Strange, "The Toronto Social Survey Commission of 1915 and the Search for Sexual Order in the City," in Roger Hall et al., eds., *Patterns of the Past: Interpreting Ontario's History* (Toronto, 1988).

48. Ann Douglas, *The Feminization of American Culture* (New York, 1977). See also Carroll Smith-Rosenberg, *Religion and the Rise of the American City* (Ithaca, N.Y., 1971); Paul Johnson, *Shopkeepers' Millennium: Society and Revivals in Rochester, N.Y., 1815-1837*, (New York, 1978); Nancy Hewitt, *Women's Activism and Social Change: Rochester, N.Y., 1822-1872* (Ithaca, N.Y., 1984); Mary P. Ryan, *Cradle of the Middle Class* (London, 1981).

49. Leonore Davidoff and Catherine Hall, *Family Fortunes: Men and Women of the English Middle Class, 1780-1850* (London, 1987), pp. 110-13.

50. Sylvanus Stall, *What a Young Husband Ought to Know* (Philadelphia, 1907 [1899]), p. 53. Note that the laborious components of domestic work, especially in the kitchen, are still thought to be exclusively female.

51. *Ibid.*, pp. 68-71.

52. Johnson, *Shopkeepers' Millennium*, shows that men who were born again in the revivals of the 1830s and 1840s fared quite a bit better in business than their unconverted counterparts, partly because of the formal and informal credit and business links forged among members of the same congregation.

53. See Sander Gilman, *Difference and Pathology: Stereotypes of Race, Sexuality, and Madness* (Ithaca, N.Y., 1985).

54. I have adopted the term "moral regulation" from Philip Corrigan and Derek Sayer, *The Great Arch: English State Formation as Cultural Revolution* (Oxford, 1985). However, they do not differentiate between moral and other modes of social regulation; by contrast, I restrict the term to mean the formation of ethical subjectivity.

■ QUESTIONS FOR CRITICAL THOUGHT

1. What is social control? Formal social control? Informal social control? What is the essence of Chunn and Gavigan's critique of this model? How is their critique relevant to the study of crime, deviance, and the state?

2. What does Sangster see as the benefits and limitations of a Foucauldian approach to crime generally, and to women's criminality specifically? Why does she argue against fully decentring the state and power?

3. What is Corrigan drawing from Durkheim? From Marx? How do these various ideas combine to form "moral regulation"? What does moral regulation do that none of these theories does on its own?

4. What do Valverde and Weir take from Corrigan in their approach to moral regulation? What about Corrigan's definition do they critique? What is their definition of moral regulation? What is the difference between "the state" and "the nation," and how does this difference affect Valverde and Weir's approach to moral regulation?

5. In what ways is sexual regulation linked to moral regulation? For Kinsman? For Valverde and Weir? For Valverde?

6. How do moral tropes, such as pure milk and white snow, help to construct "morality" as white, as well as middle-class and heterosexual? Can you think of contemporary examples of this kind of association?

■ FURTHER READINGS

Mary-Louise Adams. "'In Sickness and In Health': State Formation, Moral Regulation, and Early VD Initiatives in Ontario." *Journal of Canadian Studies* 28, 4 (1993):117-130.
This essay may be considered another "coming of age" study in moral regulation. Here, the tensions about whether moral regulation is a practice of the state, and the meanings of regulation are also played out, as Adams, like Kinsman and Valverde, investigates the relationship between the state, sexuality, and the formation of subjectivities.

Philip Corrigan and Derek Sayer. "Introduction" to *The Great Arch: English State Formation as Cultural Revolution.* London: Basil Blackwell, 1985, 1-13.
As with Corrigan's original essay, this Introduction is the classic, and perhaps most often cited, contribution to moral regulation scholarship. Here, moral regulation as a theory of state formation is explicitly laid out.

Alan Hunt. *Governing Morals: A Social History of Moral Regulation.* Cambridge: Cambridge University Press, 1999.

If Valverde's book represents the first full-length study of moral regulation, Hunt's is the most recent monograph in this body of scholarship. In this wide-ranging study of moral regulation in Britain and the United States, Hunt reminds readers of the limits of social control, the importance of Foucauldian concepts of power and regulation, and the benefits of moral regulation as a form of scholarship.

Alan Hunt and Gary Wickham. "An Introduction to Foucault." *Foucault and Law: Towards a Sociology of Law as Governance.* London: Pluto Press 1994, 3-38.

As the title suggests, this essay is designed to introduce readers to Foucault. It provides an excellent overview of his key contributions and terms, such as discourse, knowledge, power, genealogies, governmentality, with a particular view to highlighting the significance of Foucault to understanding issues of legal and extra-legal forms of regulation. This text is very useful for those not familiar with Foucault's project and terminology.

PART II

STUDYING MORAL REGULATION:
PUTTING A CONCEPT TO WORK

This section offers a range of different applications of moral regulation by Canadian scholars. These scholars study a broad expanse of legal and extralegal constructions of normal and deviant behaviours and/or populations in different times and different locations across the country.

The readings are grouped through their primary interests: the making of moral subjects, the construction of "deviant" subjects, and the moral regulation of place and space. These themes introduce the reader to the diversity of moral regulation scholarship, and further explore the concerns introduced earlier.

Renisa Mawani's essay underscores the fact that regulatory projects do not merely punish the "bad" or "deviant" populations. In fact, they deliberately target and regulate the "good" or "respectable" classes and motivate them to continue to police themselves and others in the maintenance of "normalcy." Mawani demonstrates one of the key tenets of moral regulation scholarship: the production of "ethical citizens" through discursive, non-coercive projects of "making normal."

Franca Iacovetta's essay continues this theme by demonstrating how the most apparently mundane of tasks—such as grocery shopping—is actually a moralized project through which concepts of "good" citizenship are constructed. Iacovetta illustrates the salience of race, ethnicity, and gender to the construction of the "respectable" Canadian citizen.

Joan Sangster offers another view of moral regulation. She examines the regulation of those deemed to be "morally suspect." Sangster's analysis of the *Female Refuges Act*, which enabled authorities to incarcerate young women who were merely at risk of bad behaviour, demonstrates the perils of ignoring moral messages—especially for those made vulnerable by material relations of gender, class, and race. Sangster's analysis of coercive forms of regulation also returns the reader to two central points of contention in moral regulation scholarship: (1) the degree to which regulation is achieved discursively, and (2) the degree to which state mechanisms of order enforcement are key to the containment of that which is constructed as "deviant."

Margaret Little's examination of welfare recipients similarly forces consideration of the role of the state in the regulation of "deviant" subjects. Little also draws our attention to the ways that both state and non-state actors play a role in this form of regulation. Women on family benefits have their "moral worthiness" assessed by neighbours, school officials, and community members as well as by official welfare agents. The network of surveillance that is meant to distinguish the deserving from the undeserving poor is thus widened considerably.

The remaining readings in this section point to the significance of moral regulation for space and place. Mary Louise Adams's article demonstrates the ways in which the regulation of spaces—in this instance, the Toronto waterfront and the islands in the 1940s—can operate as a form of regulation of populations, such as young, heterosocial couples. She further demonstrates that the same space can take on different moralized meanings when used at different times, or by different people. Thus, a park bench can be a setting for wholesome family picnics or for furtive teenage petting.

Jennifer Nelson's essay on Africville, Halifax's black "slum," demonstrates the intimate links between space, moralized assessments of citizenship and belonging, and race. Nelson exposes everyday practices, such as zoning laws and the allocation of urban services, as racialized forms of moral regulation. For example, the location of the city dump in Africville made tacit moralized links between "dirt" and "blackness" which justified the unequal treatment of Africville's residents. At the same time, the theme of resistance re-emerges, as Halifax's black population contests the moral assessments of its communities.

CHAPTER 7

REGULATING THE "RESPECTABLE" CLASSES:
VENEREAL DISEASE, GENDER, AND PUBLIC HEALTH INITIATIVES IN CANADA, 1914–35

Renisa Mawani

The late 19th and early 20th centuries were formative periods in Canadian history, with the nation experiencing massive societal shifts, including urbanization, industrialization, and increased immigration.[1] In response to these changes and their potentially disastrous effects, government officials, social reformers, and various professionals became increasingly preoccupied with the illusive goals of building a settler colony that reflected British ideals and values.[2] As several scholars have noted, the making of the nation was not narrowly defined in terms of capital, labour, or industry, but rather it combined British and distinctly Canadian assumptions about suitable roles and appropriate conduct for European women and men.[3] In their efforts to construct a strong country, and in endeavouring to fill it with "good citizens"—who were white, middle class, married, and monogamous—the state became more and more intrusive. At this historical juncture, Canadians witnessed assiduous state initiatives to regulate behaviour in all aspects of public and private life including employment, sexual and non-sexual pleasure, and familial relations.[4]

As many Canadian historians have suggested, the state and its legal apparatus were not the singular source of social and/or legal regulation in the country.[5] Much of the historical writing produced by socio-legal theorists in Canada reminds us that regulation—in its manifold guises ranging from legal coercion to moral persuasion—did not always arise out of state concerns. To the contrary, professionals from various fields were often at the forefront of social reform initiatives, forging complex and sometimes contradictory alliances with state officials in the process. For instance, Mariana Valverde's important work on social reform in English-speaking Canada has demonstrated how philanthropic agencies and professional organizations also acted as regulatory agents which, in many cases, significantly altered the state's reform agenda.[6]

In this chapter I analyze the anti-venereal disease campaigns that emerged in Canada during the interwar period. Drawing primarily from pamphlets and advice literature, which were circulated extensively by medical practitioners, religious authorities, and other professionals across the nation, I probe the ways in which public health education was used as a strategy for regulating sex and (re)constituting subjectivities among the "respectable classes." The study of venereal disease provides an important example of the interface between state and non-state reform initiatives. It is illustrative of the ways in which medical practitioners, (s)experts, and professional organizations influenced—and in many cases facilitated—state interest in the treatment and control of venereal disease (VD) and in public health more generally at both national and provincial levels. Since public health literature was widely disseminated in most provinces, I suggest that VD control can best be understood through a broad geographical focus that transcends individual regions. Thus, my chapter concentrates on moral reform initiatives across the country.

[...]

Throughout this chapter I contend that efforts to control the spread of disease were directed not only at incorrigible populations, but at *all* Canadians—women and men, young and old, moral and disreputable. But while anti-VD initiatives were diffused across society, I am not suggesting that regulatory practices were evenly deployed by state and non-state officials, or had similar implications for all their subjects. On the contrary, as Carolyn Strange and Tina Loo remind us, in late 19th- and early 20th-century Canada, "virtue was seen to be distributed unevenly, [and] the efforts at making good had to be as well."[7] Thus, in the name of public health, "foreigners," prostitutes, young single women, and working-class men did in fact find themselves disproportionately at the receiving end of many punitive strategies. And while state officials and health professionals agreed that strong legal measures were necessary for the regulation and ultimately the reform of these "deviant" groups,[8] they also invested considerable amounts of energy into non-legal forms of intervention—such as advice literature—endeavouring to constitute "moral subjects" who were white, middle-class, able-bodied, monogamous, and heterosexual.

Whereas regulatory strategies aimed at "good" and "bad" Canadians differed significantly, it remains problematic to assume—as some historians have done[9]—that "good" women and especially men were beyond the reach of anti-VD initiatives. While Chunn and others have pointed to the ways in which fears of disease precipitated greater intervention into the lives of "respectable" women,[10] few scholars have investigated the regulatory strategies aimed at their equally reputable male counterparts. Although state officials rarely directed the law and other formal mechanisms of control at "good" men, I suggest that professionals who wrote and disseminated prescriptive literature were concerned, albeit for different reasons, with constructing normative heterosexualities for men as well as women.[11] While a double standard of sexuality remained a pervasive feature of anti-VD campaigns, reformers and health professionals insisted that monogamy, marriage, and heterosexuality were the desired and necessary attributes of a moral life for *both* sexes. Just as the law was routinely invoked to deal with "bad" behaviour, prescriptive literature was directed at (re)constructing and shaping moral subjectivities by encouraging decency and conformity among the public at large. Throughout the interwar years, health professionals hailed public health education as a promising strategy, not only for reducing rates of VD, but more importantly, for teaching Canadians about health, hygiene, and marital heterosexuality, and ultimately for (re)making them into "good citizens."

■ THE VENEREAL DISEASE CRISIS IN CANADA

In 1922, Dr. Gordon Bates, the general secretary of the Canadian National Council for Combating Venereal Disease (CNCCVD)—formerly the military officer in charge of venereal diseases—made a speech to the Hamilton Social Hygiene Council. Bates was a long-standing advocate of public health initiatives and VD control,[12] and his address was one of many that he would make to other social hygiene committees across the country. With typical flourish, Bates emphasized to his audience the prevalence and danger of venereal diseases and urged the Hamilton council to organize a strong campaign within the community for effectively dealing with them. "Venereal diseases," he warned, "constitute the greatest single public health problem of our modern times. Foul and sinister manifestations of our failure to attend to the organized study and care of our growing young people, their devastating influence is more marked than that of war itself." He continued his lecture cautioning the Hamilton council of the grave implications that followed disease: "These diseases are significant in that their end results are not only disability and death, but far reaching social results which affect social organization and human happiness in a way characteristic of no other diseases."[13]

In this same speech, Bates told the council that the origins of VD were not confined to the spirochete or the gonococcus. Rather, as a staunch supporter of public sex education, he insisted that their causes were much broader and were dispersed throughout the social order. Consequently, treating the micro-organism, argued Bates, was simply not enough. Efforts to eliminate disease had to be far greater, aimed at reconstructing the core of society itself. As Bates explained:

> The fact that venereal diseases are an index of the immorality of a community, that they are the common result of a misdirection of the efforts of nature to ensure the carrying on of the race—the fact that with unerring precision their very existence points to widespread departure from the ideals which should actuate men and women in their responsibility to one another and in their joint responsibility to the race—this means that in attempting to solve the disease problem we must also tackle social organization as well.[14]

Whereas medical clinics were necessary to treat those men and women who were unfortunate enough to contract VD, Bates believed that they were insufficient to effectively eliminate the scourge. Rather than invest money in treatment after the fact, he emphasized the need for prevention through education: "The definite training of children not only that they may be an economic success but that they may be guided towards ideals which will mean a correct attitude towards life, and towards one another is necessary. This will mean in the long run not only citizens who are longer lived and who are free from disease but contented, happy units in a well balanced state."[15] [...]

Venereal disease emerged as a public health concern across Canada during the early 20th century. The preoccupation and frenzy surrounding VD in the Canadian context and elsewhere in the Western world became a metaphor linking larger societal concerns about social and racial degeneracy. Venereal disease personified both state and professional anxieties about sex, vice, and immorality. As Lucy Bland has suggested in the British context, VD became an index for "all of the contemporary fears of national deterioration, degeneracy, and 'race suicide.'"[16] While concerns about social hygiene first manifested themselves in the pre-war era, the "sensitive" nature of VD, and its intricate connection to sex and vice, created reluctance among reformers to discuss it publicly.[17] During the First World War, however, apprehensions about disease intensified and began to leak into public discourse. While health professionals and reformers were initially concerned about the consequences that accompanied public discussions of social diseases, large numbers of infected soldiers outweighed these concerns, leaving them with few alternatives.

During the war, army officials reported disturbingly high rates of venereal infection among all Allied soldiers, and among Canadians in particular. Of all the Western countries, Canada had the most troops infected with the "leprosies of lust."[18] [...] As Canadian reformers and health professionals became increasingly alarmed about the growing number of soldiers who were infected with VD and would soon be coming home, levels of panic escalated. A high rate of infection among the military, combined with the loss of labour power resulting from war, and state and non-state endeavours aimed at protecting and making the nation, created a fertile climate for the intensification of VD control during the interwar period.

Throughout Canada, anti-VD initiatives were diverse, disparate, and contradictory. Professional and state organizations, while concerned with disease and race suicide, lacked a persistent and unified approach for dealing with the VD problem. Thus, efforts to regulate the disease in Canada were far less state-directed than in Britain and the United States.[19] However, from British Columbia to the Maritimes, government sponsorship of anti-VD programs was in evidence in various forms and degrees. The state provided financial assistance, for example, to a number of organizations involved in initiating and organizing public health strategies, including the National Council of Women, the YMCA, YWCA,[20] and later the Canadian National Council for Combating Venereal Disease (CNCCVD). For the most part, doctors and health professionals led the campaigns to eradicate VD. By the post-First-World-War period, VD had become less a mark of sin and more a disease with identifiable symptoms and cures. The medicalization of VD did not eclipse moral discourse, but rather resulted in a hybrid medico-moral regulatory regime. Health professionals and medical practitioners still relied upon their moralistic views, but now used scientific "facts" to strengthen their claims about the relationship between (im)morality, "illicit" sex, and disease.

[...]

For many authorities, the law was a necessary tool for the eradication of vice and disease, as these officials argued that VD could be eliminated only if the sources of infection were locked up. During the First World War, health professionals and reformers began urging provincial and federal governments to enact legislation for the prevention and control of venereal disease. By the post-First-World-War period, venereal disease prevention acts were implemented in all provinces except Prince Edward Island.[21]

[...]

Treatment was believed to be another essential weapon in the fight against disease. Not only did health professionals lobby the government for mandatory treatment legislation, but they also urged state authorities to provide free treatment to all those infected with VD. By the end of the First World War, the federal government had agreed to intervene in the business of regulating venereal disease and the domain of public health more generally.[22] The Dominion Department of Health was established in 1919, with one division responsible for overseeing VD control.[23] Throughout the early 1920s, the Dominion provided the provinces with approximately $100,000 per year for the prevention and control of venereal disease.[24] Altogether, the department was involved in administering 102 VD clinics across the country.[25] Furthermore, the Department of Health ensured that an adequate supply of antiluetic drugs was available for the purposes of VD control. While great numbers of people were treated in these public clinics, many Canadians—especially the wealthy—continued to seek treatment from private physicians.[26]

After the First World War, experts estimated that approximately 15 to 20 percent of civilian Canadians were infected with syphilis and/or gonorrhea.[27] Doctors and health professionals began to rapidly lose faith in existing VD control strategies. [...] First, venereal disease was difficult to diagnose and treat, especially in women. Second, treatment was prolonged and painful, and patients often disappeared before they were fully cured. Third, and most important, clinics were beset by a number of problems including overcrowding, inadequate facilities, and lack of expertise.[28]

These exigencies led many health professionals to emphasize prevention. While a large number favoured public health education, they regarded it as being complementary to, rather than a replacement for, pre-established legal regulation and treatment. Although few denied the necessity of both legal and medical control—and while professionals like Bates agreed that government had performed a vital service in establishing clinics and passing compulsory treatment legislation—a general consensus emerged among state officials and health experts that public education was the way of the future. As Bates put it, "What is badly needed [in Canada] is the growth of a great popular social hygiene movement—in the direction of studying, preaching and establishing a more normal environment, particularly for young people."[29]

■ THE CANADIAN NATIONAL COUNCIL FOR COMBATING VENEREAL DISEASE

The idea of a public health campaign flourished during the post-First-World-War era. While health professionals had in earlier years been reluctant to talk about sex and disease, concerns about social and national reconstruction, alongside the growing appeal of eugenics and social hygiene, helped advocates to promote anti-VD education.[30] By the 1920s, health professionals generally agreed that public health education was the most promising strategy for the elimination of disease. Reformers and medical practitioners alike had reached the conclusion that ignorance and misinformation presented two major obstacles to the eradication of VD. Leading the campaign for public education, Bates argued that proper knowledge was the only way Canadians could effectively deal with the scourge. As he wrote in 1921: "The best means for achieving this end [the elimination of VD] will be general education work on as large a scale as possible. The facts as to the seriousness of venereal diseases and as to their prevalence should be put before people generally as soon as possible ... Although we now have venereal disease legislation in most of the provinces, much of it is not enforced."[31] For the most part, reformers and health professionals agreed that public education must move beyond the "facts" about syphilis and gonorrhoea. According to Dr. J.J. Heagerty, who was appointed chief of the Dominion's Division of Venereal Disease Control in 1919,[32] educational initiatives had to be far more ambitious in their scope and objective: "The object of education in this campaign is not so much the dissemination of knowledge of venereal disease as the development of standards of conduct and the formation of character. A knowledge of venereal disease alone will not prevent illicit sexual intercourse nor its consequences; there must be, in addition, sound ideals which act as a basis for the control of sexual appetite."[33] Clearly, professionals including Bates and Heagerty had larger aspirations. It appears that they embraced public health initiatives as necessary not only for educating individuals, but also for (re)shaping their sexual desires and their inner selves to mirror a "moral subject" who was white, middle-class, heterosexual, married, and monogamous.

The VD public health campaign was unprecedented in this country. Canadians had never seen anything like it.[34] Much of the educational work was undertaken by the Canadian National Council for Combating Venereal Disease (CNCCVD), a voluntary body organized in May 1919 and modelled after the British society of the same name. The mandate of the CNCCVD was to "combat venereal disease by whatever means seem desirable," including education, legislative, and administrative reforms, and the implementation of treatment facilities for those persons infected.[35] The council's membership included both individuals and organizations. Although a national establishment, the council had various provincial and municipal committees that were responsible for overseeing public health initiatives in all the provinces.

Upon creation of the CNCCVD in 1919, Gordon Bates was appointed as the council's general secretary.[36] Along with his role in disseminating knowledge about VD through public lectures, published articles, and reports, Bates was also responsible for soliciting funds to support the organization's work. [...]

The CNCCVD, led by Bates, played a pivotal role in the organization of public health work in Canada. Among other things, the council was responsible for publishing and circulating pamphlets and periodicals at the national level. But their publishing efforts were constrained by an ongoing scarcity of resources. Although the CNCCVD made vigorous efforts to issue its own prescriptive literature—and did indeed manage to generate an impressive volume of material—it was forced to rely largely on the publications of British and US organizations with which it maintained close connections.[37] "Suitable" pamphlets from both these countries were enlisted to educate the Canadian public. Advice literature from the US was widely distributed in Canada, particularly in British Columbia where social hygiene work was influenced by events taking place south of the border.[38] The council was especially reliant on the American Social Hygiene Association, and made arrangements to distribute its pamphlets, cards, exhibits, films, and slides in Canada.[39] Public health literature was written mostly by medical practitioners and public health nurses. Sex-specific instruction through radio broadcasts, public lectures, moving pictures, and lantern slides was also instrumental to mass education, and its authors and promoters claimed to draw from a variety of medical and "scientific breakthroughs" in the field of disease control.[40] Yet, despite these efforts to scientificate and medicalize educational initiatives, the VD advice literature was saturated with moralistic undertones.

[...]

■ CREATING A CAMPAIGN FOR PUBLIC EDUCATION

Although the content and aims of anti-VD educational initiatives were sex- and age-specific, some points of convergence were apparent. According to the CNCCVD, public health literature was designed to meet several objectives. First, officials urged that public education was needed to ensure Canadians had adequate knowledge about the signs, symptoms, and consequences of VD. Reformers and health professionals argued that since the symptomatology of syphilis and gonorrhoea was often mild and undetectable, people were not always aware of their infectious state. Thus, medical practitioners who authored advice literature commonly described the physical manifestations of gonorrhoea and syphilis as follows:

> The first sign of syphilis is the appearance of a small ulcer, or chancre, on or about the sex organs two to four weeks after intercourse with an infected person, although it may be earlier or later. This chancre may be thought of no importance because it may not be painful and may even clear up without special treatment. But through it the organisms of syphilis have made a gap in the body's defenses and are thus able to spread to vital parts.[41]

Health professionals encouraged readers to check their "private parts" for these sorts of symptoms, reminding them that illiteracy about VD posed a serious risk to themselves and the nation. Yet, in practice, not all members of the population were equally privy to knowledge about VD. The distribution of educational materials was clearly gender-stratified, as descriptions of VD-related symptoms were more frequently found in literature for men than for women.[42]

The second function of education was to convince those persons infected with venereal disease to come forth for testing and treatment. As Bates put it, educational initiatives would ensure that "infected persons or persons who have exposed themselves to infection may be informed of the necessity for undertaking treatment at the earliest possible moment."[43] Patients who attended public clinics were routinely provided with propaganda, in the form of pamphlets and cards, advising them that it was their national responsibility to undergo treatment until cured. Indeed, the implicit message was that "good citizenship" was equated with strong, (re)productive, disease-free bodies. As one source asserted, "We want all to realize that it is the imperative duty, not for his or her own benefit only but as a civic obligation, of every man or woman who has been exposed to sexual infection to get treated at the earliest possible moment and for as long as it is necessary."[44] Women and men were warned by health professionals, and in advice literature, that their failure to comply with treatment would be followed by grave consequences. In many cases, public health nurses were routinely sent out to make home visits and were mandated by law to report incorrigibles who discontinued treatment to the provincial authorities.[45]

The third and perhaps most important function of educational initiatives was to provide women and men with "proper" knowledge about social and sexual hygiene. The dominant view among public health officials characterized VD as a pivotal link between vice, disease, and sexuality. In spite of efforts by some health professionals to extend the list of potential sources of infection beyond "illicit" sex to include unclean dishes, table cutlery, towels, and public lavatories,[46] the dominant view was that VD was principally the product of sexual immorality and promiscuity. The Health League of Canada, for example, insisted that VD could not be acquired innocently, as "scientific breakthroughs" confirmed that these diseases could be contracted only through sexual relations. As one Health League publication counselled, "If we [Canadians] abstain from free-and-easy intercourse we need not fear that we shall contract the disease."[47]

Reformers generally agreed that public education was not only necessary for the prevention of disease, but also crucial for the shaping of an individual's inner essence—morals, character, and sexual nature. Drawing from examples of educational strategies undertaken in Britain and the US, Bates underscored the urgency of pursuing similar programs in Canada: "Education has not been confined to the imparting of knowledge as to the physical results of venereal disease, but every effort has been made to go as far beyond this as possible in the inculcation of the view that correct moral standards are fundamental in all classes of society if the venereal disease problem is to be solved."[48] Health professionals argued that instructing women and men about the "correct" standards of good health—in matters of sex and society—was the only way that the venereal peril and the looming threat of race suicide could be eliminated. Thus, Bates and his followers resolved that (re)shaping morality among women and men was the key to solving "the greatest of our public health problems."[49] Experts believed that inculcating the public with "respectable" ideals would not only create and promote "the health and happiness of the average citizen," but more importantly would ensure that Canada would assume its rightful status as a strong and virile nation.[50]

Anti-VD initiatives constructed the prevention of disease as a national responsibility. While state and professional organizations were enjoined to fight the great scourge of social disease, advice pamphlets commonly articulated to female and male readers alike that it was their civic duty to remain free from infection. Just as prescriptive literature reminded the readership that attaining treatment was the responsibility of all Canadians, authors of anti-VD propaganda also told them that continence and good health in both sexes were necessary for national health and security. [...]

Since doctors and (s)experts believed that sexual immorality was a root cause of the social problems that plagued Canadian society, shaping sexual behaviour among the populace became crucial to the construction of "citizens" and to the making of the nation. As the Health League of Canada explained, "People are realizing that the greatest health and happiness can be attained only through complete physical, mental, and spiritual development, and that such development is possible only when the sex instinct is used for the up building of the individual and the race."[51] Moreover, as Dr. W.A. Lincoln remarked in the popular journal *Social Welfare*, the only cure for the social evil was "a high standard of morals" that would "instill in the minds of young men and women that the sexual functions" were for a high and noble purpose—namely, marriage, and replenishing the race.[52] Furthermore, public health authorities often reiterated the latter point of racial reconstruction by underscoring the disastrous consequences of the First World War in Canada, including a mass depletion of her citizenry.[53]

Advice literature frequently called upon medical professionals to discuss matters of sex and, more importantly, to draw the parameters of "normal" sexual behaviour. Professionals did not espouse a purely repressive view of sex. Rather, they made explicit distinctions between "bad" sex and "good." While "bad" sex was often defined in terms of sexual immorality, perversity, and pleasure, its converse—"good" or "normal" sex—was always synonymous with marital heterosexuality and was determined through abstinence, except for the purposes of reproduction. The Health League of Canada and other organizations took the matter of sex very seriously, repeatedly reminding its readership that conforming to "good" sex would drastically reduce an individual's chances of contracting VD: "The marriage of one man with one woman has come to be considered the best method of carrying on the life of the race. Through such a relationship, the sex instinct finds its most wholesome satisfaction ... More than this, indulgence in sex relations among persons who are not married to each other exposes them to serious physical danger: they are likely to become infected with venereal disease."[54]

While authorities admonished that "good" sex protected women and men against VD and also encouraged individual and national progress, they cautioned that "bad" sex inevitably resulted in disease and imperial decline. The definition of "bad" sex throughout public health literature was often broad and ambiguous. Generally, health professionals and reformers suggested transgressive intercourse included all sexual relations that deviated from the prescribed norms of heterosexuality, marriage, and reproduction.

Sex for pleasure commonly fell under the definition of "bad" sex and, thus, was universally condemned by public health workers. Health officials argued that sexual pleasure was lustful, dangerous, and, moreover, served no social purpose. Although medical practitioners agreed that sex was a natural or primordial human characteristic, they urged that it had a time, place, and function. "While the sexual instinct is one of the primal instincts," explained a 1917 pamphlet published by the Nova Scotia Department of Health, "It differs from the other primal instincts, as hunger and thirst, in that its purpose is the perpetuation of the species rather than the preservation of the life of the individual." The pamphlet concluded that while sex was indeed an important aspect of life, "its satisfaction is not necessary to the health of the individual."[55] Experts repeatedly drew upon such medico-moral discourses to maintain that all extramarital sex was abnormal and unsafe, and virtually guaranteed exposure to VD.

While all Canadians were warned about "deviant" sex and the dangers that followed, public health literature was tailored for specific audiences who, according to health professionals, required "special" information. Parents, young women and men, physicians, nurses, clergymen, employers, and sailors were among these target groups. A number of social factors mediated the messages conveyed to these audiences.[56] Gender, for instance, had an enormous impact upon the kind of information that was conveyed about venereal disease and social hygiene more generally. But while Allan Brandt is generally correct in his claim that venereal disease meant very different things for women and men,[57] these gendered divisions were never entirely clear-cut. Although gender mediated discussions of disease and (im)morality, it did not predetermine them. For example, it was not always women who were construed to be "dangerous" and "diseased." To the contrary, both women and men were constituted by authors of prescriptive literature as "victims" and "perpetrators" of diseases at various junctures. While men were frequently portrayed as the victims of "deviant" women such as professional and clandestine prostitutes, the roles were often reversed when "lustful" men (husbands included) were seen to contaminate women with their depravity and disease.

■ EDUCATION FOR WOMEN

Until the early 20th century, a dominant perception among health professionals was that women were child-like in emotional quality and intellectual capacity. Doctors and lay reformers agreed that knowledge about such matters as venereal disease and sexuality was deemed to be unsuitable for women, as it was for children. Physicians and other experts held that the typical woman was too "virtuous" to discuss questions of sex and sexuality, and hence needed to be spared the experience of being exposed to such "salacious" topics. Many claimed that knowledge of this kind was likely to put a woman in danger, as too much knowledge would corrupt her innocence and entice her into a life of promiscuity, vice, and disease.

By the end of the First World War, however, medical practitioners had begun to change their views and emerge from this "conspiracy of silence." As estimated rates of venereal infection rose precipitously among both sexes after the war, and as fears of widespread infection and imperial decline escalated, health professionals and feminist reformers began to insist upon VD education for women. [...]

In the postwar era, feminist reformers and health professionals alike maintained that only through the spread of knowledge could women be safeguarded from immorality and disease. Feminists contended that an understanding of sex, disease, and morality could protect women from deceitful men who seduced them and led them astray through promises of marriage. Medical practitioners and professionals, including Bates, became increasingly supportive of these entreaties.[58] As one source suggested in the *Public Health Journal*: "There is a large number of girls who, because of lack of home care and protection, and because of incomplete ignorance as to the sex organs and instincts, have not the slightest idea as to why certain liberties with their persons are not to be permitted, and are enticed early by boys of the neighborhood."[59] Drawing from emerging feminist discourses about the causes of sexual immorality, doctors and other professionals enlisted educational initiatives to warn young women of "dangerous" men. As explained by the Health League of Canada:

> Because the sex instinct, which may bring the individual the greatest joy, is sometimes misused, a girl should exercise great care in the choice of men with whom she associates. Chance acquaintances often invite girls on automobile rides and to the use of liquor, with the intention of leading them into sexual relations. Such invitation should be refused. A girl does not wish to be considered an easy mark, or to put herself in a position where a man may take advantage of her.[60]

Women therefore needed to be eternally vigilant. Educational materials such as a 1922 pamphlet authored by the American sex educator Bernard McFadden warned that "one act of folly," even if just a kiss, could propel women into a life of corruption, prostitution, and disease.[61]

By the early 1920s, health professionals generally agreed that knowledge about sex and VD was vital not only for the protection of women's virtue and health, but more importantly for race preservation and growth. After the war, estimates suggested that married women and children had the highest rates of VD among all categories of Canada's civilian population. According to one article published in the *Canadian Medical Association Journal*, "There exists more gonorrhoea among married women than among prostitutes."[62] Gonorrhoea was believed to be so common among married women that many health professionals, including Dr. J.J. Heagerty, who was appointed president of the CNCCVD in the mid-1920s, facetiously referred to it as "honeymoon appendicitis."[63] Heagerty believed that venereal disease among women contributed significantly to the diminishing birth rate and to the population decline that Canada was experiencing during the Great Depression. While the physical health effects of gonorrhoea were unknown, professionals argued that syphilis, the less common of the diseases, was responsible for nearly half of the accidental miscarriages in Canada, not to mention blindness, deafness, and mental deficiency among young children.[64] Not surprisingly, these apprehended high rates of disease among "innocent" women and children elicited enormous concern among health experts, and among Canadian officials who were preoccupied with the projects of nation-building and "race preservation."

Health professionals also believed that education for women was ultimately the only protection against the prospect of "race suicide." The assumption was that if women were properly instructed about the signs and symptoms of gonorrhoea and syphilis, they would be in a better position to identify their afflictions and seek treatment at an early stage. According to Dr. Patterson from the Toronto division of the CNCCVD, "Many hundreds of women in our city have had operations on their womb and ovaries caused, unknown to most of them, by gonorrhoea in their husbands."[65] Since VD had devastating consequences for women's reproductive ability, and moreover was believed to be transmitted in utero, its prevention through the education of women was integral to the nation's health, security, and future prospects. One publication by the federal Department of Health framed the question as follows: "In the past years the discussion of sex hygiene and venereal diseases has been avoided, with the result that most girls have grown up in ignorance as to conditions which are of vital importance to them ... Knowledge is power. For her to know the truth about her maternal organs and the diseases which may affect them, is giving her power to guard not only her future health but also that of her children."[66]

[...]

Educational initiatives for both sexes were based on prevailing assumptions about the properties of femininity and masculinity. Prescriptive literature for women emphasized sexual passivity and the "true" ideals of femininity, including motherhood. Drawing from social and moral beliefs about female sexuality, doctors and other professionals typified "respectable" women as innocent, virtuous, altruistic, and maternal. Educational initiatives for women encouraged them to conform to these desired norms, and to embrace and fulfill their expected roles as wives and mothers. Experts especially encouraged self-control and passivity in matters of sex. They warned women that failures of discipline not only would result in disease, but would jeopardize their prospects for marriage and motherhood, and ultimately would prevent them from fulfilling their patriotic duties to produce good, healthy "citizens" for the state.

Health professionals valorized motherhood through various educational initiatives that targeted women. Government officials, professionals, and lay reformers in many Western nations in the period after the First World War constituted women as the "mothers of the race," fusing gendered, racist, heterosexist, and nationalist ideals of the period.[67] Slightly revised messages were conveyed within prescriptive literature, in which motherhood not only was an obligation that women needed to fulfill for themselves and their country, but was conceived as the most joyous experience a woman could undergo. [...]

The advice literature for women cautioned that one simple mistake could prevent the reader from ever experiencing "such joys," and could catapult her into a life filled with debauchery, immorality, and disease. Yet another pamphlet—this one from the

Department of Health—warned that a "woman who sacrifices herself for physical plea-sure or mercenary gain leads herself to disaster and sacrifices the opportunity for the greatest love in life."[68]

Throughout the literature, Canadian women were constructed as the moral guardians of the imaginary white nation. According to health professionals, it was a woman's responsibility to herself and the race to be selective about the men with whom she associated. Every woman was to choose a "decent" man for marriage and to demand from him the highest forms of chastity and cleanliness. As the Health League of Canada urged:

> Girls and women have a special job to do ... in helping to build up a high standard of sex conduct. They must demand clean living from the men with whom they as-sociate. Frank, wholesome companionship on the part of the girl will encourage the same sort of companionship from the man. Good manners are born of respect for one's self and for others. A handshake extends a friendly greeting. A kiss should mark a pledge of love. A girl who does not value these expressions highly and use them sparingly makes herself cheap and weakens her power of self-protection.[69]

Although, as noted earlier, women were sometimes constructed as the "victims" of libidinous men, they were also the ones charged with the responsibility for promoting the nation's health, as the advice literature also emphasized women's accountability for policing the morality of men. Their future, and more importantly the fate of their children and country, depended on it.

■ EDUCATION FOR MEN

Just as advice for women was built upon pervasive beliefs about "appropriate" femi-ninity, education for men was constructed around prevailing assumptions about masculinity. Based on authoritative ideas about the "true" natures of "normal" men, public health literature aimed at male audiences had two broad purposes. Ac-cording to the Ontario Board of Health, the first aim was to provide "accurate in-formation concerning syphilis and gonorrhoea and how and why to avoid them," while the second was to "clear up false ideas concerning self-abuse or masturbation, seminal emissions and sexual indulgence."[70] Doctors devoted enormous efforts to re-educate men about sex. Throughout the late 19th and early 20th century, men were encouraged to abstain from extramarital sexual relations and to save them-selves for marriage.

As one medical practitioner explained, absolute continence was as necessary in men as in women: "The advantage of preventative medicine, and the far better understanding of the conditions of health and bodily vigour which obtains to-day, have put the whole subject of masculine chastity in a new light. It is *now absolutely known* that *complete continence is consistent with perfect health*, and, indeed, that continence is *necessary for the highest development of bodily strength and endurance.*"[71]

While education for men encouraged them to maintain purity and chastity, it also warned about the dangers of masturbation. "Onanism" was characterized by health professionals as both physically and mentally injurious to a man's well-being. It could even lead to homosexuality.[72] Medical practitioners cautioned that "illicit" sex could precipitate a myriad of sexual and social dysfunctions. Professionals repeatedly advised men that an excess of sexual emissions would lead to the loss of sexual enjoyment and ultimately to impotence. [...]

Extramarital sex had far graver consequences than merely the reduction of sexual desire. As the advice literature for men admonished, promiscuity inevitably resulted in disease among men, which in turn would cause grievous suffering for their prospective wives and children. According to the Ontario Provincial Board of Health, a man "who has illicit sexual relations may get venereal disease THE FIRST TIME. The only safe way is to use common sense and not to indulge in any illicit sexual intercourse."[73] Ignoring the protection afforded by condoms, medical practitioners insisted that abstention from masturbation and other forms of "illicit" sex was the sole means by which men could be guaranteed a life of good health, virility, and vigour.

Although education for men did not stress the imperatives of fatherhood to nearly the same degree as motherhood was emphasized for women, men were nonetheless warned of the numerous ways in which VD would prevent them from fulfilling their paternal obligations. Many of the pamphlets for men cautioned them of the disastrous consequences that syphilis and gonorrhoea could harbour for the well-being of their children, their family, and the nation more generally. As Charles Eliot professed, "It is clearly understood that the consequences to offspring of lack of chastity in the father may be just as grave as those of lack of chastity in the mother; and that the happiness and security of family life is quite as apt to be destroyed by want of purity and honor in the father as in the mother. Thus, the lack of children, or the limitation of children to one or two in the family, is not infrequently the direct result of immorality in the male."[74]

In this fashion, pamphlets reminded men of their familial and civic obligations to remain robust and disease-free. To quote a wartime pamphlet published by the American Social Hygiene Association, a man's "patriotic duty is to be strong, able-bodied and healthy in order that [he] may now protect the flag that has protected [him]."[75]

Just as public health initiatives enjoined men to fulfill their responsibilities to themselves, their families, and the nation, they also warned men to avoid contact and commerce with "dangerous" women. Whereas reformers such as Gordon Bates made numerous attempts to construct venereal disease as the product of general immorality rather than prostitution per se, health professionals nevertheless continually made reference to the risks posed by infected women.[76] In a typical pamphlet, the federal Department of Health described gonorrhoea as "caused by a germ (gonococcus) which a man gets in sexual intercourse with a diseased woman."[77] This category of "diseased woman" referred not only to professional prostitutes, but also to "loose women" who were seen to engage in clandestine or occasional acts of sexual promiscuity. Health professionals counselled men that any woman who could be easily encouraged to have sex was probably infected with VD. In fact, the "loose woman" was in many cases more dangerous than the professional prostitute. As one source volunteered:

> A woman who will enter in the sexual relation with a man who is not her husband, we must term a loose woman. She may come of good family. She may move in the best social circles. Her license in these matters may not be known publicly. She may have social standing, but she nevertheless is a woman of loose character. The young man must realize that any woman who enters into this relationship with him is liable to enter into it with other men. Physicians today tell us that women of this kind are diseased at some time or other.[78]

Whatever the role allegedly being played by "promiscuous" women, however, men were depicted as the responsible agents in the transmission of venereal disease. According to professionals, it was primarily the immoral sexual behaviours of men that lay behind the alarmingly high rates of disease among women and children. Dr. Ernest Hall, a reformer from British Columbia, concluded that "germs contracted in the bawdy house" by men were almost certainly carried home, thereby linking together the "prostitute and the virtuous woman."[79]

As noted above, at the same time as the advice literature warned men of the hazards posed by venereal disease and dangerous women, health professionals also emphasized the need for "character-building." While women were channelled into domesticity, femininity, and motherhood, men were told about the importance of physical and mental self-control. Men were exhorted away from "illicit" sex and into healthier forms of masculine recreation including outdoor sports and adventure reading.[80] The experts informed men that the "strength of manhood" could be attained only through the exercise of self-constraint.[81] Educational endeavours for men encouraged them not only to act "purely," but also to think "pure" thoughts. Sanitary bodies and moral minds were necessary for the prevention of VD and the attainment of virility, vitality, and citizenship.

■ CONCLUSION

A study of venereal disease control policies, discourses, and activities during the early 20th century offers several insights about modalities and methods of socio-legal regulation across the country. First, it suggests that the law was not the only, or even the most pervasive, form of regulatory practice that people experienced during this period. To the contrary, as regulation theorists have suggested, a plethora of institutional structures and cultural forces—manifest in both public and private spheres—operated to prescribe and limit social conduct.[82] In the context of anti-VD initiatives, public health literature was, in many cases, far more pervasive than legal doctrines or sanctions. While the law was preserved as a "last resort" to deal with "deviants" who could not be reformed, public health literature was aimed at the entire population. Throughout these initiatives, health professionals and medical practitioners attempted to (re)construct and shape "legitimate" moral and sexual identities and practices for women, men, and children. As several scholars have observed, moral regulation functions, *inter alia*, by constructing certain behaviours as "natural" and "normative" while marginalizing all others.[83]

A second conclusion emanating from this analysis is that regulation was not always manifested by the state, nor was it contained within specific geographical boundaries. In the case of VD control in early 20th-century Canada, it was medical practitioners and health professionals rather than state officials who were responsible for organizing public health strategies in general and VD prophylaxis in particular. While the state did participate in efforts to control disease, most government involvement was the result of pressure applied by organizations like the National Council for Combating Venereal Disease and the National Council for Women. Although the various provinces had their own specific public health techniques, certain aspects of VD control—most notably public education—were dispersed across the nation. While state and non-state initiatives to suppress disease were uneven, disparate, and contradictory, it is important to remember that advice materials were often shared across provincial and national borders.

Third, the study of VD control demonstrates that "respectable" middle-class women and men were included as subjects of regulation within anti-VD initiatives. Although health professionals and reformers tended to approach the "respectable" classes with kid gloves (in contrast to the blunt instruments reserved for the "unworthy"), middle-class women and men were nonetheless regulated through the medium of advice literature aimed at shaping them into "good" productive citizens who manifested the desired characteristics of whiteness, heterosexuality, marriage, and monogamy.

Fourth, whereas regulatory practices were routinely mediated by gender, these gender boundaries were never completely clear. Rather, public health education transmitted contradictory messages about the absolute and relative blameworthiness of women and men. Some feminist historians have claimed that women were always believed to be responsible for the spread of VD, and hence were subject to more invasive regulatory techniques than were men.[84] But while medical practitioners feared the consequences that venereal disease held for "respectable" women, the threat of disease among "respectable" men was also an abiding concern. In the Canadian context at least, attributions of responsibility for the spread and containment of VD, and expert depictions of culprits and victims, were socially contingent and multifaceted in their relation to gender. Both women and men were variously depicted as victims and perpetrators. As Jay Cassel observes, anti-VD education cannot be construed as yet another "purity crusade, nor can it be viewed as a straightforward presentation of 'Victorian' morality."[85] Rather, educational initiatives were immersed in a litany of complex and nuanced discourses and practices that resist simple reduction to gender relations alone.

■ ACKNOWLEDGMENTS

The research and ideas for this chapter originated in a Master's thesis at the School of Criminology, Simon Fraser University. I would like to thank Dorothy Chunn for her guidance and support during the research and writing of the thesis. For their various contributions, my thanks also go to John McLaren, Carolyn Strange, and the three reviewers from UBC Press and the Aid to Scholarly Publications Programme. In addition, I would like to thank the staff at the National Archives of Canada and the United Church Archives at UBC and the University of Toronto. I am especially grateful to Dorothy Chunn and Robert Menzies, who edited and supported this work with much enthusiasm and generosity.

■ NOTES

1.   Jean Barman, *The West Beyond the West: A History of British Columbia* (Toronto: University of Toronto Press, 1996); Robert A.J. McDonald, *Making Vancouver, 1863-1913* (Vancouver: UBC Press, 1996).

2. Kay Anderson, "Engendering Race Research: Unsettling the Self-Other Dichotomy," in *Body Space*, ed. Nancy Duncan, 197-211 (New York and London: Routledge, 1996), 201, 208. On the making of Canada as a "white settler society," see Daiva Stasiulis and Radha Jhappan, "The Fractious Politics of a Settler Society: Canada," in *Unsettling Settler Societies: Articulation of Gender, Race, Ethnicity, and Class*, ed. Daiva Stasiulis and Nira Yuval-Davis, 95-131 (Thousand Oaks: Sage, 1995).

3. Stasiulis and Jhappan, *ibid.*, at 97; Mariana Valverde, *The Age of Light, Soap, and Water: Moral Reform in English Canada, 1885-1925* (Toronto: McClelland & Stewart, 1991).

4. Carolyn Strange and Tina Loo, *Making Good: Law and Moral Regulation in Canada, 1867-1939* (Toronto: University of Toronto Press, 1997), 9.

5. Angus McLaren, *Our Own Master Race: Eugenics in Canada* (Toronto: McClelland & Stewart, 1990); Strange and Loo, *ibid.*; Valverde, *The Age of Light, Soap, and Water*.

6. Valverde, *ibid.*

7. Strange and Loo, *Making Good*, 36.

8. *Ibid.*

9. See Adams, "In Sickness and in Health"; McGinnis, "Law and the Leprosies of Lust"; Buckley and McGinnis, "Venereal Disease and Public Health Reform in Canada."

10. Dorothy E. Chunn, "A Little Sex Can Be a Dangerous Thing: Regulating Sexuality, Venereal Disease, and Reproduction in British Columbia, 1919-1945," in *Challenging the Public/Private Divide: Feminism, Law, and Pubic Policy*, ed. Susan Boyd, 62-86 (Toronto: University of Toronto Press, 1997); Renisa Mawani, "'Educational Prophylaxis': Venereal Disease Control and the Regulation of Sexuality in British Columbia and Canada, 1900-1930" (MA thesis, Simon Fraser University, 1996).

11. Normative constructions of sexuality were indeed gendered. While professionals emphasized the need for chastity and denounced promiscuity among women, for men they emphasized heterosexuality and monogamy while condemning homosexuality.

12. Jay Cassel, *The Secret Plague: Venereal Disease in Canada, 1838-1939* (Toronto: University of Toronto Press, 1987), 119.

13. Gordon Bates, "The Venereal Disease Problem," *Public Health Journal* 13, 6 (1922): 265.

14. *Ibid.*

15. *Ibid.*

16. Lucy Bland, *Banishing the Beast: English Feminism and Sexual Morality, 1885-1914* (London: Penguin Books, 1995), 245.

17. Buckley and McGinnis, "Venereal Disease and Public Health Reform in Canada," 338.

18. Cassel, *The Secret Plague*.

19. Chunn, "A Little Sex Can Be a Dangerous Thing."

20. Major J.G. Fitzgerald. "The Advisory Committee on Venereal Diseases for Military District No. 2," *Public Health Journal* 5, 2 (1918): 49.

21. Cassel, *The Secret Plague.*

22. Buckley and McGinnis, "Venereal Disease and Public Health Reform in Canada," 342; Cassel, *The Secret Plague.*

23. Janice Dickin McGinnis, "From Health to Welfare: Federal Government Policies Regarding Standards of Public Health for Canadians, 1919-1945" (Ph.D. thesis, University of Alberta, 1980).

24. Buckley and McGinnis, "Venereal Disease and Public Health Reform in Canada," 346.

25. Cassel notes that by the mid-1930s eight clinics had been established in different areas in BC: *The Secret Plague,* 177. See also Janice Dickin McGinnis, "From Salvarsan to Penicillin: Medical Science and VD Control in Canada," in *Essays in the History of Canadian Medicine,* ed. Wendy Mitchinson and Janice Dickin McGinnis (Toronto: McClelland & Stewart, 1988), 127.

26. According to one report made by the federal department for the year 1921, 9,900 cases of VD were treated in clinics across Canada, while 15,189 cases were dealt with by private practitioners: *Venereal Disease Report for the Department of Health, Ottawa,* 1921, National Archives of Canada [hereinafter NAC], RG 29, vol. 216, file 311, vol. 3-19.

27. L.C. Gilday, "The Social Diseases in Their Relation to Public Health," *Social Welfare* 2 (1919/20): 165.

28. Cassel, *The Secret Plague.*

29. *Ibid.,* 266.

30. For a discussion of eugenics and social hygiene in Canada see McLaren, *Our Own Master Race.*

31. Gordon Bates, "The Relation of the Canadian National Council for Combating Venereal Disease to the Programme of Venereal Disease Control," *Public Health Journal* 12, 4 (1921): 160.

32. Cassel, *The Secret Plague,* 169.

33. J.J. Heagerty, "Venereal Disease Situation in Canada," *Public Health Journal* 13, 10 (1922): 485.

34. Cassel, *The Secret Plague,* 207.

35. *Ibid.,* 158-59.

36. *Ibid.,* 171.

37. Cassel, *The Secret Plague,* 209.

38. *Ibid.,* 200.

39. Bates, "The Relation of the Canadian National Council for Combating Venereal Disease to the Programme of Venereal Disease Control," 161.

40. Brandt, *No Magic Bullet;* Cassel, *The Secret Plague.*

41. Health League of Canada, "What are the Venereal Diseases?" (Toronto, n.d.), 3. UCA, Victoria College, University of Toronto [hereinafter VC, U of T], Pam RA G44, VA A4.

42. There were several possible reasons for this. For example, reformers and health professionals might have felt that women would be incapable of tolerating such loathsome subjects. Alternatively, since VD was more difficult to detect in women, perhaps doctors were simply unable to identify early symptoms of disease.

43. Bates, "Essential Factors in a Campaign against Venereal Disease," 389.

44. T. Barlow, "Brotherhood and the Fight against Venereal Diseases," *Social Welfare* 2 (1919/20): 333.

45. Brown, "Venereal Disease Control in Ontario," 7-8.

46. Bates, "The Relation of the Canadian National Council for Combating Venereal Disease to the Programme of Venereal Disease Control."

47. *Ibid.*

48. Bates, "The Relation of the Canadian National Council for Combating Venereal Disease to the Programme of Venereal Disease Control," 156.

49. *Ibid.*, 157.

50. *Ibid.*, 162.

51. Health League of Canada, *Healthy Happy Womanhood* (Toronto, 1929), 2-3. NAC, MG 28 I 332, vol. 81, file 3.

52. W.A. Lincoln, "Venereal Diseases among the Civilian Population," *Social Welfare* 1 (1919/20): 32.

53. The nation has commonly been constructed in terms of white womanhood. See Anderson, "Engendering Race Research." See also Anne McClintock, *Imperial Leather: Race, Gender and Sexuality in the Colonial Contest* (New York and London: Routledge, 1995), especially "Introduction."

54. Health League of Canada, *Healthy Happy Womanhood*.

55. Department of Public Health, *The Venereal Diseases* (Nova Scotia, May 1917), 3. UCA, UBC, Hugh Dobson Papers, box A3(2), file N.

56. Mawani, "Educational Prophylaxis," 13.

57. Brandt, *No Magic Bullet*.

58. Bates, "Essential Factors in a Campaign against Venereal Disease," 392.

59. R. Yarros, "The Prostitute as a Health and Social Problem," *Public Health Journal* 11, 1 (1919/20): 610-11.

60. Health League of Canada, *Healthy Happy Womanhood*.

61. Bernarr McFadden, *Talks to a Young Girl about Sex*, Sex Education Series No. 4 (New York, McFadden Publications, 1922), 29. NAC, MG 28 I 332, vol. 80, file 26.

62. O. Wilson, "Venereal Diseases: Their Treatment and Cure," *Canadian Medical Association Journal* 9 (1919): 137.

63. J.J. Heagerty, "The Necessity for a Medical Certificate of Physical and Mental Health as a Pre-Requisite to the Securing of a Marriage License," *Social Welfare* 6 (1924): 242.

64. E.A. Morgan, "Syphilis, Its Relation to Infant Mortality and Child Welfare, with a Discussion of Present Day Methods for Its Control," *Canadian Medical Association Journal* 11 (1921): 851.

65. R.H. Patterson, "Some Social Aspects of the Venereal Disease Problem," *Public Health Journal* 11, 12 (1920): 568.

66. Department of Pensions and National Health Canada, *Information for Young Women about Sex Hygiene* (Ottawa, n.d.), 3. NAC, MG 28 I 332, vol. 81, file 3.

67. Anna Davin, "Imperialism and Motherhood," *History Workshop* 5, (1978): 9-65; Mariana Valverde, "'When the Mother of the Race Is Free': Race, Reproduction, and Sexuality in First Wave Feminism," in *Gender Conflicts: New Essays in Women's History*, ed. Franca Iacovetta and Mariana Valverde (Toronto: University of Toronto Press, 1992).

68. Department of Pensions and National Health Canada, *Information for Young Women about Sex Hygiene*, 4.

69. Health League of Canada, *Healthy Happy Womanhood*; see also Bland, *Banishing the Beast.*

70. Ontario Provincial Board of Health, *Facts on Venereal Diseases for Young Men* (Toronto, 1920), 2. NAC, MG 28 I 332, vol. 81, file 7.

71. *Ibid.*, 9-10.

72. For a discussion of this point see Gary Kinsman, *The Regulation of Desire: Homo and Hetero Sexualities*, 2nd ed. (Montreal: Black Rose Books, 1996).

73. Ontario Provincial Board of Health, *Facts on Venereal Diseases for Young Men*, 9.

74. Eliot, *The Double Standard of Morals and the Social Diseases*, 10.

75. American Social Hygiene Association, *Keeping Him Fighting Trim*, (New York, 1917), 8. UCA, University of British Columbia, Hugh Dobson Papers, box A(3), file N.

76. Bates, "Essential Factors in a Campaign against Venereal Disease," 389.

77. Department of Pensions and National Health Canada, *Information for Men: Syphilis and Gonorrhea* (Ottawa: National Health Publication, 1929), 3-4. NAC, MG 28 I 332, vol. 81, file 3.

78. Bernarr McFadden, *Talks to a Young Man about Sex*, Sex Education Series No. 3 (New York, McFadden Publications, 1922), 24. NAC, MG 28 I 332, vol. 80, file 26.

79. "Venereal Diseases under Discussion," *Victoria Colonist*, 23 March 1922, 4.

80. "Report of the Commission on Venereal Diseases, Ontario, 1919," *Social Welfare* 2 (1919/1920): 53.

81. Ontario Provincial Board of Health, *Facts on Venereal Diseases for Young Men*, 2.

82. See Mariana Valverde, *Studies in Moral Regulation* (Toronto: Centre of Criminology, 1994).

83. *Ibid.*

84. *Ibid.*, 70; McGinnis, "Law and the Leprosies of Lust"; Mawani, "Educational Prophylaxis."

85. Cassel, *The Secret Plague*, 207.

CHAPTER 8

RECIPES FOR DEMOCRACY?
GENDER, FAMILY, AND MAKING FEMALE CITIZENS IN COLD WAR CANADA

Franca Iacovetta

During the past several decades, feminist and left scholars of immigrant and refugee women and women of colour have exposed—both through empirical documentation and careful rethinking of conventional categories of nation, immigrant, and citizen—the material and ideological processes central to the "making" of nation-states and national identities. Many now acknowledge that nation-building is premised on the political and social organization of "difference," and that it creates both citizens (or potential citizens) and non-citizens denied rights. That First World nations in the EU and NAFTA champion globalization and free trade zones while at the same time "police" their borders against "others" (especially Third World migrant workers) speaks volumes on the topic.

Studies of contemporary migration note the growing female presence among migrant workers around the world, while those focused on Canada show how racist, class-based, and heterosexist paradigms continue to define mainstream notions of Canada and Canadian. This situation prevails despite the long history and enduring impact of immigration to Canada, and its increasingly multiracial profile—especially since the 1970s. Immigrant women of colour from the Caribbean, Asia, Africa, and other "Third World" nations—who are exploited as temporary workers but discouraged from settling permanently and stereotyped as sexually promiscuous single mothers undeserving of citizenship—experience most directly the cruel hypocrisy of liberal capitalist countries that promise opportunity and freedom to all, while simultaneously creating pools of unfree labour and perpetuating damaging race and gender stereotypes. Immigration and citizenship policies are also sexualized and shaped by bourgeois and heterosexual norms regarding reproduction and motherhood. Lesbian women face particular challenges in the face of hetero-normative discourses, and women of colour are eroticized in ways that affect adversely their claims to citizenship.

Specialists of migrant, immigrant, and refugee women workers in Canada have sought to disrupt the dominant liberal construction of Canada as "an immigrant nation" that has always opened its doors to the world's peoples. As their work documents, liberal histories of Canada erroneously depict state-sanctioned racist policies, such as the infamous Chinese Head Taxes and other laws prohibiting the entry of wives and children of Chinese male workers, as blips in an otherwise smooth and linear development towards mature nationhood. Similarly, nationalist boosters, past and present, see the presence of "successful" white ethnic and "non-white" Canadians as proof of even greater national progress. We must remain aware of the critical distinctions between, on the one hand, an official liberal and highly flawed policy of multiculturalism, and, on the other, Canada's historical and continuing transformation into a multi-racial society and the reality of many Canadians who in daily practice live multi-cultural, multi-racial lives.

As a historian of post-World War II Canada, I wish here to tackle the dominant liberal framework of Canada as a land of genuine opportunity, where all hardworking newcomers can prosper, contribute to the country's rich cultural mosaic, and eventually join the Canadian "family." Such portraits of Canada as a place where everyone can be both "different" and "equal" ignore the fact that, as Tania Das Gupta and I observed elsewhere, Canadian immigration and refugee policy have long been exclusionary and discriminatory with regard to so-called "undesirables." But I want also to take the point further. The liberal "we are an immigrant nation" discourse (which perhaps only the U.S. has more aggressively promoted) also ignores or downplays the more invidious aspects of gatekeeping efforts to remake into something else even those newcomers ostensibly "welcomed" into the nation.

In addressing this theme, my article shifts the focus from the present to the recent past, and from the exclusionary practices described above to the immigrant and refugee reception and citizenship campaigns of the early postwar and Cold War decades before 1965. More specifically, it examines the gendered nature of reception activity, and nation-making after 1945. And rather than addressing forms of outright exclusion—such as screening for Communists or deporting newcomers deemed politically or morally suspect, or deemed potential burdens on the state—I adopt an analytical framework central to the emerging social and gender histories of Cold War capitalist societies: domestic containment. By focusing on women, nutrition, food, and gender and family ideals, I explore here how the dominant gender ideologies of liberal democracies in the early Cold War—including a bourgeois model of homemaking and food customs and family life—informed reception work and social service activities among immigrant and refugee women. By domestic containment, I mean of course both state-sanctioned and volunteer efforts within western countries to police not only the political but also social, personal, moral, and sexual lives of its citizens—a process that, ironically, involved the repression in liberal western democracies of individual rights and freedoms in the name of democratic rights and freedoms. The Cold War, as U.S. scholars such as Elaine Tyler May and Canadian historians such as Gary Kinsman have documented, witnessed the resurgence of a conservative and hegemonic family ideology that "normalized" an idealized bourgeois Anglo-Celtic nuclear family, and that in turn served as an (unrealistic and oppressive) standard against which "non-conformists" were harshly judged, harassed, and punished.

I have documented elsewhere that even as Canada's social welfare elite boldly declared the birth of the brave new world, they also debated at length the fragility of postwar democratic society and swore to attack all threats—from within and without—to democratic "decency." The threat of the atomic bomb, the Soviet Empire, and homosexual spies were marked features of the Cold War, as were working mothers, juvenile delinquents, (especially but not exclusively gang girls), women deemed sexually promiscuous, and male "sex perverts," and they legitimated a corrupted democracy in which the state, and its civilian accomplices, was obliged to censor its citizenry. Historian Geoffrey Smith has effectively used the metaphor of disease to describe how the U.S. state waged a dirty war against all those considered sources of contamination—godless communists, gay civil servants, marginal African-American welfare mothers, and others. Similar patterns obtained in Canada; indeed, recent research on the domestic side of the Cold War, made possible in part because of recent access to security intelligence materials (such as RCMP case files), has begun to challenge the conventional wisdom that Canada's Cold War was essentially, or comparatively, benign.

Mariana Valverde's *The Age of Light, Soap, and Water: Moral Reform in English Canada 1885-1925* showed how Canadian nation-building in an earlier era required more than protective tariffs, backroom political deals, and a transcontinental railway. It also involved various moral campaigns aimed both to encourage middle-class white Canadian women to procreate (or face "race suicide") and to ensure the moral "uplift" of working-class immigrants and racialized Canadians deemed inferior on both moral and mental health grounds. The desire for a healthy body politic, both literally and figuratively, also fueled nationalist boosters and social and psychological experts committed to national reconstruction after the Second World War. While hardly the sole cause of these post-1945 agendas, the arrival of the Cold War did impart a particular kind of political and moral urgency to campaigns meant to ensure the long-term physical, mental, and moral health of Canada's current and future citizens. Both men and women were targeted by such campaigns, but women, as in the past, were more vulnerable to moral assessment and branding.

My research on immigrant and refugee women and families offers another lens through which we can explore some of these key issues. Here, I take one thematic slice—nutrition and food campaigns and what front-line health and welfare workers called "family life" projects intended to improve poor and immigrant children's lives and remake their mothers. In tackling this topic, I have considered a wide range of players and activities. They include, on the one hand, a variety of gatekeepers, from front-line settlement house workers, citizenship activists, adult literacy workers, and women's organizations to professional social workers, psychologists, and government bureaucrats; and, on the other, the more than 2,000,000 women, men and child immigrants and refugees, especially but not exclusively from Europe. Taken together, the activities under scrutiny were many and varied: from the more explicitly ideological work of the Citizenship Branch and the RCMP, both of which engaged in the political surveillance of the left ethnic press and organizations, to the numerous English classes, social agency services, and neighbourhood "projects for newcomers" undertaken in these years, particularly those aimed at low-income immigrant mothers and children in inner-city neighbourhoods in Toronto.

■ "SELLING" CANADIAN ABUNDANCE AND MODERNITY TO EUROPE'S "BACKWARD" WOMEN

As the Second World War ended, the media alerted Canadians to the widespread hunger, starvation, and health disasters affecting people from around the world. Canadian newspapers, for instance, contained graphic and heartbreaking images and tales of emaciated Holocaust survivors, flood and disaster victims in Europe and beyond, and malnourished mothers and children from towns ravished by war. Indeed, a central theme emerging in these early years stressed the great gap between Canada as a land of modest affluence and a devastated Europe.

With the coming of the Cold War, this theme also served ideological ends. Among the most popular texts of the day were what I call "iron-curtain escape narratives"[1] published in newspapers and magazines. Highly dramatic, these stories featured the trials and tribulations of those who had escaped "Red" countries, risked health and death to trek across frontier border towns, and eventually reached the western zone in Europe, finally settling in countries like Canada. A *Toronto Star* front-page story (25 Sept 1950) that told about the escape of a "pretty little Czech girl" who "outwitted Soviet Police," and "waded mountain snows" to reach Canada is emblematic. A Ph.D. student from Prague, 23-year-old Irene Konkova, had been arrested "for not conforming to Communist dictates." After escaping jail, she gave the Soviet police the slip at a remote inn and finally reached safety in West Germany. There, she worked in the U.S. zone as a physical education director with the YWCA-YMCA until taking a YWCA job in Winnipeg. Though worried about her parents, Konkova told reporters she was "looking forward to the Canadian way of life," which she associated with western modernity and affluence. When asked what most impressed her about Canada, she noted the "smart clothes and immaculate appearance" of Canadian women and abundance of food. She loved it all: "hot dogs and potato chips impressed her as much as steaks, cakes and candy."

Both U.S. and Canadian propaganda material contrasted the good fortunes of mothers in North America, where liberal capitalism permitted them to raise and nurture well-fed and moral children, with those mothers working far away from their children and in other ways struggling under the exploitation and scarcity prevailing in "Iron Curtain" countries. From stoves to one-stop grocery stores, boosters sang the praises of Canadian modernity. In the displaced persons and refugee camps, on ships sailing overseas, and in locales across Canada, women newcomers confronted these messages of Canadian affluence and modernity everywhere: in films, pamphlets and newspapers, in English and citizenship classes, and in settlement house mothers' clubs and YWCA meetings. Cooking lessons, sermons, and health "interventions" sought to reform both Canadian and New Canadian women's cooking regimes and food customs, household management, and child welfare. Indeed, health and welfare experts offered their version of the postwar, bourgeois homemaker ideal, with their middle-class and sexist denunciations of married women and wives who worked for pay—among them, huge numbers of refugee and immigrant women.[2] Canadians were encouraged to embrace the newcomers but also teach them the superior values of democracy, "freedom," and, not least of all, the well-balanced Canadian meal.

After 1945, Canadian nutritionists, food writers, and health and welfare "experts" focused much of their attention on the hundreds of thousands of Europeans who figured prominently among the more than 2,500,000 newcomers who had entered the country by 1965. Food and health campaigns aimed at immigrant women and their families were varied and numerous. They were part of larger campaigns intended to "improve" the homemaking skills of all women—resident or soon-to-be resident—in Canada. When, for example, British war brides were offered health lectures and cooking classes, both in England and Canada, they were not only taught to measure ingredients the Canadian way (i.e., the British measured liquids by weight, North Americans by volume), but were deliberately being "trained" for their new role as wives and mothers of Canadian husbands and children. Media coverage of the war brides' resettlement in Canada, a major government undertaking in which the military and Canadian Red Cross played important roles, garnered enormous public attention, and was everywhere punctuated by the image of the fresh faces of young, white British women and their ruby-cheeked children. By contrast, the non-British war brides, including Dutch and Italian women, and their children never attracted as much attention.

Central to these health and welfare campaigns were certain overriding concerns: preaching the value of a well-balanced diet, efficient shopping and household regimes, planned menus, and budget-conscious shopping. Much of the food advice prioritized middle-class ideals regarding preparation and consumption—clean and uncluttered homes, formal dining rooms or kitchen "dinettes," and a stay-at-home wife and mother. This was a far cry from the crowded and sub-standard flats, low and vulnerable incomes, and harried and tired working mothers that were the hallmarks of many newly arrived immigrants and refugees in Toronto and other urban locales.

■ CANADIAN CULINARY WAYS

As Valerie Korinek's important new book, *Roughing It in the Suburbs: Reading* Chatelaine *in the Fifties and Sixties* well illustrates, Canada's top-selling woman's magazine offers us an indirect but excellent source about postwar food and health campaigns. In saying this, I am not suggesting a direct causation between immigrant women, *Chatelaine* magazine, and changed habits. Rather, the magazine's food features and recipes provide valuable glimpses into the images, assumptions, messages, recipes, professional advice, and other features of postwar health and homemaking campaigns. Korinek persuasively argues that the magazine, despite its image as a conventional woman's magazine, was not composed exclusively of "happy homemaker" images. She also cautions against simple and reductionist theories that assume women readers are passively duped by bourgeois women's magazines. Still, as she adds, the food advertisements and features did provide many conventional images of traditional middle-class femininity—including images of mothers who showed their love in part by baking bread, shopping well, and producing a grand variety of cheap but well-balanced meals, nicely presented on table-clothed tables. The ads that delivered such messages also reflected the interests of food corporations whose much-needed funds kept *Chatelaine* afloat. Central images emerged in these food features. For example, the "Canadian way" (as Korinek and I detail elsewhere) was usually portrayed by attractive, white, middle-class Canadian women pushing overflowing grocery carts down aisles with well-stocked shelves, or cooking meals in modern and well-appointed kitchens using canned, frozen, and other ingredients from their well-stocked pantry shelves, freezers, and refrigerators. Recipes featured affordable meals using cheap cuts of meat—hamburger, for example, in the ever ubiquitous casserole (though by the 1960s curry chicken casseroles actually hit the pages!) and on occasion, fancy hors d'oeuvres and brunches.

By the early 1960s, the magazine began to feature more "ethnic" recipes and even discuss the plight of working wives and mothers, but these were very modest concessions. A case in point is Italian food. U.S. food historians such as Harvey Levenstein and immigration historians such as Italian specialist Donna Gabaccia have documented both that Italians were among the most resistant of the immigrants in the U.S. when it came to pressures to change their food customs and that Italian foods, including pasta, were among the most successfully "mainstreamed" ethnic foods in the U.S. diet. For the U.S., the conflicts and accommodations involving immigrant and particularly Italian foods occurred in particularly dramatic ways during the interwar decades, following the mass migration of Southern and Eastern Europeans to the U.S. during the period from the 1880s to the 1920s. Levenstein and Gabaccia trace the promotion of Italian and other ethnic foods that were inexpensive, nutritious, and filling—in food magazines, food corporation ads, and also the military, where large numbers of young American men were first introduced to Italian foods. That process invariably involved modifying "foreign" or "exotic" foods for the more timid palates of North American consumers by removing pungent cheeses, or other offensive ingredients, and perhaps including more recognizable ones (cheddar cheese instead of parmesan, for instance). Similar developments occurred in Canada especially though not exclusively during the post-1945 era, when the country witnessed its mass migration of incoming newcomers. Yet, it's also clear that Canadian women did experiment with ethnic recipes, particularly by the 1960s. By then, *Chatelaine* also began featuring (white) "ethnic" women, including working mothers, and their recipes, although this did not preclude a reliance on "cute" and patronizing racial-ethnic and sexual stereotypes.

■ NURSING INNER-CITY KIDS, PATHOLOGIZING IMMIGRANT MOTHERS

In contrast to media depictions of ethnic foods, the records of Canadian health and welfare experts from the 1950s and 1960s are less ambiguous with respect to the "problems" posed by the huge influx of immigrant and refugee mothers and their families. Indeed, they are replete with examples of the ways in which Canadian experts singled out immigrant women for special attention or blame, particularly those from more impoverished and "peripheral" rural regions of Southern Europe. Invariably the "experts" stereotyped these humble immigrants and low-income mothers (and fathers) as too ignorant, isolated, backwards, stubborn, and/or suspicious to access "modern" health care, secure their children's health needs, and otherwise raise their children appropriately as future Canadians.

Such themes emerge in a popular postwar food guide, *Food Customs of New Canadians*, that was prepared by professional home economists and nutritionists for use by health and welfare personnel working with newcomers. Although presented as a scientific and objective assessment of the food customs of racial-ethnic groups, the guide sought to equip front-line activists with ways of encouraging immigrants to adapt their food patterns to Canadian foods, recipes, equipment, and eating regimes. Some recommendations—drink more milk, for instance—were intended for everyone. Overall, however, the guide reflected middle-class, pro-capitalist, North American assumptions such as the wisdom of a three-meals-a-day pattern because it was well-suited to Canadian school and work hours. It also reflected the superiority of Canadian utensils, equipment, and modern appliances.

The guide isolated particular problems for each group under review and assigned teaching suggestions for eliminating them. No group received an entirely negative (or positive) evaluation. For example, while the Chinese scored poorly in hygiene on what the experts considered insufficient cleaning of pots and shared use of chopsticks, they scored well overall on their use of fresh foods, including vegetables. Overall, North-Western Europeans generally fared much better, though there was room for improvement here too. The guide referred to the propensity of "Czechs" to be overweight because of their love of dumplings, and Austrians were cited for consuming too many sweets, and so on.

More problematic were the Italians and Portuguese. Italian immigrant women emerged in the guide as uneducated and primitive peasants who were forced to cook on outdoor clay or brick ovens and whose homes lacked the necessary equipment of a modern household: a gas or electric stove, a refrigerator, and storage space. Although praised for their ability to "stretch" meats through use of pastas and other starches, Italian women in Toronto were chastised for spending too much of their modest family income on purchasing specialty foods from Italy such as fine-grade olive oil when cheaper Canadian substitutes were available! (Curiously, only the Italian entry refers explicitly to the possibility that the high rate of female labour participation meant that, after migration, Italian women had less time to produce food.) Similarly, Portuguese women were criticized for buying fresh fish from the market because it was more expensive than the frozen variety. Professional nutritional experts appear to have prioritized their professional repertoire over the values and cultural preferences of their clients. Italian mothers, I should add, were also singled out for their "bad" habit of serving their children a bit of wine with dinner. Their advice, of course, ran counter to that of today when we are told to more closely emulate various features of the continental European diet.

Many of the recommendations contained in the guide reflected the concern of nutrition experts to determine the capacity of immigrant women in low-income families to produce well-balanced meals. Since family economic need pushed many of them into the paid force, these women had even less time for "improving" homemaking skills. Thus, even while public and professional campaigns intended to raise homemaking standards were aimed at the entire female population, class distinctions, which overlapped with racial-ethnic ones, accounted for some differing remedies. Regrettably, home economists have long assumed that poor people's diets were more the result of their ignorance of nutrition and food preparation than material scarcity. Proposed solutions usually meant imposing austere diet and meal plans on the poor, while the approved diets and advertised meal plans for middle-class families permitted various frills and luxuries. In postwar Toronto, experts serving immigrant neighbourhoods were routinely asked whether people in the area seemed aware of general health guidelines such as, The Canada Food Rules, cod liver oil for children, what constitutes adequate hours of sleep, and so on. School nurses and child welfare workers held differing expectations for the mother and children of bourgeois and poor families. On one level, this was a reasonable response: as Cynthia Comacchio observed for an earlier period, it was insulting to teach the finer points about child personality training, or food fussiness and toy fetishes, to poor immigrant mothers who could not even afford "decent" housing. Yet, rather than attack class inequities, the experts focused on teaching mothers the fundamentals of health—cleanliness, nutrition, fresh air—as though mothers alone could prevent ill health.

Toronto provides a valuable case study for considering how low-income immigrant and refuge women were both given some critical assistance by front-line social workers and health and welfare personnel keen to improve health care among struggling working-class immigrants—and also pathologized by the experts. Front-line social and welfare personnel identified several major problems. They worried about the ill effects of crowded and substandard housing on low-income immigrant families and the special burdens that inadequate wages imposed on women who, whether housewives or working mothers, had to stretch inadequate pay checks to cover rent, food, drugs, clothing, furniture, and other necessities. If the family had purchased larger ticket items like furniture on credit (which became more accessible to low-income people in these years), there was the burden of additional bills and collection agencies that would demand payment. The lack of proper cooking facilities in many substandard rental flats encouraged unhealthy eating. Furthermore, the budget item that invariably appeared most flexible was food. To pay the bills, women, it was feared, turned to cheap, usually starch-heavy, foods while cutting out comparatively more expensive and healthy alternatives. The result, claimed nutrition experts, was malnutrition, which might not be detected for years but would nonetheless take its toll on the mental, emotional, and physical health of immigrant adults and children. An additional concern was that as more middle-class Canadians abandoned the urban core for the suburbs, cities like Toronto would become host to "decaying" inner-city neighbourhoods. In response, experts basically applied old remedies to the current context—home visits, family budgets, meal plans—and tried to attract particularly stay-at-home immigrant mothers into their cooking and nutrition programs. Some modest successes were scored, but the main response recorded is continuing frustration with absenteeism.

A related problem earmarked by health and welfare experts was that immigrants' seeming ignorance of Canada's social services, combined with their needless suspicion or distrust of outsiders, meant that many immigrant parents, especially mothers, were unwittingly neglecting their children's health. When both parents worked, mothers were unavailable or too exhausted to tend to their children's needs. Social workers referred to the "tremendous job" required to educate the newcomers about the value of nursery school, summer camps, parent education, and other valuable services "new" and "strange" to them.

Once again, rural non-English-speaking immigrants transplanted to major urban centres were considered most pathetic. In the heavily Portuguese neighbourhood of Parkdale, the International Institute of Metropolitan Toronto (IIMT), the city's largest immigrant aid society, opened up an extension office in 1961 to reach these women. The project supervisor, veteran social worker Edith Ferguson, collected fieldwork notes and produced case histories meant to illustrate the value of social work interventions. One such case involved a mother who told the visiting caseworker that her daughter had infected tonsils but could not afford to have them removed. Although the family had been registered with the Ontario hospital plan, the mother, who had recently undergone an operation, erroneously assumed that time had to elapse before they could return to hospital. They could not afford a private surgeon's fee because they held a heavy mortgage on a recently purchased house and the husband was sidelined by a workplace injury. Their 17-year-old daughter was the family's only income earner.

In response, the IIMT caseworker contacted the girl's school nurse, who, wrote Ferguson, saw the child immediately, determined her tonsils were badly infected, and referred her to Toronto Hospital for Children. Having secured the parents' trust, they could assist with other things—completing the husband's workman's compensation application, enrolling him in a training course, and checking out job possibilities for a nephew wishing to come to Canada. They also found the daughter, who had been earning a dismal factory wage, a better-paying clerical job in a new local pharmacy interested in a Portuguese-speaking employee.

Like the *Food Customs* manual, front-line workers also stressed the lack of pre-natal instruction for immigrant and refugee women. While the guide focussed on the absence or inadequate pre-natal education in the women's homelands, front-line caseworkers dwelt on a continuing widespread ignorance about modern childfeeding and childrearing methods among immigrant women. Immigrant women, they argued, suffered needless "complicated pregnancies" for lack of doctor appointments. Those convinced to go to out-patient clinics or pre-natal courses learned very little as the lectures and mimeographed diet and instruction hand-outs were in English. When "costly vitamins or medicines" were prescribed, women "seldom" took them "because of a lack of understanding of their worth." Too often, community social workers had had to convince parents to rush a sick child to hospital.

In response, experts searched for better ways to reach immigrant women, including translating information pamphlets and more systematic home visiting. Public health workers also began enrolling in Italian and Portuguese language classes, while others lobbied for more local pre-natal and child nutrition clinics. However, the initiatives of professional nutrition and health experts determined to reshape immigrant behaviour were not always effective. For example, city settlement records in the early 1960s commented on the high rates of absenteeism in courses organized for recently arrived newcomers.

Health and welfare personnel also frowned on what they dubbed the inadequate, makeshift daycare arrangements of immigrant working mothers who reportedly left babies and toddlers in the care of grandparents, siblings, and others sitters incapable of providing proper supervision, nutritious meals, healthy recreation, or moral guidance. While all working mothers were vulnerable to such criticism, non-English-speaking immigrant and refugee women were considered particularly prone to bypassing modern daycare centres for informal, often kin-based arrangements. The result in downtown areas was a so-called "epidemic of inadequate child care arrangements." Home visitors reported on a range of inappropriate sitters: an old-age pensioner who lived next door, a six-year-old child in charge of a two-year-old, and harried mothers with their own children.

Determined to raise the standard of child care in the community, St. Christopher House (SCH), along with the neighbouring Protestant Children's Home and the Victoria Day Nursery, began experimenting in 1962 with small daycare programs "in specially selected family settings." Like other social welfare programs, including progressive ones intended to support low-income working mothers, a carrot-and-stick approach characterized this scheme: all participating mothers had to attend SCH sessions on child care and homemaking.

By the early 1960s, efforts aimed at inner-city immigrant mothers included downtown experiments intended to "strengthen family life" by addressing "part of a complex of problems of family living," namely, meal planning, food purchasing on limited funds, and child and adult eating habits. In 1961, SCH (whose neighbourhood was bounded by Queen St, Bathurst St., College St., and Spadina Avenue), participated in a hot lunch program with Toronto Board of Education and the Metro Toronto Social Planning Council at Ryerson Public School. An important program that deserves praise for addressing the needs of low-income children, the hot lunch project nevertheless came with conditions: a dozen "undernourished" children from the neighbourhood were given money subsidies (donated by the Rotary Club) to purchase nutritious hot lunches at school provided that their mothers agreed to attend fortnightly classes at St. Christopher House for "help in nutrition and meal planning." The children were selected in consultation with school and St. Christopher House staff, who could supply "knowledge of family conditions," while a family life worker hired by St. Christopher House conducted follow-up visits. The hot meals were not described but likely consisted of conventional cafeteria fare of this era, such as hot roast beef sandwiches with peas and carrots or cooked ham with (canned) pineapple and (canned) vegetables, and, of course, milk.

According to St. Christopher House staff, the hot school lunch produced positive results for both children and mothers. Within a year, they reported a general increase in the number of students buying hot lunches at Ryerson Public School. Meanwhile, the mothers of the subsidized children had shown much "enthusiasm" for their meetings and their "excellent" instructor, a nutritionist from the Visiting Homemakers Association who used a good mix of films, kitchen demonstrations, and lectures. Two years later, a report claimed that teachers had "observed improvement in the health of the children and in the quality of their work in school," while their mothers had "gained practical knowledge through their contact with a nutritionist and a social worker." Furthermore, the classes had provided the women with "their only social experience in an otherwise drab existence" and given them "the feeling that somebody cared." On a more negative note, nutritionists expressed "some concern about finding methods to ensure that the families are taking full advantage of the subsidy to purchase the lunches at school"—suggesting that some immigrant mothers, by choice or circumstance, were spending the money on other items.

The Hot Lunch campaign quickly became incorporated into a more intrusive two-year Family Life project launched at SCH in 1962. With funds from the Laidlaw Foundation, this project too aimed to "reach" rural immigrant women now transplanted to an urban centre and provide them with "a very basic type of adult education eg., consumer buying, citizenship etc." The primary target was the growing number of Portuguese newcomers in the Kensington market area, though Italian, Chinese, Caribbean and other newcomers were also contacted. A full-time Family Life worker and a Portuguese-speaking nutritionist with experience in Home Economics education in Angola were hired. The IIMT also collaborated on the project.

Like other community experiments with inner-city immigrants, the Family Life Project produced mixed results. Also, like other front-line work with newcomers, it reflected and perpetuated the marginal status of women from rural, impoverished, and formally uneducated Old World backgrounds.

■ IMMIGRANT AND REFUGEE WOMEN'S RECIPES FOR "CANADIAN" LIVING

Although anecdotal, the available evidence suggests that refugee and immigrant women also responded selectively to postwar health and homemaking campaigns, even if they could not control the terms of their encounter with social welfare personnel. Like surviving written sources, oral testimonies[3] attest to the critical importance of food to immigrants and refugees and to women's efforts to negotiate a complex culinary terrain. Immigrant and refugee women had their own versions of European scarcity and Canadian abundance: their recollections contain horrific tales of starvation in Nazi camps and heroic ones of gentiles and partisans who risked their lives to get food to hungry prisoners across Europe. Some testimonies offer us humorous recollections of the joys of eating Canadian bread and fruit upon arrival in Halifax, while others record the serious complaints and protests of refugees clearly disgusted by what they saw as over-indulgence and the (sinful) throwing out of leftovers. In addition, immigrant women's cooking and their families' food-eating patterns varied greatly during these years and thus defy easy categorization: some immigrant mothers steadfastly stuck to "traditional" meals in the home while others were keen to experiment with Canadian recipes or convenience foods. The example of Polish Jewish survivors who responded differently to Canadian food customs and the availability of many commercial products suggests too the importance of individual choice. One woman explained her insistence on cooking traditional "Jewish food" in part as a concrete way of continuing to defy Hitler's Final Solution; the other embraced Betty Crocker and other U.S. as well as Canadian products because these newfangled things offered her one of several ways of putting behind the past and moving forward.

While these briefly summarized testimonies are highly suggestive, the gender and generational dynamics involved still require more research and closer scrutiny. Here again, my research sheds some light on various intriguing patterns. For example, some immigrant and refugee husbands pressured their wives to stick to familiar meals and insisted that their children eat their homeland foods at home. In some cases, this gender dynamic overlapped with political as well as ethnic or cultural tones. During the early Cold War years, for instance, left-wing Ukrainian Canadians who belonged to the Farm-labour Temple in Winnipeg evidently insisted on eating Ukrainian as a sign of their continuing resistance to a repressive Canadian state—but they also left it to women to do the time-consuming labours involved to prepare the food. By the same token, certain immigrant or ethnic Canadian men deliberately encouraged their wives to incorporate some Canadian foods because they wished to "embrace" Canada; other times, the opposite pattern emerged. Children also played a role, usually by pressuring their mother to "try" or "buy" Canadian goods—with hot dogs, hamburgers, and pop being favourites. In short, the evidence, though fragmentary, points to a seemingly endless number of permutations of hybrid diets in the households of working-class and middle-class immigrants who increasingly combined familiar foods with Canadian foods and "ethnic" foods from other homeland origins.

Particularly for cities like Toronto, immigrant foods (and ethnic restaurants) have clearly changed the city's culinary landscape even as the immigrants' own food customs have themselves been modified. But we still need to trace more closely and to develop a sharper analysis of what some have called the "yuppification" of ethnic foods.

I find it especially ironic that the foods that had caused me much embarrassment as a child—spicy and pungent salami, prosciutto, strong and smelly cheeses, dense and crusty bread—have become markers of middle-class taste. But they have also been embraced by people from diverse racial-ethnic and class backgrounds, many of whom, in my view, are not merely using food to affect a certain sophisticated, worldly, or snobbish big-city style. Rather, they (we) clearly value the sensuality involved in eating a range of foods, of experimenting with new smells and tastes, of embracing food practices that see eating as a social and cultural practice, not merely a biological function, during which people talk, laugh, argue, debate, and in this and other ways spend hours making and re-making community.

Equally important, we cannot deny the power politics embedded in food wars and customs—to make only brief mention of the so-called "wok wars" that recently received media attention in Toronto, when a WASP Canadian couple complained bitterly and publicly about their Chinese neighbour's cooking habits and "smells." Nor can we omit the role that food corporations, saturation-advertising, and capitalist imperialism have played in shaping women's cooking and shopping habits and family eating customs—how else can we explain what I have called the postwar Dole Pineapple conspiracy? As suggested by the New Left scholars of the late 1960s and the 1970s, who exposed the insidious links between U.S. imperialist ambitions in Latin America, the creation of so-called banana republics, and multi-national food corporations' aggressive promotion of their various tinned and packaged citrus fruits to (North) Americans, the political economy of food must inform our analysis of the social and gender practices surrounding the purchase, production, and consumption of food.

So too do people matter; their curiosity, willingness to experiment, in short their agency—should also figure in our efforts to discern key changes in food customs, including the recent rise of "multicultural" eating in Canada. Nevertheless, when we focus on the immigrant and refugee women and families who encountered Canadian nutrition and food experts on their doorsteps or in their children's schools, health and welfare offices, hospitals or settlement houses during the early post-1945 decades, a particularly strong theme looms large: working-class immigrant women residing in inner-city neighbourhoods bore the brunt of professional discourses that attributed women's failure to conquer the kitchen and ensure "quality" food and family life to ignorance and distrust of modern standards and distrust of social service interventions.

I am indebted to Valerie Korinek for sharing her research materials and ideas with me. We have co-authored a lengthy article on related themes, entitled "Jello Salads, One-

Stop Shopping, and Maria the Homemaker: The Gender Politics of Food," submitted to book-in-progress, Marlene Epp et al., eds., Sisters or Strangers?: Immigrant Women and the Racialized Other in Canadian History. *Very warm thanks to Cynthia Wright for inviting me to submit this piece and to her and Ian Radforth for their speedy and valuable feedback. Finally, thanks to CWS/cf editor Luciana Ricciutelli and staff for their patience with a scholar who refuses to install the latest information technology at her cottage!*

Franca Iacovetta, a professor at the University of Toronto, is the author of Such Hardworking People: Italian Immigrants in Postwar Toronto *and the co-editor of several books in the areas of immigrant, women's and social history. She is currently writing a new book on immigrant/refugee women in Cold War Canada.*

■ NOTES

1. See, for example *The Toronto Star* from 1945-65.
2. Sources listed in order of appearance in the text: Toronto City Archives: Social Planning Council (SC) 40, Box 53 File 3A-International Institute Parkdale Branch (IIPB) 1961-63, Report on School Principals at Grace, Alexander Muir, Old Orchard, Charles E. Fraser, and Lansdowne Public Schools; SC 24 D Box 1 University Settlement House, Executive Director's Reports, 1939-1975, Head Resident's House Report, 14 Feb. 1952; Executive Director's Monthly Report, 28 May 1956 on Housing and Suburbs: National Federation of Settlements Conference; St. Christopher House, SC 484 IA1, Box 1, Folder 5, Minutes 1951-1952: Annual Report 8 Feb 1951; SC 484 IA1 Box 2 St. Christopher House Folder 1 Minutes 1959, dated 23 April 1959; Box 1 Folder 7 Minutes 1955; Folder 8 Minutes 23 May 1956; SC 40, Box 53, File 3 A-IIPB 1961-63, Report from Parkdale Branch, International Institute (Edith Ferguson) to School Principals at Grace, Alexander Muir, Old Orchard, Charles E. Fraser, and Lansdowne Public Schools; SC 484 IB2 Box 1 Folder 6 "Briefs and Reports 1962-1970" St. Christopher House to the Select Committee on Youth. Oct 1964; Box 2 folder 4 Minutes 1962; Folder 6 "Briefs and Reports 1962-1970" Draft Presentation of the St. Christopher House to the Select Committee on Youth. Oct. 1964 (description of School Lunch Committee, Child and Family Section, Social Planning Council of Metropolitan Toronto, May 1964; Box 2 Folder 5 Minutes 1963, 24 Jan 1963; Report filed by Family Life worker Miss Spadafore regarding Visiting Homemakers Nutritionist.
3. The oral testimonies were selected from a larger database of more than 100 interviews with post-1945 immigrants culled from the Oral History Collection, Multicultural

History Society of Ontario). My sample here is of 28 interviews, most of them conducted in the 1970s, with immigrant women and couples asked about food customs, with the following breakdown: European (18), including European Jewry (4), Asian (2), Caribbean (1), and South Asian (India) (3). I also drew on a few anecdotes collected from numerous colleagues and members of audiences who have heard me speak about this research. I thank them for sharing their stories with me.

■ REFERENCES

Adams, Mary Louise. *The Trouble with Normal: Postwar Youth and the Making of Heterosexuality*. Toronto: University of Toronto Press, 1997.

Belmonte, Laura A. "Mr. and Mrs. America: Images of Gender and the Family in Cold War Propaganda." Paper presented at Berkshire Conference on the History of Women, Chapel Hill, North Carolina, June, 1996.

Brienes, Wini. *Young White, and Miserable: Growing Up Female in the Fifties*. Boston: Beacon, 1992.

Comacchio, Cynthia. *Nations Are Built of Babies*. Montreal: McGill-Queen's University Press, 1993.

Gabaccia, Donna. *We Are What We Eat: Ethnic Food and the Making of Americans*. Cambridge: Harvard University Press, 1998.

Gleason, Mona. *Normalizing the Ideal: Psychology, the School and the Family in Postwar Canada*. Toronto: University of Toronto Press, 1999.

Iacovetta, Franca. "Gossip, Contest and Power in the Making of Suburban Bad Girls, Toronto 1956-60." *Canadian Historical Review* 80 (4) (Dec 1999).

Iacovetta, Franca. "Making Model Citizens: Gender, Corrupted Democracy, and Immigrant Reception World in Cold War Canada." *Whose National Security? Canadian State Surveillance and the Creation of Enemies*, edited by Gary Kinsman, Dieter K. Buse, and Mercedes Steedman. Toronto: Between the Lines Press, 2000.

Iacovetta, Franca and Tania Das Gupta, eds. "Whose Canada Is It?" *Atlantis* 24 (2) (Spring 2000).

Kingston, Anne. *The Edible Man: Dave Nichol, President's Choice and the Making of Popular Taste*. Toronto: McFarlane, Walter, & Ross, 1994.

Kinsman, Gary. *The Regulation of Desire: Homo and Hetero Sexualities*. Montreal: Black Rose Books, 1987. Revised edition 1996.

Kinsman, Gary and Patrizia Gentile et al. "'In the Interests of the State': The Anti-Gay, Anti-Lesbian National Security Campaign in Canada." A Preliminary Research Report. Laurentian University, April 1998.

Korinek, Valerie. *Roughing It in the Suburbs: Reading* Chatelaine *in the Fifties and Sixties.* Toronto: University of Toronto Press, 2000.

Levenstein, Harvey. *Revolution at the Table: The Transformation of the American Diet.* New York: Oxford University Press, 1988.

Levenstein, Harvey. *Paradox of Plenty: A Social History of Eating in Modern America.* New York: Oxford University Press, 1993.

May, Elaine Tyler. "Gender, Sexuality, and Cold War: For the U.S." *Homeward Bound: American Families in the Cold War Era.* New York: Basic Books, 1988.

Meyerowitz, Joanne. "Beyond the Feminine Mystique: A Reassessment of Postwar Mass Culture, 1945-58." *Journal of American History* 79 (March 1993).

Meyerowitz, Joanne, ed. *Not June Cleaver: Women and Gender in Postwar America, 1945-1960.* Philadelphia: Temple University Press, 1994.

Parr, Joy, ed. *A Diversity of Women: Ontario, 1945-1980.* Toronto: University of Toronto Press, 1995.

Smith, Geoffrey S. "National Security and Personal Isolation: Sex, Gender, and Disease in the Cold-War United States." *The International History Review* 54 (2) (May 1992).

Toronto Nutrition Committee, *Food Customs of New Canadians.* 2nd ed. Archives of Ontario, International Institute of Metropolitan Toronto Collection, MU6410, File: Cookbook Project, Booklet. Published with funds from Ontario Dietic Association. 1959, 1967.

Valverde, Mariana. *The Age of Light, Soap, and Water: Moral Reform in English Canada, 1885-1925.* Toronto: McClelland & Stewart, 1991.

Visser, Margaret. *Much Depends on Dinner: The Extraordinary History and Mythology, Allure and Obsessions, Perils and Taboos, of an Ordinary Meal.* Toronto: McClelland & Stewart, 1986.

Whitaker, Reginald and Gary Marcuse. *Cold War Canada: The Making of a National Insecurity State: 1945-1957.* Toronto: University of Toronto Press, 1994.

CHAPTER 9

INCARCERATING "BAD GIRLS":
THE REGULATION OF SEXUALITY THROUGH THE FEMALE REFUGES ACT IN ONTARIO, 1920–1945

Joan Sangster

In 1935, Judge McKinley of the Ottawa Family Court sent more than one young woman to the Mercer Reformatory for Women for "idle and dissolute" behavior. Mildred, a single woman of 19 who had left school at 14 and claimed "no occupation," was sentenced to one year nine months. The judge said female probation officers working with her had had "no results," and the purpose of a jail term was to treat her venereal disease and "teach her some discipline."[1] Juliette, age 21, had one illegitimate child and was pregnant with a second when she was sentenced by McKinley to 15 months: she was "not strong enough to face the world without help."[2] And Dorothy, only 16, was sentenced after her mother swore out a statement against her, saying she was "incorrigible and immoral."[3] Dorothy's mother anguished over the imprisonment of her daughter but still embraced this strategy of control, claiming she had no other option given her daughter's sexual misconduct.

The incarceration of these young women was made possible by Section 347 of the province's Female Refuges Act, first enacted in 1897 to regulate the Industrial Houses of Refuge that held women sentenced or "*liable* to be sentenced" by magistrates under local bylaw or Criminal Code infractions.[4] Instituted specifically for women between the ages of 16 and 35, who were too old for industrial schools, the Female Refuges Act (FRA) provided for low-security correctional institutions, where women were offered shelter, work, and reform as an antidote to "unmanageability and incorrigibility."[5] The initial FRA allowed a sentence of up to five years, until this was amended to two years, less a day, in 1919.[6] Accompanying this reduction, however, came a new clause giving magistrates and judges wide-ranging powers to incarcerate young women for immoral behavior. "Any person" could bring before a magistrate "any female under the age of 35 ... who is a habitual drunkard or by reasons of other vices is leading an idle and dissolute life." All that was needed was a sworn statement about the woman's incorrigibility: no formal charge was needed, and hearings were in private, though written evidence was supposedly required. A 1942 amendment allowed sentences to be appealed before the Court of Appeal—though this appears to have been little used—and in 1958 these sections were finally deleted.[7] Criticism of the clauses did not appear to be the cause of their repeal; instead, politicians accepted the minister's claim that "these sections are already dealt with adequately in the Criminal Code and other federal and provincial statutes."[8]

From 1920 to the late 1950s these provisions in the FRA allowed parents, police, welfare authorities, and the Children's Aid Society (CAS) to use incarceration as a means to regulate the sexual and moral behavior of women perceived to be "out of sexual control." For rebellious teenagers already serving time in industrial schools, the act could increase their punishment by sending them to the Mercer Reformatory for Women as soon as they were 15 or 16 years old, for up to two more years. Indeed, rather than send convicted women to refuges like Toronto's Belmont House, which had a dormitory setup and minimum security, some magistrates simply fast-tracked women into the reformatory. After Belmont closed its doors as an industrial refuge, this practice became standard. And if a woman started off at Belmont and refused the discipline there, she could easily be transferred to the reformatory under the FRA.

The process of sexual regulation through the FRA, as it was articulated in the peak years of FRA prosecutions, the 30s and early 40s, is the focus of this article. I want to uncover the dominant definitions of *idle* and *dissolute* used by the court and analyze why these definitions of sexuality dominated. How did the FRA operate to define and construct "bad" girls' sexuality as opposed to the ideal of feminine sexuality—both inside and outside the prison? How were the women incarcerated literally created as criminals, pathologized on the basis of their sexuality, and offered "cures" that only replicated their existing patriarchal and material oppression? What can the operation of the FRA also tell us about the way in which women's punishment for being idle and dissolute was grounded in patriarchal, class, and ethnic divisions? Finally, how did women themselves respond to these constructions of their sexuality as immoral: Did their strategies for coping involve rejection of the moral assumptions behind the FRA?

■ MORAL REGULATION

The draconian use of these FRA clauses could be characterized by the term *moral regulation*; that is, the processes whereby some behaviors, ideals, and values were marginalized and proscribed while others were legitimized and naturalized. These processes were central to social relations of power, reinforcing dominance and subjection, though there is extensive scholarly debate within moral regulation studies about the origin and operation of such practices.[9] While economic imperatives, state power, and ideology remain important themes in Marxist analyses of the creation of a moral culture within the context of bourgeois economic relations,[10] scholars following Foucauldian and post-structuralist approaches have concentrated more on how discourses define immorality and expert knowledge normalizes certain behaviors, producing disciplinary power that crosses the boundaries of state and civil society.

These debates are linked to recent critiques of social control theories and alternative arguments for the use of moral regulation as the organizing paradigm to explain sexual regulation.[11] Marxist-inspired studies of the law have been critiqued for either downplaying gender or ignoring the subtle forms of non-state regulation that shape everyday life, while critical social control theories (drawing on neo-Marxist and New Left ideas) have also been disparaged, even by their early proponents, as too essentialist, all-encompassing, determinist, conspiratorial, and top-down in their approach.[12] Feminist appropriations of these theories that insist that women are controlled by a patriarchal legal system, contend some theorists, have also veered toward essentialism, erroneously assumed a mythical separation between the private and public spheres of women's lives, and ignored contradiction, negotiation, struggle, and resistance in the making of the law and social policy.[13] As Mary Odem's work on juvenile delinquency has shown, for example, the courts were not the sole authority shaping the fate of delinquent daughters; women's interests were fractured by age, class, and race as well as gender; and the efforts of reformers were sometimes misappropriated by the state, with the unintended, contradictory effects of punishing working-class women.[14]

The charge that social control theories were used like a "hammer" is not without justification.[15] Nonetheless, though now scorned as passé in comparison to post-structuralist insights, social control theories did wrestle with the crucial question of how "powerful groups consciously or unconsciously attempt to restrain, induce conformity, even assent among less powerful, who then come to monitor their own behavior."[16] Moreover, they offered two potentially worthwhile legacies: they attempted to bring the state back in to challenge liberal, uncritical, pluralistic views of the production of conformity, and their proponents often articulated a political, partisan objection to the more oppressive consequences of social control, suggesting an alternative vision of justice, equality, and socialism.[17]

Drawing more decidedly on post-structuralist and especially Foucauldian theories, moral regulation studies have extended our gaze beyond the state, dissected power (including the relations between the regulators and the regulated) as a multidimensional, complex process, and analyzed the emergence of disciplinary practices from discourses associated with systems of expert knowledge. This research has also brought the regulation of gender and sexuality to the foreground. Using discourse analysis, for instance, Carolyn Strange has effectively deconstructed the legal, medical, and reform doctrines defining the problem of the single working girl in Toronto at the turn of the century. These moralizing texts, she argues, worked to "organize meaning" and the social practices shaping working women's lives; they revealed both the "relentless sexualization of women's behavior" and the way in which women's pleasure was equated with immorality and social disorder.[18]

In understanding sexual regulation in particular, feminist-Foucauldian insights have been invaluable, illuminating the way in which medical, social science, and legal discourses criminalize and pathologize certain women.[19] Such a perspective accentuates the ways in which women's bodies, though culturally constructed, also become "saturated with sex" and "the objects of discipline," in the view of experts.[20] Both of these insights are evident in the case of women incarcerated under the FRA. And as Foucauldian scholars have emphasized so well, penal punishment is also part of a broader web of moral regulation: the meanings of normal female heterosexuality constructed and circulated through laws like the FRA imprisoned all women's psyches, for this knowledge pervaded wider social groups, ordering all women's self-discipline and self-repression.

Concentrating on the discourses that define and construct moral regulation, however, should not obscure the political economy and social relations framing them. Some of the more general misgivings about Foucauldian theory articulated by feminists and Marxists may be relevant here. Michel Foucault's description of normalization, comments one critic, "seems to work as a neat historical trick,"[21] producing "docile bodies" and allowing for little admissible evidence of women's own expression or experience.[22] Feminists have been wary of Foucault's assumption of an ever-increasing, irrational urge to disciplinary power that avoids the central questions of who the agents and benefactors of power are, where the "headquarters" of power reside.[23] This question of centralized power is critical in terms of the FRA: we need to know which social groups promoted, used, and endorsed this form of regulation, why, and how their consent was secured. The tendency to stress the discursive rather than nondiscursive side of Foucault's analysis may also obscure the economic and social relations of privilege framing these processes of regulation.[24] And we should be wary of Foucault's tendency to dismiss the importance of the state: after all, in the case of the FRA, the police and courts often encouraged families to incarcerate their daughters using this legislation.

The concept of social censure, coined by socialist criminologists, may provide a valuable alternative means to analyze the sexual regulation articulated through the FRA. Censuring processes of demarcating the good/bad, holy/demonic, they argue, are intrinsic to all knowledge systems, and order social relations with political and moral judgments that simultaneously enforce power relations based on "hegemonic masculinity" as well as race and class power.[25] As Colin Sumner notes, "Censures, as categories of denunciation," are "lodged within historically specific moral debates and practical conflicts" that are ideological in nature and are connected to the dynamics of class, as well as gender and race relations.[26] Though drawing heavily on Foucauldian notions of normalization and the power/knowledge alliance, this approach emphasizes that the particular behavior designated as criminal, wicked, and dangerous is a contested question of economic, political, and ideological constitution. Social censures are "not descriptive as much as acculturated terms of moral judgment," and the discourses describing the immoral and criminal must be read in relation to the economic, political, and cultural "reality" that they represent. Regina Kunzel's examination of the competing discourses defining out-of-wedlock pregnancy in the United States, for instance, tries to strike such a balance, situating the narratives of both the social workers and the pregnant women in the broader spheres of power shaped by class, race, age, and gender.[27]

Given the overlapping possibilities of these theories, what is perhaps most important is to develop a framework, however named, that does not operate as an all-encompassing, determinist, analytical construct. Our conceptualization must encompass the historical specificity of the processes of regulation, explicating the patterns of resistance, struggle, and accommodation as well as control, drawing us toward the ideological overlap and relations between informal and formal controls, opening out into explorations of how and why consent to regulation is organized. In the case of the FRA, these questions require an exploration of the specific historical, materialist context and the related discursive practices that together shaped the gendered power relations of sexual regulation through the courts.

■ THE CONTEXT FOR REGULATION

Ironically, this particular draconian clause of the FRA only came into being after World War I, when sexual morality supposedly became more open and liberal for both working- and middle-class women. As Christina Simmons has argued, however, the characterization of the Victorian period as sexually repressive and the postwar one as liberal is highly problematic.[28] Anxieties about working-class sexuality and reproduction were still strong in the interwar period[29]: in fact, the peak of FRA prosecutions came during the 1930s and World War II.[30] By the interwar period, argues Strange, Canadian middle-class reformers were more preoccupied with working girls' transformation into efficient, healthy, moral mothers (especially Anglo and white mothers) of the future,[31] having forsaken their earlier obsession with the inherent moral dangers of wage work for single urban women. Yet, the FRA convictions after World War I betrayed persisting, underlying fears that working-class girls were in danger of becoming unruly, overly sexual women, either led astray or leading men astray. A fear of female sexual assertiveness could still be mobilized as a metaphor for social disorder—and not just in large urban centers like Toronto.[32]

Not coincidentally, this was also the period when legal reformers pressed for family courts in Ontario, which also attempted to regulate working-class morals and normalize certain family forms.[33] Ironically, the emergence of more liberal correctional philosophy did not necessarily lessen the chances of women's incarceration for moral offenses. Indeed, some professionals advocated more institutionalization, along with probation and social work, as a means of deterring working-class girls at risk. Young women especially had longer indeterminate sentences at the Mercer Reformatory, sometimes handed out by the very female magistrates whom suffragists had recently pressured the state to appoint.[34] These magistrates believed that the good example, discipline, and retraining provided in reformatories run by maternal feminists like themselves would offer young women positive benefits.[35] Finally, social workers, psychologists, and doctors were increasingly involved in the correctional system; they used scientific measures, such as intelligence tests or family assessments, to diagnose women's sexual deviancy. These methods, as Kunzel has argued for the American context, may have actually resulted in the sexual lives of working-class women becoming more closely scrutinized and objectified by these experts.[36]

Some of the anxieties about working-class women's sexuality may have been reinforced by ongoing changes in their work and family lives: during the interwar period, more single women were working for wages and they were more likely to live away from home as the rural areas depopulated. During the Depression, anxiety about joblessness led some politicians and social workers to worry that youngsters would abandon their sexual morality along with the work ethic.[37] Yet, even during the more prosperous war years, anxiety about women's sexuality did not decrease: it merely altered its form. Now, women's nontraditional work, public wartime roles, and even new fashions engendered anxieties about their sexuality.[38]

In these peak years of FRA operation, there are certain characteristics common to many convictions. Youth is the most distinguishing feature of all the women who were summoned before the court; indeed, the act specifically targeted young women under 35, presumably because these were women's more active sexual and reproductive years. Almost all those convicted were under 21, and 70 percent were teens from 16 to 19 years old. The vast majority of women were of Anglo-Celtic background, and many were Canadian-born. There was a significant minority of British immigrants in this sample, but not inordinate numbers considering the influx of such immigrants to Ontario just before the First World War and the tendency of immigrants to face economic and social dislocation.[39]

Almost all the women also came from either working-class or poverty-stricken backgrounds, though their families crossed the spectrum from the criminal classes to the skilled artisan. They generally had left school by 14 or 15, and their occupations, if they had them (and they often did not), were listed as domestic or, less often, waitress, sales clerk, factory worker.

A few incarcerated women were impoverished or destitute or had run away, but for the overwhelming majority, *dissolute* was equated with errant sexuality. Significantly, almost half of the women either had an illegitimate child or were pregnant with one when they entered the reformatory.[40] Just over a third—perhaps more—were treated for venereal disease.[41] Many also had stiff sentences; on average, they received from a year to two years, and women did not secure release easily, serving about two-thirds of their sentences.

Although the person who originated the case was not always stated, it is clear that parental complaints supported about a third to a half of the actions against these young women.[42] A significant minority of the girls came directly from some kind of state care, such as a foster home, refuge, or industrial school, and many also came from single-parent or reconstituted families. Parental divorce, separations, and single parenthood were thus often offered as explanations for girls' wayward behavior by social workers. Rather than question the poverty of single-parent families or the alienation of foster care, the authorities, and even families themselves, looked to a mythical nuclear family along with the penal discipline as a means of curing the women imprisoned.

Finally, it is important to remember that the numbers of women actually convicted under this act were small; even within the prison population, these women were a minority. We can claim far too much by looking at court cases for certain legal infractions, which were, after all, only the very tip of the iceberg in terms of sexual relations. Moreover, sexual and moral regulation changed over time, taking on various garbs, and it may be presumptuous to claim that a period was characterized by more intense regulation simply by noting the statistical increase in conviction for certain sexual offenses. The case files of the convicted are also highly mediated, problematic sources; they are biased by the recorder's views, are incomplete, and may encompass justifications, fabrications, or supplications on the part of the state official or the prisoner.[43]

What such case files can do, as Julie Matthews points out, is highlight the polarized constructions of good and bad femininity and sexuality created and justified by those with medical and legal authority, and the way in which women were measured against these ideals.[44] The "subtle dialectic"[45]—and sometimes the not-so-subtle antagonism—between those with moral authority and the women incarcerated also becomes apparent as we explore women's actual encounters with sexual regulation.

◼ CENSURING SEXUAL NONCONFORMITY

The vast majority of FRA incarcerations resulted from three things, which were often intertwined: sexual promiscuity (better termed *nonconformity*), illegitimate pregnancies, and venereal disease.[46] Young women under parental control could be sent away on the flimsiest of evidence regarding their promiscuity. One 17-year-old, for example, was given two years, less a day, after her mother had simply sworn that she was "not doing what was right. She borrowed money because she was in difficulty with a man. She goes out at night and is not obeying me."[47] Cases like this one may omit discussion of earlier run-ins with the police or probation officers, thus obscuring the fact that the FRA incarceration came as the culmination of a series of problems, but even where there were more details of the woman's activities, it is clear that sexual promiscuity was defined very broadly.

The sexual activity of young women became a problem for parents and authorities when the women left home or stayed out all night without parental consent, when they got venereal disease, or when they were perceived to have too many partners or the wrong kind of partner. "Drinking and keeping late hours with undesirable companions are her special weaknesses," noted a sentencing report when a landlady informed on a CAS foster child working for her as a domestic.[48] One father testified before the magistrate that his 17-year-old, who had already had an illegitimate child, was "leaving home for weeks on end," was drinking in beverage rooms, and was staying out late with men. Her mother added that she could not believe her daughter was mentally sound given her actions. They agreed with the magistrate that the only hope of reforming her was to offer the discipline served up at the Mercer.[49]

Multiple partners—even more than one—were seen as a serious problem denoting promiscuity. "Her main misfortune appears to be truck drivers," noted one file (though taxi drivers also seem to figure in the files); "she spends nights with them and would go on drinking sprees in Chatham and St. Thomas .... She could not say no to their associates, or men she met from time to time."[50] A woman's choice of partner sometimes tainted her own character: "very hard and a tough specimen of humanity," noted one northern magistrate who in the same breath claimed the woman was sleeping with lumberjacks who were "tough specimens."[51]

[...]

Even one partner, however, could be one too many if the parents objected to the man and felt he was a bad influence on their daughter. Parents from a northern Ontario town went to the court, claiming they were "having difficulty with [their daughter] through a fellow" who was encouraging her sexual promiscuity. "[He] should be here [in court] .... He is a reptile," the mother charged vehemently. The parents claimed he was leading their daughter, who was "weak-minded" and a bit slow, astray, getting her drunk at dances and then introducing her to other men of dubious morals.[52] In this case, the daughter was unusually vocal in court, defending her right to control her own social and sexual life: "I don't know why I'm here. I did not do anything wrong last night .... He is better than some around here. I phoned him up and wanted him, and that's that."[53]

[...]

When women were found with Chinese men, parental and police anxiety was even more intense; in the early 30s, a 17-year-old described by her foster mother as "boy crazy, with no regard for the truth" was found in a "bawdy house with a Chinaman."[54] Magistrate Margaret Patterson immediately remanded her into psychiatric care, a procedure that was not uncommon in FRA cases and that underscores the way in which women's sexual nonconformity was literally equated with their insanity.

There are also other cases where daughters are clearly acting out against parents who admitted that they had very strict rules and who brought the daughters before the court to "scare [them] with the threat of reform school," as one Cornwall father put it.[55] Both his daughters worked at the local textile mill but were staying out all night with boyfriends. "People think I am a man that may chain them to a collar," he admitted in court, "but the only reason they hate me is because I put a stop to them coming in at 6, taking a piece of toast and going off to the mill to work." Yet, testimony from a social worker at the local mental health clinic who knew the family, as well as from the younger daughter, Joan, demonstrated a shared perception of the father as an overbearing patriarch. "It doesn't matter what boy I am with, my father finds something wrong with him," Joan complained. The magistrate's decision about the case neatly summed up the way in which the law punished girls' "precocious sexuality"[56] but ignored boys' sexual exploits—indeed, promiscuity was defined only as a female problem. "I'm not going to have anything to do with the boy .... It is the daughter I am concerned with," concluded the magistrate. Because of Joan's illness (she was epileptic) and her sexual behavior, he prescribed 18 months in the reformatory to "save" her: "When a girl starts at 16 sleeping out all night no good will come of this," he concluded in his judgment.

A refuge or reformatory, it was claimed by the magistrate as well as many CAS workers and police, would teach discipline, self-control, new morals, and some work skills for domestic life or feminine occupations. Correcting bad language; learning respect for others, especially elders; learning cleanliness; and working every day at a job were all part of the program to help women improve their moral character and thus ultimately control their sexual behavior. Saving girls from themselves was the paternalistic rationale for incarceration that many magistrates and judges used in their sentencing reports. Preventing girls' slippery slide into prostitution was often cited as the primary grounds for a term in the reformatory.

[...]

Throughout such proceedings there was a somewhat voyeuristic pleasure as male interrogators questioned young women about their sex lives. They appeared to be simultaneously fearful and fascinated, repulsed and attracted, to women's stories.[57] A classic question asked by police and magistrates was, How many times did you have intercourse with different men? The legal authorities were excessively preoccupied with this question, and in certain cases seem only to egg the women on: "How many times, would you say 50, 100?"[58] One assumes that one method of rebellion for the women was to exaggerate the numbers, simply to horrify those in authority or to put an end to their questioning.

In assessing the incarceration of these young women, one also has to take into account parents' active participation in the process and thus the broader question of how consent to the law was organized. Many parents who testified against their daughters described themselves as "nearly beside themselves,"[59] near nervous breakdown, desperate, having no other option, and so forth. They objected to the defiance and disobedience of their daughters; in some cases, parents and daughters were clearly involved in massive battles for control of resources and for power (as when one mother hid all her daughter's shoes and clothes so she could not go out; the same daughter stole money from the mother to buy forbidden high-heeled shoes).[60]

[...]

Some of the most disturbing FRA cases are those where parents seek out the help of the police, but then quickly find the process moving beyond their control as the greater authority of the legal experts takes precedence over their wishes. These parents wanted help restricting their daughters' actions, not a jail sentence. In one case, a teenager who was a first offender was sentenced to two years despite her mother's attempts to ask the police and the magistrate for alternatives. Evelyn was described as mentally slow and childish after a severe case of sleeping sickness. Her father was unemployed, and, although two sons worked, the mother could barely feed her eight children. She was still reluctant to lose her daughter, whom she saw as essentially "a good girl" but one who got "led astray" when she ran off to a local town. The mother just wanted to keep her "out of trouble" and asked for placement in an industrial school. Once in court, however, the police provided evidence that the girl had venereal disease, and the magistrate strongly pressured the mother until she agreed that the reformatory was the only place Evelyn could go. [...]

Sexual nonconformity was most often evidenced by sex out of marriage, multiple and frequent partners, or single women sleeping with married men. In a few cases, it was also linked to homosexuality or to liaisons with men from other ethnic or racial groups. Homosexuality, though largely unacknowledged by the reformatory authorities, undoubtedly existed within the prison itself.[61] It could also become one reason for incarcerating young women in the first place. One 16-year-old foster child, sentenced under the FRA, came from the Galt Girls Training School, where she was "considered a menace to the other girls." The superintendent claimed she ran away three times and engaged "in homosexual practices, pursuing the girls .... When they reported it to me, I interviewed her and she admitted it."[62] Originally sent to a training school for skipping school and trying to hitchhike to her original home in Timmins, the girl was examined by psychiatrists before being sent to Mercer.

Finally, sexual nonconformity was linked to sex with non-white men. One 22-year-old, who immigrated from England as a nursemaid, claimed her sister pressured her to become a prostitute by forcing her to "have intercourse with Italian and Chinese men"; she was ordered deported after her sentence was over as "she has been going around Hamilton with Chinamen and other men and is now pregnant."[63] In a northern Ontario community, a young woman's relationship with a Native man was central to the court's anxieties about her sexuality. Ironically, her mother was seen, on the one hand, as a bad example since she was living common-law, but the mother also participated in the complaint against her daughter, who she charged was "running around with an Indian boy and would not get a job." Mabel claimed that her boyfriend "wanted to marry her" but became abusive "and threatened to kill her if she saw anyone else." The magistrate, despite his disbelief in her charges of violence and coercion, agreed that "Mabel's conduct was satisfactory until she started seeing a young Indian boy .... We will put this girl in a home. We can't have her running around with Indian boys like that."[64]

[...]

Both the working-class families involved and the court officials perceived non-white men and women as more sexually promiscuous and feared whites would become tainted or seduced by these lax morals (though in the few cases involving Chinese men, it is clear that fears centered on their supposed roles as pimps and drug pushers). One father swore out a statement against his 19-year-old, a mail clerk at Simpsons in Toronto: the main complaint was that she was "keeping bad company ... she is now with a coloured man and pregnant by him." The case was originally brought to the attention of the police by a Catholic welfare agency whom the girl contacted, hoping for assistance so she could keep her baby. They alerted the police, talked to the parents, and urged the woman to give up her baby, facilitating her return home to her parents after her sentence.[65] Although it was invariably the woman who was incarcerated, these cases also indicate the extent to which the sexuality of non-white men was viewed suspiciously and regulated and censured more stringently than that of white men.[66]

[...]

The various perceptions of different ethnic groups in sentencing reports were more complex. The authorities were often interested for deportation purposes in whether the person was a recent immigrant: such women were most likely to be Irish, Scottish, or English, not from other areas of Europe. What most concerned the court, regardless of ethnicity, was a woman's willingness to support herself; whether she was considered feeble-minded, what her sexual practices were, and the role she played in the family. Ethnicity, however, was still intertwined with judgments about sexuality and morality in the pronouncements of some magistrates, police, and social workers. It is significant that the designation white, British, or English was absent from the majority of case files: whiteness and an Anglo background were never considered important rationalizations for women's immorality. In contrast, if there were non-Anglo people involved, ethnicity was more likely to be mentioned, with the implication that this explained the presence of immorality.

[...]

■ ILLEGITIMACY AND VENEREAL DISEASE AS RATIONALES FOR INCARCERATION

Next to sexual promiscuity, the two most significant factors in women's files are illegitimate children and venereal disease. Some officials literally used the Mercer as a home for unwed, poor mothers. A Hamilton magistrate sent a pregnant twenty-year-old with no parents and no means of support, as the father of her first child had left, to Mercer: "This girl has no one to care for her and seems unable to look after herself. She gave herself up at the police station as she was ready to be confined."[67]

Married and older women were more likely to be incarcerated after they had produced too many illegitimate children, less likely to be incarcerated for promiscuity. As one judge noted: "It is not often we have a married woman with two children up [for promiscuity] ... but if there is anybody leading an idle and dissolute life, this woman is leading it."[68] The married woman in question was seen as a particular problem because she was not living with her husband and family but, rather, had an apartment that she and her friends used for sexual encounters—in particular, she had supposedly encouraged the sexual activity of a teen who was a minor. Despite evidence of alcoholism, poverty, and lack of housing for her family, the court was more concerned with "how many" men she had slept with. In court, she claimed the police had "got her all excited" and encouraged her to exaggerate these numbers. Nonetheless, she clearly failed the "how many is too many test"; this, along with the fact that her sexual liaisons were with soldiers from nearby Camp Borden, clinched her incarceration.[69]

[...]

The most angry denunciations of women with illegitimate children often came from welfare authorities or CAS officials, who saw these children as a further burden on the state. Sometimes they tried to block these women's paroles back into the community.[70] These cases were especially noticeable during the Depression, but they were not entirely limited to it. In a small town near Windsor, the mayor, who happened to double as the relief officer in the 30s, had a woman with four illegitimate children charged.

Though the mother claimed "she took care of her children and had a house," she was on relief, a cause of considerable aggravation to the mayor, especially since the woman refused to name all the fathers of her children, claiming one was just known to her as "Harry" and another had married her girlfriend, whom he also got pregnant.[71] Such narratives, implying a nonchalant view of sex, only fueled the antipathy of the welfare or CAS authorities involved. After being pronounced mentally defective, this woman was later sent to the Cobourg Asylum indefinitely.

[...]

Incarceration for producing illegitimate children could also happen to young teens. If there was no obvious father/potential husband in sight, her pregnancy was seen by some parents as evidence that their daughter was out of sexual control. Even more upsetting to families was a second pregnancy, which was far from uncommon; for prison officials the second pregnancy signaled the need for an IQ test. The high number of women incarcerated who also delivered babies while in jail is very striking, and the experience of being transported, under guard, from a jail to the hospital to give birth without friends or family must have been a frightening and alienating experience. [...]

Finally, the FRA was also used as a means of enforcing treatment for venereal disease, though again this was often intertwined with a pregnancy and charges of promiscuity. City solicitors, public health officials, and CAS workers all appealed to magistrates to have girls and women taken away because they had either rejected medical treatment or refused to stop having intercourse. Magistrates also ordered investigations for venereal disease, either before or after imprisonment for sexual offenses. Presumption of venereal disease was so strong in the case of multiple partners, in fact, that women were sometimes treated even if their tests were negative. "She did not test positive," noted one report, but "we gave her three months of vaginal treatment anyway."[72] Some were treated for both syphilis and gonorrhea even though the tests were negative.[73] Little wonder that one woman "ran away from the Toronto General Hospital as she was afraid of continued painful treatment for VD."[74] [...]

■ EXPLAINING WOMEN'S SEXUAL NONCONFORMITY

The FRA case files tell us more about how these women were perceived by those in authority than about the convicted women's own perceptions. Even the statements of parents are often overshadowed by the final judgments supplied by police, CAS officials, and the magistrates themselves. The latter group clearly saw these women as aberrant and abnormal and as potential if not real criminals. They believed women's sexual behavior was pathological and harmful both to the women themselves (who they thought had little self-respect) and to the larger community (by encouraging bad moral standards). A woman's sexual identity and desire were thus not private matters: they were the focus of intense scrutiny and management by "these engineers of the human soul,"[75] whose expert status and legal authority invested them with tremendous power to censure what was criminal, immoral, good, or bad.

At first glance, the FRA sentencing reports appear to reflect, above all else, patriarchal definitions of female sexuality.[76] The creation of categories of good and bad girls, and of moral and immoral women, through the raw power of the legal system, proscribed women's sexuality within the bounds of a gender order defined by hegemonic masculinity and the sanctification of the nuclear, father-headed family. Though these norms are often equated with the middle class, they were clearly shared, to a degree, by working-class families. Again and again, it was women's perceived promiscuity, sometimes accompanied by their venereal disease or their production of illegitimate children, that was the crowning reason for their imprisonment. Women's public poverty might be tolerated; their sexual license would not be.

Yet the constructed definitions of women's immorality by those in authority are not without internal contradictions: the FRA women are sometimes seen as potential sexual victims, sometimes as a sexual danger. Still, if any unity can be discerned, it is the focus on women's sexuality being out of control, beyond the bounds of family, propriety, and morality: these women were more likely to be portrayed as sexual aggressors and as purveyors of disease rather than as victims of seduction and betrayal.

[...]

Attempts to regulate female sexuality were class- and race-specific. In social work discourses the very concept of "sex delinquency" used to diagnose and censure these women had become fused with images of working-class, poor (and often non-Anglo) women.[77] The categories of idleness (refusing to fit into the work ethic of capitalist society) and dissoluteness (refusing to accept dominant notions of sexual morality) were often closely intertwined and condemned in the eyes of the authorities. Moreover, the material and social positioning of the women arrested—who were overwhelmingly poor and working-class—had a direct bearing on how their sexual morality was regulated. As Foucault argued, sexual control is often most "intense and meticulous when it is directed at the lower classes."[78]

The explanations offered by these experts in the sentencing reports for women's misdeeds often drew on a medical, rational, and scientific language, but they were also clearly ideological, working to create meanings of women's behavior that perpetuated a double standard and portrayed women's sexual activity as dangerous if it was expressed outside of marriage. Despite their attempts to probe the social causes of the woman's downfall, many legal and medical assessors ultimately could not resist presenting women as "authors of their own unhappy fate, or victims of internal pathological processes."[79] Moreover, the experts' definitions of the environmental causes of immorality simplistically assumed those with disabilities were "innately promiscuous,"[80] read feeble-mindedness into women's behavior, or condemned divorce, separation, and common-law relationships as causing immorality. The criteria measured by social workers in their home visits to the women's families—including educational level, leisure pursuits, language, stable employment—also indicated inherent class and race biases. Metaphors of pollution and decay and the inevitable linking of poverty to immorality in their assessments betrayed both the distance between the experts and the women jailed, as well as the way in which the experts' scientific explanations collapsed into subjective moral judgments.

[...]

Women's claims of family violence were duly noted, and could be perceived negatively, but violence commanded little explanatory power as a reason for women's alienation and rejection of their proper sexual roles. One woman who the authorities admitted was "mature" and intelligent, ran away at 15 from parents who "used excessive physical punishment." Her escape from the home was cemented by a marriage to a 23-year-old soldier (which she later regretted); when discovered, she was sent to a girls' training school and then to Mercer because she became more and more rebellious, with "tantrums and emotional outbursts." What was a rational strategy for the girl—leaving violent parents and trying to escape through marriage—was constructed as incorrigibility by the authorities. No wonder the girl protested all the more vehemently, claiming "she has not committed an offense and can look after herself."[81]

The same insensitivity to violence was sometimes found in women's stories of rape, which were often discounted because these women had already been defined as promiscuous. One woman who claimed to have been gang-raped at one point, for instance, has a "story to tell":[82] the authorities clearly did not place much confidence in her account of events. Perhaps most disturbing was the disinclination to take all incest cases seriously. Incest was seen as reprehensible, but sometimes both the police and the CAS avoided rather than confronted its existence, and there was little inclination to see in-cest as one reason for girls' rejection of the dominant sexual mores.

[...]

◼ WOMEN'S RESPONSES

In response to descriptions of their immorality in court, the majority of women simply remained silent, refusing to respond or cooperate, or they agreed with the magistrate that they had been immoral. Their silence and acquiescence, however, could be read as resignation and a realization of the power of the court rather than acceptance of the judgments being made. A minority of women, though, rejected some of the sup-positions of those sentencing them. Some, like the women above, offered their own explanations for their behavior, citing overbearing, excessively strict parents, unhappy foster care, or domestic violence as their reasons for rejecting social norms.

[...]

The fact that this minority of women offered up frank comebacks, exaggeration, and bravado does suggest they attempted to create their own sexual standards, resisting those being articulated by the court. When one woman was offered an escape hatch by the magistrate, who wanted to know if her late nights were simply forgetfulness or willfulness, she answered abruptly, "Willfulness." She was incarcerated.[83] [...]

Many teens being accused of promiscuity cited peer pressure as an explanation for sexual activities, but still with a measure of defiance. Explaining her wild night in Peterborough, the Lindsay girl described above simply said she needed recreation: "I need some friends," she shot back at the judge when he was lecturing her.[84] Another teen refused to let the magistrate define her activities. "Q: Were you in the habit of hav-ing intercourse with boys? A: Not in the habit. It happened a few times. Q: Is W, your girl friend, wild too? A: She is not wild, but she has a lot of fun in her. Q: What led you astray? A: I don't know what you mean, I just picked up with a crowd that thought this kind of thing was smart. Q: You found out your mistake now? A: silence."[85]

Women who were in court for having too many illegitimate children sometimes also challenged the verdict. Some refused to give the name of the father even if they knew it.[86] Others tried to suggest that pregnancy was a private matter and no business of the court, as long as they worked or supported themselves. A pregnant woman in her twenties, with a history of two illegitimate children given up to the CAS, tried to point out that the latest father would support her if she could find housing, and in response to the magistrate's claim that she was "having a high old time" sleeping with many men, she countered angrily that "she worked pretty well every summer night and day." The magistrate noted disapprovingly that her sister also had an illegitimate child (as if this was an inherited problem), and charged that she would become a burden on welfare: "This girl has not been working, is living off relations and could not work .... But the main feature is her continuing relations with men despite two illegitimate children." The woman, however, had the last word, offering pragmatic disregard for the magistrate's standards of sexual propriety. "Why do you continue to have intercourse with this man?" he demanded about the latest father. "I'm already in the family way," she shrugged. "What does it matter now?"[87]

Finally, once in the reformatory, some women continued their rebellion. Many of the women who started off at Belmont House were actually transferred to the Mercer because of their attempts to run away, throwing bedsheets out the window to climb down or breaking windows, and so on. Others were transferred after swearing at the matrons and sometimes hitting them or other prison attendants. In the Mercer, a few tried to disagree with the doctors who were interviewing them, offering up alternative assessments of their problems; others confronted the petty rules with daily disobedience. The more courageous tried to escape the prison altogether: the married woman convicted for sleeping with too many Camp Borden soldiers attempted a bold escape that led to demands by the matron that she be "strapped."[88] Indeed, these women appeared to have a high number of misdemeanours and punishments within the correctional system, which were all the more noticeable because of the overwhelming pressure in such institutions to conform in order to secure parole, as well as to avoid solitary confinement.[89]

■ THE FINAL CURE

Some women, who made no response at all to their sentences, may not have been consciously resisting the court's assessment, for some FRA women were simply broken and unresponsive human beings: they were completely destitute, alcoholic, or disabled. One woman, for example, apparently mentally slow and unable to work, was found in a chicken coop living on scraps of food. For this woman, the FRA was used as a last resort to ease her poverty, as it was also used as a last resort for the promiscuous woman. In both cases, however, incarceration was a drastic, irrational, and certainly unjust response to these women's lives.

Once incarcerated, the cures offered to the women assumed that their dissolute and idle behavior could be eliminated with an emphasis on hard work, good manners and

clean language, and personal self-control and discipline.[90] A central part of this training reinforced an ideal of female domesticity as well as sexual passivity. Women were
trained in household skills, or sometimes in female-type jobs, and many were released
to become domestics.

Behind the language of reform and personal change used by the reformatory was
the stark and brutal reality of discipline designed to coerce the woman's psyche and
soul into a new mould. Far from a subtle process, this could well be called social control—with all its implications of one group using its inordinate power to refashion the
morals and character of another group. The second chance the women received in the
Mercer included punishment (sometimes solitary confinement) for bad language, disobedience, or physical rebellion; isolation from friends and family, with limited visiting
days; circumscribed and limited reading material; forced and uncomfortable medical
treatment and work; sometimes control of access to their babies; and curbs put on sexual and intimate relationships with other women prisoners.

As other historians have pointed out, the coercive side of penal discipline was combined with a modicum of nurturing, care, and personal attention, including basic food
and medical care. One revisionist current even lauds the Mercer Reformatory for the
kind, maternal care provided by the matrons.[91] Even if it was run by women with good
intentions, this cure was not a home as much as a prison with high walls around it.
Ultimately, both strategies of kindness and coercion were designed to alter the will of
the subjects, so much so that they would then come "to monitor and correct their own
deviation."[92]

How much these women completely absorbed their disciplinary cures is difficult to
say; even though the majority did not return to the Mercer, some may have simply hidden their sexual activities better than before. Scholars studying marginalized women
have recently pointed to the problems in measuring women's resistance to such discipline and, indeed, in "finding direct access to their experiences and subjectivity."[93]
Their voices come to us through the enigmatic, sometimes contradictory narratives
they and their regulators left for us; such case histories, as Kunzel points out, indicate
how difficult it is to disentangle "women's experiences from the narrative means they
used to represent themselves."[94] Nonetheless, their stories do illuminate the relations
of power, the discord and antagonisms framing the relations between the woman condemned and those looking for her ritual confession. And whatever the constructions of
women's sexual nonconformity both by the authorities and by the women themselves,
we should not forget that the ensuing discipline they faced involved a denial of liberty
and freedom and an appalling level of punishment to body and to soul. Their experiences included condemnation of their values and lives, giving birth alone without
family or friends, and the social isolation, pain, and despair of incarceration in a cold

jail cell. The few who attempted to escape or the many who tried to conform may have all been acting with one goal in mind: securing release from a regime of punishment designed to censure their errant sexuality.

■ CONCLUSION

A short list of the qualities most condemned in the FRA women tells us much about the dominant ideals of femininity and its polar opposite, the bad woman in the 1930s and early 1940s. The FRA women most rebuked were those who were described as willful, stubborn, disobedient to elders and family, overly sexual or easily led to engage in sex, lacking in sexual guilt, having no sense of appropriate sex partners, and disrespectful of marital boundaries with regards to sex.

If this was the definition of the bad woman, then one must assume that women's proper role was to acquiesce to their conventional marital and maternal role, to accept traditional lines of familial authority, to avoid premarital and extramarital sex, and assume a position of sexual passivity rather than assertiveness in response to men. If located outside of these boundaries, women's sexuality was potentially a danger. Some elements of this image, particularly the emphasis on sex only within the proper bounds of women's familial role, resembled 19th-century legal and social prescriptions,[95] but it was now articulated in an era that claimed some sympathy for women's sexual fulfilment and autonomy.

These prescriptions for sexual behavior created a locus of discipline that cast its net far wider than the legal and correctional system. As Foucauldian scholars have emphasized, penal punishment becomes part of a broader system of moral regulation within the larger cultural formation by normalizing some behaviors, pathologizing others, and setting out definitions of good/bad, abnormal/normal for all of society. The definitions of women's sexuality bolstering the FRA, given authority and prestige by legal and social science discourses of the time, "permeated all social groups, so much so that punitive powers of moral enforcement were dispersed throughout civil society, ordering self repression for all, even of the repressors themselves."[96]

Though couched in the expert language of clinical analysis, the definitions of women's sexual perversity or promiscuity were also at heart moral, indeed, ideological judgments that went far beyond mere condemnations of sex in cars: they reinforced notions of inherent differences between male and female sexuality, linking natural female sexuality to passivity and premarital purity. Connected to these moral anxieties were other fears at the core of FRA prosecutions: it was also an attempt to preserve the prevailing form of nuclear, patriarchal family in which the wife was monogamous and played a domestic role and the daughter a dutiful and chaste apprentice. The protection of these roles, which had both material and social power attached to them, were inextricably linked to the regulation of women's sexuality.

Moreover, the sexual nonconformity of these women triggered other anxieties linked to class, race, and eugenic concerns. For one thing, women's material impoverishment always encouraged the likelihood of their arrest under the FRA, and their lack of economic support was tied to images of dissolute behavior. Also, police, social workers, and judges had clear suppositions about what constituted a moral home; invariably, the material and social measurements they applied saw working-class—and especially the poorest working-class—homes, or those with people of color in them, as more likely to produce immorality and illegitimacy. Third, these experts were also determined to limit the reproduction of these women, whom they saw, in eugenic terms, as less fit.

While the dominant definitions of sexual morality were endorsed, first and foremost, by the legal, medical, and social work professionals interrogating the women, they were shared by many working-class parents who also saw a precarious line between sexual immorality and respectability. Accepting some of the same suppositions about the patriarchal family and female sexuality, they applied similar—though not always identical—standards to their own daughters. The process of censuring women's sexuality, though organized and institutionalized by the state, was also created in informal spheres such as the family, with consent to this regulation organized around the reassurance that women were being protected and the family preserved.

The process of censuring women's sexuality must thus be located within the material and social inequalities of an ethnocentric class society; how this was worked out ideologically, though, had much to do with the dominant culture of "masculinist hegemony."[97] The meanings of women's sexuality, which were constructed, reinforced, and applied in the courtroom, reflected a set of power relations that ultimately authorized patriarchal social relations. The representation of women's sexuality and reproductive capabilities, and their discipline with stiff jail terms, reflected a power structure that controlled women's reproduction and also punished female sexual desire, assertiveness, and experimentation in a manner quite distinct from the formal and informal sexual regulation of heterosexual men.[98] No equivalent law was used to incarcerate heterosexual men between the ages of 15 and 35 for promiscuity. And the familial model the law implicitly reinforced stressed adult and masculine authority structures.

While some Foucauldian scholars eschew the designation *repressive* to describe the process of disciplining sexual behavior, the word does have some symbolic resonance with regard to this very extreme, coercive example of the FRA. And though we should preferably employ the concept of social censure rather than the discredited social control to characterize the FRA, the latter may be a fitting political metaphor of protest for a process that took away women's most basic liberties, encouraged their sterilization, and discouraged them from keeping their children. There are certainly examples of women's resistance to this law and of their ambiguous attempts to redefine their own sexuality, but the power of their resistance did not, at least in this instance, match the authority of the law.

■ NOTES

My thanks to Lykke de la Coeur, Bryan Palmer, Tamara Myers, Marg Hobbs, and Karen Dubinsky for comments on an earlier version of this article.

1. Archives of Ontario (hereafter, AO), Ministry of Correctional Services, Mercer Reformatory for Women, RG 20, D-13, Case File 7372 (hereafter, Mercer Case Files).

2. AO, Mercer Case File 7474.

3. AO, Mercer Case File 6932.

4. Emphasis is mine. Women did not have to be convicted of a crime to be sentenced to an industrial refuge. See Allan Dymond, *The Laws of Ontario Relating to Women and Children* (Toronto, 1923), pp. 82–111. For a description of the different correctional institutions, see Ontario, Royal Commission on Public Welfare, Report (Toronto, 1930). Belmont was privately run, but received a per capita grant from the provincial government and also the city.

5. As Dymond notes, women could also be incarcerated if, because of "bad habits" like drunkenness, they were unable "to protect themselves" (Dymond, p. 84).

6. This change came after an inquest into the suicide of a young woman in a house of refuge in Toronto (*Globe and Mail* [April 12, 1919]).

7. Royal Statutes of Ontario (RSO), 1897, c. 311, *An Act Respecting Houses of Refuge for Females*; RSO 1919, c. 84, *An Act Respecting Industrial Refuges for Females (The Female Refuges Act)*, see esp. sec. 15; RSO, 1927, c. 347, secs. 15, 16, 17.

8. Ontario, Legislative Assembly Debates (March 1958), p. 742.

9. Mariana Valverde, "Introduction," in *Studies in Moral Regulation*, ed. Mariana Valverde (Toronto, 1994), p. v. See also Mariana Valverde and Lorna Weir, "The Struggle of the Immoral: Preliminary Remarks on Moral Regulation," *Resources for Feminist Research* 18 (1988): 31–34.

10. For example, Philip Corrigan and Derek Sayer, *The Great Arch: English State Formation as Cultural Revolution* (Oxford, 1985). The earlier work of E.P. Thompson and Douglas Hay delineated how the definitions of crime, justice, and mercy were ideological legitimations for the rule of "bourgeois" law in society—though these notions have been used as a means of resistance to class power. See Douglas Hay, ed., *Albion's Fatal Tree:*

Crime and Society in Eighteenth-Century England (London, 1974). On ideology, see also Paul Craven, "Law and Ideology: The Toronto Police Court, 1850–80," in *Essays in the History of Canadian Law*, ed. David Flaherty (Toronto, 1982), 2:248–307. For comment on the Marxist tradition in regard to women, see Shelly Gavigan, "Marxist Theories of the Law: A Survey, with Some Thoughts on Women and the Law," Criminology Forum 4 (1983): 755–90; or for a review of Canadian works, see Brian Young, "Law in the 'Round,'" *Acadiensis* 16 (1986): 155–64. For a comparative view of Marxist and Foucauldian interpretations of punishment, see David Garland, *Punishment and Modern Society: A Study in Social Theory* (Chicago, 1990).

11. These debates are problematic because of the multiple, differing definitions of social control, social censure, and moral regulation that confuse the field. The actual differences between social control and moral regulation are not always spelled out in great detail by many scholars; many authors assume the concepts are different—but not for the same reasons. In fact, like moral regulation, social control was never a unitary "theory" but encompassed debates and various approaches. Some Foucauldian explanations for the "engineering of the soul" like Nicholas Rose's *Governing the Soul: The Shaping of the Private Self* (New York, 1990) sound more top-down to me than social control theory; some writing using social control theory, like Nicole Rafter's *Partial Justice: Women in State Prisons, 1800–1935* (Boston, 1985), takes better account of gender than Foucauldian theory, for example.

12. For the definition of critical (or revisionist) social control theory, see Stanley Cohen, "The Critical Discourse on 'Social Control': Notes on the Concept as a Hammer," *International Journal of the Sociology of Law* 17 (1989): 347–57. See also essays critical of social control in Stanley Cohen and Andrew Scull, eds., *Social Control and the State: Historical and Comparative Essays* (Oxford, 1983).

13. Dorothy Chunn and Shelly Gavigan, "Social Control: Analytical Tool or Analytical Quagmire?" *Contemporary Crises* 12 (1988): 107–24. See also Linda Gordon, "Family Violence, Feminism and Social Control," *Feminist Studies* 12 (1986): 453–78; Dawn Currie, "Feminist Encounters with Postmodernism: Exploring the Impasse of Debates on Patriarchy and Law," *Canadian Journal of Women and the Law* 5 (1992): 63–86.

14. Mary Odem, *Delinquent Daughters: Protecting and Policing Adolescent Female Sexuality in the United States, 1885–1920* (Chapel Hill, NC, 1995).

15. See Cohen for an attempt to move beyond an "essentialist" use of the concept and one that is based on empirical and specific questions.

16. Rafter, *Partial Justice*, p. 157.

17. Cohen, pp. 349–50.

18. Carolyn Strange, *Toronto's Girl Problem: The Perils and Pleasures of the City, 1880–1930* (Toronto, 1995), pp. 12, 213.

19. For example, see Carol Smart, "Disruptive Bodies and Unruly Sex: Historical Essays on Marriage, Motherhood and Sexuality," in *Regulating Womanhood: Historical Essays on Marriage, Motherhood and Sexuality*, ed. Carol Smart (London, 1992), and *Feminism and the Power of the Law* (London, 1989); and Irene Diamond and Lee Quinby, eds., *Feminism and Foucault: Reflections on Resistance* (Boston, 1988). As Susan Bordo has noted, some of the visionary power attributed to Foucault on some of these issues—like the social construction of women's bodies—was already a part of feminist pre-Foucault thinking. See Susan Bordo, "Feminism, Foucault, and the Politics of the Body," in *Up against Foucault: Explorations of Some Tensions between Foucault and Feminism*, ed. Caroline Ramazanoglu (New York, 1993), pp. 179–202.

20. Michel Foucault, *The History of Sexuality: An Introduction*, vol. 1 of *The History of Sexuality*, trans. Robert Hurley (New York, 1980), p. 45.

21. Colin Sumner, "Foucault, Gender and the Censure of Deviance," in *Censure, Politics and Criminal Justice*, ed. Colin Sumner (Philadelphia, 1990), p. 29. This problem may not be true in feminist appropriations of Foucault. See Jana Sawicki, *Disciplining Foucault: Feminism, Power and the Body* (New York, 1991), pp. 33–48.

22. Lois McNay, *Foucault and Feminism* (Boston, 1992), p. 47.

23. Nancy Hartstock, "Foucault on Power: A Theory for Women?" in *Feminism/Postmodernism*, ed. Linda Nicholson (New York, 1990), pp. 157–75. See also Karlene Faith, "Resistance: Lessons from Foucault and Feminism," in *Power/Gender: Social Relations in Theory and Practice*, ed. H. Lorraine Radtke and Henderikus J. Stam (London, 1994), pp. 36–66.

24. What Foucault thought about the "extra-discursive" is open to contention. For one view, see Maureen Cain, "Foucault, Feminism and Feeling: What Foucault Can and Cannot Contribute to Feminist Epistemology," in Ramazanoglu, ed., pp. 73–96.

25. Colin Sumner, "Re-thinking Deviance: Towards a Sociology of Censure," in *Feminist Perspectives in Criminology*, ed. Lorraine Gelsthorpe and Allison Morris (Philadelphia, 1990), pp. 15–40. See also his later "Foucault, Gender and the Censure of Deviance"; and Paul Roberts, "Social Control and the Censure(s) of Sex," *Crime, Law and Social Change* 19 (1993): 171–86.

26. Sumner, "Re-thinking Deviance," pp. 28–29.

27. Regina Kunzel, *Fallen Women, Problem Girls: Unmarried Mothers and the Professionalization of Social Work, 1890–1945* (New Haven, CT, 1993), pp. 5–6.

28. Christina Simmons, "Modern Sexuality and the Myth of Victorian Repression," in *Passion and Power: Sex in History*, ed. Kathy Peiss and Christina Simmons (Philadelphia, 1989), pp. 157–73.

29. Angus McLaren, *Our Own Master Race: Eugenics in Canada, 1885–1945* (Toronto, 1990); Jennifer Stephen, "The 'Incorrigible,' the 'Bad' and the 'Immoral': Toronto's

Factory Girls and the Work of the Toronto Psychiatric Clinic," in *Law, Society and the State: Essays in Modern Legal History*, ed. Susan Binnie and Louis Knafla (Toronto, 1995), pp. 405–42.

30. About 327 FRA case files have been examined for these four decades. However, the act was primarily used in the 1930s (about one-third of the cases) and the 1940s (40 percent of the cases). Just over 60 percent of all incarcerations took place during the Depression and war years. I have focused on these years as the peak of FRA prosecutions; some variations in the cases—including the incarceration of more Native women—were apparent by the 1950s, and I discuss them in another article (in progress).

31. Strange, *Toronto's Girl Problem* (n. 18 above), pp. 175–208. Similarly, Odem implies that there was declining concern with sexual delinquency after World War I (*Delinquent Daughters* [n. 14 above], p. 189).

32. See Strange's excellent explication of the way in which working-class women's sexuality was seen as a metaphor for social disorder in the period before World War I in *Toronto's Girl Problem*. The FRA case files I use come from across the province.

33. Dorothy Chunn, *From Punishment to Doing Good: Family Courts and Socialized Justice in Ontario* (Toronto, 1992).

34. Wendy Ruemper, "Locking Them Up: Incarcerating Women in Ontario, 1857–1931," in Binnie and Knafla, eds., pp. 351–78.

35. Dorothy Chunn, "Maternal Feminism, Legal Professionalism and Political Pragmatism: The Rise and Fall of Magistrate Margaret Patterson, 1922–34," in *Canadian Perspectives on the Law and Society: Issues in Legal History*, ed. W. Wesley Pue and Barry Wright (Ottawa, 1988), pp. 91–118.

36. Kunzel (n. 27 above), pp. 63–64. For discussion of this problem in the Progressive era, see Odem, pp. 128–56.

37. Margaret Hobbs, "Gendering Work and Welfare: Women's Relationship to Employment, Unemployment and Social Policy during the Great Depression" (Ph.D. diss., University of Toronto, 1994).

38. Ruth Roach Pierson, *They're Still Women after All: The Second World War and Canadian Womanhood* (Toronto, 1986), pp. 169–87.

39. Many of the case files are incomplete in terms of such information. An immigrant was often noted if there was a possibility of deportation.

40. About 45 percent of women incarcerated in the 1930s had an illegitimate child; some of these women had more than one.

41. Again, the records are not complete. Some of these women were treated for venereal disease, though their tests were negative.

42. Where there is clear evidence, about 30 percent were initiated or supported by parents, but the number is probably even higher.

43. The problems and possibilities of using such case files are explored in Linda Gordon, *Heroes of Their Own Lives: The Politics and History of Family Violence* (Boston, 1988), pp. 13–17. See also Steven Noll, "Patient Records as Historical Stories: The Case of the Caswell Training School," *Bulletin of the History of Medicine* 69 (1994): 411–28. On women's use of narrative in the courtroom, see my "Pardon Tales from Magistrates Court: Women, Crime and the Courts in Peterborough County, 1920–1960," *Canadian Historical Review* 74 (1993): 161–97.

44. Jill Julius Matthews, *Good and Mad Women: The Historical Construction of Femininity in Twentieth-Century Australia* (Sydney, 1984).

45. Noll, p. 412.

46. I use words like *promiscuity* and *immorality* in an ironic sense throughout this article.

47. AO, Mercer Case File 6282.

48. AO, Mercer Case File 10294.

49. AO, Mercer Case File 9617.

50. AO, Mercer Case File 10708.

51. AO, Mercer Case File 10943.

52. AO, Mercer Case File 8110.

53. *Ibid.*

54. AO, Mercer Case File 6972.

55. AO, Mercer Case File 8115.

56. Steven Schlossman and Stephanie Wallach, "The Crime of Precocious Sexuality: Female Juvenile Delinquency in the Progressive Era," *Harvard Educational Review* 48 (1978): 65–95.

57. As Joy Danousi suggests in another context, such male voyeurism also constructed masculine identity through their fears of and fascination with the "other" (Joy Danousi, "Depravity and Disorder: The Sexuality of Convict Women," *Labour History* 68 [1995]: 30–45). It is worth noting that in a few cases, female social workers displayed the same voyeurism.

58. Another example also makes this clear: "Q: 'How many men in your life have you had improper relations with?' A: 'Four.' Q: 'Count them up carefully now, remember you are under oath, I want to know the truth'" (AO, Mercer Case File 9097).

59. AO, Mercer Case File 8123.

60. AO, Mercer Case File 8153.

61. Some prison discipline regarding women who had friendships with other women (e.g., prohibition of passing notes, etc.) was probably directed at women suspected of homosexual behavior. For some discussion of this in American prisons, see Estelle Freedman, *Their Sisters' Keepers: Women's Prison Reform in America, 1830–1930* (Ann Arbor, MI, 1981), pp. 139–41.

62. AO, Mercer Case File 7733.

63. AO, Mercer Case File 8634.

64. AO, Mercer Case File 9404.

65. AO, Mercer Case File 8700.

66. For related discussion, see Odem (n. 14 above), pp. 80–81; Strange, *Toronto's Girl Problem* (n. 18 above), pp. 155–56; Karen Dubinsky, *Improper Advances: Rape and Heterosexual Conflict in Ontario, 1880–1929* (Chicago, 1993), pp. 88–89.

67. AO, Mercer Case File 8989.

68. AO, Mercer Case File 9900.

69. As a similar file noted, "Strange as it may seem, her husband is willing to take her back" (AO, Mercer Case File 7829).

70. AO, Mercer Case File 8133.

71. AO, Mercer Case File 8710.

72. AO, Mercer Case File 6630.

73. AO, Mercer Case File 6811.

74. AO, Mercer Case File 8129.

75. Nicholas Rose, *Governing the Soul: The Shaping of Private Self* (New York, 1990), p. 3.

76. Despite the critique of patriarchy, as a universalizing and ahistorical concept, I think the word is still useful in this context to denote a gender system in which the dominant family form reflects the material and/or ideological justification of adult and male power and a system in which women's reproduction and sexuality are regulated within an ideology of masculine hegemony and power.

77. In the United States this paralleled anxieties about the sexual mores of immigrant and "foreign" women (Kunzel [n. 27 above], p. 61).

78. He also argues they escaped "the deployment of sexuality" and its amorphous, extensive economy through the body (as opposed to "the alliance of sexuality" that tried to regulate the bourgeois family and the economic order, i.e., property, legitimacy, etc.) longer than middle classes (Foucault [n. 20 above], 1:121). By this time period, however, both these processes of regulating sexuality are evident in women's incarcerations. See Smart's discussion of how the deployment of alliance and deployment of sexuality are relevant to working-class women at different times and in different ways than middle-class women ("Introduction" in Smart, ed. [n. 19 above], p. 32).

79. Unfortunately, this bears similarity to a recent study: Dorothy Chunn and Robert Menzies, "Gender, Madness and Crime: The Reproduction of Patriarchal and Class Relations in a Psychiatric Court Clinic," *Journal of Human Justice* 1/2 (1990): 41.

80. This had been true since the late 19th century. See Nicole Rafter, "Chastising the Unchaste: Social Control Functions of a Women's Reformatory, 1894–1931," in Cohen and Scull, eds. (n. 12 above), pp. 288–311.

81. AO, Mercer Case File 8956.

82. AO, Mercer Case File 8110.

83. AO, Mercer Case File 8140.

84. AO, Mercer Case File 8111.

85. AO, Mercer Case File 8147.

86. AO, Mercer Case File 7851.

87. AO, Mercer Case File 9097.

88. AO, Mercer Case File 9900.

89. As Bronwyn Dalley argues, we should take care not to overemphasize resistance within the institution, when penal discipline so emphatically encouraged and secured the opposite ("Following the Rules? Women's Responses to Incarceration, New Zealand, 1880–1920," *Journal of Social History* 27 [1993]: 309–26).

90. The actual treatment of women in prison could be the focus of another paper. For some discussion of the Mercer's regime in the 1920s, see Carolyn Strange, "The Velvet Glove: Maternalistic Reform at the Andrew Mercer Reformatory for Females, 1874–1927" (Master's thesis, University of Ottawa, 1986).

91. Peter Oliver, "'To Govern with Kindness': The First Two Decades of the Mercer Reformatory for Women," in *Essays in the History of Canadian Law*, ed. Jim Phillips, Tina Loo, and Susan Lewthwaite (Toronto 1994), 5:516–71.

92. Rafter, *Partial Justice* (n. 11 above), p. 157.

93. Strange, *Toronto's Girl Problem* (n. 18 above), p. 11.

94. Kunzel (n. 27 above), p. 103.

95. For example, Dubinsky (n. 66 above); and Constance Backhouse, *Petticoats and Prejudice: Women and Law in Nineteenth-Century Canada* (Toronto, 1991). This is not an argument that these definitions are timeless. On the contrary, many of the FRA files underline how sexual "danger" is historically constructed, for some of the condemnations of women in the 1930s would not be considered reason for incarceration today.

96. Michael Ignatieff, "The State, Civil Society and Total Institutions: A Critique of Recent Social Histories of Punishment," in Cohen and Scull, eds. (n. 12 above), p. 93.

97. Sumner, "Foucault, Gender and the Censure of Deviance" (n. 21 above), p. 37.

98. The sexual regulation of heterosexual men, as this article makes clear, was also fractured by race and ethnicity: liaisons between white women and non-white men were condemned, sometimes terminated, by the incarceration of the women.

CHAPTER 10

"MANHUNTS AND BINGO BLABS":
THE MORAL REGULATION OF ONTARIO SINGLE MOTHERS*

Margaret Hillyard Little

O ntario Mothers' Allowance or Family Benefits was one of the first pillars of welfare state legislation in Canada and helped to lay the groundwork for the state's
involvement in the moral scrutiny of the poor. This article illustrates that the
moral regulation of the poor, often associated with the Victorian era, continues today
through the administration of this policy. Government administrators, neighbours,
and other welfare recipients are all encouraged to examine and report on the daily
behaviour of poor single mothers.

■ INTRODUCTION

> It is time to realize that the poor are neither "worthy" or "unworthy," they are
> simply poor.
>
> (Ontario, 1988: 129)

Every day poor single mothers come face to face with a welfare system which creates
a hierarchy of deservedness. Every day they try to convince their neighbours, teachers of their children, and social workers that they are worthy of the monthly welfare
cheque. Since the introduction of Ontario Mothers' Allowance in 1920, low-income

single mothers have struggled to prove their worthiness as good mothers. This welfare policy, now called the Family Benefits Act (FBA), was initially enacted to support poor widows but later expanded to include deserted, divorced, unwed, cohabiting mothers, mothers with incapacitated husbands, and single fathers. Each new category has called for new types of regulation in order to determine who is and is not worthy. These administrative procedures help to stigmatize the poor and encourage all those around them to scrutinize their daily behaviour. As Josephine Grey, a single mother and leading anti-poverty activist, explained, "When you live on social assistance, you live in Stalinist Russia—your neighbour, your [social] worker, even your friend might report you. You live with all kinds of terrorist fears" (Grey, 1991). These fears have escalated as the Ontario government has begun to cut existing welfare programs and increase the policing of recipients. As of July 1993, single mothers with children over the age of 12 years are pressured to seek work. And *Turning Point*, the most recent government White Paper on social reform, advocates financial incentives for those who find retraining or employment. This article will focus on the contemporary concerns, frustrations, and rebellions of Family Benefits recipients as expressed in interviews with 61 single mothers from six areas of the province and a number of long-term anti-poverty activists, community legal workers, and social workers. Although this policy has liberalized and expanded to some extent over the last 73 years, what is perhaps most surprising is how today's applicants, much as the poor single mothers before them, must submit to intrusive investigation and continually prove their worthiness in order to receive this monthly benefit.

■ MORAL REGULATION AND ITS APPLICATION

Ontario Mothers' Allowance (OMA), enacted in 1920, was one of the first pillars of welfare state legislation in Canada, and helped to lay the groundwork for the state's involvement in the moral scrutiny of the poor. This moral investigation of welfare recipients has not been adequately explored by most welfare scholars. Moral concerns about the poor are generally associated with charity work prior to the 20th century. Many assume that this type of moral scrutiny withered with the emergence of the post-World War II welfare state (Guest, 1980; Splane, 1965). But the history of OMA or Family Benefits suggests that moral questions continue to dominate some areas of welfare legislation. British scholars Philip Corrigan and Derek Sayer and their Canadian colleagues Bruce Curtis, Mariana Valverde, and Lorna Weir have explored what they term the *moral regulation* of citizens. Influenced by Durkheim, Weber, and Foucault, these scholars explore the ongoing processes by which the state and social agencies organize social life. They observe how these practices become a project of normalizing, of rendering natural unequal relationships between the rulers and the ruled. These moral regulatory practices may reinforce class, gender, and/or race interests (Corrigan and Sayer, 1985; Curtis, 1988; Valverde, 1991; Valverde and Weir, 1988).

In a number of ways the concept of moral regulation helps to emphasize certain aspects of this 73-year-old policy which have long been neglected or minimized by other welfare scholars. It is true that there were clear social and economic interests behind the enactment of OMA. There was a deep concern about the growing number of unemployed soldiers; there was also a desire to replace the losses on the battlefield with healthy future citizens, particularly of Anglo-Saxon stock. The gender politics of this era also played a role in the formation of this policy. Women had increased their role in the public arena. They had participated in the job market during the war and were encouraged to return to the home following the war, losing these jobs to men. They had also demanded and achieved the federal vote in 1918. Mothers' allowance provided a neat solution to these social, economic, and gender problems. It could persuade women to leave the paid work to the men, reducing the unemployment problem. It granted public value to the role of motherhood, to the delight of newly enfranchised maternal feminists. At the same time it ensured the continuance of healthy male workers and healthy future workers. As such this policy encouraged women into an economic, social, and sexual dependent relationship within the family.

But these economic interests do not explain the intrusive features of this policy. Charity women played a pivotal role in the introduction of mothers' allowance and consequently the formation of the Canadian welfare state. At the turn of the century a wide range of charity leaders had become anxious about the growing poverty caused by rapid industrialization. These philanthropists believed economic deprivations were at least partly due to drinking, promiscuity, and unsanitary habits. In order to curb these tendencies these social leaders played an intrusive role in the lives of the impoverished. Women performed a pivotal role in these charity organizations and were active in both the naming of the problem and the creation of a solution. As middle-class white women they naturally defined the issue in their own terms. Ensconced in maternal feminist ideals, they condoned mothers who were forced to work outside the home. Through charity organizations they participated in an international campaign which urged the state to recognize the value of child-bearing and alleviate the need for mothers to work by introducing mothers' allowance legislation (Strong-Boag, 1979).

In many ways Ontario Mothers' Allowance closely resembled charity work. First enacted to support poor widows, the Act stipulated that recipients must be "fit and proper persons" (OMA Act, 1920). This allowed for both intrusive scrutiny of the women's lives and enormous discretion on the part of the OMA administrators. Investigators, as the early social workers were called, were encouraged to conduct extremely thorough investigations. In some "particularly difficult" cases it was noted that investigators visited "daily to advise on everything from bedding, care of children, sleeping arrangements, etc." (OMA, 1921–22: 30),

Over time this policy was expanded to include a variety of single mothers. Each category was placed upon a hierarchy of worthiness. Widows were considered most deserving and received the least scrutiny. Women with incapacitated husbands were the second group to receive the allowance and were generally approved provided a medical certificate could prove that their husband was "totally and permanently incapacitated." Deserted wives, on the other hand, were considerably less worthy according to the OMA administrators. Originally the deserted mother had to swear that she had not seen or heard from her husband in *seven* years. This time restriction was a barrier for many impoverished women and children; after considerable protest the period was reduced, but it was not finally removed until October 1991. Similar to deserted women, divorcees were treated with suspicion and were not eligible until 1951. In 1955 the policy expanded to include unemployable single fathers, mothers whose husbands were imprisoned, and unwed mothers. The latter was one of the most controversial groups to receive the allowance. Initially a two-year waiting period was enforced to ensure that these mothers were "fit" to care for their children and that they did not continue their "improper" sexual practices. Eventually this was reduced to three months, but only in October 1991 was this time restriction removed. Separated mothers became eligible in 1979, single able-bodied fathers in 1983, and mothers who cohabited with a man in 1987. The latter amendment was highly contentious and several stipulations were attached to this group. These women can receive the allowance for three years provided the man they live with is not the father to any of the children. After three years of cohabitation they are no longer eligible and the allowance is cut off. Each of these amendments has resulted in both a more inclusive policy but also new methods for morally regulating the lives of poor single mothers.

■ THE VOICES OF POOR SINGLE MOTHERS

Throughout the history of this policy poor single mothers had to prove themselves both financially and morally deserving of the allowance. Based on interviews with groups of poor single mothers this section will focus on their contemporary experiences of the policy. Most of the single mothers interviewed requested that pseudonyms be used to protect their anonymity. Their experiences suggest that they, like single mothers before them, must continually prove their worthiness.

Financial Matters

The boundaries between financial and moral worthiness for a poor single mother have often been blurred. Throughout the history of this policy single mothers were forced to meet the contradictory expectations of both raising and providing for their children. The allowance has always been below subsistence, forcing these mothers to work at least part-time. But paid work always interfered with their other prescribed role as mothers dedicating their lives to domestic duties. Thus poor single mothers have had to juggle two incompatible responsibilities and have often been criticized when they were not up to the task.

In the 1990s financial concerns dominate many poor single mothers' lives. As government budgets are squeezed single mothers experience increased financial scrutiny of their lives. One single mother in Kitchener said her bank book is constantly examined. "Every time they [the social workers] come, they see your bank book. They have a release form, so [they] have access to your bank account at any time" (Mothers and Others Making Change or MOMC, 1991; Hannah, 1991). Others recalled "interrogations" because they had received a gift of furniture, groceries, or clothing from a friend or relative. Still others have their cheques withheld if they are not home when the social worker makes a surprise visit (di Salle, 1991).

Because the monthly benefit remains woefully inadequate, many single mothers spoke about the many ways they survive. Food is one of the few non-fixed items in a single mothers' monthly budget and therefore the one sacrificed to meet rent, hydro, and phone payments. Given the inadequacy of the Family Benefits cheque most mothers do not have enough money to meet the basic Canada's Food Guide requirements (see Figures 1 and 2). Everyone agreed that the last ten days of the month are the toughest. "That's when I hear the rumble in my stomach. That's when there's no milk in the fridge and I have to give my kids dry cereal to eat," said one Kitchener mother (MOMC, 1991), "Those last ten days are really bad for groceries," remembered another mother from North Bay. "I would be counting the slices in a loaf of bread to make sure my son had at least two slices a day but I just couldn't make it" (Low Income People Involvement or LIPI, 1991). Many women said they had to use their food money to pay the rent and then visited the local food bank to make up the difference. Many food banks, however, have placed conditions on the use of their services. In North Bay single mothers on OMA are only permitted to visit twice a month and then they can only receive enough food for three days. In Belleville "you have to show your stub of assistance and [explain] where the money went and if your reasons don't meet with their satisfaction, they say no," explained one single mother (Hannah, 1991). And at least one Salvation Army food bank in downtown Toronto has told FBA recipients that they should only attend once every three months. "They've told us that their food is *really* for those who are newly unemployed—not for us," said one single mother (Fight Back Metro Coalition, 1992).

Table 10.1 Barbara da Silvas's basic monthly budget, single mother with two children

Monthly FBA cheque	$856.40
Rent	441.00
Phone	20.00
Hydro	22.00
Total	483.00 (56.4%)

Paying the above bills at a total of $483.00 taken
from the monthly cheque of $856.40 leaves a
balance of $373.40 (44.6%) to cover all other needs.

Other essentials including clothing, extra medication, personal care, and transportation	$198.02
Subtract $198.02 from $373.40	$175.38
Add baby bonus	64.82
Total	240.22

With $240.22 left for groceries based on a 30-day month,
therefore, Barbara can only spend $2.67 per meal, or 89¢
per meal per person.

Source: Consumer Focus Group Project, Advisory Group on New Social Assistance
Legislation, Ontario government, Toronto, 1992.

Other single mothers find alternative ways to make ends meet between FBA
cheques. For some, bingo provides a way to make a little extra money and socialize at
the same time (Ross, 1984: 212). But bingo participation is often heavily scrutinized.
Single mothers in North Bay have to beware of the "bingo police" or social workers who
attend bingo events, take account of the winners, and then automatically subtract the
amount from the Family Benefits cheque (LIPI, 1991). In Elgin County, neighbours,
referred to as "bingo blabs," are encouraged to tell the Family Benefits office who attended the game (D'Arcy, 1991).

Some single mothers work "under the table" in the underground economy. They
babysit, sell items from mail order catalogues, collect empty beer bottles, whatever they
can to survive. Some set up extra bank accounts or give money to a relative or friend for
safekeeping. "That's called abuse but we don't call it abuse, we call it survival," explains
Jennifer Myers, a long-time anti-poverty activist from Kitchener (MOMC, 1991). A few
single mothers said that their social workers have helped them hide money (MOMC,
1991; Women's Weekly, 1991b).

Table 10.2 Barbara da Silvas's basic meal costs	
Breakfast	
Milk	$1.19
Hot cereal (including sugar)	0.50
Toast	0.17
Juice	0.37
Total	$2.23
Lunch	
Soup	$0.54
Sandwich	
Bread	0.17
Peanut butter	0.12
Honey	0.24
Vegetables — carrots	0.42
Milk	1.19
Total	$2.23
Supper	
1 box of Kraft macaroni and cheese	$0.79
1 lb. ground beef	2.70
1 can of peas	0.69
1 can of corn	0.79
Milk	1.19
3 apples	0.42
Total	$6.58

These meals follow Canada's Basic Food Guide. The cost of all three meals is $11.04. Multiply this by 30 days equals $331.20.

Barbara's grocery money for the month	$240.12
Cost of the above groceries	$331.20
Balance	−$91.08

While Barbara has only $240.12 for groceries, Canada's Food Guide insists you spend at least $331.20 a month for the least expensive meal. How is Barbara supposed to feed herself and her children when she receives only 72.5 percent of the money she needs to feed her family?

$240.22 − 331.20 = 0.725 \times 100 = 72.5\%$

Source: Consumer Focus Group Project. Advisory Group on New Social Assistance Legislation, Ontario government, Toronto, 1992.

Retraining and employment are other arenas for financial scrutiny. Until recently Family Benefits' recipients were only permitted to work part-time. But welfare programs have experienced enormous pressure to reduce costs as a result of the federal government cuts in Canada Assistance Plan funding, the push towards global economic competitiveness, and the popular demand for a reduced and privatized state. Consequently, the provincial government has initiated a number of full-time employment schemes for single mothers and has produced several reports calling for more action in this area. The 1993 White Paper on social reform recommends a form of partial workfare which includes increased scrutiny of recipients and differentiated payments based on retraining and employment (Evans and McIntyre, 1987; Ontario, 1988; 1993). If implemented this plan will exacerbate a growing distinction between the deserving and undeserving, blaming the victims of this devastating recession.

Single mothers have voiced a number of concerns regarding these employment initiatives. Many women said they were unable to participate in such training programs because they could not find subsidized child care and those who had daycare considered themselves exceptionally lucky (LIPI, 1991). Carole Silliker, a long-time anti-poverty activist from Kitchener, is a strong opponent of retraining programs:

> Retraining is a farce. It is [a] band-aid solution .... You learn to be things that the market is saturated with—it makes no sense at all. And they think they're doing us a favour—and it's our fault when there is no job out there at the end. It's a big scam to make them look good. (MOMC, 1991)

There are many other single mothers from rural areas or one-industry towns like Carole who are discouraged by the lack of jobs available.

Those fortunate enough to find paid work have discovered that their new job does not make them more financially secure. Because of their job they have lost their drug benefits, housing subsidy, and child-care subsidy. Most of the single mothers who have jobs work for minimum wage with few, if any, fringe benefits to offset the FBA services they have lost. Since 1975 the purchasing power of minimum wage has declined by 22 percent, leaving a single mother with less ability to make ends meet (Ontario, 1988: 289). One mother explained her frustration during the SARC hearings.

> Even though I'm working I'm making less than if I'd be on Mothers' Allowance which is very discouraging to me. I'm trying to raise four teenagers on a very small budget and I feel I'm sinking lower and lower all the time. (Ontario, 1988: 291)

Single mothers who have found jobs have moved from the unemployed poor to the working poor. They are no longer scrutinized by their social workers or neighbours, but they do continue to live below the poverty line.

While poor single mothers have always had to juggle the incompatible responsibilities of caring and providing for their children, this contradiction will in all likelihood become more profound in the near future. With the increase in unemployment and the reduction in child-care spaces and other support services it is unlikely that most FBA recipients will find jobs. But this emphasis on retraining and employment may encourage the public to blame single mothers who do not find full-time work. This may also result in reduced welfare payments to those who, for whatever reason, remain on Family Benefits.

The persistence of moral regulation

This financial scrutiny of poor single mothers' lives is intertwined with moral issues. It is the visits by the workers and the whispers from the neighbours about how they talk, dress, manage their homes and their children which most irritate and humiliate the FBA recipients interviewed. Even those who now have full-time paid work will never forget the scrutiny they experienced during their years on FBA. At the end of the interview with Sally she said, "This has left such a scar. It's 10 years later and just talking to you—I want to go and cry. It's brought up such terrible memories" (LIPI, 1991).

The blurring of financial and moral scrutiny is most obvious in the case of women with absent male partners. Whereas widows are considered deserving, other mothers experience more intensive investigations to prove their worthiness. In keeping with the male breadwinner ideology, the state demonstrates its reluctance to financially support single mothers when fathers could do so.

In the case of desertion, mothers who know the whereabouts of their husbands are now eligible for the allowance but experience considerable difficulty from the social workers. Deserted mothers complained about social workers pressuring recipients to pursue the man through the Court system. "There's nothing in this battle for me. When I charge him he gets mad and comes after me. And even if he agrees to pay me support I have to claim it as income so I'm no further ahead," explained one mother (Women's Weekly, 1991a). Another recipient remembered the court procedure as both lengthy and emotionally exhausting.

> It was really embarrassing to go through the personal stuff before the lawyer and then the Court. And then the judge said, "If you had two children by him, he can't be all that bad." (Women's Weekly, 1990)

Other mothers try to arrange under-the-table support payments from their husbands, but these agreements are also difficult, as one mother described:

> My Ex pays $100 a month under the table and says he'll stop paying this if I tell Mothers' Allowance—and if I tell Mothers' Allowance they'll go after *me* for fraud. He gets off. I get the blame. (Women's Weekly, 1991a)

The women at one single mothers' group agreed it was best to tell the social worker you did not know the husband's whereabouts. "You're better off saying you got drunk and got raped by several guys than to say there was one," claimed one recipient (Women's Weekly, 1991a).

Unwed mothers also experience intense scrutiny from social workers. One single mother, Dorothy, recounted her story of the social worker's attempt to discover the name of the father.

> The social worker asked, "Well did you *actually* go out with him [the father]?"

> I said, "No, I screwed him on the bar stool—what the hell do you think."

> Then the worker asks, "Do you know his name?" I said I only have his first name, Frank. So she writes that down on her form: F-R-A-N-K. Then she says, "Well have you gone looking for him?" Well yeah, like I'm going to run across the country yelling, "Frank, Frank." (Women's Weekly, 1991b)

Another group which is carefully watched by social workers is women who live with men. The 1987 amendment which permitted cohabitation for a three-year period has done little to reduce home investigations. According to the FBA manual, workers are expected to investigate *every* complaint. "This is an open warrant to investigate a recipient's home at any time, over and over again if they wish," said John Clarke, provincial organizer for Ontario Coalition Against Poverty (Clarke, 1991). And the definition of cohabitation is so broad that it includes eating meals together, babysitting, washing dishes together, going anywhere together (D'Arcy, 1991). This definition provided for FBA workers is not generally made available to FBA applicants and promotes confusion and fear. As one mother said, "I was frightened to have my brother to stay over the night .... No one told me I could" (Women's Weekly, 1991b).

Most of the women interviewed had their own experience of what some call the "manhunt." The bathroom investigation was the most common.

One worker looked behind the shower .... He [the worker] was looking at absolutely everything. They ask to use your washroom, they go through your shaving cream, razors, three toothbrushes. Those are the things they looked for. (Women's Weekly, 1991b)

Another mother recalled a boot investigation at her home.

I had to try on my boots in front of them [social workers] because I took size 11. I had cougar winter boots which could be unisex. It was so humiliating. (LIPI, 1991).

Social workers have also been known to check for tire tracks in the snow, examine fridge notes, search for hunting equipment and evidence of dogs, stake out parking lots at night, throw sand on the doorstep in order to trace footprints—all in an effort to confirm that a man is living in the home (Clarke, 1991; LIPI, 1991; Gunness, 1991).

Many community workers and anti-poverty activists expect these home investigations to escalate as more and more FBA recipients reach the three-year limit for cohabitation. As one legal aid worker warned, "We'd better get used to it because now they're going to start enforcing the three year stuff. I had a meeting with FB workers who hated the new rule, they couldn't wait to get these single moms" (LIPI, 1991).

As well as direct supervision of a woman's intimate relationships, there are also indirect forms of scrutiny. The current FBA regulations in regard to a single mother's sexual practices are contradictory at best. The cohabitation amendment would suggest that the policy now allows a mother to be sexually active, provided it is not with the father of her children. The three-year cohabitation limit encourages short-term rather than long-term relationships, yet the drug plan does not allow for the purchase of a variety of reproductive products. The birth control pill is the only reproductive device permitted by the drug plan. In the era of the AIDS epidemic, condoms are not covered by the drug plan. Binkie, an FBA recipient, is exasperated by this regulation:

I'm 36 years and they would give me the pill but I had to pay for my own diaphragm and gel. Even though I had a doctor's certificate saying I need a diaphragm they still won't pay for it. (Women's Weekly, 1991b)

Concerns about cleanliness, which dominated charity work at the turn of the century, still persist in FBA administration today. As one mother stated,

> Children's Aid Society, cops, society—everyone judges you on cleanliness. The
> teachers in the school system. How they see them [the children] dressed .... (Wom-
> en's Weekly, 1991b)

Another single mother believes social workers expect your house to be especially spotless
if you do not have paid work (LIPI, 1991). Ontario anti-poverty activists and single mothers interviewed acknowledged that social workers continue to comment on a recipient's
cleanliness or lack thereof (di Salle, 1991; Women's Weekly, 1991b; Mott, 1991). A recent
case involving the regulation of poor mothers' cleanliness has occurred in subsidized
New Brunswick housing. Poor women, predominantly single mothers, living in this
housing are forced to take lessons in cleaning which involve childlike picture lessons and
include a 12-step quiz on the cleaning of toilets (see Figure 10.1). These lessons include a
surprise investigation of the resident's home to ensure that she is following the prescribed
regulations. If residents do not take these lessons or do not pass the class they can be denied subsidized housing (New Brunswick Housing Corporation, 1992).

Attitude was very important to early charity workers and still remains significant.
Several mothers interviewed agreed that a humble, grateful attitude was essential when
dealing with the social workers. As one mother explained, "I'm not human to them,
and I have to be subservient, or they just won't even talk to me" (Ontario, 1992).

Race and ethnicity

Whereas all FBA recipients receive a certain degree of financial and moral scrutiny,
women from ethnic minority backgrounds tend to experience a disproportionate
amount. In northern communities many francophone and First Nations single mothers
have difficulties with the FBA administration. In the District of Nipissing 28 percent of
the population is Franco Ontarian and yet there are social workers who do not speak
French and cannot understand the questions of their clients (LIPI, 1991). In regard to
First Nations applicants, few qualify for the benefit, suggesting that the rules and the administration of this program are not sensitive to First Nations' issues (Ross, 1987: 136).

Women of colour also experience racism from social workers. Carolann Wright, a
Toronto activist, has encountered racism both as a poor black single mother and as an
advocate for others.

> I've seen their [the workers'] racist attitudes. Women of colour say that they're
> treated poorly. The workers automatically assume you're not Canadian. You are
> not given enough information. They make disparaging comments. The women
> of colour have more trouble than white women getting the money and any ad-
> ditional benefits. (Wright, 1991)

This racism can also be camouflaged in bureaucratic regulation. When FBA worker Kathleen Lawrence was reassigned to a new work area she noticed that there was a great deal of discrepancy in child-support deductions taken from the monthly FBA cheque of single mothers. These deductions are made when an FBA worker determines that a client did not make adequate attempts to obtain child support from the father. When Lawrence explored the cases of 311 single mothers she discovered that racial minority mothers were six times more likely than white recipients to experience these deductions, regardless of the similarity in their situations. Also she found the deductions charged to racial minority recipients to be considerably higher than those charged to white women (Lawrence, 1990). These bureaucratic decisions reinforced the racist stereotype of the absent and irresponsible black father.

CLEANING THE TOILET

1 Flush the toilet
2 Lift toilet seat
3 Pour in bleach
4 Place warm water and cleanser in a pail
5 Use clean cloth to wipe top of toilet seat
6 Wipe bottom of toilet seat
7 Wipe rim of toilet
8 Wash outside of toilet
9 Scrub bowl with long-handled brush
10 Place brush in holder
11 Flush toilet
12 Replace toilet paper if necessary

Agents of moral regulation

Social workers are not the only people to morally scrutinize FBA recipients' lives. Today FBA workers carry a case load of approximately 330 cases and therefore rarely see the majority of their clients (Ontario, 1988: 241). Others, however, are willing to volunteer to oversee a single mothers' activities. Teachers, landlords, neighbours, police, and charity workers have all been known to spy on FBA recipients and report to social workers. Over and over again the mothers interviewed emphasized that there are very few people they can trust. As one mother explained, "You try not to tell anyone you're on FBA. You feel very threatened" (Women's Weekly, 1991b). There are several instances of social workers bribing FBA recipients to inform on other recipients (di Salle, 1991; Women's Weekly, 1990; 1991b).

Moral scrutiny is particularly rampant in small communities or low-income housing projects. As one woman from North Bay explained, "Small town politics makes it really hard on single moms—there's an awful lot of social stigma. People know what side of the tracks you are from and they never forget it" (LIPI, 1991). Low-income housing projects in urban centres have many similar traits to small-town life. One single mother in Toronto moved out of a housing project and spends almost twice as much money to rent a townhouse in Scarborough. She saw this as the only way to give her children a fighting chance against stigmatization. As she reasoned, "In metro housing there's lots of spying.... The neighbours go to the worker. If you're dressing up too much, they think you're doing drugs or selling them" (Women's Weekly, 1991b).

From the interviews conducted it is clear that FBA recipients encounter moral judgment from a variety of sources. Whether it be the teacher at school, the store owner at the corner, or the neighbour next door, single mothers live with a great deal of moral scrutiny. It is no wonder that single mothers live in fear and self-censor their own activities. Because of the high level of distrust for others and the discretionary nature of FBA administration, single mothers devise complex strategies in order to guarantee their monthly cheque.

■ CONCLUSION

Throughout the history of this policy, poor single mothers have had to prove time and again their worthiness. Although the policy has expanded over its seventy-three-year history to now include a variety of single mothers, with these amendments have come new types of regulations. This is not to deny that change has occurred in this policy, but what is perhaps most remarkable is how Ontario Mothers' Allowance or Family Benefits continues to be intrusive and moralistic, based on discretionary criteria which allow social workers to separate the worthy from the unworthy. These regulations and the relationship between the regulator and the regulated help to reinforce dominant race, class, and gender interests in society at large. Through Mothers' Allowance both the state and other social organizations have been involved in a lengthy process of normalizing the stigmatization and intense scrutiny of poor single mothers.

◼ REFERENCES

Clarke, John. Ontario Coalition Against Poverty. Toronto, Ontario, November 18, 1991.

Corrigan, Philip and Derek Sayer. *The Great Arch: English State Formation as Cultural Revolution.* Oxford: Basil Blackwell, 1985.

Curtis, Bruce. *Building the Educational State: Canada West, 1836–1871.* London: Althouse Press, 1988.

D'Arcy, Richard. Community legal worker. Community Outreach Programs of Elgin County, St. Thomas, Ontario, November 22, 1991.

di Salle, Nick. Former FBA worker, Toronto, Ontario, November 22, 1991.

Evans, Patricia and Eilene McIntyre. "Welfare work incentives and the single mother: An interprovincial comparison." In Jacqueline Ismael, ed., *The Canadian Welfare State: Evolution and Transition,* pp. 101–25, Edmonton: University of Alberta Press, 1987.

Fight Back Metro Coalition. Single Mothers' Workshop, Toronto, Ontario, April 11, 1992.

Grey, Josephine. Low Income Families Together (LIFT). Speech at Democracy Conference, York University. Toronto, Ontario, April 18, 1991.

Guest, Dennis. *The Emergence of Social Security in Canada.* Vancouver: University of British Columbia Press, 1980.

Gunness, Patty. Neighbourhood legal workers. Neighbourhood Legal Services, London and Middlesex County, London, Ontario, November 19, 1991.

Hannah, Laurie. Chair of Citizens for Action. Belleville, Ontario, December 10, 1991.

Lawrence, Kathleen. "Systemic discrimination: Regulation 8—Family Benefits Act: Policy of reasonable efforts to obtain financial resources." *Journal of Law and Social Policy* 6 (1990): 57–76.

Low Income People Involvement (LIPI). North Bay, Ontario, November 28, 1991.

Moscovitch, Allan and Jim Albert, eds. *The "Benevolent" State: The Growth of Welfare in Canada.* Toronto: Garamond, 1987.

Mothers and Others Making Change (MOMC). Kitchener, Ontario, November 19, 1991.

Mott, Ruth. Women for Economic Justice, Toronto, Ontario, December 3, 1991.

New Brunswick Housing Corporation. *Home Orientation and Management Program.* Fredericton, New Brunswick, 1992.

Ontario. "Ontario Mothers' Allowance Act." *Statutes of Ontario,* First Session of the 15th Legislature, Chapter 89, 1920.

———. "Second annual report of the Ontario Mothers' Allowance Commission." *Ontario Sessional Papers*, Vol. LV, Part VIII, 1921–22.

———. *Transitions: Report of the Social Assistance Review Committee.* Toronto: Queen's Printer, 1988.

———. *Consumer Focus Group Project.* Advisory Group on New Social Assistance Legislation, Final Report. Toronto: Queen's Printer, 1992.

———. *Turning Point: New Support Programs for People with Low Incomes.* White Paper, Ministry of Community and Social Services. Toronto: Queen's Printer, 1993.

Ross, Becki. "A feminist reconceptualization of women's work and leisure: A study of Kingston mother workers." M.A. thesis, Kingston: Queen's University, 1984.

Ross, Heather. *First Nations Self-Government: A Background Report.* Prepared for the Social Assistance Review Committee, Toronto, 1987.

Splane, Richard. *Social Welfare in Ontario.* Toronto: University of Toronto, 1965.

Strong-Boag, Veronica. "Wages for housework: Mothers' Allowances and the beginning of social security in Canada." *Journal of Canadian Studies* 14(1): 21–34, 1979.

Valverde, Mariana. *"The Age of Light, Soap, and Water": Moral Reform in English Canada, 1885–1925.* Toronto: McClelland and Stewart, 1991.

Valverde, Mariana and Lorna Weir. "The struggles of the immoral: Preliminary remarks on moral regulation." *Resources for Feminist Research* 17(3): 31–34, 1988.

Women's Weekly, discussion group for low-income women. Toronto, Ontario, May, 1990.

———.Toronto, Ontario, June 19, 1991a.

———. Toronto, Ontario, December 11, 1991b.

Wright, Carolann. Women for Economic Justice, Toronto, Ontario, December 3, 1991.

■ NOTES

*I would like to thank Janet Borowy, John Clarke, Josephine Grey, David Kidd, Leo Panitch, Mariana Valverde, and members of the Toronto Sex History Group for comments on an earlier draft of this paper. Most importantly, I would like to acknowledge the generosity of a number of single mothers across the province who gave their time and details of their lives. Please address all correspondence and offprint requests to Professor Margaret Little, Department of Political Studies, University of Manitoba, 532 Fletcher Argue Building, Winnipeg, Manitoba, R3T 2N2.

ALMOST ANYTHING CAN HAPPEN:
A SEARCH FOR SEXUAL DISCOURSE IN THE URBAN SPACES OF 1940s TORONTO

Mary Louise Adams

In this essay, postwar discourses about urban spaces are investigated for the ways in which they led to the regulation of particular spaces as well as the people who used them. The focus of this research is on Toronto in the late 1940s, when teenagers were one of the primary targets of spatial regulation. In this analysis, moral regulation is as much a product of social meanings as it is of the legislation and policies that such meanings make possible.

This is a paper about urban spaces and the things that people do in them. It is about the way that notions of mortality and sexuality lend meaning to local geographies and amusements. The reputations of places, it will be shown, can have a very real, regulating effect on the people who frequent them.

Moral regulation is often thought of as a product of legislation and policy, restrictive or permissive, that directly targets specific individuals or actions (Corrigan, 1981; Corrigan and Sayer, 1986; Valverde and Weir, 1988). But we also need to look at moral regulation as a consequence of more subtle, less direct processes, in this case discursive constructions of specific types of places as "bad." While this paper does include discussions of legislative measures, it deals primarily with "smaller," less glamorous forms of regulation, from simple expressions of social disapproval to crude neighbourhood "clean-up" attempts. What is important here is that unlike turn-of-the-century moral reform campaigns, many of these postwar efforts did not focus specifically on people but on their environments (Valverde, 1991). Others, while applying directly to specific people, did not necessarily assume the immorality of those individuals, but were intended to protect them from the dangers of an overdetermined local geography. In either case, as we will see, both the environment and those who used it suffered regulatory effects.

■ ON THE WATERFRONT

Waterfronts have a particular role to play in the sexual and moral history of many cities, and so this project begins on the Toronto Islands, an interesting conflation of urban waterfront and seaside resort. When the ferryboat crosses Toronto's harbour it docks at a large but tranquil city park, with acres of grass and trees, public beaches, picnic areas, and bicycle paths. A tiny community of homes, a children's amusement park, and a petting zoo are all that remain of what was once a bustling nightspot and vacation resort (Gibson, 1984). From the late 1800s through the first half of this century, wealthy and middle-class Torontonians escaped urban heat and pollution with annual treks to the island, where their summer homes ranged from tents and small seasonal cottages to large waterfront estates. Hotels and boarding houses catered to the un-propertied vacationer while commercial amusements provided evening and weekend entertainment for those unable, for reasons of money or time, to take extended breaks from the city.

As late as the 1930s, writes island historian Sally Gibson, crowds were coming to Hanlan's beach to dance, to try out the mechanical rides and to take advantage of the many free attractions, from concerts to dancing elephants to whippet races (1984: 181). At that time, she says, Centre Island was a "mecca for sociable, unattached young Torontonians" who lived together in shared rooms and who set the streets of Centre Island "humming" after work hours. Grocery stores, a Dominion Bank branch, dairy services, laundries, and several restaurants catered to seasonal residents.

In the mid-1930s, the population of the island's permanent community was only 300 people. But by the end of World War II, that figure rose to more than 2,000 as city politicians tried to find solutions to Toronto's severe housing shortage (Gibson, 1984: 218; Lemon, 1985). The city had to extend ferry service. Stores began to stay open all year. The Manitou Hotel grew crowded with teenagers and adults alike. In 1950, a 700-seat movie theatre opened on Iroquois Avenue, though its tenure there was to be a short one.

Perceptions of the island as either tawdry pleasure park or romantic small-town resort could lead to widely divergent moral pronouncements on both the place itself and the people residing or visiting there. And, of course, moral pronouncements could have concrete ramifications in terms of people's behaviour and activity. Places, in and of themselves, have no meaning. Without human activity and social discourse, a particular park, alleyway, or commercial amusement centre is no more "immoral," "romantic," or "sexually charged" than another. The island, with its conflicting definitions, is a good example of how social discourse operates to naturalize socially ascribed meanings.

At the turn of the century, C.S. Clark, chronicling the underbelly of Toronto, claimed that young women intent on making "haphazard acquaintances with gentlemen they know nothing about" frequented the island and its commercialized amusement areas. He further suggested, with disapproval, that if one were to frequent the island on Saturday nights one might find numerous couples (presumably heterosexual ones) "en flagrante delecto" [sic] (Clark, 1970). In the 1950s, this sordid image was brought up to date as reporters made reference to "Bohemia on the Bay." In an alliterative frenzy, columnist Hugh Garner referred to people on the island as "denizens of that jerry-built demi-paradise of the deserted, defeated, and demi-mondaine" (Garner, n.d.). Although separated by 60-odd years, Clark and Garner both draw on their audiences' knowledge of urban vice to cast the island in a distasteful sexual light. Contrast their conceptions of the island as seedy urban space with this mid-60s nostalgic recollection of the island as a pleasure-filled, romantic resort:

> In 1946 five ferries were carrying nearly 2,500,000 passengers in the summer. Torontonians flocked to the Islands for canoeing, bicycling, turning blue in Lake Ontario and pink on the hot sands, making love, feeding ducks, riding the merry-go-round, sipping sodas at Ginn's Casino … and listening to Eddie Stroud's dance band. (*Canadian Weekly*, 1963)

Or contrast them with a 1957 prediction in the *Globe and Mail*, attributed to Metro's Parks Commissioner T.W. Thompson, that "[t]he Islands of the future would not feature the hurdy-gurdy sounds. There would be 'necking in the lagoons as usual,'" and "the Islands would be quiet places." In these two examples, the island remains a place of sexual activity, but now we are talking about sex in the context of a summer beach resort, a daytime place. There's also a distinction being made here between sex as romance (making love in the sand) and sex as the "dirty" manifestation of carnal desires ("en flagrante delecto," in the "demi-monde"). It is a distinction rooted in the relationship between the class of those having the sex and the class of those commenting upon it.

Conflicts over the moral character of the island contributed to the protracted battle between city (after 1953, Metro[1]) politicians and island residents that led, eventually, to the levelling of island homes and businesses. In the late 1930s the tackiness of the amusement area on Hanlan's succumbed to progress and the construction of the island airport. Then, during the early 1950s, politicians (with the public support of people like Hugh Garner) began pushing for the eviction of island residents and the transformation of the island's 760 acres into parkland, a family-oriented place that would benefit all Toronto's citizens. This sudden interest came after years of the city neglecting island services. The ensuing state of deterioration was then given as evidence of the need for a massive clean-up. Residents—the Bohemians by the Bay—who had weathered the flooding and the mud were, in some odd way, viewed as part of the decay.

In the late 1950s, after most of the island's businesses and homes had been demolished, Metro's Parks Commissioner told the *Telegram* that his department was "aiming for the tidy untidiness of the average well-kept place." Islanders, on the other hand, perceived Metro's efforts as an "official sterilization" (Gibson, 1984: 252). But modern cities needed modern facilities and wholesome places for families to pursue their recreation. Toronto, like other North American cities in the 1950s, was in need of a new image to reflect its postwar prosperity. In 1948, the city was dubbed "Canada's most important money market"; in 1951 unemployment was only 1.3 percent (Lemon, 1985: 85); between 1945 and 1946, manufacturing wages doubled (Francis et al., 1992: 338); retail sales receipts rose from $400 million in 1941 to $1 billion in 1951, in spite of an unremarkable growth in population (Lemon, 1985: 90). The ramshackle, small-town feel of the pre-demolition island didn't fit the updated version of an increasingly affluent city. Torontonians of the 1950s were tired of make-do wartime facilities. Cleanliness and modern design were prized after two decades of material hardships. Furthermore, the island's reputation as a good-time place was at odds with mainstream 1950s discourses that privileged the home and hearth over outside entertainment. While these factors weren't the only reason for the evictions and the bulldozers, they certainly eased their way. In constructing a pastoral landscape, politicians were able to domesticate both geography and a community.

The amusement park and bathing pavilion at Sunnyside was Toronto's other "Lake Shore Playground" and beach resort in the postwar years. Just west of downtown, Sunnyside was built in 1922. Like the island, it was a place of lakeshore recreation for those city dwellers stuck in the downtown heat and humidity. According to the Toronto *Star* (1956), Sunnyside was known as the "unemployed man's Riviera" during the Depression. Promoted as "Canada's Coney," it catered to 1,500,000 visitors over its 25-week season (*The Standard*, 1949). On especially hot days, 100,000 people might crowd the beach and pool. A flyer for the park reads, "If you haven't seen Sunnyside Beach, you haven't seen Toronto" and describes it as "One of the Best Equipped and Most Modern Amusement Resorts on the Continent." But among many local young people, the park's claim to notoriety was based on its sexual possibilities. Sunnyside was a place close to home for dating and for finding dates. A Toronto *Star* editorial (1956) called it "a naively glamorous 'hang-out' for teenagers."

As an amusement park, Sunnyside's identity was at least partially coloured by popular fears about corruption and vice. In 1949, the notion that linked amusement parks with moral danger permitted *Chatelaine* readers to make sense of the amusement park setting in a moral tale about a girl's near fall from grace (Shallit, 1949: 26–27ff.). The mechanical rides, the games, the mixed-class crowds, the litter and noise of the amusement park brought to mind the atmosphere of a travelling carnival (Kidd, 1971). And as Hazel Elves (1977) points out in her autobiography of Canadian carnival life after the war, carnivals were often thought to house and cater to the immoral and the easy. In the case of Sunnyside, one of the apparent justifications for this opinion—and a sign that the park encouraged a general "letdown in morals"— was the fact that the annual Miss Toronto contest was held there, an event at which "young women would expose themselves in ... a public way" (McAfee, 1947).[2] Girls from "nice families" were warned away from the park because it was "too tacky" and not a "good" place for them to be (R.J. interview, 1992). However, some nice girls went there anyway, without telling their mothers, so they could hang out looking for boys (Adams, personal communication). Again, class fears were fuelled through sexual connotations.

While the park was assumed to be dangerous (with all the sexual connotations of that word) for girls on their own, it was painted as a romantic *endroit* for heterosexual couples. Members of Toronto's Parks Commission took this perception into account as they debated the merits of wood versus concrete for resurfacing the two-mile long boardwalk. The *Globe*'s (1949a) story on their final decision lauds Parks Commissioner Walter Love (sic) who "has struck a blow for romance and refuses to replace the Sunnyside boardwalk with cement which would be cheaper and more durable." Even the rides at the park were thought to provide a setting for romance and physical intimacy:

> When Waldo pays 40 cents to take his girl on the coaster he knows that when they reach the top of the first hill she's going to be looking for masculine protection. So, when the coaster rockets downward, Waldo (who was probably looking for something to hold onto anyway) grabs his girlfriend, she grabs him and everybody is happy. (*Globe and Mail*, 1946c)

Whether one was talking of danger or romance, Sunnyside was a place of sexual potential. The difference in perspective depended on the age of the visitor and the time of the visit.

After the sun went down, Sunnyside was famous for its dance spots. Although the open air floor at the Sea Breeze could hold 3,500 people, there was often a line-up. Admission was five cents per couple per dance until 1945 when entry fees of 50 cents for men and 35 cents for women allowed dancers access to the floor for the entire night. Gross receipts for 1945, from the dance floor alone, were over $61,000 (Taylor, 1946). Next door to the Sea Breeze was the Palais Royale where, during the 1940s, some 2,000 dancers a night would pay a 10-cent admission charge and five cents a dance. Across the street was the Club Top Hat and a mile down the road the huge Palace Pier Ballroom.

While all of these dance spots exploited romantic ideas about the relationship between love and moonlight and water, none did so as blatantly as the huge Palace Pier. Modelled after large seaside developments in England—which had their own reputation as sexy holiday spots (Urry, 1990)—the Palace Pier was designed to be a spectacular pleasure spot and "outstanding landmark" on the western edge of the city. A promotional piece in the 1931 Toronto Yearbook heralded the development which would provide "high-class entertainment" for residents and visitors alike:

> Brighton wouldn't be Brighton without its Palace Pier or West Pier, nor would Blackpool continue to hold the same attraction for its hundreds of thousands of visitors if its three Piers were no more. Even Atlantic city—America's playground for the wealthy—regards Steel Pier and The Million Dollar Pier as two of its greatest drawing cards.
>
> And now Toronto is to have a pleasure Pier at the mouth of the Humber that will surpass in architectural beauty, solidity of construction and scope of entertainment, any similar enterprise either in the Old Country or U.S.A.... (CTA, n.d.)

In spite of this grand pronouncement, only the ballroom was completed and it eventually burned down in 1963. In 1976, a Toronto real estate company ignored this one important detail as it re-invented the history of the Palace Pier in ads for an apartment complex of the same name to be built on the same site:

> The girls in their light cotton dresses. The boys in open collared shirts and lavishly pleated trousers. The daring ones smoked cigarettes. Red lipstick looked black in the moonlight. And the clandestine scent of Evening in Paris mingled with the clean creosote smell of the tar that protected the pier from the lake.

They came to hear a little night music. To flirt. To spoon. To fall in puppy love. To court. To escape the stern Victorian masonry and manners and the hot streets of the city.

... The old Palace Pier has disappeared. A new skyline has grown in Toronto. And now, just to the west of the city's hub, at the very edge of the lake, another tower reaches toward the stars. (CTA, 1976)

Like the island, Sunnyside and the other nightspots along the western beaches were sacrificed by politicians to an ever-changing, ever-demanding modernity. In 1951 city controllers and aldermen agreed that the amusements had to move for a new "super highway." One controller complained about concessionaires protesting the loss of their businesses: "they can't stand in the way of progress" (*Telegram*, 1951). A few years later, Metro Chair Frank Gardiner claimed: "We can't have this honky-tonk at the main entrance to the city on both sides of the main expressway. It should be completely cleared away" (cited by Kidd, 1971). By 1956 everything was gone except the pool, the Palais Royale, and the Palace Pier down the road. The site of the old amusement park lay in the shadow of the expressway that would take Frank Gardiner's name.

With the building of the expressway close to the lakeshore and across the full length of the city, Torontonians without cars were geographically cut off from the waterfront and from both the romance and the tawdriness of its various reputations. While the prime goal of those who developed the Gardiner was to ease traffic congestion along Lakeshore Boulevard, they also managed to curtail a significant measure of the city's summer night life. For young people who could get away to the Kawarthas or the Muskokas or to the broad beaches on Lake Huron and Lake Erie, the "sound of the waves" would continue to provide the backdrop to their romantic and sexual liaisons. But as the shore of Lake Ontario was tidied up and drained of excitement, those of less fortunate economic circumstances had to find romance and sex in more urban, more strictly regulated, surroundings.

◾ REGULATING URBAN SEX

Writing about single women who lived in Toronto during the earlier years of this century, Carolyn Strange (1991) says that unsupervised places of amusement—dance halls, roller rinks, amusement parks—provoked moral indignation and concern among Toronto's reformers. She also notes that "commercial amusements were conflated with commercial sex." Certainly both of these positions continued to hold ground through the 1940s. An editorial in the *Globe and Mail* (1946a) discussed efforts by the police commission to study poolrooms "and other such places where youth congregate .... Indeed, there are some who feel that the poolrooms, as well as some hamburger restaurants, are a menace and should be closed altogether." In a surprising display of social awareness, the *Globe and Mail* countered these suggestions by inverting the relationship they proposed between the social and the environmental: "Like dance halls, beverage rooms and some other places where people meet for entertainment, the conditions under which the places are run are the important factors."

In recognizing the potential for "places" themselves to be neither "good" nor "bad," the *Globe* cut short discussions of simple, blanket solutions for the variety of "youth problems" that came under the headings of delinquency, vice, and immorality. More typical were arguments that a particular spot would inevitably lead to immorality. For instance, in 1945, a member of the Ontario Training School Advisory Committee wrote to the Attorney-General complaining about the Silver Slipper Roadhouse in Swansea, more popularly known as the Kingsway:

> If you were to go down ... any Sunday night between 7 and 8 o'clock, you would see a long queue, four wide, largely of teenage youngsters waiting to get into this roadhouse. Our information is that they sit around and drink "coke" and what have you, until 12.01 AM when the dance starts.

> It is quite obvious that the habit of these teenage young people, spending Sunday evening this way and not getting home until the wee small hours of the morning, is having a very detrimental effect not only on their health but on their future, and we feel that it would be advisable for your Department to investigate and see if something can be done to stop this, as juvenile delinquency is becoming a terrific problem and this place is only a feeder to further delinquency.

> ... in the opinion of the writer this dance hall (and I assume there are others like it) is doing more harm to the young people of the city than any gambling place.... (Terry, 1945)

In 1946, a writer for the Toronto tabloid, *Justice Weekly*, made similar connections between dance halls and vice in a story about a 16-year-old girl caught in a hold-up attempt:

> While Grand Juries, temperance cranks, jurists and social welfare folks are blaming beverage parlours, both men's and women's, as being responsible for much of

the crime, immorality and drunkenness so prevalent these days, overlooked are the dance halls where just as much, if not more crime, immorality and drunkenness get their start. In most of these dance spots, no attention is paid to the ages of the patrons, many of whom come stag and "pick up" members of the opposite sex for dancing purposes, and then, in many cases, almost anything can happen and does happen. (*Justice Weekly*, 1946: 13)

This focus on dance halls emphasizes their primary difference from other "bad" places: dance halls catered to, indeed they depended on, young women as well as young men. As places where young people of both sexes would gather, they had the potential to foster not simply delinquency, but heterosexual delinquency and immorality.

Delinquency for both boys and girls was often a case of being found in the wrong kind of place—somewhere without "any adult guidance or control" (Rogers, 1945: 82). But while boys were arrested for a variety of offences (theft, vandalism, trespassing, assault, etc.), girls were usually brought to court on vague, non-property-oriented crimes like vagrancy, incorrigibility or immorality (Toronto Family Court, 1947). Girls, it seems, became "immoral" while boys committed crimes or joined gangs. This isn't to say, however, that boys' sexuality was left unexamined; boys, as well as girls, could be referred to as "sex delinquents." Still, the sexual aspect of boys' troubles was not widely discussed. In a report on street gangs in Toronto prepared by the Big Brothers, workers found the older boys to be "abnormally sex conscious." And though they found evidence of "filthy language, obscenity, relatively open immorality (heterosexual and homosexual)" they chose not to use these incidents to illustrate their report: "We can not see that doing this would serve our purpose any more than the selections used [which were mostly about idleness, petty thieving, and gambling]" (Rogers, 1945: 20). Unlike girls, boys were rarely labelled delinquent for sexual reasons alone (although the delinquency label implied questionable sexual morals). Sexual activity was just one of the ways that boys' delinquent characters could be manifest. Social critics regularly made broad moral pronouncements about delinquent boys without ever mentioning their sexual conduct—the same would have been impossible for girls.

According to Carolyn Strange, turn-of-the-century girls out for an evening's entertainment were equated with prostitutes whether they were actually looking for paid sex or not. Similar equations were put into play during World War II when the "pick-up" became synonymous with the "amateur girl" or unpaid prostitute (Pierson, 1986). Boys, it goes without saying, were rarely considered to be "pick-ups" (whether they were getting picked up or not). In a piece on delinquency in *Saturday Night* magazine, Gerald Zoffer (1946: 7) writes,

> In the beverage room of cheap hotels that may be found in any fair-sized Canadian
> community, one comes in contact with the female of the species, young girls from
> every walk of life who flock to the beer parlours every night to seek excitement,
> and escape .... Get to know any one of these girls and you will invariably find her
> to be a pleasant, likeable girl with ordinary tastes and desires, and who is merely
> out to "have a little fun" after working hours. They enter the beverage rooms in
> groups ... and generally sit for hours with a glass of beer in one hand and a ciga-
> rette in the other, chatting gaily ... they are quite willing to admit that one of the
> main reasons they come to the beverage room is to be picked up.... Yet these very
> same girls are outraged if someone refers to them as prostitutes. "What's the mat-
> ter with having a good time with some fellow?"

It's not the beer and the cigarettes that have Zoffer upset, it's the presumed heterosexual activity that follow them. But the structure of his argument reflects both the
sexual propriety of his day as well as the fact that places were heavily inscribed with
social meaning.

It almost goes without saying that commentary on juvenile delinquency was produced and circulated within the middle class while the majority (though certainly
not all) of those so labelled were working class. For the most part, views expressed
on the issue were liberal enough to avoid the suggestion that the delinquent was
inherently bad or immoral. Unlike earlier believers in eugenics, most postwar experts argued that social and environmental conditions had led to the delinquent's
downfall and it was the social conditions—not the person—that were inherently
immoral. A Big Brothers worker wrote of the downtown neighbourhood that lay
between Bloor and Carleton streets, Yonge and Sumach (Cabbagetown and its surrounding area):

> There are many connecting lanes running at the back of [the] side streets and
> parallel to them. These lanes are excellent warrens of refuge for activities which
> shun the light of day. The eastern half of the area is a congested area teeming with
> Anglo-Saxon children.
>
> The people of this area make a very interesting study. It abounds with "people
> of the shadows." In an area of this kind the comedy and tragedy of life rub el-
> bows every day: all the excesses and weaknesses of the flesh are exhibited ...
> In the eastern half of the area the people are mainly English, Irish and Scotch.
> These people are sturdy working class people, inclined to be suspicious, many of
> them decent and clean, others, physically dirty and morally corrupt. Children

growing up in an area of this kind are exposed to influences which exaggerate the evils of life. Bad language, gambling, drunkenness, prostitution, are all too familiar. (Rogers, 1945: 47)

To counter the bad influences of their backgrounds, young people (mostly working-class boys) were to be offered healthy amusement and supervised, "attached" (to a club, a church, or a school) recreation (Cavallo, 1981). It was hoped that good amusement in good places would make a dent in the delinquency rates.[3] In 1944 there were at least 71 organizations offering youth services in Toronto, and the city spent $208,697 on playgrounds and $82,000 on rinks. But still, a *Globe* reporter complained, there were "children running the streets in gangs, operating floating crap games, indulging in petty thefts, picking up social diseases and running foul of the law" (*Globe and Mail*, 1946b). W.R. Cockburn, chair of the school board, said, "There's been too much emphasis placed on play as a means of curbing juvenile delinquency" (*Telegram*, 1946). Despite his concerns, more coercive measures for regulating youth had not been abandoned.

When it seemed that organized recreation was not solving the delinquency problem to their satisfaction, some civic officials and social commentators proposed other solutions. If delinquency was about children and young people being in the wrong kinds of places, then why not regulate social space to limit access?

The most drastic effort to regulate young people's access to the streets was a proposal for a curfew put forward by the city council. In the spring of 1944, council made an official request to the police and the Juvenile Court to enforce the provisions of a seldom-used provincial statute, The Children's Protection Act. The act banned anyone under 16 "from places of entertainment after 9 p.m., unless accompanied by his parent or guardian" (*Globe and Mail*, 1944). The idea behind the curfew was to keep young people off the streets and out of commercial places of entertainment, like movie houses or dances. While council voted in favour of the idea, parents reacted negatively. The response of community groups was not quite so clear. Although a conference of service organizations felt that a curfew wasn't necessary, "at the same time, the conference recommended 'wholesome and discretionary enforcement of the Children's Protection Act' to prevent children loitering on street corners, in refreshment places and around places of entertainment after 9 p.m." (*Telegram*, 1944). Their statement alludes to the perceived problem of young people hanging out in beverage rooms, dance halls, and hamburger "joints"—all places most likely to be frequented by working-class youth, all places where sexual temptation was thought to exist. As two 15-year-olds wrote to the Toronto *Star* (1944):

> Why don't they clean out all the cheap dance halls where not only 'teen-age young-sters but also the older crowd go. These dance halls represent one reason for making the curfew and causing all this disturbance. We 'teen-agers go to school five days a week and have two hours' homework each day. We visit the library once a week and when the weekend comes we like to go out for some good clean entertainment, such as movies, bowling, rollerskating, concerts or even school affairs.

The writers did not need to add that in the 1940s, "high school kids" (as opposed to vocational or "tech" kids), was a category that included more middle-class than work-ing-class youth.[4] Common sense notions about "middle-classness"—as some kind of indicator for perseverance, maturity, responsibility—meant that middle-class youth were, to some extent, assumed to be self-regulating, that is, to stay out of serious trou-ble. They were not the ones for whom the curfew was intended.

Nothing ever really came of the curfew. The police enforced it for a short while, but then they eased off. Calls for curfews in later years were equally unsuccessful. But there remained other, less dramatic, more easily implemented strategies for regulating the use of and access to public space in the fight against immorality. For instance, the school board refused to permit mixed (boys and girls) swimming in the pools under its jurisdiction (*Globe and Mail*, 1949b) and the city refused to turn the lights on at public skating rinks on Sundays. As Frank Tumpane wrote in his column in the *Globe* (1948), "the principal argument [about the rinks] seems to be that in some manner 'moral standards' would be lowered." Amusement parks and resort areas were also subjected to Sunday closing laws. Some people suggested that Sunday closing regulations, en-acted to protect Christian "moral standards," were in fact encouraging delinquency. Without proper recreation, kids would become idle and engage in unsupervised activi-ties. At one point in 1946, the city recreation department brought together a group of young people to brainstorm around the types of things teenagers might actually be permitted to do on a Sunday (CTA, n.d.).

Like the curfew, Sunday closings were more likely to affect working-class than middle-class youth. On Sundays, middle-class youth were not dependent on downtown commercial amusements: they could spend the day visiting each other in comfortable homes or backyards, or in parks that grew more spacious outside the downtown core. It is also important to remember that for many people in the 1940s, Sunday was the only day off in a six-day work week. And, on that day, teenaged wage-earners were prevented access to the amusements that high school students without jobs were free to enjoy on Saturday. The point here is not that middle-class teenagers were not subject to moral regulation, but that they were thought to be generally capable of regulating themselves, while working-class young people needed external controls.

But the moral regulation of young people who worked went beyond their leisure time. The Factory Act prohibited children under 14 from working in certain types of places, while children 14 to 16 could work at the restricted places before 6:30 in the evening. In 1944, the acting Deputy Minister of Public Welfare wrote to the Minister to inform him that moves were afoot to strengthen the restrictions:

> I am advised by the Department of Labour that restaurants are listed as one of the places in which employment is so precluded or limited. Bowling alleys, theatres, and bingo halls, do not fall within the excluded places. I am further advised by the Department of Labour that there is presently under consideration an amendment to the Factory Act which will enable that Department to control the employment of children in any places not presently listed.[5]

Yet another, more subtle, means of regulating public space was the use of "morality lights." Apart from their peculiar name, there was nothing special about these spot-lights which were affixed to school buildings and mounted in some parks. Although the lights were probably most useful in protecting properties from vandalism, this was not necessarily the main motivation for their installation. In 1947 school board chair Isabel Ross claimed that "Evening patrolmen are no substitute for 'morality lights' in preventing school yards from becoming lovers' lanes" (*Globe and Mail*, 1947). At a cost of $900 per school per year, the decision to mount the lights wasn't made lightly. In 1950, parent-teacher associations at Jarvis and Humberside Collegiates requested lights because "darkness" on school grounds was "conducive to immorality." Opponents of the lights claimed "that what goes on in the shadows of school grounds at night is certainly not educational and therefore public school supporters should not be required to pay for guarding the morals of the public at large." But Mrs. Ross, who by this time had finished her term as chair, represented majority opinion, reminding the dissenters that, "I cannot forget that I am my brother's keeper" (*Globe and Mail*, 1950). The lights went up.

Certainly the moral regulation of sexuality through restrictions on access to or use of public space isn't something that only affected young people. Other marginal groups were subjected to some of the same restrictions. When it became known that gay men were cruising along Philosophers' Walk at the University of Toronto, morality lights were installed along the pathway. For similar reasons, the bushes were cut down at Queen's Park and at the Hanlan's Point beach.

Social worries about prostitution led to a bylaw establishing women-only beverage rooms along Jarvis Street. The idea behind the bylaw was that drinking rooms without men would limit women's chances of being "picked-up," for money or otherwise. Of course, women who wanted to continued to find men while, at the same time, lesbians (some of whom were prostitutes, some of whom were not) were happy for the women-only space, like the tavern in the Rideau Hotel.

In the early 1950s, a North Toronto parents' group used similar tactics to deal with people they called "sexual perverts." In a brief to the Royal Commission on the Criminal Law Relating to Criminal Sexual Psychopaths (1954), the chair of the group wrote:

> In our particular part of Toronto, Lawrence Park, a natural ravine playground has become a menace to young children in particular, and to their parents and teachers vicariously, because it becomes an area where unsavoury persons lurk. Several incidents of indecent exposure and accosting of little girls and boys have taken place, with no apparent correction under law enforcement. In an effort to make this ravine (a city park) safer as a recreational area, a group of parents in our school has enlisted the support of neighbourhood organizations in having civic authorities clear out underbrush, and provide ready access for police patrol of the ravine .... We intend to continue our vigilance toward maintaining this natural asset in our community.

In this case, efforts to "protect the children" resulted in another "sterilization" campaign and an increased police presence in a residential area. The clearing of bushes functioned much in the same way (although on a smaller scale) as did the construction of the Gardiner Expressway and the levelling of Sunnyside and the Centre Island community. In trying to eliminate unsavoury elements from their neighbourhood, members of the Lawrence Park Ravine Project also eliminated secluded places for their children to play and laid open all members of the community to increased surveillance by each other and by the police. Similar efforts have recently been carried out in Toronto's Cawthra Square Park, a popular gay cruising area. The argument in this contemporary case is that the bushes had to be cut to protect gay men from gay bashers. The result has been the destruction of a piece of gay-appropriated public space and the homogenization of the urban landscape.

■ CONCLUSION

This paper began with the recognition that moral regulation takes many guises and is directed at various kinds of targets. The moral regulation of postwar urban spaces has been analyzed to examine its implications for the moral and sexual regulation of the people who used those spaces. In looking at young people in postwar Toronto, I am interested in the "how" of moral regulation and in the way that moral and sexual discourses operated to curtail possibility and to construct particular kinds of sexual subjects. In *The Great Arch*, Philip Corrigan and Derek Sayer talk about how moral regulation works to erase differences and to limit the forms of expression we have available to us. Clearly the regulation of the spaces we use, the imposition of "clean" banality on our environment, can play a part in this.

Discourses about public space are simply one example of many that could be investigated for their regulatory effects. In putting my primary focus on the conduits of regulation as opposed to their targets, I want to highlight the pervasiveness of moral regulation. I also want to show the potential of this method for looking at the similarities in how different groups are morally regulated, at the similarities in the relationships various marginal groups have with the so-called centre. In understanding marginal groups as subjects of and subjected to the same processes, we gain a better understanding of the centre—the norm—and the ways that hegemonic discourses regulate our lives.

■ NOTES

*I would like to thank my sex/history study group (Debi Brock, Karen Dubinsky, Julie Guard, Margaret Little, and Becki Ross), Keith Walden, and Mariana Valverde for comments on earlier drafts of this paper. I'd also like to thank SSHRC for financial assistance. Please address all correspondence and offprint requests to Mary Louise Adams, Department of Sociology, Queen's University. Kingston. Ontario, K7L 3N6.

1. Metropolitan Toronto was created in 1953 from an amalgamation of the City of Toronto and its surrounding suburbs. The 26 municipalities combined to facilitate planning and development and to coordinate services. See Lemon (1985: 108–11).

2. In opposition to the Miss Toronto contestants, Miss Beautiful Toronto contestants (who also competed at Sunnyside) were required to appear in skirts, sweaters, stockings, and medium-sized heels. While the sponsors of the Miss Toronto contest were members of the working-class Police Association, the sponsors of the Miss Beautiful Toronto contest were well ensconced in the middle-class Young Men's Board of Trade.

3. Ironically, the actual numbers of delinquents brought before the courts peaked in 1942 at 1,861 cases. In 1943 the numbers were down to 1,811; in 1944 they were 1,344; in 1945 they were 1,165; in 1946 they were 793; in 1947 they were 830; in 1949 they were 920; and in 1950 they were 1,013 (The Toronto Family Courts, Reports. CTA, RG47, Box 135).

4. In Canada in the mid-1940s, only one-quarter of Canadian young people were in school after the age of 16 (Canadian Youth Commission, 1948: 176). In Toronto, by 1952, six out of ten students were leaving high school after only one or two years, as soon as they turned 16, so they could go to work (Toronto Star, 1952).

5. Memo from B.W. Heise, acting Deputy Minister of Public Welfare to R.P. Vivian, Minister of Public Welfare, 7 January 1944. AO, RG4-02, File 22.7. In 1944, Bill 64 amended the Factory, Shop and Office Building Act so that the definition of shop was extended to include bowling alleys, pool rooms, and billiard parlours.

■ REFERENCES

Adams, Betty. Personal communication. n.d.

Canadian Weekly. "Look what they've done to Toronto's island." 24 August, 1963.

Canadian Youth Commission. *Youth, Marriage and the Family.* Toronto: Ryerson, 1948.

Cavallo, Dominick. *Muscles and Morals: Organized Playgrounds and Urban Reform, 1880–1920.* Philadelphia: Temple, 1981.

City of Toronto Archives (CTA). *The Toronto Yearbook: The Story of a City, 1931.* Xerox, vertical file, "Palace Pier." n.d.

———. "Informal discussion by young people representing a cross-section of the youth of Toronto, on recreation needs and problems as they see them, Monday, May 13th, 1946." Part 2. RG 12A, Box 78, File 3, 1946.

———. Advertisement for A.E. LePage (Ontario) Limited, December. Source unknown, vertical file, "Palace Pier," 1976.

Clark, C.S. *Of Toronto the Good.* Toronto: Coles, 1970. [originally published 1898].

Corrigan, Philip. "On moral regulation: Some preliminary remarks." *Sociological Review* 29(2) (1981): 313–33.

Corrigan, Philip and Derek Sayer. *The Great Arch: English State Formation as Cultural Revolution.* Oxford: Blackwell, 1986.

Elves, Hazel. *It's All Done with Mirrors: A Story of Canadian Carnival Life.* Victoria: Sono Nis, 1977.

Francis, R. Douglas, Richard Jones, and Donald B. Smith. *Destinies: Canadian History Since Confederation,* 2nd edition. Toronto: Holt, Rinehart and Winston, 1992.

Garner, Hugh. "An island tunnel: Undermining the Bohemians." Undated newsclipping. City of Toronto Archives, SC 47, Box 1, File 1, n.d.

Gibson, Sally. *More Than an Island: A History of the Toronto Island.* Toronto: Irwin, 1984.

Globe and Mail. "Every one bewildered by city's curfew move." 5 April, 1944.

———. "Community centres an answer." Editorial. 3 January, 1946a.

————. "Now is the time to fight juvenile delinquency." 7 January, 1946b.

————. "Carnival boom bulges tills in record year." 9 August, 1946c.

————. "Lights till wee hours to banish lovers' lanes nip school vandalism." 19 June, 1947.

————. "Commissioner Love is for romance." 8 January, 1949a.

————. "Reject Junction club's bid for mixed splash parties." 18 January, 1949b.

————. "Put up morality lights at 2 schools, committee asks." 30 March, 1950.

————. "Quiet lagoons, parks in Island plan." 12 April, 1957.

Justice Weekly. "16-year-old girl plans dummy hold-up with youths picked up in dance hall." 5 January: 13, 1946.

Kidd, George. "Sunnyside ... a time and a place gone by." *Toronto Week* 10 April, 1971.

Lawrence Park Ravine Project. Brief presented to the Royal Commission on the Criminal Laws Relating to Criminal Sexual Psychopaths by the Lawrence Park Ravine Project, April 2. National Archives of Canada, RG 33/131. Box 1, File: Appendix, Montreal-Toronto, Exhibit 91, Page 1806, 1954.

Lemon, James. *Toronto Since 1918: An Illustrated History.* Toronto: James Lorimer, 1985.

McAfee, J.V. "We rang the bell on beauty contests." *Globe and Mail,* 8 October, 1947.

Pierson, Ruth. *"They're Still Women After All": The Second World War and Canadian Womanhood.* Toronto: McClelland & Stewart, 1986.

R.J.. Interview, March, 1992.

Rogers, Kenneth. *Street Gangs in Toronto.* Toronto: Ryerson, 1945.

Shallit, Rebecca. "The brass ring." *Chatelaine* (April): 26–27ff, 1949.

Strange, Carolyn. "The perils and pleasures of the city: Single wage-earning women in Toronto, 1880–1930." Ph.D. dissertation, Rutgers University, 1991.

Taylor, E.E. Superintendent of Concessions to F.R. Scandrett, General Manager, Toronto Harbour Commission, 15 February. Toronto Harbour Commission Archives, RG 3/3, Box 300, Folder 8, 1946.

Telegram. "Curfew hour held unneeded in queen city." 14 April, 1944.

————. "Too much stress on play." 30 April, 1946.

————. "Moving Sunnyside for new highway council hot potato." 23 May, 1951.

Terry, H.J. H.J. Terry to Hon. Leslie E. Blackwell, Attorney-General, 5 January. Archives of Ontario (AO), RG4, 4-02, File 24.4, 1945.

The Standard. "Canada's Coney." 23 July, 1949.

The Toronto Family Court. "Report for the Year 1947." CTA, RG 47, Reports, Box 135, 1947.

Toronto Star. "Many leave school too early." Editorial. 11 August, 1952.

————. "Good-bye to Sunnyside." Editorial. 23 January, 1956.

Tumpane, Frank. "At City Hall." *Globe and Mail,* 11 January, 1948.

Urry, John. *The Tourist Gaze: Leisure and Travel in Contemporary Societies.* London: Sage, 1990.

Valverde, Mariana. *The Age of Light, Soap, and Water: Moral Reform in English Canada, 1885–1925*. Toronto: McClelland & Stewart, 1991.

Valverde, Mariana and Lorna Weir. "The struggle of the immoral: Preliminary remarks on moral regulation." *Resources for Feminist Research* 18(3): 31–34, 1988.

Zoffer, Gerald. "'Underworld' evils breed juvenile delinquency." *Saturday Night* 12 January: 7, 1946.

CHAPTER 12

THE SPACE OF AFRICVILLE:
CREATING, REGULATING, AND REMEMBERING THE URBAN "SLUM"

Jennifer J. Nelson

> There is a little frequented part of the City, overlooking Bedford Basin, which presents an unusual problem for any community to face. In what may be described as an encampment, or shack town, there live some seventy negro families ....
>
> The citizens of Africville live a life apart. On a sunny, summer day, the small children roam at will in a spacious area and swim in what amounts to their private lagoon. In winter, life is far from idyllic. In terms of the physical condition of buildings and sanitation, the story is deplorable. Shallow wells and cesspools, in close proximity, are scattered about the slopes between the shacks.
>
> There are no accurate records of conditions in Africville. There are only two things to be said. The families will have to be rehoused in the near future. The land which they now occupy will be required for the further development of the City.
>
> —G. Stephenson, 1957[1]

This chapter traces a series of events that demonstrate how the space of Africville, Nova Scotia, was legally regulated by the City of Halifax throughout its existence. This space remains a contested site—a reminder to the city that burial of past injustice requires diligent maintenance. Through exploration of several events over time, it becomes clearer that the notion of a united black community, which exists on its own terms and is subject to the same rights and freedoms as the greater white community, was and remains inconceivable. The dislocation of Africville residents from their land and community was more than an isolated, finite project; on the contrary, the process has been one of ongoing eviction, suppression, and denial.

The role of a spatial analysis becomes clear in three ways throughout the discussion. First, the legal regulation of space governs what can and cannot happen within it, in ways that may not be obviously defined as racist in law itself, nor perhaps to a community not directly and negatively affected by such regulation. Second, the regulation and limitation of spaces of resistance are easily masked as a necessary measure to protect the public, a reasonable and equitable measure that applies equally to all citizens, rather than targeting any specific group. Third, the violence inherent in the regulation of racialized space is rendered invisible when law is conceived as being a product of consensus of liberal social values. The inequities can only be heard when the differing stories of those involved are allowed to emerge. Thus, this chapter makes an argument for context-specific considerations of wrongdoing that go beyond an assumed consensus of "fairness" to a series of legal actions that were planned and carried out by one group against another.

While there are many elements to the Africville story that tell a tale of spatial and racial discrimination, for the purposes of length and poignancy, I have selected a few key moments from a broader and ongoing struggle to demonstrate the inconceivability to a racist society of an enduring communal Black presence.

As a white writer, I believe it is important to make clear my choices in directing the study's conceptual bent towards whiteness-as-dominance, rather than attempting to replicate "the black experience" of Africville, a story which is not mine to tell. While not intended to alienate or exclude, I acknowledge that this form of analysis and the conclusions I make embody a critique directed to the white community, which people of colour may not find to be "new" or illuminating. Further, I do not mean to suggest at any stage of analysis that resistance and opposition were absent among Africville residents themselves. Certainly, organization against the city's plans took place at the time of Africville's forced dislocation, and various events and projects that seek justice, encourage remembrance, and celebrate resistance have been underway ever since. I am merely choosing here to focus on the dominant players whose governance made resistance insufficient to save Africville. It is the practices of the dominant group that we must critically examine if we seek to educate for change among a white community that is accountable for things done to Black communities.

■ A STORY OF UN/SETTLEMENT

> [C]onsideration of this or any other urban development must recognize the sig-
> nificance of its prior occupancy and revisit the colonial past to retell some of the
> histories of initial dispossession of the land involved .... The issue is not only one of
> initial invasion, but of ongoing dislocation and exclusion.
>
> —L. Johnson[2]

To "begin at the beginning" draws one into a complex history of Black settlement in Nova Scotia in the 18th century, a history too detailed to fully discuss here. Briefly, the means by which Black residents of the province came to form the community of Africville must be regarded in the context of a history of the displacement and enslavement of Black people by whites in North America, of hostile reception upon settlement in Nova Scotia, complete with a worldview that demanded their containment and denial, and of a young nation struggling to form its identity through the predominantly British colonial enterprise.

Although slavery was never legally instituted in Nova Scotia, some whites held slaves at the time the City of Halifax was founded in 1749 and throughout the next 50 years. The practice failed to reach the proportions of American plantation cultures, due more to a paucity of arable farmland than to widespread public opposition. The number of slaves following the arrival of slave-holding Loyalists is thought to be around 1,500. While officially frowned upon by the courts at a relatively early date, Nova Scotia's "slave culture" was undermined as the labour of incoming free Black and white Loyalists could be had for little more than the price of keeping slaves.

Soon-to-be Africville residents were among the wave of refugee Blacks who arrived after the War of 1812 and who were allotted space in rural regions, particularly present-day Preston, where rocky, inadequate soil made survival off the land impossible. The Africville site on the shores of Bedford Basin, not far from today's city centre, held the hope of diminished isolation, better employment and living conditions, and other economic opportunities. Having purchased the properties in the 1840s from white merchants, founders William Brown and William Arnold established the boundaries within which Africville would develop. Along with other early families, they established a church congregation and elementary school, a postal office, and a few small stores. Although land conditions for farming were no better than on their former plots, a few head of livestock were kept, the Bedford Basin offered a steady supply of fish, and the new location held the increased chance of obtaining waged labour in the city.[3]

Throughout the community's approximately 120-year history, Halifax's development, particularly in the industrial and disease- and waste-management sectors, encroached on Africville land. In addition to the construction of railway lines, which required the destruction of several Africville buildings, an oil plant storage facility, a bone mill, and a slaughterhouse were built. Encircling these establishments were a leather tanning plant, a tar factory, another slaughterhouse, and a foundry. Shortly after the settlement of Africville, the city established Rockhead Prison on the overlooking hillside; about 20 years later, the city's infectious diseases hospital was placed on this hill, and the open city dump was located about one-and-a-half miles away. Additional construction of railway lines to different factories dislocated more Africville families. Destruction of many surrounding industries following the Halifax Explosion of 1917 resulted in new facilities being built in their places. For decades, this waterfront region was the target of much discussion regarding expropriation for industrial expansion by the City of Halifax, a plan which became solidified in the 1947 rezoning of the city. In the early 1950s, the city dump was moved directly onto Africville land—350 feet from the westernmost home—and two years later, the city placed an incinerator only 50 yards beyond its south border.

Throughout Africville's existence, building permits to improve homes were increasingly difficult to obtain from the city government. Requests for water lines and sewers, which would bring sanitation and quality of life closer to the standards for the rest of the city, were refused. Police and fire protection and garbage collection on par with such services received by the rest of Halifax were denied. Living conditions were ironically described by city officials as intolerable and unsanitary—in short, as justification for the inevitable dismantling of the community and eviction of its 400 residents. Discussion of the dismantling continued, until finally, in the 1960s, the threat became a more serious reality. By the end of the decade, despite avid resistance and organization on the part of Africville residents themselves and in concert with other community groups, Africville was expropriated by the City of Halifax for the purposes of industrial development, as well as for the alleged benefits of "slum clearance" and "relocation" of the residents.[4]

Due to an informal system of handing down properties and housing within families and between in-laws over the years, many residents were unable to prove legal title to their land; thus, they had little recourse when faced with the proposition to sell or be evicted. Due to historical, social, and economic conditions, residents had no formal community leadership that would be seen as legitimate political representation and little access to the legal and bureaucratic bargaining tools of the municipality. Most were forced to accept the city's small compensation, or to settle for low prices offered for homes they had not been permitted to maintain and improve, located in what was defined as "the slum by the garbage dump."[5] In a seeming mockery, when moving companies refused to be hired, city garbage trucks, which had never serviced Africville, were sent to carry away the residents' belongings.

The last Africville home was bulldozed in 1970. Most of the former residents had to adjust to living in public housing facilities, struggling to pay rent for the first time in their lives, while those who owned their own homes would suffer financial difficulties in the near future. Separated from friends, family, and their strong sense of community, many Africvilleans were left with the insufficiency of welfare dollars and the meager $500 compensation they had received—defined as a "moral claim"—from the benevolent city.

■ STAGE 1: INDUCING ILLNESS

Of particular interest to a critical geographical race analysis is the manner in which the control of space and the control of bodies through control of space become tools for defining a community's physical and metaphorical boundaries, its character, and how individuals or groups will be determined through such understandings and associations. David Goldberg writes,

> The slum is by definition filthy, foul smelling, wretched, rancorous, uncultivated, and lacking care. The racial slum is doubly determined, for the metaphorical stigma of a black blotch on the cityscape bears the added connotations of moral degeneracy, natural inferiority, and repulsiveness ... the slum locates the lower class, the racial slum the underclass.[6]

In denying the community of Africville essential services that would facilitate its health and its development within the larger metro area, the city produced the community, in the "outside" public mind, as a place of dirt, odour, disease, and waste. These associations, which came to be manifested as the conflation of Africville with degeneracy, filth, and "the slum," justified the further denial of essential services on the basis of how Africville had come to be known. Working from a basic assumption that the use and characterization of space is socially determined, and that the ideologies surrounding race are socially produced, it is possible to speak of a socio-spatial dialectic wherein "space and the political organization of space express social relationships but also react back upon them."[7]

In the formation of Africville, and its regulation over time, we see an extension of this dialectic in the relationship between power–dominance and the creation of the slum. Particular race relations in this context produced certain space as a repository for all that the dominant group wanted to contain and distance itself from. In the self-fulfilling prophecy—that is, Africville becoming exactly what it was set up to become in the eyes of the outer white community—the slum legitimates dominance by offering a concrete example of filthy, intolerable conditions, a notion of helplessness, and a lack of self-determination that are seen as inherent to its inhabitants. The origins of the conditions in question and the absence of choice for the residents must be conveniently forgotten, and this forgetting is accomplished most easily when the dominant group can achieve an axiomatic yet unspoken association of blackness with inevitable demise. As Barnor Hesse discusses in terms of "diasporic outside/inside," the internal Other, as opposed to the colonial Other overseas, poses a particular problem in western societies:

> ... temporal nativization of the "other," outside/inside the West is accompanied by a spatial nativization in which people are compressed into prefabricated landscapes, the ghetto, the shanty town, and undergo a process of "representational essentializing" ... in which one part or aspect of people's lives comes to epitomize them as a whole ...[8]

At the same time that we see that observable concrete realities of poverty and deprivation exist, we see in the creation of the racial slum a set of knowledge-making practices that serve to legitimate all that we must believe about Africville in order to dominate it. As Henri Lefebvre writes:

> Space is not a scientific object removed from ideology and politics; it has always been political and strategic. If space has an air of neutrality and indifference with regard to its contents and thus seems to be "purely" formal ... it is precisely because it has been occupied and used, and has already been the focus of past processes whose traces are not always evident on the landscape. Space has been shaped and molded from historical and natural elements, but this has always been a political process .... It is a product literally filled with ideologies.[9]

The ideologies produced in the making of Africville-as-slum involve narratives about raced bodies that are tied to, but must not be conflated with, the spaces they inhabit. Take, for instance, the moving of the dump into Africville: this act was received by Africvilleans in the only way they saw possible—to make use of it, to salvage the things that others threw away, repair or clean them, and go on with life:

> ... we try to make the dump work for us .... There's all kinds of scrap metal in there that you can collect and sell .... There's ways of tellin' good stuff from bad .... We got fellas here who can get [car] parts off the dump and make the worst lookin' wreck in the world run like new .... You know what really gets up folks' behinds

out here? When those newspapers talk about us "scavenging" food and clothes off the dump. People read that stuff and think we're runnin' around diggin' week-old tomatoes and nasty rags out of that messy dump. Any fool knows you get stuff off the trucks before they throw it on the dump ... by the time the ladies out here get through workin' on second-hand clothes with their needle and thread, you'd never know they were bound for the dump. Some folks say the dump was put here to try to drive us out. If that's true, things kind of backfired, didn't they?[10]

The dump, although smelly and distasteful, becomes incorporated into social practice as a means of survival. At the same time, from "outside," Africville becomes character-ized more strongly than ever as a space of garbage, of the waste of the white commu-nity. The use of the dump can be viewed as proof that the Black community is indeed comfortable being associated with dirt, that it is natural for them to live off the waste of others. Spaces are manufactured in ways that dictate what sorts of activities can and will take place in them. Life practice, then, determines both insider and outsider perceptions of identity: from within, perhaps, emerges a sense that the community can survive against unfair odds. Black identity in the outside white public discourse be-comes intimately bound up with space/place in a negative sense—they are no longer simply people who live near the dump; they are "scavengers."

To see Others as recipients of your garbage, as *desiring* your waste, constitutes a very particular kind of relation and belief system about their place, their culture, their "peoplehood," on a dramatic level (as well as, very intimately, a belief system about your own place, culture, personhood). Dominant group members are not required to see how these relations are formed; on the contrary, "common-sense" views engender and support a sense that they are natural, that some people simply live "this way."

Many space theorists have described the way in which both marginalized groups and peripheral space signal an existence "beyond" society, apart from civilized norms, and as separate space in which undesirable activities could take place in order to pre-serve the purity of dominant, ruling space.[11] Essentializing the people and the space of Africville becomes apparent in the notion of the community as a site "outside" the rest of society, metaphorically and spatially. As Peter Marcuse makes clear in his concept of the *residual* city, racial minority spaces frequently come to house the wastes of society, be they pollutants from industrial manufacturing, sewer systems and garbage disposal areas, or houses for others deemed undesirable, such as AIDS victims or the home-less.[12] This means that undesirable places and practices are located across a boundary that is rarely crossed, or crossed for specific purposes that are "outside" the purity of the white middle-class home—for instance, the treatment of disease or exploring the red light district.[13] Specific to Africville would be the acts of buying liquor illegally[14] or disposing of waste. (Garbage, by definition, is material that is useless, has been thrown out. It is not a legitimate part of your space. It *must* be taken away from where you live, to another place.)

David Sibley's research on gypsy communities has been influential in pulling together many factors, discourses, and social sanctions that enable the construction of a marginal community as "separate," inferior, and slumlike. He speaks of the problematic of perceived "disorder," particularly in travelling communities, whose borders are never clear and require strict regulation.[15] Despite its more than 100-year history and long line of founding families, Africville residents were frequently thought of as a group of transients. In her essay on "the homeless body," Samira Kawash explores how the absence of place, while socially constituted, is seen as highly problematic and in need of legal and social systems of order-making and containment.[16] Although the Africville population was not seen in quite the same light as the homeless, their image as being outside society, undeserving of "place," and as threats to the place of the rest of the community, I believe, form some similar conceptions in the dominant public mind. Narratives of disorder become clear as well through references that are made in news reports and in the original relocation study to the community's criminal element, its potential for disease, and to the possibility that its population was composed mainly of squatters.

Goldberg discusses the making of the slum as periphractic space, characterized by "dislocation, displacement and division" from the rest of society. He concludes that this is "the primary mode by which the space of racial marginality has been articulated and reproduced."[17] At the same time, he notes that periphractic space is not physically marginal to the urban centre, but, quite the contrary, is usually central, promoting a constant surveillance of its inhabitants and conditions. He refers to Vancouver's Chinatown and other similarly positioned communities, as functions of "that set of historical categories constituting the idea of the project: idealized racial typifications tied to notions of slumliness, physical and ideological pollution of the body politic, sanitation and health syndromes, lawlessness, addiction, and prostitution."[18]

These notions help to fuel an anachronistic sense of Africville's Otherness in time and space. Consider, for instance, the quotation at the beginning of this chapter from the provincially commissioned Stephenson Report: Imposing on land coveted for "development of the city" and threatening the city's borders (even though it was there first), Africville becomes *not* part of the city. The representation of an "encampment" connotes an axiomatic impermanence, antithetical to progress and development of "society," which is already understood to be not-Africville. The abrupt solution proposed does not take into account the desires or needs of the residents themselves from their own perspectives. His sweeping disregard for any possibility of the community's survival is achieved in one brief and conclusive paragraph in a lengthy report that devotes detailed analysis to the upgrading of many other areas of Halifax, some of which are identified as exhibiting "the worst" conditions in the city.[19]

The depiction of Africville as "an unusual problem for any community to face,"[20] suggests who is considered to be—*and not to be*—"the community." One might also question what, exactly, was "unusual" about a peripheral, underprivileged, and neglected Black population in a North American urban centre with a dominant white majority. To see the situation as an isolated case sidesteps a critical interrogation of the systemic causes of racial oppression. In any case, Africville's "life apart" begs the question, "Apart from *what?*" The answer can only mean some combination of society-community-nation-progress-time-space-history. Indeed, this view must be fundamental to the description of a place as "little frequented," although 400 people were living there.

Interestingly, as the City of Halifax justified its forced dislocation of Africville residents through reference to land use and the need for industrial development, Sibley points out how outsider societies are understood to be contrary to, even the antithesis of, "development."[21] The wild and untamed lifestyle connoted in Africville's "private lagoon" was easily imagined as an outdated freedom, as an intolerable privilege of inhabiting valuable harbourfront space. Space that had to be made white.

■ STAGE 2: EUTHANASIA

> ... we knew all about segregation. But we didn't look at ourselves as a segregated community. We just looked at ourselves as a community. And when the people from the Progressive Club and others like them held out integration like some kind of Holy Grail, we told them we weren't sure exactly what integration could do for us as a community.
>
> And the fact that we would raise doubts about it—well, that kind of shocked 'em.[22]

To solidify the ideologies produced around the space of Africville, the project of racial desegregation enabled an appearance, to many whites, of good intent that relied on a mode of imposed euthanasia—that is, the necessity of putting the community out of its misery.[23] When suffering is seen as "obvious" and incurable, destruction can be looked on as a form of rescue. Investments in the inevitability of this solution are so strong that it is extremely common for white people to ask, upon hearing of this issue, what Roger Simon might call the obscene question, "Why wouldn't they just leave?"[24] This question relies on a learned arrogance that assumes the solution being offered, in this case, to live among white people, is superior, and that the notion of free choice based on a common understanding of the experience exists. The many outsider narratives surrounding the slum construct a background against which implicit and explicit understandings of the (invisibly white) self and community as legitimately dominant are formed. The logic of the slum is productive in its own death, making common-sense knowledge of the fact of its dependence and inevitable need of an outside solution.

What, then, are we to make of the role of law in carrying out the solution in question? Not surprisingly, there was little space for Africville residents to contextualize their claims within a history of poverty, racism, and colonialism inflicted upon them by the same dominant group enacting the current violence. I have struggled with the problematic of identifying the precise legal (illegal?) moves made by the city—in all the accounts I have read the destruction of the community was simply "carried out." There are no references made to specific legal rulings or principles in the historical accounts, other than the mention of a more recent law passed to prevent certain forms of public protest. Nowhere in city reports from the time of relocation have I found expressions of doubt that Africville *could* be removed. Nor does there seem to exist a concern with justifying the removal through official channels. Instead, a common-sense logic prevails, composed of interwoven themes of understandings to which "we," as rational, race-neutral beings, are assumed to adhere. I soon felt forced to realize that it may be precisely the legality of the process that is so strikingly violent. This violence of the legal process is an integral thread in the common-sense discourse of relocation that, from a relatively privileged perspective, is easy to miss. In his discussion of liberal discourses of desegregation, as applied in various contexts, Goldberg summarizes well what I felt to be the imprecision of the legal process:

> ... law's necessary commitment to general principles, to abstract universal rules, to develop objective laws through universalization, is at once exclusive of subjectivities, identities and particularities .... So when law in its application and interpretation invokes history the reading is likely to be very partial, the more so the more politicized the process becomes. And race, I am insisting, necessarily politicizes the processes it brackets and colors.[25]

I have seen no legal opening for demonstrating, for example, that to be black, poor, displaced, and faced with the threat of physical removal from your home, in a segregated city in Nova Scotia, is not the same thing as to be white, professional, and arguing that the new mall's parking lot should not be placed in your backyard. There is little framework in place within which to claim that "relocating" in this context is different from simply "moving to a new house," hoping you'll soon get to know the neighbours. Such assumed neutrality of experience in the eyes of the law is extremely imprecise and misleading, while attempts to understand injustice are made difficult when context does not come into play. As Sherene Razack demonstrates in her analysis of the murder of an Aboriginal woman working as a prostitute in the Canadian West, any attempt to suggest a context in which race, gender, white male violence or discourses around the bodies inhabiting racialized, degenerate zones, is seen to bias the case. She illustrates how this renders particular identities invisible: "Since bodies had no race, class or gender, the constructs that ruled the day, heavily inflected with these social relations, coded rather than revealed them explicitly."[26] More than a matter of having "the wrong information," which can then be corrected, the discourses that define what white individuals in positions of power can hear about the subordinate group allow a self-concept of innocence to continue. Elsewhere, Razack writes, "Storytelling as a methodology in the context of law runs up against the problem of the dominant group's refusal to examine its own complicity in oppressing others. The power of law's positivism and the legal rules that underpin it are willing accomplices in this denial of accountability."[27]

To acknowledge complicity in histories of oppression and violence would be to give up an individual and collective sense of self and place. To ensure that this toehold is intact, the appearance of accountability can be manufactured through such venues as the $500 "moral claim" given to those residents who could not prove title to their homes. Take for instance the 1994 letter from R. J. Britton, the Halifax director of Social Planning, to City Council, reviewing the options that were perceived to be available at the time: "The City can use its statutory powers to remove the blight and at the same time, temper justice with compassion in matters of compensation to families affected."[28] Britton goes on to pronounce the "official story" that is to be known about Africville in public consciousness. This includes clauses assuring city officials that the aggressive bulldozer approach taken in the 1960s was simply the accepted method of "relocation" at the time, that the utmost compassion was given at various stages of negotiation, and that, since the actual cost of relocation was in the end approximately nine times the estimated cost, they can be assured of their benevolence. (On the contrary, it could be seen as their mistake and as evidence that rehabilitating the community might have been possible after all.) Compensation is cited as "at least very fair and perhaps generous." In this telling of the official story, historical distance excuses what are seen as minor glitches in the project of "relocation," and officials are permitted to feel good about their current perspectives and their predecessors' conduct. Moreover, as the "official story" ends, these leaders move beyond compassion to a sense of friendship and celebration: "The City of Halifax does need to recognize the reality of Africville in its history, celebrate the contributions the Africville people made to the City, and to continue to seek and help in their full participation in the life of the City."[29]

It is clear that within the governmental discourses surrounding Africville, officials define their innocence based on the absence of a legal structure that would hold them accountable in any way. What is perhaps most astounding is the absolute investment in legality as a moral foundation. This investment and the uninterrogated belief in its epistemic assumptions strike one as almost childlike in their simplicity: "If something is illegal, it is *wrong*; if something is legal, it is *correct*; if something is not our legal obligation but we offer it anyway, this makes us *good*." Not only are questions of accountability erased, they are made to seem unequivocally absurd when dominant subjects can believe they have kindly gone "above and beyond" their responsibilities. What is forgotten is that Africville's residents had no part in defining what would constitute these moral parameters, nor in constructing what was a legal or moral way of thought that made racism invisible.

What are the theoretical tools that might interpret the city's intended "slum clearance" or "industrial development" as processes that had, and continue to have, consequences for a poor Black community? It is clear that straightforward *evidence* of racism, or even of what is definable as harm, will not be forthcoming. Richard Thompson Ford offers a detailed study of the manner in which segregation upholds itself even when legislative policy seeks to disband it. Were racial segregation banned, he posits, the structures in place to maintain people's links to specific areas, networks, services, and survival mechanisms devised by various communities, regardless of their differing socio-economic statuses, would see that desegregation remained extremely difficult at best.[30] Similarly, Goldberg traces the discriminatory and regulatory consequences of seemingly race-neutral legal rulings. He cites examples from South African apartheid, under which landlords could refuse to rent property to families with more than a certain number of children.[31] It so happened that Black families tended to have larger than average numbers of children, thus the areas in which they were permitted to live could be "raced" without having to name this intent.

As Africville residents were moved, some were targeted by similar policies, having to give away some of their children or break apart families, forming household structures that differed from those they had known for generations. In some cases, single mothers were required to marry the fathers of their children in order to qualify for the new housing projects,[32] thus removing their power of choice to live as they pleased and implementing a value system based on the centrality of the nuclear family, rather than on Africville's sense of community and co-operation among extended relatives and friends. There are lawful ways in which to invoke "universal" values to bolster regulatory measures, as Goldberg points out:

That the State in the name of its citizenry insists on overseeing—policing—the precise and detailed forms that housing must take for the poor and racialized suggests that we really are committed to the kinds of disciplinary culture that inform current practice. The principle of agent autonomy so deeply cherished at the core should not, it seems, extend to the periphery; the racially marginalized should not be encouraged to exercise independence (least of all with public monies).[33]

In "relocating" them to their new homes, the municipality hoped, perhaps assumed, that Africville residents would melt into their new neighbourhoods, establishing the appearance of a desegregated city regardless of the hostility they might experience from white neighbours and regardless of the great psychic expense they might suffer—an expense that would make it only too apparent "why they wouldn't just leave."

■ STAGE 3: BURIAL

Drawing on Heidegger and on architectural theory, David Harvey theorizes the *genius loci*. Taken from the Roman, *genius* refers to a "guardian spirit" which determines the essence of one's identity. Harvey expands this to explore the essence of identity and community as it is associated with specific central locations. He speaks of how buildings and places absorb relations that occur within them, that these variant relations—to environment, history, physiology, sociality, psychology—become embodied in meanings that are projected onto the *genius loci*. In part, this reading practice begs the distinction of space from "place." As I intend it, space is the more general term, referring to any conceptual or actual space, including place. Place depicts a space upon which identity is founded. While either may be political, I see place as automatically so, referring to and incorporating notions of "home," collective history, and social location in reference to an identified group or individual. Place is the more precise term, encompassing the particular meanings embedded in spaces that are of significance to those who occupy them.

Harvey describes place as having a quality of "permanence." He studies a wealthy, walled community, which insulates itself against the outside world's perceived danger and degeneracy, as an example of place-making. His "place," and that of Heidegger whose work he engages, is intimately bound up with identity, roots, belonging, continuity, and readings onto space of particular memories.[34] I do not believe that *genius loci* is limited to a connotation of positive or negative meaning-making, but that, depending on how it is used, it can incorporate the violences, inequities, or comforts of how we come to understand our "place" in the world. Harvey's walled community shifts focus to the way in which dominant subjects make their place in the world through rigid boundary-maintenance designed to keep degeneracy at bay.

In a similar vein, Kathleen Kirby examines the mapping of space as fundamental to the formation of the "Cartesian subject."[35] Speaking of the necessity of establishing identity through the mastery of unknown places, she notes how space, for the privileged newcomer, is studied and "known" while space itself is not actively permitted to "know," to act back upon, the dominant subject. When this relationship shifts, such disorder is profoundly disturbing to the privileged (usually) white male subject who "explores" and, through mapping, conquers and reformulates space into something felt to be his own. It is in the project of this expropriation, with its concomitant distancing from the environment, that dominant subjects come to know themselves. While Kirby's theory is set out among "New World" explorer narratives, a greatly similar mechanism is at work in Africville, where white panic over the possibility of an enduring Black presence is played out in a continual project of re-examining, rezoning, and reformulating the environment, making it clear who is in control and who may not achieve this subjugation of space.

A new stage in this project began in the 1980s when the city established Seaview Memorial Park on Africville's former site. Named after Seaview Church, which was destroyed before the rest of Africville, the park lies under a major bridge between the cities of Halifax and Dartmouth and winds for several acres along a stretch of waterfront. Landscaped as a gently rolling green space, the park provides benches overlooking the water and gravelly walking trails. A paved parking lot has replaced the oily dirt roads former residents have described. When the park was opened in 1985, the city's mayor announced plans to build a swimming pool there—on this site where Africville had been denied the installation of water lines throughout its existence.[36] A reunion with several hundred former Africville residents or descendants and their families takes place there each summer. In 1988, a monument was built near the park's entrance, engraved with the names of the area's first Black settlers. This monument is the only visible evidence that Africville once existed, and even its tribute does not tell the story of the destruction of this community.

Standing in the park, attempting to feel some semblance of connection to my project, I was struck by the manufactured ignorance and erasure available to someone like myself—born after Africville's destruction, white, never having been taught this element of my province's history. Attempting to map the images in photographs and stories onto the site was futile. The land is not the same shape; it is not the same colour; its contours have been altered. It could easily be seen as a park where Halifax proudly honours a founding Black family and a community that happened to blend silently into the city's past. Unless one knows, nothing in sight speaks to the history of this space.

To read the park as *genius loci*, I believe, helps to situate it as a site of evidence with multiple meanings that can be read onto it, or onto the monument itself, depending on the histories and awarenesses people bring to it. As much as the monument shapes memory and dictates how we are to remember the story it depicts, it is important to remember that socially made preconceptions interact with our interpretation of what is being presented. Obviously, those who enter Seaview Memorial Park as their "place," or as a grounded symbol of continued resistance, will define this locale differently from those who remember driving to Africville to dump their garbage. Different still are the definitions of those who have never been to the city before, who visit as tourists or newcomers and "receive" a history that has been laid out for them, even as they bring specific conceptual tools to its interpretation. For them, the space says nothing of the violence that has been enacted upon it. It is in this act of burying the true story and dramatic transformation of the land that forms a poignant link in the chain of events that evicted Africville from its own space.

In the compression of time and space embodied in the monument and in the park, what might prevent us from seeing space as possessed of a history, of seeing the land we stand on as intimately problematic? What is *buried* beneath this symbol of remembering, or what truths does it hold down? It seems that the emptiness of space, here, is another form of *genius loci* for the Cartesian subject, who is complicit or silent in Africville's dislocation. In hiding the evidence where the community once stood, the city continued to produce an ongoing regulation of space to serve the purpose of memory-making. It predetermined how the space was to be received—as recreational land, a "neutral" greenspace open to "anyone." As non-Black outsiders, we can imagine little more than a mythic existence of a Black community, either romantic or slumlike, well in the past. In knowing ourselves through its reclamation and subjugation, we return to our "place" and know that it is *not* that place, which existed only as a site of intolerable disarray awaiting our inevitable intervention and organization.

The monument and park may foster a collective white belief in a sense of innocence, or in what Jane Jacobs has called "reconciliation." Tracing the effect of "Aboriginal walking tours," which display Aboriginal cultural artworks alongside traditional colonial monuments in the urban space of Melbourne, Australia, Jacobs explores the narrative of reconciliation that underpins this public positioning of histories. In its attempt to unite historically colonized and colonizing groups under a common national identity, reconciliation "attempts to bring the nation into contact with the 'truth' of colonisation—and this includes the attendant emotional 'truths' of guilt, anger, regret and hurt—in order that there might be a certain 'healing.'"[37] The anxieties this discourse raises among non-Aboriginals as to their understandings of their past and their place in the nation's history are, in Jacobs's view, rekindling a more overt racism imbued with a sense that Aborigines now possess too much power and privilege.

Would this sort of defensive hostility result from attempts to retell the truth of Africville's history in the public forum? Do the monument and park, along with more recent acceptance of memorials in the form of plays, music, and art displays, incur a sense of reconciliation among white Halifax residents, a sense that they have gone far enough in paying tribute to "unfortunate" events of the past? Informally expressed regret, combined with the more common-sense notion that Africvilleans are "still bitter" and should "put the past in the past," fail to expose personal and collective complicity, much less to ignite a strong public legal move towards material compensation. Further, they allow a sense of personal achievement in having come to a point of understanding, of believing we relate to what happened, that we regret what those before us did, while remaining distinct from the whole mess. As in the Australian case Jacobs describes, we have seen heightened resentment against Africville residents who are making demands at the government level, while many white residents assert that the city has been generous and compassionate where there was no racism to begin with.

How might the way in which the Africville story is "told" enable a dominant, privileged audience to receive a message of complicity and responsibility? As Lefebvre writes, "Monumental space offered each member of a society an image of that membership, an image of his or her social visage."[38] To usefully explore the social visage of a community that forced the dislocation of others, it is crucial to understand the way we remember or forget, but we also must look further to determine the historical understandings and memories we bring to the Africville monument. When these remembrances are disconnected from the actual space, as they are in most white public consumption of the story, the story may retain a mythic quality, like an entertaining but "unreal" war narrative from ancient history. The potential of a physically grounded analysis, in which we can hear the story from the perspectives of former residents and connect it to their space, is lost.

■ SILENCING THE GHOSTS

In 1994, there was a resurgence of municipal panic when two brothers, former Africville residents, occupied Seaview Memorial Park. They were protesting the lack of compensation and demanding renewed claims on Africville land. The Carvery brothers, teenagers when they left Africville, set up camp in Seaview on the site of their former home for over a year, getting through a cold winter with only a tent and a few survival implements. The authorities failed in their repeated threats and attempts to evict them, which included locking the park's only public washroom.[39] Their protest took place at the same time that the city was preparing to host the G7 summit. To allow the ghosts of Africville (though in reality very much alive) to seep through the carefully managed fabric of a well-tended burial would cause Halifax worldwide embarrassment—whether over a failure to manage "its Blacks" or over leaked knowledge of its injustices is not clear.

News reports during this time reflect a daily concern with the presence of the Carvery brothers in the park and cite complaints from Halifax residents who claimed the Carverys' protest "took away from their enjoyment of the park."[40] A few months before the summit, despite widespread protest from the Black community, a law was passed that forbade citizens to camp in public parks overnight. Mayor Fitzgerald, who earlier claimed his government had "bent over backwards" in attempt to negotiate with Africville protesters, cited the new ordinance as falling under the *Protection of Property Act*. In contrast to two days earlier, when the city had had no legal recourse against those sleeping overnight in a city park, he was able to announce that "people are in the park illegally and we want them off."[40] The Carverys eventually moved their protest just outside the park's border, to an area that did not fall under municipal jurisdiction. As the city alone could not evict them without provincial and federal consent, they maintained their campsite for several more years.[42]

The city's destruction of Africville was the culmination of a moral panic at the possibility of an independent, sovereign blackness. The nation makes itself not through exclusionary practice alone, but, to borrow Sibley's term, through "geographies of exclusion."[43] Through the desecration of space as Black, the appropriation of space as white, the suppression of the story of this violence and the denial of accountability, the life of Africville is grounded upon a geography of racism and its discursive organization. Like the proverbial lie, once told, the story necessitates the telling of a chain of "maintenance fictions," complete with the management of space in such a way that the fictions prevail intact and that oppositional stories remain buried. For the purposes of demonstrable racist harm, it will never suffice to engage in a strictly information-based investigation, for it can never be proven within such a paradigm that Africville was destroyed because a Black presence was disdained.

The legal, social, and historical logic of "relocation" tells us that the city's actions were unfortunate but necessary, humanitarian, compassionate, non-racist, integrative, progressive, and, perhaps above all, innocent. A conceptual analysis of the regulation of space over time helps us look beyond this, perhaps because it asks as many questions as it answers: Why was industrial development *not* carried out? Why was "empty" recreational space created instead? Why didn't this take place in a white neighbourhood? Why is there no dump in the city's prosperous south end? Why does the city still speak of "Black areas" in derogatory ways? For it appears that the discourse of integration, never realized, is more a discourse of erasure from sight and site.

Africville's story does not begin in 1962; it does not even begin in 1862. It begins in slavery, in Preston, in the founding of Halifax and the nation, in the hunting of the Mi'kmaq by British settlers.[44] In short, our perceptions of what functions as "evidence" must shift to allow the building of a context of ongoing oppression that may inform the way such issues are approached in law, to re-examine common key assumptions about fairness and equity which, by design, will serve the case badly. Our framework must shift from one of innocence or pity to one of justice.

Legal decision-making follows social histories that include poverty and racism. Such histories rely upon complex narratives of blackness that operate in the making of the slum. In turn, legal policy is producing further histories that perpetuate racist practice. These phenomena operate as threads knotted together; to remove any one would make the story of Africville qualitatively different. To discuss any one in isolation is to belittle and betray any attempt at truth or justice. In drawing continuities along a chain of evictions, burials, denials, and complicities through time, their logical sequence becomes evident: depriving the community of essential services; defining the community as slumlike based on the conditions this deprivation promotes; dislocating both persons and space, claiming the inevitability of destruction; altering the space and redefining its purpose and use by opening a park; installing a monument to suggest a sense of reconciliation; suppressing the true story when it resurfaces, and legislating restrictions on protesters who resurrect it.

As I have tried to demonstrate, the legal moves inherent in Africville's history as a degenerate site become clearer when a spatial analysis is permitted to trace and broaden the scope of what are considered to be regulatory measures. If we want to resist the official story, we must insist that history be alive and visible, and look at Africville's destruction not as a segment of the past but as fabric in the history of the present.

■ NOTES

1. G. Stephenson, *A Redevelopment Study of Halifax, Nova Scotia* (Halifax: Corporation of the City of Halifax, 1957), pp. 27–8.

2. L. Johnson, "Occupying the Suburban Frontier: Accommodating Difference on Melbourne's Urban Fringe," in A. Blunt and G. Rose, eds., *Writing Women and Space: Colonial and Postcolonial Geographies* (New York: Guilford Press, 1994), p. 146.

3. For early historical information, I have relied on: Africville Genealogical Society, eds., *The Spirit of Africville* (Halifax: Formac, 1992); D.H. Clairmont and D.W. Magill, *Africville Relocation Report* (Halifax: Institute of Public Affairs, Dalhousie University, 1971); D.H. Clairmont and D.W. Magill, *Africville: The Life and Death of a Canadian Black Community*, 1st and 3rd editions (Toronto: McClelland & Stewart, 1974, 1999); F. Henry, *Forgotten Canadians: The Blacks of Nova Scotia* (Don Mills, ON: Longman Canada Limited, 1973).

4. For documentation of relocation, see Clairmont and Magill, *Africville*, and the Africville Genealogical Society, eds., *The Spirit of Africville*.

5. The letter of R.J. Britton, Director of Social Planning for the City of Halifax, to Halifax City Council can be found in "Letter to Halifax City: Re: Africville Genealogy Society," in the Halifax Public Library: Africville File, October 28, 1994. Housing purchase prices are listed in this letter. The amounts city council claims to have paid are seen as inaccurate by some Africville activists with whom I have spoken. There have been accusations of bribery, in which city officials are alleged to have offered residents suitcases of cash in exchange for their eviction. See J. Robson, "Last Africville Resident," *The Mail Star* (Halifax), January 12, 1970, p. 5.

6. David Goldberg, *Racist Culture* (Oxford: Blackwell, 1993), pp. 191–92.

7. Henri Lefebvre, "The Production of Space (Extracts)," in N. Leach, ed., *Rethinking Architecture: A Reader in Cultural Theory* (London: Routledge, 1997), p. 140.

8. Barnor Hesse, "Black to Front and Black Again," in M. Keith and S. Pile, *Place and the Politics of Identity* (London: Routledge, 1993), p. 175.

9. Henri Lefebvre, "Reflections on the Politics of Space," *Antipode* 8 (1876), p. 31.

10. C.R. Saunders et al., "A Visit to Africville," in Africville Genealogical Society, eds., *The Spirit of Africville*, p. 33.

11. See Goldberg, *Racist Culture*, p. 7; David Sibley, "Racism and Settlement Policy: The State's Response to a Semi-Nomadic Minority," in P. Jackson, ed., *Race and Racism: Essays in Social Geography* (London: Allen and Unwin, 1987), p. 74; David Sibley, *Geographies of Exclusion* (London: Routledge, 1995); P. Stallybrass and A. White, *The Politics and Poetics of Transgression* (Ithaca: Cornell University Press, 1986); E. Said, *Culture and Imperialism* (New York: Vintage, 1993).

12. P. Marcuse, "Not Chaos, but Walls: Postmodernism and the Partitioned City," In S. Watson and K. Gibson, eds., *Postmodern Cities and Spaces* (Cambridge: Blackwell, 1995), p. 243.

13. Sherene Razack, "Race, Space and Prostitution," *Canadian Journal of Women and the Law* 10, 2 (1998), p. 338.

14. Reports of some bootlegging in Africville are cited in Clairmont and Magill, *Africville Relocation Report*.

15. David Sibley, *Outsiders in Urban Societies* (Oxford: Blackwell, 1981).

16. Samira Kawash, "The Homeless Body," *Public Culture* 10 (1998), p. 319.

17. Goldberg, *Racist Culture*, p. 190.

18. *Ibid.*, p. 198. See also K. Anderson, *Vancouver's Chinatown: Racial Discourse in Canada, 1875–1980* (Montreal: McGill-Queen's University Press, 1991).

19. Stephenson, *A Redevelopment Study of Halifax, Nova Scotia.* The Stephenson Report focuses most intensely on the downtown region of Halifax and what might be done about the poor and overcrowded living conditions of its residents, the majority of whom would have been white.

20. *Ibid.*

21. Sibley, *Outsiders in Urban Societies.*

22. C.R. Saunders, "Relocation and Its Aftermath: A Journey Behind the Headlines," in Africville Genealogical Society et al., eds., *Africville: A Spirit That Lives on* (Halifax: The Art Gallery, Mount Saint Vincent UnIversity, 1989), p. 17.

23. Many references to the city's intended desegregation are cited in Clairmont and Magill, *Africville Relocation Report,* and Clairmont and D.W. Magill, *Africville: The Life and Death of a Canadian Black Community;* see also Britton, "Letter to Halifax City Re: Africville Genealogy Society," note 5 above.

24. R. Simon, "The Touch of the Past: The Pedagogical Significance of a Transactional Sphere of Public Memory," in P. Trifonas, ed., *Revolutionary Pedagogies: Cultural Politics, Education, and the Discourse of Theory* (New York: Routledge, 2000), p. 61.

25. Goldberg, *Racist Culture*, p. 204.

26. Sherene Razack, "Gendered Racial Violence and Spatialized Justice: The Murder of Pamela George," chap. 5 in this volume.

27. Sherene Razack, *Looking White People in the Eye: Gender, Race and Culture in Courtrooms and Classrooms* (Toronto: University of Toronto Press, 1998), p. 40.

28. Britton, "Letter to Halifax City: Re: Africville Genealogy Society," note 5 above.

29. *Ibid.*

30. R. Thompson Ford, "The Boundaries of Race: Political Geography in Legal Analysis," *Harvard Law Review* 107 (1994), p. 1843.

31. Goldberg, *Racist Culture.*

32. Clairmont and Magill, *Africville Relocation Report.*

33. Goldberg, *Racist Culture*, pp. 204–05.

34. D. Harvey, *Justice, Nature and the Geography of Difference* (Cambridge: Blackwell, 1996).

35. Kathleen Kirby, "Re: Mapping Subjectivity: Cartographic Vision and the Limits of Politics," in N. Duncan, ed., *Bodyspace: Destabilizing Geographies of Gender and Sexuality* (London: Routledge, 1996), p. 45.

36. L. MacLean, "Seaview Officially Opens," The Mail Star (Halifax), June 24, 1985, p. 1.

37. Jane Jacobs, "Resisting Reconciliation: The Secret Geographies of (Post)colonial

Australia," in S. Pile and M. Keith, eds., *Geographies of Resistance* (London: Routledge, 1997), pp. 206–08.

38. Lefebvre, "The Production of Space Extracts," p. 140.

39. M. Lightstone, "Africville Showdown Brewing," *The Halifax Daily News*, February 12, 1995.

40. C. MacKeen, "City Responds to Protest over Seaview Park Land," *The Halifax Chronicle-Herald*, May 12, 1995.

41. T.L. Paynter, "City Gives Carverys the Boot," *North End News*, March 24, 1995; M. Lightstone, "Mayor: 'No Racism in This,'" *The Halifax Daily News*, March 25, 1995; C. MacKeen, "Get Out, Protesters Warned," *The Halifax Chronicle-Herald*, May 17, 1995, p. A1.

42. Charles Saunders, "Scenes from Africville Reunion," *Halifax Daily News*, August, 8, 1999, p. 20.

43. Sibley, *Geographies of Exclusion.*

44. See Bonita Lawrence, "'Real' Indians and Others: Mixed-Race Urban Native People, the Indian Act, and the Rebuilding of Indigenous Nations" (Ph.D. diss., Ontario Institute of Studies in Education of the University of Toronto, 1999).

■ QUESTIONS FOR CRITICAL THOUGHT

1. Mawani writes that "[t]he object of education in this [V.D.] campaign is not so much the dissemination of knowledge ... as the development of standards of conduct and the formation of character." What does she mean by this? How does this link to Corrigan's observation that "all social relations have an 'educative tendency'"? How is this observation key to moral regulation studies?

2. What are some of the processes by which "normal" is produced? How does "normality" reproduce unequal class, gender, and racialized/ethnic social relations?

3. What are some of the processes by which "deviance" is produced? What are the roles of resistance, power, and agency in the production of "bad" or "immoral" behaviours? Is the state a more important player in the production of "immorality" than in "normality"? Why or why not?

4. How has Nelson specifically illustrated how race and space are connected in regulation? How does the history of Africville shape our understandings of moral regulation more generally?

5. What is the relationship between the moralization of place and the regulation of space? How does space link to the project of "nation-building" and "respectable" citizenship? What roles do agency and resistance play in the regulation of space?

■ FURTHER READINGS

Mary-Louise Adams. *The Trouble with Normal: Postwar Youth and the Making of Heterosexuality* Toronto: University of Toronto Press, 1997. In this study of the development of teenage (hetero)sexuality, Adams shows the historical and contingent nature of "normal."
This work also makes it clear that reformers, and especially non-state agents, have a distinct interest in constructing a sense of normalcy that is then actively policed in such a way that the construction and policing of it appear as normal themselves. This book shows the continuing significance of the moral regulation approach to expanding our sociological understanding of "normal" and "deviant" sexualities.

Robert Campbell. "Managing the Marginal: Regulating and Negotiating Decency in Vancouver's Beer Parlours, 1925-1954." *Labour/Le Travail* 44 (Fall 1999):109-127.
Campbell offers a thorough examination of the ways in which the regulation of bars, ostensibly practised as a way to control excessive drinking, operates as a form of the moralization of bar patrons in general, and of specific drinking populations in particular. Importantly, Campbell shows how the organization of public space, such as the men's and the "ladies and escorts" sides of bars, is informed by, and grants naturalizing

power to, existing social relations of class, race, and gender. However, he also shows that these regulated spaces are resisted in ways that demonstrate that moral regulation is always a contested practice.

Becki Ross. "Destaining the (Tattooed) Delinquent Body: The Practices of Moral Regulation at Toronto's Street Haven, 1965-1969." *Journal of the History of Sexuality* 7, 4 (1997):561-95.

In addition to further exploring the issues raised by Sangster, Ross's analysis of young "delinquent" women in Toronto in the late 60s alerts us to the significance of the body to practices of regulation. Ross demonstrates that outward appearances, such as the lack of tattoos, are read as signifiers of moral subjectivities. In addition, Ross reminds us of the significance of "deviant" sexualities to the class-based, gendered, and racialized assessments of morality.

Carolyn Strange. *Toronto's Girl Problem: The Perils and Pleasures of the City, 1880-1930.* Toronto: University of Toronto Press, 1995.

Through an exploration of the moral discourses that surrounded the young, single working girl in turn-of-the-century Toronto, Carolyn Strange demonstrates not only the centrality of moral-sexual conduct to the regulation of young women, but also the centrality of the discourses about young women themselves to the broader project of morally regulating the city of Toronto.

PART III

THE LIMITS OF MORAL REGULATION AND BEYOND

This final section returns to the original debates established at the beginning of the text, asking again about the value and limitations of moral regulation.

The tensions documented throughout the reader divide into two divergent forms of inquiry. The first is governmentality studies, a Foucault-inspired form of analysis that focuses on the making of new, responsible, and self-regulating citizens in a neoliberal context. The second stream of inquiry reaffirms the significance of the power of the state in the regulation of problematic populations, whose regulation is largely external and punitive or coercive. These two streams of thought demonstrate the significance of moral regulation to the development of new forms of sociological analyses of deviance, normalcy, and ethical citizenship.

Mitchell Dean's interpretation of moral regulation offers a sharp contrast to that offered by many other scholars. Dean critiques Corrigan's approach to moral regulation as overly concerned with the state. Instead, Dean argues for a more Foucault-inspired analysis of the formation of self in relation to political practices. In this way, Dean's approach also acts as an important bridge between moral regulation and governmentality studies.

Mariana Valverde's examination of the practices of Alcoholics Anonymous offers a concrete example of many of Dean's theoretical formulations. As Valverde argues, AA offers the quintessential instance of this form of regulation because its philosophy embraces a form of ethical self-formation. This emphasis on the governance of the self illustrates the shift, among some scholars, from moral regulation to governmentality.

By contrast, Dorothy Chunn and Shelley Gavigan, who earlier critiqued social control, now apply that same critique (of overuse and methodological vagueness) to moral regulation. They use the contemporary legal regulation of welfare recipients as their case study. They argue that the state, coercion, and materialist analysis are as helpful in understanding recent shifts in welfare regulation as is the moral regulation emphasis on non-state governance and discursive formations of moral subjectivities. Chunn and Gavigan suggest that both moral regulation and a materialist analysis of social control are necessary to understand the punitive forms of contemporary regulation.

David Garland's essay returns us to the original questions surrounding the sociological analysis of deviance and crime. Garland questions whether theories of governance—especially discursive, non-state forms of regulation—explain the control of populations deemed criminal. Garland argues that there is a difference between "agency"—that is, the will to act—and "freedom"—that is, the ability to act in ways of one's choosing. This distinction offers a neat summation of the tensions evident in the development of moral regulation scholarship. It also raises the question of what areas the sociology of deviance, control, and regulation can next explore.

CHAPTER 13

"A SOCIAL STRUCTURE OF MANY SOULS":
MORAL REGULATION, GOVERNMENT, AND SELF-FORMATION

Mitchell Dean

This article explores different ways of thinking about the general problem of the interconnection between self-formation and political and governmental practices and processes. It first explicates the thesis of the relation of moral regulation and state formation advanced in the writings of Philip Corrigan. It argues that, despite its strengths, this formulation has several difficulties: its reliance on a culturalist account of the work of moral regulation; its undue focus on the state; and its inability to approach domains of self-formation at a distance from the state. It further argues that many of the problems raised within this framework can be formulated more effectively by developing the analytic of governmentality provided by Michel Foucault. Such a framework allows us to understand how processes of political subjectification are dependent upon, if irreducible to, both governmental and ethical practices of self-formation.

> In all willing it is absolutely a question of commanding and obeying, on the basis, as I have said already, of a social structure composed of many 'souls' .... (Nietzsche, 1973: 31)[1]

After Durkheim, sociology might be described as a "natural science of morals" (cf. Turner, 1992) in that it presupposes the primacy of society over the individual in accounting for causes or origins of moral values and conduct. Moreover, it construes this as a process immanent to the development of societies. In his lectures on civic morals, Durkheim discusses the subsumption and the promotion of the individual by the state as a "law of moral mechanics ... just as inevitable as the laws of physical mechanics" (1992: 60). In contrast, Philip Corrigan's use of the term "moral regulation" seeks to overcome this naturalistic formulation of sociology by stressing the constructed and contested character of what is taken to be natural and normal including, presumably, the necessity of social determination itself. In other words, it is not sufficient to assert the causal prima- cy of "the social" as a sociological *a priori*; rather, it is necessary to show *how* this primacy occurs in particular cases in such a way as to make it appear as necessary, inevitable, and natural. Sociology cannot, then, ground itself in general notions of social causality; to be effective, it must begin with a sense of the contingency of what appears as inevitable.

On this basis, Corrigan found an elision within Durkheim's thought:

> There is a slippage between the categories "moral" and "social," and between "State" and "Society"; taken together, these result in systematically suppress- ing the constrained *but-constructed* features of human sociation in favour of their naturalisation as normalised states of human life (*any* human life). Thus if we compare such texts as *The Division of Labour* and *Suicide* or *Professional Ethics ... and Moral Education*, we find the former title in each couple elaborating in more par- ticular terms that which the latter has (quite literally) *socialized*. (Corrigan, 1990: 106, original emphasis)

What Corrigan seeks to address, then, is not the process by which "Society" necessarily stamps itself on the personality of individuals but the means by which "constructed" identities come to be formed, re-formed and taken to be natural and normal. It is this naturalizing and normalizing process that is at the core of Corrigan's specification of the concept of moral regulation. This concept concerns a) the naturalization and nor- malization effects of b) the external and constraining force (after Durkheim) of c) social relations on d) identities and subjectivities. Nevertheless, *pace* Durkheim, or at least a certain typecasting of him, Corrigan (1990: 114) insists on the multiple nature of identity, without which we cannot understand "the fragility, permeability, difficulty, agony, and yet poetic energy of most human lives which result from attempting to live with and through the contradictory combination of a variety of possible social classifi- cations, possible identities."

A preliminary point to note here can be raised by asking the question, "why moral"? This is something that needs to be clarified in the following discussion if we are to be clear as to what separates this term, and the analysis it makes possible, from a revamped version of that old sociological faithful, social control. However, it is not the neologism that makes Corrigan's thought interesting. It is the attempt to rethink the linkages between the regulation of conduct and the state. This attempt is embodied in what might be called "Corrigan's formula." This formula is present already in the title of his doctoral thesis (Corrigan, 1977), "State formation and moral regulation ...," and is given greater clarity in the opening pages of *The Great Arch* (Corrigan and Sayer, 1985: 4), where it is stated that "moral regulation is coextensive with state formation." The agency of moral regulation for Corrigan is, above all, the state. What is interesting, although not novel—given the work of Norbert Elias (1978; 1982; 1983) and, more recently, Michel Foucault—about this formula is the attempt to think of the state as an historical process of formation linked to the formation of individual and collective capacities, identities, and conducts. This paper will deal with both sides of Corrigan's formula, for it is not possible to think about one without the other, and what I am most interested in is the development of the insight that there is a relation or overlap between the two disparate processes of state-building and individual citizen-formation.

I wish, however, to dissent from key aspects of Corrigan's approach. I dissent not from Corrigan's attempt to make intelligible the naturalization and normalization of socially formed identities but from his account of the *means* by which this occurs. I suggest that this account is deficient in three major ways: its dependence on the language and framework of "culture"; the manner in which it conceives the state, particularly its "state-centredness"; and the absence of a concerted approach to domains of self-formation that operate at a distance from the state. Many of the problems raised within the terms of Corrigan's formula can be reformulated more effectively in what amounts to the open analytic space provided by a full appreciation of the thematics of governmentality that appear in Michel Foucault's later writings, lectures, and interviews.

In the first section, I consider Corrigan's formula, particularly in *The Great Arch*, and expand upon and illustrate the limitations just noted. In the second, I ponder the possibilities of developing a morals/ethics contrast as one between a set of principles or codes, on the one hand, and practices of self-formation and regulation, on the other. I argue that it is in this last regard that the Foucauldian theme of governmentality as the intersection of practices of ethical self-formation and practices of government provides an instructive analytical framework rather than a general social theory. What follows is hence an interpretative description of some of the major features of that analytic and illustrations of its use, and an exposition and transformation of the conceptual language appropriate to it. In particular I address what I call the problem of "political subjectification" from the perspective of a concern with practices of governmental and ethical self-formation. I also consider how that framework differs from its nearest sociological counterpart, the theory of the sociogenesis of the modern form of self provided by Norbert Elias's historical sociology.

In a brief conclusion, I summarize the argument with respect to the limitations of the Corrigan thesis of the identity of moral regulation and state formation and the relative strengths of Foucault's account of ethical and governmental self-formation. I suggest that the mode of political subjectification in liberal-democratic states (i.e., the treatment of political subjects as if they were autonomous citizens within self-governing political communities) should be understood as (at least in part) conditioned by various practices of governmental and ethical self-formation operating from a variety of locales both within and outside the state.

■ 1

During the heyday of work on the *theory* of the state in the 1970s there was little discussion—with the notable exception of Nicos Poulantzas's attempts (1978: 63–75) to incorporate Foucauldian themes—on questions of identity and individuality and practices and process of individualization. It may be that a similar point can be made about the more recent turn to an historical sociology of the state. This is a massive oversight. [...]

In this regard, Corrigan and Sayer's historical sociology of English state formation, *The Great Arch* (1985), may be, if not unique, at least exceptional. Unlike much of the historical sociology of the state, this book eschews both a comparative method and the attempt to establish a causal thesis about the formation of the state. Rather it seeks to introduce considerations of individuality, identity, and subjectivity into the heart of an account of the development of the English state. In this it is remarkably successful. The limitations of the book derive from what amounts to a *culturalist* understanding of many of the features of state activities and power it examines. Its principal thesis, echoed in its subtitle, is that English state formation is cultural revolution. I take this to mean that the narrative of the state cannot be divorced from the regulation and even constitution of particular cultural forms, and that the state itself is constructed within such forms. At the heart of such a problematic is the attribution of meaningful identities by state practices and processes and the material and historical forces—of class, gender, race, religion, and so on—that give rise to such meanings.

A crucial part of this cultural transformation, and at the core of the way these authors consider the effects of the state, is the process of moral regulation. This is where the thesis of the common topography of moral regulation and state formation is introduced. Indeed, if one were to give the Corrigan and Sayer thesis a theoretical form, it is that state formation effects cultural transformation through the mechanism of moral regulation. However, in keeping with their general approach, the notion of moral regulation is presented in terms of culture. Thus, returning to an earlier paper, we find that Corrigan conceived (1990: 111) the work of moral regulation as the reproduction of particular forms of expression that attempt to fix as normal representations of types of experience, and that the "means of moral regulation" are thus "expressive forms and norms."

In *The Great Arch* moral regulation is above all a project of normalization and naturalization of the premises of a specific social order. It concerns the *meaning* of state activities for the constitution and regulation of social identities and subjectivities (Corrigan and Sayer, 1985: 2). This moral regulation centrally takes place by giving "unitary and unifying expression" to "multifaceted and differential historical experiences of groups, denying their particularity" (1985: 4). It legitimizes forms of individual and collective identity as it denies the legitimacy of other forms, as well as the realities of inequality of class, gender, ethnicity, age, locality, occupation, and belief.

Corrigan and Sayer inflect what could be a quite straightforward Marxist account of the representation of individuality within "bourgeois" state forms with two manoeuvres. The first is borrowed from a reading of Foucault's writings on governmentality and the second from Durkheim's conception of the state. First they argue that moral regulation has a "totalizing" and "individualizing" aspect (Corrigan and Sayer, 1985: 4–5). It is totalizing in that it represents "people" as members of an illusory and imaginary political community in notions of nationality and citizenship. It is individualizing in so far as it represents people within various categories of identity, such as citizens, taxpayers, jurors, parents, consumers, voters, and so on. The crucial terms in their account of how these identities are represented and how they have determinate effects are the "routines" and "rituals" of state. The routines embody these forms of identity, treating people as if they fall within such categories. The rituals of state, on the other hand, broadcast these identities, particularly the totalizing ones, in a grandiloquent form and so naturalize and normalize them as a part of national identity. There are problems with this notion of representation and its mechanisms I shall return to in a moment. Simply note now that the effectiveness of state formation on moral regulation is restricted to the ways in which identities are constructed in various forms of *representation* and the consequent meaning "people" (a highly naturalistic term if ever there was one) attach to their experiences, activities, lives, careers, and relationships.

The second inflection within Marxism comes from its marriage with Durkheimian thought on the nature of the state as an organ of social thought and moral discipline, at first a parasite on the *conscience collective*, which it then comes to regulate (Corrigan and Sayer, 1985: 6–10). The dual sense of the French word *conscience* as conscience and consciousness comes into play in the analysis. Collective representations are both forms of description of social identities and relations and also normative prescriptions of the legitimate forms of existence possible. The state becomes a focus of such representations, taking an active role in the regulation of those collective representations which prescribe the limits of what is permitted as they describe forms of identity. Combining Durkheim with Marx, the authors conclude that the state project concerns the construction of aspiration and the internalization of bourgeois norms as constitutive of personalities (1985: 194–95). As a result, capitalism, for example, is not simply an economy but a "set of social forms of life" regulated through the state (1985: 188). *The Great Arch* is a highly interesting attempt to introduce questions of individuality, identity, and subjectivity into problems of the state and its consequences for social life. However, there are several weaknesses that follow from the way it constructs an account of moral regulation; these become pertinent in our account of Foucault's rubric of governmentality.

The first problem involves the range of effects of what we might call a *culturalist* conception of the work of moral regulation. The way in which these authors conceive of moral regulation as a cultural process presupposes, first, a realm of experience grounded in material relations (Corrigan and Sayer, 1985: 7) and, second, an ideal domain of the representation of experience. Cultural processes, in such a framework, are ones in which experiences can be expressed, denied, excluded, or distorted at another level, that of meaning or representation (or, in other versions, ideas and values). Corrigan and Sayer use this dual-level framework of experience and meaning in a complex manner. Both realms are thoroughly historicized and pluralized and the representation of experience is a contested domain. [...]

Nevertheless there are general difficulties with maintaining this dual-level structure of experience and meaning. Not the least is that the very category of experience invokes a residual naturalism that belies the attempt to examine processes of naturalization. This naturalism takes the form of a philosophical anthropology of the human subject as a cultural being, i.e., as a being endowed with a capacity to attach and bestow meaning to its experience. [...] This presupposition limits the analysis of self-formation to a process by which human subjects, as a matter of course, come to bestow meaning on or to represent their experience. It thus forecloses the analysis of the multiplicity of the practical, technical, and discursive *means* by which self-formation occurs and the possibility that the meaning-giving subject of its own experience itself is a particular social and cultural category and dependent upon definite social-historical and intellectual conditions. [...]

* * * * *

To frame the question of moral regulation in terms of the representation of experience is thus to ignore or at least underplay the various ways in which specific governmental and administrative practices operate both singly and in concert to direct the life-conduct of actors whether as clients, claimants, or subjects, of the state, and the degree to which this direction has come to be dependent on the definition of what might be called life-choices (this is especially clear in the administrative devices concerning social welfare assistance, debates on poverty traps, notions of "active systems" of income support, etc.). [...] To think of moral regulation in terms of the (mis)attribution of meaning to experience is to remain within a general theory of language and representation and thus to foreclose the complex analysis of the relation between specific political and governmental discourses and rationalities, and administrative techniques, practices, rituals, and routines.

If there is a tendency to conceive moral regulation as a component of the state as a cultural form in *The Great Arch*, there is also a tendency—this time contrary to Durkheim's stress on the complexity of the state (1992a: 48)—to overemphasize the unity of the state and its consequences. [...] The state takes the place of the philosophical subject in the moral regulation of individuals, i.e., as the principal agent of the representation of experience and bestowal of meaning to it. In any case, Corrigan's insight into the fragile construction of individual identity needs to be complemented by a greater sense of the fragmentary character of state formation and the difficulty (and, in a sense, fruitlessness) of seeking to locate a division between "the state" and its outside. This restriction to the state is problematic in several ways. Above all, it ignores the multiplicity of agencies and authorities involved in the governance of the life-conduct of individuals, families, groups, and populations. This is clearly illustrated by the multiple and overlapping jurisdictions involving local, regional, national, international, and global authorities within which actors are located. It is evidenced by the widespread development of non-profit community and social services in advanced liberal democracies which are funded partially by the national state but run by citizen associations, and by the neo-liberal use of corporations, charities, and families, to achieve governmental objectives (e.g., the provision of welfare and domestic care, the establishment of prisons, job-centres, etc.). It can be also instanced by the introduction of management and efficiency norms modelled on the supposed operations of the private corporation into state employment and organization. Moreover, this form of analysis does not allow for dispersion of the policies and strategies enunciated within various sectors of the state (say, between the national treasury and a women's unit of a regional Department of Health) and the possibility that moral regulatory strategies could be similarly dispersed and dissonant (e.g., between the forms of sexuality sanctioned within the military and within anti-discrimination legislation). The oft-used caveat implied by the word "contradiction" [...] cannot do justice to this dispersion of both strategies, their intended consequences, and their range of (intended, semi-intended, unintended, and indeed perverse) effects, and the dissonance within and between specific strategies, programs, policies, and their consequences.

A third set of problems with the Corrigan formula stems from the fact of this dispersion of policies, practices, effects, and their consequences. If this is accepted, then there would be reason to examine the activities and consequences of other agencies and authorities in regard to the formation of identities. Not to do so is at odds with Durkheim (1992a: 47–50), who stresses the importance of "secondary organs" and "special groups," as well as "social currents" unconnected to the state, in the networks of social governance. Not only are there other agencies involved in practices of the governance of the conduct of individuals that exist in various relations (legal, regulatory, fiscal, financial, diplomatic, etc.) to sectors of the nation-state, but there are also other practices and techniques which centre on moral regulation, which have a highly variable relation to the state. These "practices of the self" run the gamut from the "acceptable" ones promoted by "psy" disciplines, social work, medicine, education, established religion, forms of sport and physical culture, to the plethora of practices associated with cults of self-liberation and self-improvement (from martial arts to sexual realization) and "how-to" programs in work, business, money, marriage, and love. Indeed, it may be that by bringing these practices and techniques of the self into focus in relation to a consideration of governmental powers and administrative practices that we are led to a problematization of the notion of the state *per se*, i.e., as a unitary entity concerned with the production or reproduction of a particular social order based on definite forms of subjectivity, and as the agent of social control.

Finally, with regard to *The Great Arch*, it might be observed that amid all the emphasis on moral regulation and the production of individualities, the nub of the problem of citizenship is not addressed: how political government can be conceived in terms of a community of self-governing citizens when governmental and ethical practices are bound up with the creation, shaping, and promotion of the capacities of these citizens. Surprisingly little attention is paid to the status of the self-governing citizen not only in Corrigan and Sayer but also all the recent literature on the historical sociology of the state. Yet it is precisely this issue that suggests a possible interconnection of that historical sociology with central issues of political thought.

In the next section, I want to suggest that a fuller appreciation of the ramifications of Foucault's thought on discipline in particular, and governmentality more broadly, can help us move beyond the limitations of this conception of moral regulation.

■ 2

Despite the limitations I have noted in the preceding section, Corrigan's (and Sayer's) account of moral regulation is significant in that it seeks to address the problem of the intersection of political and governmental processes of state formation with types of self-formation. There is, however, the issue of the force of the adjective "moral" and the difference between moral regulation and an account of social control as the formation of personality types through the agency and practices of the state. To clarify this, it is worth considering the problem of the use of "moral."

Consider the distinction between morals and ethics. As a first illustration, Durkheim's sociology as a science of morality shares something with its virtual contemporary, Nietzsche's genealogy of morals (1969), which uses the German term *Moral*. Both seek to locate the social and historical origins and present purposes of systems of morality, i.e., of codes of good and bad, right and wrong, etc. "Morals" refer in these, as in common use, to codes of evaluation. In both cases, however, the stress is on the practical rather than theoretical form of morality. For Durkheim, moral individualism is a matter of practice, of morals insofar as they are embodied in social institutions (1992a: 59). For Nietzsche, the codes of morality are subordinate to the practices of self-formation, what he called the "morality of mores." It is "with the aid of this morality of mores and the social straitjacket man was actually *made* calculable" (Nietzsche 1969: 59). Nietzsche's task may be understood as a "revaluation" of values and codes by reference to the social, political, ethical, and ascetic practices in which they are embedded. In this sense he is close to Kant who, as Ian Hacking points out (1986: 239), uses the term *Sitte* in numerous titles, which is translated as ethics but refers to customs and practices not exclusively moral. Weber, who owes much to both Kant and Nietzsche (Hennis, 1988), uses the term *Ethik* in his writings on the economic ethic of world religions which he defines as "the practical impulses for action which are founded in the psychological and pragmatic contexts of religions" (Weber, 1970: 267).

Without seeking to homogenize the work of these different thinkers, there is something to be learnt here for our present purposes. In so far as we seek to address issues of the direction of conduct within social practices, then what we are concerned with is less the explicit, codified system of evaluations than with self-formation within practical and pragmatic forms and contexts of everyday life, less with the theoretical artifice of commandments and law than with the practical conduct of life. In this sense, we are concerned less with morality and more with ethics, or, to be more precise, we are concerned with morality as it codifies and is inscribed within and modified by ethical practices.

* * * * *

This shift in our discussion to issues of ethical self-formation highlights the problems of the very term "moral regulation." The adjective "moral" remains indeterminate because it delineates no clear domain that is (even relatively) autonomous from forms of political regulation and state power. It might be suspected that the term simply continues the sociological preoccupation with the state as the agency of social control and only differs by having a more complex account of how that control occurs, i.e., by the naturalizing and normalizing of certain forms of identity through the representations inscribed in state routines and broadcast in state rituals. This brings us back to the third problem outlined above, the inability of the language of moral regulation to address the existence of spheres of self-regulation and self-formation that are not immediately po-litical (unless that term is to encompass everything and so become meaningless). The formation of political identity—"political subjectification"—can only be made fully in-telligible if placed in relation to the irreducible domains of ethical self-formation and governmental self-formation. One key implication of the discussion thus far is the need to develop an analysis that is capable of understanding the diversity of processes of self-formation, in particular the autonomy and interrelationship of governmental and ethical practices in this regard, and the relation between these practices of self-forma-tion, on the one hand, and political subjectification, on the other.

To clarify, by political subjectification I mean the practices and discourses that treat individuals *as if* they were political subjects in their diverse forms, particularly the treat-ment of individuals as sovereign subjects or citizens within a self-governing political community under the conditions of liberal democracy (cf. Hindess, 1991). Governmental self-formation refers to the ways in which various authorities and agencies seek to shape the conduct, aspirations, needs, desires, and capacities of specified categories of individu-als, to enlist them in particular strategies and to seek defined goals; ethical self-forma-tion concerns practices, techniques, and discourses of the government of the self by the self, by means of which individuals seek to know, decipher, and act on themselves. These three terms allow us to distinguish analytic domains that, while not mutually exclusive, may condition and presuppose one another in specific circumstances.

Following both Weber and Foucault, then, it is possible to recast the problem of so-ciology itself as one of the ways in which social practices, customs, habits, and beliefs are implicated in diverse processes of self-formation. While processes of political sub-jectification constitute an autonomous domain for critical thought, they draw upon, and intersect, various forms of self-formation—not only the governmental and ethical practices explored in this paper but also discursive practices and practices for the pro-duction of truth (e.g., Foucault, 1982; 1993).[...]

One might wish to reread Foucault's great popular work, *Discipline and Punish* (1977), as a set of variations on this theme of political subjectification. Drawing broadly on that text, we can note several clarifications Foucault's analysis offers us on the problems outlined in the first section. Firstly, the analysis of political subjectification should be more cautious toward a presumed *identity* of "moral regulation" with "state forma-tion." Processes of political subjectification are not necessarily located within the state but are constructed from practices operating from multiple and heterogeneous locales (citizen associations, charities, trade unions, families, schools, workplaces, etc.). These practices are not immediately political and have diverse historical origins and uses—military, pedagogical, religious, ascetic, bureaucratic, medical, economic, and so forth. While they are intensified and refined by their application within enclosed institutions (schools, factories, hospitals, asylums, etc.), they "swarm" within the social body. To restrict attention to the way in which the state is involved in political subjectification is to ignore the way in which governmental practices of self-formation come to colonize, compose, and transform the state itself.

Second, rather than political subjectification entailing processes of meaning and (mis)representation of the experience of the subject, for Foucault it involves the use and application of different types of self-relation. To take a well-known example, the forms of surveillance promoted by discipline, and exemplified in Bentham's Panopticon, do not work by attachment of (ideological) meaning to one's activity but by the inducement within the subject of "a state of conscious and permanent visibility that assures the automatic functioning of power" (Foucault, 1977: 201). This is achieved through the organization of power within definite forms of time-space. In Bentham's case, the very design and architecture of the enclosure is constructed according to the principle of the visibility and unverifiability of power. Political subjectification works by the establishment of forms of self-relation through disciplinary practices and techniques of surveillance, and through the material organization of conduct in time-space. Thus the citizen—the self-governing subject of rights—and the "docile and useful" individual sought by disciplinary practices are reciprocal conditions of one another in Foucault's account of representative democracy (1977: 222–23). Indeed, following Deleuze (1988: 99–103), one might think of Foucault's notion of the self by means of a spatial metaphor as involving the "folding" back of exterior relations of power and governance to create an "interiority" that can act of itself. One might further speak of a tissue of foldings by which the self is constituted as an independent self-governing entity, a free subject, that can act on itself through "practices of the self" as it is acted upon in practices of government. While *Discipline and Punish* (Foucault, 1977: 26–29) is concerned with the folding back of the "political technology of the body" to encompass a space of self-reflexivity, and so provides a "genealogy of the modern soul," it is in the latter volumes of his *History of Sexuality* (1985; 1986a) that the foldings in which the self acts on itself, knows and deciphers itself, are fully addressed.

Finally, these forms of political subjectification operating through particular techniques of government are specified within forms of normalizing and scientific discourse or, as he puts it, an entire "scientifico-legal complex" (Foucault, 1977: 23). Foucault would seem to be emphasizing the "routines" rather than the "rituals" of power as the key to political subjectification. Indeed, his account of the transformation of punitive practices within a changing complex of "power-knowledge" is sketched against the background of the diminution of the significance of the ritual form of sovereignty manifest in the spectacular of torture (*supplice*). The crucial point, however, is that these routines do not simply operate according to more or less arbitrary classifications and categories of individuals but are the loci of the formation of definite types of rationality and knowledge, which in turn are linked to governmental programs and operate as the means of strategy. The governmental routines of self-formation conditioning political subjectification cannot be made intelligible apart from the forms of knowledge (the normalizing discourses of the human sciences) which are invested in them and on which their operation depends.

This history of disciplinary practices as a key to political subjectification is subsumed under a much more general theme of the practices, techniques, and mentalities of government in Foucault's later lectures. The key term here is "governmentality." A glance at how Foucault uses this term immediately reveals the multiplicity of its domains and the way they traverse a similar territory to that marked out by Corrigan. In a seminar in Vermont, he defined governmentality as "the contact between the technologies of domination of others and those of the self" (Foucault, 1988d: 19; cf. 1993), and so captured its role at the fulcrum of his political and ethical problematics. Again, in an interview after the publication of the second and third volumes of *The History of Sexuality*, he suggested that governmentality implies the ethical relation of self to self, and that it concerns strategies for the direction of conduct of free individuals (Foucault, 1988a: 19–20). What makes Foucault's later studies pertinent to the present discussion, I would suggest, is condensed in this notion of governmentality. It defines a novel thought-space across the domains of ethics, government, and politics, of the government of self, others, and the state, of practices of government and practices of the self, of self-formation and political subjectification, that weaves them together without a reduction of one to the other.

This term can act as the general heading of two related transmutations of Foucault's thought in these years. On the one hand, the "microphysics of power"—exemplified by the disciplinary techniques which find their point of application in the minutiae of the comportment of the human body—becomes, in his lectures, a genealogy of governmentality, with its concerns for the complex historical trajectory of forms of political rationality (e.g., his Stanford lectures, Foucault, 1988c) and their relation to techniques and technologies of government, particularly in the context of the history of liberalism and the analysis of neo-liberalism (Foucault, 1989: 110–19). On the other, his history of sexuality becomes a genealogy of the desiring subject, concerned with a kind of morphology of the historical forms of ethical practice grounded in practices and techniques concerned with self-cultivation and

self-stylization (Foucault, 1985; 1986a). The notion of governmentality, encompassing the government of the state, the government of others, and the government of
self, is the fulcrum around which Foucault proposes to think the linkages between
these historical domains of practice. It is also the angle from which he proposes to
reflect upon the formation of political subjects, citizens, and communities.

Foucault establishes a common approach to each of these domains. In keeping
with Weber and Nietzsche, he gives primacy to the forms of governmental and ethical *practice* over their legal and moral codification and formalization. More importantly, he elaborates a methodology germane to the analysis of the government of
oneself and the government of others. In relation to the genealogy of ethics, this
methodology isolates four dimensions (Foucault, 1985: 26–28; 1986a: 238–39;
1986b: 352–57; 1988d; 1993): that of ontology, concerned with *what* we seek to
govern in ourselves and others, the "ethical substance" worked on by the respec-
tive techniques (e.g., the pleasures or *aphrodisia* in Greece, the flesh in early Christianity, sexuality in contemporary liberation ethics); that of ascetics, concerned
with *how* we govern this substance, the work on self, or the self-forming activity or
"forms of asceticism" (e.g., the employment of the various "techniques of the self"
such as dialogue, listening, meditation, prayer, training of memory, mortification
rituals, diary-keeping, self-examination, and, of course, confession, that comprise the
Hellenistic and Christian cultures of the self, Foucault, 1988d); that of deontology,
concerned with the "mode of subjectification," with the positions we take or are
given in relation to rules and norms, with *why* we govern ourselves or others in a
particular manner (e.g., to live a noble and beautiful life in antiquity, to submit to
God's law in Christianity, to become universal rational beings in Kantianism, to
fulfil our potential in contemporary liberation movements); and that of teleology,
the aim, end, goal, design, or *telos* of these practices, of the mode of being we hope
to create, of what we hope to produce (e.g., self-mastery through moderation for the
Greeks, salvation through self-renunciation in Christianity, the emancipation of the
self for contemporary liberation movements).

While this methodology is made explicit in relation to ethical practices in *The Use
of Pleasure*, it can be applied to what might be more narrowly regarded as governmental practices. To exemplify this, we have to go no further than the account of
"modern" punitive practices found in the first chapter of *Discipline and Punish* (Foucault, 1977: 16–31). There the substance of the punishable element is less the criminal act than the "soul" of the criminal—the circumstances, instincts, passions, desires, and effects of environment or heredity. The work of punishment becomes one
of the supervision, management, and normalization of the individual. The criminal
is subjectified as delinquent, deviant, or maladjusted, as one capable or incapable of

normalization. Finally, the *telos* of modern systems of punishment is not to be found in the internal history of criminal justice itself. Rather the *telos* refers to how the penalty is incorporated in a pattern of activities and knowledge leading to a specific end, a specific mode of being or, as Weber would have put it, conduct of life. The *telos* of punishment then is discipline itself, the new "political technology of the body" designed to operate on the body so that the subject will govern him or herself as a docile and useful individual.

Two aspects of this schema and mode of analysis of ethical and governmental practices are germane: first, both sets of practices are analyzed by similar tools concerned with the substance, work, mode, and end of practices of self-formation; second, that while both can be subject to parallel forms of analysis, they are quite distinct domains. For Foucault's thought on the relation between practices of government and self-formation, there is no one single schema, or type and direction of causality. There is simply the supposition that both can be understood in terms of the forms of self-relation they presuppose and enact and that it is possible to discuss the interconnection between the two domains. This then is less a theory of the relation between state and individual, or state formation and moral regulation, and more an analytic of differential domains of practice.

If we are to turn this analysis toward one of political subjectification, we should note that no analysis of the formation of political subjects is possible without a full account of both the way in which various authorities seek to direct the conduct of individuals and groups and the ways in which individuals and groups seek to act on themselves. Nevertheless, we should also note that political subjectification cannot be reduced to these governmental and ethical practices: voluntary association, political participation of various kinds, community action, public demonstrations, etc., are all means of formation of citizens and collective solidarities quite distinct from practices of government and practices of the self. However, the capacities used in such activities crucially depend on various governmental practices, from literacy and numeracy to a modicum of economic security, and ethical practices, e.g., ones concerned with "assertiveness," "self-esteem," and "consciousness raising."

* * * * *

The notion of governmentality is pivotal because it allows us to follow two crucial sets of continuities in Foucault's thought. First, there are the continuities between the microphysics of power (and the political technology of the body) and the concerns of the government of nations, populations, and societies. Second, there is a continuum established between both of these and the practice of ethics as a form of government of the self. The notion of governmentality implies, then, first a project for the analysis of the state which would no longer rely on the juxtaposition of micro- and macro-levels of power, and the conceptual antimony of an analytics of micropowers and the theory of sovereignty. It also, however, suggests a domain of the investigation of the relation between the government of the self by the self, of one's own existence, and other agencies and spheres of the government of conduct, including but not limited to forms of political government. It is in the delineation of such a domain that the problem of political subjectification can be raised.

This triple domain of self-government, the government of others, and the government of the state, is captured by Foucault's concern to mobilize an earlier sense of the term, in evidence in 16th-century Christian pastorals, neo-Stoicism, pedagogy, and advice to the prince. Here government encompasses the government of oneself, of souls and lives, of children and households, as well as the art of conducting affairs of state (Foucault, 1979a: 5). Moreover, Foucault's general characterization of government as *la conduite de la conduite*, or the conduct of conduct (Gordon, 1987: 296), suggests that the term marks out a massive domain between the minutiae of individual self-examination, self-care, and self-reflection and the techniques and rationalities concerned with the governance of the state.

I want simply to draw out several points regarding Foucault's approach to each of these domains and to suggest how they may be used to open up further a critical historical sociology of political subjectification.[2] First, the genealogies of government and the self not only effect a displacement within Foucault's thought, but also within conventional forms of ethics and political analysis. Thus Foucault juxtaposes an analytic of the practices of government to the theory of the state and remarks that he refrains from the latter as one might abstain from an indigestible meal (Gordon, 1991: 4). He also juxtaposes ethical practices, or practices of the self, to moral codes, suggesting that the history of moral codes reveals little about changing modalities of ethical self-relation and self-formation. In both cases, instead of focusing on a unitary entity ripe for a general explanation, Foucault approaches the problem from the perspective of a multiplicity of practices as distinct events that can be arranged and followed in their lineages and series. Second, these lineages interweave at certain points and direct us to key questions for historical and sociological analysis. Thus [...] we might pose the question of the relation between cults of personal liberation in recent decades and the rise of a neo-liberal critique of the welfare state with its notions of the "enterprise culture" and the "entrepreneurial self."

* * * * *

Third, all these examples demonstrate a constant cross-referencing from one domain to the other. On the one hand, ethics as an action of "self on self" is linked to the practice of government, the government of others as well as oneself. Similarly, the problem of government cannot be dissociated from a reflection on the relation of individuals to themselves, whether as self-governing citizens in Athenian and other versions of democracy, or in the reflection on limits to government that are coextensive with what we call liberalism. At base, and of utmost importance, the rights of resistance, of the governed to protest the actions of various forms of government, and of the governed to various forms of information, are ethical ones. [...]

Finally, the problem of both politics and ethics is one of the use and practice of freedom. Foucault suggests that "liberty is the ontological condition of ethics. But ethics is the definite form assumed by liberty" (1988a: 4). That is to say, ethics is simply not possible without freedom and that as a practice it seeks to shape freedom. Power—or at least the forms of power that compose liberal practices of government—comes to operate on and through the conduct of the governed. It seeks a more or less subtle direction and shaping of conduct rather than a violent or gross form of corporeal domination. In this sense, the microphysics of power may have been overstated if it gave the impression of a determinism of power operating upon the body. Here, governmental power assumes a "free subject," not an individual existing in an essential space of freedom, but one whose subjection is consistent with forms of choice. [...] The distinctive features of any liberal mode of government is that it seeks to prevent the collapse of types of rule into mere domination by invoking the capacities and powers of the self governing individual, while at the same time undertaking to foster, shape, and use those same capacities and powers.

* * * * *

The entwinement of complex domains of practice in Foucault provides an analytic framework of the relation between types of governmental self-formation, types of ethical self-formation, and—although I have not developed this theme here—the constitution of the self in relation to "games of truth," i.e., veridical discourses or discourses charged with saying the truth. Power, self, and truth are the three points of the "Foucauldian triangle." It is from this non-reductive genealogy of their interconnection that Foucault challenges us to the formation of historical studies that are *critical* in that they problematize forms of identity that are taken as natural and given, and *effective* in so far as they refuse to provide a safe haven for any other form of identity. It is quite remarkable that he was to undertake such a project during the period when sociologists such as Norbert Elias and indeed, Corrigan and Sayer, were sketching out the domain of the relation between the forms of authority of the state and the formation of modern forms of identity. The real challenge of Foucault's thought here may lie in its capacity to drive these questions further than a newfound interdisciplinary domain of historical sociology.

■ 3

Foucault's own work on governmentality remained in a relatively undeveloped state, although this has been somewhat rectified by the exemplary work of more recent social analysts (e.g., the articles contained in Burchell et al., 1991; Rose and Miller, 1992). Of course, Foucault's work in this area is not immune from criticism. We might want to investigate how, having broken with state-focused analysis, we can reconceive aspects of the nation-state, particularly the sphere of law and legality, in terms of this concern for the practices of government, or how, more generally, we are to rethink the relation between government and politics. In this paper, however, we have demonstrated the broad consistency of Foucault's own illumination of the spheres of government and ethics: the primacy of ethics over morality; the privilege accorded the means and mechanisms of government over the form of the constitutional, territorial state; the emphasis on practical questions of the conduct of life in self-formation; and the posing of the general problem of political subjectification.

It should be clear that several of the limitations noted in Corrigan's formula of the identity between moral regulation and state formation are overcome in Foucault's theme of governmentality. The latter does not rely on the *a priori* of a cultural subject attaching meaning or representations to its experience; it shows instead the historical conditions of political subjectification in ethical and governmental practices of self-formation. Its emphasis is not on meaning and representation but the practical relations between governmental and ethical practices and the development and formation of human psychological and corporeal capacities. It is able to analyze the nation-state as one, albeit special, agency among others, e.g., international governmental organizations, transnational corporations, non-state welfare organizations, businesses, trade unions, sporting associations, and media organizations. It enables us to pose questions of the government of the economy, families, bodies, the conduct of life, and of one's relation with oneself, and to analyze the governmentalization of the state.

Moreover, if the theme of governmentality refuses the reduction of government to the state, we must also refuse the reduction of political subjectification to government. On the one hand, there are forms of militancy and participation (in unions, parties, social movement organizations, demonstrations, citizen associations) that have consequences for forms of political identity. On the other, there are the non-governmental, ethical practices that are implicated in self-formation and have consequences for political subjectification. The classic examples, of course, are the political and economic consequences of the modes of self-formation inscribed in religious ethics and the practice of religious sects revealed by Weber's sociology of religion. To take a recent illustration, it may be simply not possible to analyze the emergence of the "enterprise culture" in isolation from the myriad practices of self-formation and self-cultivation that have pervaded liberal democracies in recent decades (the "Californian" cult of the self, New Age enthusiasms, mass sporting rituals, martial arts, "Eastern" cults, the "self-stylization" that followed the implosion of the counter-culture into the "Me generation").

It is clear that the problem of political subjectification cannot be resolved in the context of historical sociological analysis. For it is at this point the discussion goes beyond the particular ways in which individuals are constituted as various forms of political subject, e.g., citizen, migrant, voter, taxpayer, client, consumer, claimant, juror, parent, or worker. What is at stake is the multiple status of the political subject: on the one hand, the ideal, specified in our political rationality, of autonomous citizens in a self-governing political community; on the other hand, the space defined by the means and apparatuses of the government of self and others, of practices of government and practices of the self. The problem of political subjectification at its most general level is how we address the dissonances between these constituents of the free individual or citizen that are supported by various governmental and ethical practices and forms of political reason, and that give shape to our political and social existence.

That problem goes beyond the boundaries of the present paper. What is also clear, however, is that Foucault has increased the intelligibility of this free political subject. This subject is constituted by our political rationality and governmental techniques as both a self-governing citizen and an object of fostering, welfare, and care. Yet this division presupposes a more primary folding. The ways in which the subject works upon itself, the relation of self to self, must also be taken into account and linked to the most general forms of government. The citizen is formed not only as an active member of a political community and a dependent subject but also as one who works on her or himself and is, as a consequence, an ethical being. The well-governed commonwealth can no longer be divorced from the commonwealth of many souls that is the self.

■ NOTES

1.   In this section, Nietzsche repeatedly returns to an analogy between the social structure of the self and a "well-constructed and happy commonwealth." The will is com-

pared to a ruling class that establishes its command over "under-wills" or "under-souls." This analogy seems to me entirely useful and germane to the discussion of moral regulation if for no other reason than that concept must include means for the promotion of such a "social structure of souls."

2.   I have recently sought to develop the implications of Foucault's methods of genealogy and archaeology, and his conception of the history of the present, for historical sociology, and social-theoretical understandings of history, under the title of *Critical and Effective Histories* (Dean, 1994).

■ REFERENCES

Burchell, Graham, Colin Gordon, and Peter Miller, eds. *The Foucault Effect: Studies in Governmentality.* London: Harvester Wheatsheaf, 1991.

Corrigan, Philip. "On moral regulation: some preliminary remarks." In *Social Forms/Human Capacities.* London: Routledge, 1990.

———. "State formation and moral regulation in nineteenth-century Britain: sociological investigations." Ph.D. thesis, University of Durham, 1977.

Corrigan, Philip and Derek Sayer. *The Great Arch: English State Formation as Cultural Revolution.* Oxford: Basil Blackwell, 1985.

Dean, Mitchell. *Critical and Effective Histories: Foucault's Methods and Historical Sociology.* London: Routledge, 1994.

Deleuze, Gilles. *Foucault.* Trans. S. Hand. Minneapolis: University of Minnesota Press, 1988.

Durkheim, Emile. *Professional Ethics and Civic Morals.* Trans. C. Brookfield. London: Routledge, 1992.

Elias, Norbert. *The Civilizing Process.* Vol. 1. *The History of Manners.* Trans. E. Jephcott. New York: Urizen, 1978.

———. *The Civilizing Process.* Vol. 2. *State Formation and Civilization.* Trans E. Jephcott. Oxford: Blackwell, 1982.

———. *The Court Society.* Trans. E. Jephcott. Oxford: Basil Blackwell, 1983.

———. *Involvement and Detachment.* Ed. M. Schrotter, trans. E. Jephcott. Oxford: Basil Blackwell, 1987.

Eribon, Didier. *Michel Foucault.* Trans. B. Wing. Cambridge, Mass.: Harvard University Press, 1991.

Foucault, Michel. *Discipline and Punish: The Birth of the Prison.* Trans. A. Sheridan. London: Allen Lane, 1977.

———. "Governmentality." *I and C* 6: 5–21, 1979a.

————. *The History of Sexuality.* Vol. 1. *An Introduction.* Trans. R. Hurley. London: Allen Lane, 1979b.

————. "The subject and power." In *Michel Foucault: Beyond Structuralism and Hermeneutics,* edited by H. Dreyfus and P. Rabinow. Brighton: Harvester, 1982.

————. *The Use of Pleasure.* Trans. R. Hurley. New York: Pantheon, 1985.

————. *The Care of the Self.* Trans. R. Hurley, New York: Pantheon, 1986a.

————. "On the genealogy of ethics: an overview of the work in progress." In *The Foucault Reader,* edited by P. Rabinow. Harmondsworth: Penguin, 1986b.

————. "Politics and ethics: An interview." In *The Foucault Reader,* edited by P. Rabinow. Harmondsworth: Penguin, 1986c.

————. "The care for the self as a practice of freedom." In *The Final Foucault,* edited by J. Bernauer and D. Rasmussen. Cambridge, Mass.: MIT Press, 1988a.

————. "The political technology of individuals." In *Technologies of the Self: A Seminar with Michel Foucault,* edited by L.H. Martin, H. Gutman, and P.H. Hutton. London: Tavistock, 1988b.

————. "Politics and reason." In *Politics, Philosophy, Culture,* by M. Foucault, edited by L.D. Kritzman. New York: Routledge, 1988c.

————. "Technologies of the self." In *Technologies of the Self: A Seminar with Michel Foucault,* edited by L.H. Martin, H. Gutman, and P.H. Hutton. London: Tavistock, 1988d.

————. *Résumé des cours 1970–1982.* Paris: Julliard, 1989.

————. "About the beginnings of the hermeneutics of the self." *Political Theory* 21(2): 198–227, 1993.

Gass, James. "Towards the active society." *OECD Observer* June-July: 4–8, 1988.

Giddens, Anthony. *The Nation-State and Violence.* Cambridge: Polity, 1985.

Gordon, Colin. "The Soul of the citizen: Max Weber and Michel Foucault on rationality and government." In *Max Weber, Rationality and Modernity,* edited by S. Whimster and S. Lash. London: Allen and Unwin, 1987.

————. "Governmental rationality: An introduction." In *The Foucault Effect: Studies in Governmentality,* edited by G. Burchell, C. Gordon, and P. Miller. London: Harvester Wheatsheaf, 1991.

Hacking, Ian. "Self-improvement." In *Foucault: A Critical Reader,* edited by D.C. Hoy. Oxford: Basil Blackwell, 1986.

Hennis, Wilhelm. "Max Weber's 'central question.'" *Economy and Society* 12(2): 135–80, 1983.

————. 1988. Max Weber: *Essays in Reconstruction.* London: Allen and Unwin.

Hindess, Barry. "Imaginary presuppositions of democracy." *Economy and Society* 20(2): 173–95, 1991.

Mann, Michael. "The autonomous power of the state: Its origins, mechanisms and results." In *States, War and Capitalism: Studies in Political Sociology.* Oxford: Basil Blackwell, 1988.

Miller, Peter. *Domination and Power.* London: Routledge and Kegan Paul, 1987.

Nietzsche, Friedrich. *On the Genealogy of Morals.* Trans. W. Kaufmann and R.J. Holingdale. New York: Random House, 1969.

———. *Beyond Good and Evil.* Trans. R.J. Holingdale. Harmondsworth: Penguin, 1973.

OECD. *The Future of Social Protection.* Paris: Organisation for Economic Co-operation and Development, 1988.

Oestreich, Gerhard. *Neostoicism and the Early Modern State.* Cambridge: Cambridge University Press, 1982.

Patton, Paul. "Taylor and Foucault on power and freedom." *Political Studies* 37 (1989): 260–76.

———. "Le sujet de pouvoir chez Foucault." *Sociologie et sociétés* 24(1) (1992).

Poulantzas, Nicos. *State, Power, Socialism.* Trans. P. Camiller. London: New Left Books, 1978.

Rose, Nikolas and Peter Miller. "Political power beyond the state: problematics of government." *British Journal of Sociology* 43(2) (1992): 173–205.

Turner, Bryan S. "Preface to the second edition." In E. Durkheim, *Professional Ethics and Civic Morals.* Trans. C. Brookfield. London: Routledge, 1992.

Weber, Max. *The Methodology of the Social Sciences.* Trans. and ed. E.A. Shils and H.A. Finch. New York: Free Press, 1949.

———. *From Max Weber: Essays in Sociology.* Trans. and ed. H.H. Gerth and C. Wright Mills. London: Routledge and Kegan Paul, 1970.

———. *The Protestant Ethic and the Spirit of Capitalism.* Trans. T. Parsons. London: Unwin, 1985.

CHAPTER 14

THE POWER OF POWERLESSNESS:
ALCOHOLICS ANONYMOUS'S TECHNIQUES FOR GOVERNING THE SELF

Mariana Valverde

Although generally ignored by social science, Alcoholics Anonymous has been the subject of a number of studies. Some of these, written by addiction specialists, attempt to evaluate AA's success rate. Others, less policy-oriented studies, use data from AA to illustrate quite general, pre-existing theories—about the domination of psychotherapy in contemporary life and/or about the use of personal narratives to construct an identity.[1] This form of philosophical idealism, so common in sociology, can be avoided by paying close attention to the specificity of AA practices for governing self and others. This chapter therefore attempts to study AA in a loosely anthropological vein, describing rather than evaluating, and paying much closer attention to the techniques used by AA groups and individuals than to the theoretical claims made in its literature. The analysis of some of AA's rich storehouse of techniques for sobriety will occupy most of the second half of this chapter, but it may be useful to state at the outset that the most striking feature of these techniques, taken as a whole, is that, despite the organization's basis of unity in alcoholism, the governance of alcohol is not the main focus of AA. It is the soul of the member that is the main object of AA's innovative approach to ethical governance, an approach relying primarily on *self*-governance rather than on advice or exhortation. Insofar as the liquid consumption of the member is being governed, drinking is governed for the sake of the soul.

■ BETWEEN ETHICAL WORK AND CLINICAL PRACTICE: AA AS A HYBRID TECHNOLOGY

Alcoholics Anonymous describes itself not as a movement but as "a fellowship," and it positively refuses to engage in political and social change, to lobby for or against legislation, or to participate in the public arena in any way.[2] This explicit refusal of a public image, unusual in the context of American philanthropic or spiritual organizations, is best explained as a reaction to the old temperance movement. Despite possessing complex organizational forms, successful fundraising techniques, and powerful lobbying tools, the North American temperance movement had become, by the 1930s, ridiculous: a symbol of everything that was either wrong or simply impractical in the American tradition of moral reform. AA was founded very shortly after the repeal of Prohibition in the United States, and the Protestantism of its founders was markedly more modern, more non-denominational and much less proselytizing than that of their parents. They thus sought to consciously distance AA from temperance; and there was no more effective way of doing this than refusing to participate in public debates, perhaps especially debates about liquor legislation.

AA's early success thus owed a great deal to its insistence that individuals, even individuals collected together in cohesive groups, could and indeed should confine their ethical work to changing themselves and, at most, supporting others who had also made the decision to change.

Paradoxically, the very success of AA contributed to normalizing the heavy drinking that became common in the 1940s and 1950s across class and gender boundaries, in North America and in other developed countries. AA shared the view held by social and medical scientists in the 1940s and 1950s that the problem of alcohol was not to be located in alcohol itself, but rather in the souls of that minority of drinkers who could not control their drinking. Much as today's legalization of gambling casinos is implicitly validated by the sudden discovery of "the pathological gambler"[3] for whom treatment has to be provided even as governments open up more gambling venues, so too the popularization of the alcoholic identity likely legitimated increasingly high levels of alcohol consumption for the (non-alcoholic) public at large.[4] This historical paradox is not discussed within AA circles, probably because one of the few dogmas they adhere to is that the distinction between alcoholics and "normies" (normal drinkers) is an ontological one, not one produced by legal or cultural regulation.

Thus, the interests of AA are not necessarily opposed to those of the liquor industry: AA did not challenge the general post-World War II project that earlier in this book has been called "enlightened hedonism." And indeed, if AA had set itself squarely against the liquor industry or against consumerism in general, it probably would have melted into oblivion, given the historical defeat not only of temperance but of what became disparagingly known as "puritanism." Thus, although AA is in some ways an anti-consumer organization, and certainly challenges the project of American entrepreneurs of the soul to develop a for-profit psychotherapy market, it does not explicitly challenge either liquor advertising or the more general cultural inducements to drinking that were always denounced by temperance activists.

If AA has a contradictory relationship to the practices of the consumer marketplace, it has a similarly ambivalent relationship to the other major institution governing drinking and eating practices in Euro-American cultures, namely medicine. This ambivalence with respect to medicine is precisely what makes AA an excellent site in which to study the complex ways in which the powers of various medical gazes (the clinical gaze, the epidemiological gaze, etc.) are simultaneously amplified and challenged in extra-medical circles. There are certainly other practices and social sites upon which a variety of contradictory medical and scientific gazes converge, but if we are interested not only in complexities and contradictions *within* medicine but also in the ways in which non-professionalized forms of expertise have challenged the authority of physicians and scientists, few sites could be as fruitful as AA. Today we have AIDS activism, breast cancer survivor self-help groups, and other situations in which "consumers" and activists seek to wrest control of health problems from traditional institutions, but none of these is as old or as rooted in working-class life as AA. And indeed, purposively or not, most of the consumer/survivor mutual-help organizations that exist today owe a major debt to AA. It was AA, not women's health or anti-psychiatry activists, that invented the mutual-help, leaderless group; it was AA that came up with the notion that physicians should not have the monopoly on disease; and it was, to my knowledge, AA that first succeeded in turning a disease into a full-fledged, lifelong social identity. The reflections on AA's practice offered in this chapter are thus written both to do justice to an organization that has been generally dismissed or ignored by both medical and social experts *and* to open up avenues for studying the complex interactions of medical, spiritual, psychological, and "common-sense" means for understanding and changing one's own life, in the hopes that other researchers also interested in the formation and circulation of non-professionalized knowledges may continue the task.

Insofar as the men who started meeting together to help one another stop drinking had a theory of their situation, the basis of that theory was the statement that "alcoholism is a disease." The insistence that alcoholism was neither a sin nor the inevitable result of alcohol availability, but was rather a condition afflicting a specified minority of drinkers, would appear to bring AA into the domain of the medicalization of deviance. But, although AA was certainly borrowing some of the prestige of medicine when it chose to define alcoholism as a disease, it was by no means a puppet of the medical profession.

Indeed, it could be argued that AA's peculiar definition of alcoholism as *a non-medical disease*, while at one level amplifying the authority of the medical model by labelling the vice of alcoholism as a disease, is nevertheless, at another level, one of the most successful challenges to the authority of medical and psy experts that this century has seen—a challenge that is particularly significant because it was unique for its time.[5]

On the one hand, then, alcoholism was defined as a disease; and, to corroborate this claim, a physician was asked to write an authoritative preface for the first edition of the Big Book endorsing AA's curative powers, a preface still reprinted in the current edition. Official AA discourse is uniformly conciliatory toward medicine and physicians. For instance, the 1996 survey of its North American membership carried out by AA itself notes, with implicit pride in its good relations with medicine, that "73% of members' doctors know they are in AA," and that "39% of members said they were referred to AA by a health care professional."[6] But this conciliatory stance is somewhat misleading. Although AA as an organization has always sought to cultivate good relations with all health professionals, the fact is that it casts all professionals in a supporting role. Physicians and other health system workers are supposed to support AA and to refer patients to the organization; they are not allowed to diagnose alcoholism or to treat anything other than severe physical problems.

In sharp contrast to the official AA project of building cooperative relations with physicians, many members, particularly blue-collar men, freely vent their anger at the superciliousness of male physicians, seeing their allegiance to AA as a form of resistance against medical power. A 38-year-old auto worker who dropped out of high school, when asked if he had ever sought help for his drinking problems from the health system, said:

> I never used no other method—I don't believe in doctors, they're full of shit. What do they know about alcohol addiction? I never went to no detox place because I heard stories about guys that go in there and climb the walls—I didn't want to be locked up like no animal so I stayed clear of that shit. No ... I did it the tough way. I faced it head on. I knew I was in trouble and I knew where to get help—from other guys who knew where I was coming from—who had been where I had been. Not some rich snotty doctor who never done hard time in his life.[7]

Within AA, alcoholism is said to be a disease, or an illness,[8] but it cannot be defined by absolute quantities of alcohol consumed or by any specific clinical criteria. Alcoholism is defined as a *subjective* experience of lack of control: being unable to stop drinking when one truly wants to stop. And since only *you* know whether you really want to stop, only you can diagnose yourself.[9]

One might conclude that AA's self-diagnosis abolishes medical expertise by universalizing it, in a move paralleling the Protestant Reformation's laicization of priestly authority. But AA goes further than simply rejecting the authority claims of physicians and priests: the organization has levelled a profound challenge not only to the qualification process but even to the techniques taken for granted by those professionals. The 19th century clinical/disciplinary techniques described by Foucault—hierarchical observation, classification, and so forth—are overtly refused. In AA, there is a positive refusal to collect information about anyone but oneself. Similarly, the 20th-century techniques that have, within the field of alcohol studies, largely displaced the clinical gaze—epidemiological measures and predictions—are also refused. Members do not observe others, and neither do they collect aggregate information about their groups for purposes of risk management. There is a membership survey that AA carries out in the United States and Canada, but it is done only every three years and it provides only the most basic demographic information, and it is devised and administered by AA itself, not by sociologists or survey specialists.

Although organized around alcoholism as a disease, the gaze of AA is first and foremost an ethical one. It observes and judges, but what is being observed, judged, and transformed is one's own spiritual progress, not the body of medicine or the mind of the psy sciences. This spiritual progress has a positive, if somewhat vague, content; it is not reducible to the behaviour of not drinking. The ultimate goal of AA is not the already ambitious one of helping people stop drinking; it is the even more ambitious one of helping people achieve inner peace. That is why members sometimes speak of "dry alcoholics"—people who no longer drink but who still have the old behaviour patterns (typically, egoism, boastfulness, and a misguided feeling of power). There is even a term—the "dry bender"—to designate the sort of emotional turmoil that, in AA discourse, indicates that one has become dry but not yet *sober*. Sobriety is thus more than the absence of drinking: it is a difficult-to-define but nevertheless positively existing state.

This explicitly spiritual rationality of self-government might lead one to classify AA with the religions and hence outside of medicine, as Paul Antze's insightful anthropological study does.[10] But if we are interested in analyzing, rather than pigeon-holing, the myriad ways in which various types of knowledges coexist and interact in the practical world, we may want to describe AA's internalized gaze as a hybrid one. For instance, while in most ways opposed to clinical practices, AA sometimes legitimates its knowledge with the same manoeuvre used by clinicians against the knowledge of scientific research. Just as GPs sometimes invoke their years of experience to generate a clinical judgment that is at odds with statistical studies or textbook definitions,[11] so too do members of AA often appeal to a quasi-clinical criterion of "what works" in order to further a rationality of self-governance that is primarily spiritual.[12]

The hybridity[13] of AA's approach to knowing and managing alcoholism is apparent in its ambiguous use of the term "disease," as explained above. It can be further illustrated by looking at two terms that help to operationalize the general notion of a non-medical disease and that recur constantly both in texts and in group and individual discussions: one is "self-control" and the other is "recovery."

Self-control acts to constitute the hybrid zone between the clinical and the ethical. It is primarily an ethical term, rooted in spiritual practices of self; but it also appears in some medical discourses, for instance in case descriptions and diagnostic criteria for drug dependence or obsessive-compulsive disorder. Self-control is a wonderfully useful term precisely because it is a hybrid, partly moral, partly physiological, as Roger Smith has pointed out in respect to the closely related term "inhibition," which has been used to denote both a neurological fact and a moral/cultural process.[14] In AA talk, the Protestant overtones of self-control tend to prevail over the scientific or psychiatric ones: God is often invoked and it is common for AA group meetings to end with the Lord's Prayer. Thus, the analyses of self-control and its perils provided in meetings and in conversation by individual members are inevitably tinged with religious meaning. Nevertheless, it is not a question here of classifying AA's discourse as *either* scientific or spiritual, medical or moral. AA makes full use of the rich semantic resources of terms such as "self-control." When members discuss their efforts to use the Higher Power to regain self-control, the history of scientific efforts to locate and measure the will and map the dysfunctions of inhibition and control, while remaining in the background, is not rejected. Members are no more aware of the long and complex genealogy of addictive and compulsive disorders than anyone else, but nevertheless this genealogy had already shaped alcoholism before AA was invented. The developments outlined in previous chapters thus contributed significantly to the meaning and effectivity that words such as "self-control" have, both for the speaker and for the audience, in today's AA group meetings.

Another key term involved in the constitution of AA's hybrid terrain is "recovery." Recovering alcoholics are not on the way to being cured: AA firmly believes that "once an alcoholic, always an alcoholic," and the North American 1996 membership survey tells us that almost half of the 7,200 respondents are still active in the organization even though they have been sober for over five years.[15] In contrast to medical usage, then, recovery does not mean getting healthy or becoming normal. It means learning to live with one's dysfunction as peacefully as possible. The concept of recovery that has spread beyond AA to a myriad other self-help groups, and indeed to the general population, giving rise to such joking terms as "a recovering Catholic," constitutes a hybrid terrain on the borderlands of medicine. On the one hand, the term "recovery" is drawn from medical usage, and hence implicitly appeals to or evokes the paradigm of disease; but it simultaneously undermines that paradigm by breaking the medically created link between cure and recovery, since AA members believe they can be healthy without being cured, happy without being normal.

How, then, does one set out to recover? AA's pragmatic eclecticism allows its members a wide latitude in choosing remedies that work, including drugs or psychiatric care. But it is stressed that neither medical treatments nor religion on its own will work in the long run. The only lasting solution lies in the "12 steps"—not in *believing in* the 12 steps, but in "*working*" the 12 steps.[16] Members speak of "working the program"; and by this they mean first and foremost the 12 steps, with activities such as church attendance or seeing a professional counsellor regarded as options that individual members might include in their programme, but that never substitute for any of the 12 steps. And, although members sometimes express personal discomfort with one particular step, they cannot pick and choose: the steps are a package. In AA literature, the steps are always reprinted together, without any emphasis on some to the detriment of others, and in every group meeting the 12 steps are read as a single text. Group meetings (particularly those designated as "closed" meetings, that is, meetings excluding observers and meant only for those who already see themselves as alcoholics) do often concentrate on one step or on a group of steps. But the group will move through all of the steps at various points. A group that wanted, for instance, to exclude the 12th step (which is a promise made to other alcoholics to go out and help them) could not be an official AA group. There is wide latitude given to both individuals and groups to interpret the steps (and the accompanying slogans that form much of the material for group reflection) as they see fit; but the text of the 12 steps is treated as fixed for all time.

Drinking itself, as noted at the outset, is barely mentioned in the 12 steps. The first step is acknowledging one's individual powerlessness over alcohol: "We admitted that we were powerless over alcohol—that our lives had become unmanageable." This then leads to letting one's decisions be guided by the personalized counsel of one's divine entity, the Higher Power (steps 2 through 4). Alcoholics are told to assume responsibility for harm they inflicted on others (steps 5 through 9); and finally, the last few steps stress that this new relation of self to self has to be followed by the traditional ethical work of helping others, the lifelong activity known as "12-stepping." Activity is the key term here: although driven by beliefs and dogmas to an extent perhaps not recognized by most of its members, AA is nevertheless an anti-intellectual, and particularly an anti-scientific, organization. Its knowledge is always justified by reference to the subjective experience of its members, not to either scientific logic or factual truths. Stepping is an activity, and the steps are something one *works* on; the steps as a whole are a programme for governing one's life, a programme that, as they always emphasize, is compatible with a large (although not infinite) number of belief systems.

The 12 steps are complemented by the "12 traditions," also read at most AA meetings, which specify the practices to be followed by the organization in the same way that the 12 steps specify the techniques for individual ethical practice. Most of these have to do with internal democracy, anonymity, refusing the temptations of money and fame, and avoiding political controversies that might either divide the organization or alienate potential alcoholics. Compared with the 12 steps' strongly spiritual, even religious flavour, the 12 traditions are prosaic and businesslike, but they too have a quasi-sacred status within the organization. People might debate how to interpret this or that tradition, but they do not seek to revise the basic text.

If despite the obviously religious flavour of much AA talk (including the repeated mention of God in the 12 steps) I still see AA as fundamentally different from established religions, it is because it does not attempt to universalize its ethical techniques. That is why it does not, as an organization, preach from pulpits or from our TV screens; neither does it solicit money nor tell anyone that they should join. Members may suggest to friends who drink that they might find AA useful, but they are expected to let each alcoholic make his/her own decisions. While cultivating a hands-off, when-you-are-ready stance toward people who admit having drinking problems, AA members are even less interested in changing the behaviour of those who do not report problems with drinking. In sharp contrast to most ex-smokers, AA does not seek to change the behaviour of normal drinkers—for example, they do not necessarily advocate alcohol-free social occasions.[17] They believe that it is up to alcoholics themselves to become either sufficiently strong to manage occasions in which drinks are served, or wise enough to avoid such situations. AA provides a design for living that is presented as an absolute necessity for those who are alcoholics—"AA saved my life" is a comment frequently heard in AA circles. But although their zealous enthusiasm for the 12 steps, particularly when expressed to researchers who do not appear to have a drinking problem, suggests that they believe that the 12 steps are more like vitamins than like medicine, that is, good for everyone, they nevertheless do not explicitly make universal claims for their programme.

A key feature of the programme is that it manages to articulate the once-in-a-lifetime experience of "spiritual awakening" or rebirth,[18] the extraordinary features of evangelical conversion, with the humdrum, non-sacred, even banal practices of self-management of everyday life. An early leader of AA expressed this two-edged character of the programme as follows: "AA is first a way back to life, and then a design for living."[19] The "way back to life" trope connects with the evangelical discourse of "I once was lost and now I'm found" that resonates so powerfully even with secularized Christians; while the "design for living" encompasses the little techniques of self-management that AA shares with such non-spiritual programmes as advice on smoking cessation. Putting them together in one sentence, and in a single programme that is simultaneously spiritual and practical, is AA's brilliant stroke.

Let us now go on to analyze in some detail a few of the techniques that make up AA's sophisticated toolkit of devices for caring for oneself in such a way as to change one's whole life. This will form the bulk of the chapter; by way of conclusion I will offer a few remarks regarding the conceptual resources available for this study—resources which, to anticipate the conclusions, are simultaneously too many and too few.

■ POWERLESSNESS

The first and most important of the 12 steps begins: "We admitted that we were powerless over alcohol …"

Many therapy and self-help groups are geared to empowering their members. Such groups as Codependents Anonymous fit very well with the general culture of neo-liberalism. The aim of the self-esteem industry is to foster individual capacities so as to constitute individuals who will make a successful enterprise out of their lives: helping other people or creating a collective consciousness is not on the self-esteem agenda. When a woman at her first meeting of Codependents Anonymous states: "I don't know what I'm powerless over, yet, but I'm sure I'll find out,"[20] she means that powerlessness is a bad state, one caused by the effect of a dysfunctional family on the primeval innocence of her inner child.[21] Such a woman would typically use the group to first define and then overcome this powerlessness. But when an AA member speaks of powerlessness, he/she means that alcoholics are by definition forever powerless over alcohol. For AA members, therefore, powerlessness is not something to be blamed on one's parents and overcome with the help of experts and books: it is a permanent feature of one's self that cannot be eradicated, but can be managed with the all-important support of the collective.

To this extent, AA indirectly subverts the neo-liberal discourse of personal entrepreneurship and perpetual improvement.[22] Members are perpetually in recovery, always working on their souls, but they do not imagine they will ever re-make themselves from scratch, in contrast to the neo-liberal illusion that the poor can become business executives by sheer willpower. AA goes so far as to challenge American individualism by regarding exaggerated views of one's power as part of the very illness of alcoholism. Alcoholism is, some AA texts tell us, born out of a delusion that we can indeed stop drinking when we want to or otherwise control our behaviour. "In our drinking days, we believed, we had such control. In sobriety, we realize that we didn't have control. We learn that we can make choices about what *we* do and little else."[23] The statement made by one member of AA that "people with low self-esteem can have very big egos" is, in its own low-key way, a telling critique of some assumptions of neo-liberalism.[24]

■ ANONYMITY

The requirement that AA members remain anonymous, particularly in their relation to the media, is also at odds with the culture of enterprise. Initially, anonymity was crucial in recruitment, since the stigma of alcoholism was such that few people would attend a group unless there was an iron-clad guarantee of confidentiality. This aspect of anonymity is still important for many people. But anonymity is perhaps less essential now to protect the individual—in some circles, being a recovering alcoholic is no longer stigmatized, and may even bring some cachet—than to ensure that the group does not succumb to the temptations of money, fame, and power that have crippled other organizations. "Anonymity nurtures humility," writes an AA member, in a book that will not contribute to his personal fame, since he does not use his last name. "Anonymity keeps us focussed on principles rather than personalities. There are no 'stars' in AA."[25] External anonymity is thus closely linked to one of its key traditions, namely the refusal to own property.[26] The tradition of "corporate poverty"[27] is so sacred that the worldwide AA organization recently refused to exercise any sort of intellectual property claim over their symbol—the triangle inside the circle—even as recovery entrepreneurs were making large sums of money selling trinkets with that symbol.[28]

Anonymity is one of a panoply of AA techniques enabling members to maximize the democratic potential of the organization by exercising a certain self-denial—a despotism not so much over one's own desires, as in traditional Protestant ethical forms, but over some dominant trends in contemporary culture.

■ NO CROSS-TALK

AA groups work partly because potentially hurtful opinions about other members are firmly repressed. If any newcomer is tempted to make judgmental remarks on other people's comments, he/she is told that "cross-talk"—editorializing or judging—is not allowed. The groups observed followed the "no cross-talk" rule to a remarkable extent, even when some people's accounts of their drinking miseries teetered on the edge of bragging about drunken exploits. Members, particularly women, will make disparaging remarks outside of meetings about "drunkalogues";[29] but the meeting itself tolerates an extremely wide range of speech forms and emotional contents, and judgmental comments about others are kept to a minimum.[30] Since the success of AA in attracting a wide variety of people of all classes, ages, and socioeconomic conditions clearly depends on its ability to remain, if not non-judgmental, at least more non-judgmental than the main alternatives—religion and medicine—it is clear that the prohibition on cross-talk is a crucial mechanism for the perpetuation and growth of AA.

The prohibition on judging others may be particularly crucial in attracting to the organization older, white working-class or lumpen males, who at least in our local study make up the majority of group membership and take up more than their share of talk time at open group meetings.[31] Men who have in the past felt judged by doctors, or who for class-specific reasons reject "psychobabble,"[32] are pleased to find that AA does not expect newcomers to have the sort of middle-class cultural capital that is routinely assumed in therapy groups and in feminist or left-wing organizations. Indeed, AA actually encourages the sort of plain English—peppered with homey folk sayings, somewhat trite metaphors, and the occasional four-letter word—that reminds the observer of the institution inhabited by many AA members in their previous life, namely the bar or pub. Unlike most voluntary organizations in civil society, which tend to level upwards and systematically privilege those with professional backgrounds, AA tends to level downwards.

■ TELLING ONE'S STORY

AA is one of the many movements in today's world that rely heavily on autobiographical narratives. First-person accounts of the movement from alcoholism to sobriety form a large part of the Big Book, and open group meetings have at least one or two autobiographical segments.

It would not be very helpful, however, to simply impose the paradigm of confession on AA. First of all, the telling of one's story is not always confessional. It approaches the confessional in step five work, the one-to-one discussions between members and their sponsors about the harms done by the alcoholic member to others. Even in that more private context, however, the sponsor is unlikely to monopolize the power to interpret or the power to forgive, as is the case in the confessional practices found in the institutions of the church, the criminal law, and psychoanalysis.[33] In group meetings, the key feature distinguishing "telling one's story" from confession is that the people listening do not either interpret or judge the speaker. There is, of course, a certain element of catharsis and forgiveness, but the interaction between group members differs from the hierarchical confessional practices studied by Foucault.

Storytelling in AA more closely resembles the "coming out stories" that are basic building blocks of the gay movement, or the narratives of violence and abuse that constitute various survivor groups. In those contexts, as well as in AA, the storytelling functions as much to bind the group together and create a sense of commonality as to build up individual identity. But the role of storytelling in AA is more limited than it is elsewhere. Such practices as reciting the Lord's Prayer and reading out the 12 steps and the 12 traditions, which most groups perform, function as supra-individual rituals, closer to the format of a church service than to the free-for-all practices of most self-help groups.

It is also important to note that some group meetings discourage personal storytelling altogether, and organize themselves around the process of moving through the 12 steps. Such meetings can focus either on a single step or on a related group of steps. Either way, the step meetings effect a different sort of unity than the more autobiographical ones. The steps provide members with a long-term sense of direction and progress; and, since it applies to members who no longer struggle with drinking on a daily basis, the 12-step process unifies the organization by keeping newcomers and oldtimers together. While members might well tell anecdotes about themselves in the course of step meetings, the purpose of the meeting is not to solicit unique narratives but rather to forge an alcoholic identity whose common features are regarded as more important than that which distinguishes individuals. Although AA has certainly felt the pressures of identity politics, making some limited room for groups that describe themselves as catering largely to women, to gays, or to aboriginals, no group that excludes people on the basis of identity can call itself an AA group and be listed in the directory that phone volunteers use to direct interested callers. Those aspects of one's life that distinguish one from other alcoholics are to be kept firmly in the background:

> Whenever, wherever, one alcoholic meets another alcoholic and sees in that person first and foremost not that he or she is male or female, or black or white, or Baptist or Catholic or Jew, or gay or straight, or whatever, but sees rather another alcoholic to whom he or she must reach out for the sake of his or her own sobriety—so long, in other words, as one alcoholic recognizes in another alcoholic first and foremost that he or she is alcoholic and that therefore both of them need each other—there will be not only an Alcoholics Anonymous, but there will be the Alcoholics Anonymous that you and I love so much and respect so deeply.[34]

These days, however, AA members belonging to groups with strong identity politics have to constantly justify their solidarity with alcoholics of all (other) identities. An urban aboriginal man who finds AA useful reports being criticized by his aboriginal friends:

"They tell me I'm selling out to the white man because some of my friends now are white. They say that the white god won't hear me, but I don't listen. I know what I know."[35]

Storytelling in AA, then, bears little resemblance to a psychoanalytic inquiry into the deep self. Storytelling functions rather as a way to enlist individuals in AA's pre-existing narrative of alcoholism. Sexual escapades, drug addictions, domestic violence, and other events that feature prominently in many members' lives are left firmly in the background, not only in group meetings but even in interviews (in which more time was available).[36] The sometimes rigid emphasis on alcohol, or rather on AA's prior views on alcoholism, to the exclusion of other problems in people's lives may be doctrinaire, but it probably helps to explain why so many AA groups survive for decades. By contrast, the Adult Children of Alcoholics groups observed by Elayne Rapping, which gvie their members encouragement to engage in free-ranging and usually self-serving autobiography, tend to self-destruct.

Younger people, more influenced by both psychotherapy and the practices of identity politics, can be seen at group meetings highlighting certain features of their life other than alcoholism: they might make more of their ethnic identity or their addiction to substances and behaviours other than drink, for instance. They are also more likely to focus on psychological causation, mentioning their dysfunctional family of origin, whereas the oldtimers tend to speak about alcohol itself, not about their parents or their own psyches, as having caused their problems. But even the younger generation only rarely seeks to form groups that are only for a certain type of alcoholic. They too—and this is something that is palpable when observing a meeting—share and help to reproduce AA's custom of backgrounding differences in favour of fostering the solidarity of all alcoholics with one another.

Stories about the self can and do function in very different ways, and help to enact different outcomes. Telling one's story is not a single technique with an invariable meaning and effectivity, even within a single organization. It is a very flexible technique that can be deployed in contradictory ways. It can solicit individual uniqueness, or it can create group solidarity; stories about oneself can be deployed to validate the authority of the analyst, or, on the contrary, to replace analysts with self-help groups; storytelling can be used to elicit sympathy for one's pain, or simply to gain approval for one's abilities as an entertainer.

■ THE HIGHER POWER

The explanations given in the Big Book and in semi-official histories of AA suggest that the term "Higher Power" was chosen in order to refer to the Protestant God without offending non-Christians or agnostics. Alcoholics were and are exhorted to give themselves up to the Higher Power, or, synonymously, to "God as we understood him"; this power is that which will make up for the alcoholic's admitted lack of power over alcohol. The chapter addressed to agnostics in the Big Book explains that it does not matter what precise content one gives to the term "Higher Power"; the point is simply to provide the alcoholic with a name for that supra-individual source of strength that can be drawn upon to effect what the individual's willpower had not managed to accomplish.[37]

AA members today justify the Higher Power language in the same terms as those used in the Big Book, as if the concept had remained the same over the years. But there are indications that the deistic notion of the Higher Power that the original members constructed has quietly given way to a different technique for transcending the limits of ordinary human willpower. In meetings, people talk not about "the" Higher Power but rather about "my" Higher Power—as in the phrase heard at a meeting, "my Higher Power must have a sense of humour ..."[38] The vaguely divine force acknowledged by many agnostics and lapsed Christians and Jews is difficult to define; but whatever it is, it is singular. The proliferation of individualized higher powers would suggest that today's AA members believe in guardian angels without believing in a God that guarantees the truth of angels, a development in keeping with today's tendency to liberalize religion to the vanishing point. This tendency is visible in the advice given in a recent AA book: "It has been suggested that we simply pray 'To whom it may concern.'"[39]

Through their work on the first few steps, AA members develop a sense of a powerful and protective force that is always available, always beside them. As Paul Antze shows, AA's divinity is unusual in being purely benevolent: the judgmental, wrathful aspects of the Judeo-Christian God have been expelled and ascribed solely to the demon alcohol.[40] But this benevolent force does not rule over the world, or even over all alcoholics. Its power is strictly limited to acting through and with that particular individual. While in some ways AA bucks the dominant cultural trends, in respect to the God term, it appears to be converging with New Age spirituality, with its emphasis on syncretism and individual consumer choice in religious beliefs.[41]

Consumer choice in imagining one's Higher Power is not free of all determinations, however. The origins of the alcoholics' Higher Power in the Protestant God often break through the discourse of choice and autonomy. A woman who was marginalized within her AA group, particularly by the women members, because she was known in her small town to earn money through prostitution, explained that when she was told that it was up to her to define the Higher Power, she told her group that she didn't want to imagine a masculine deity.

> I had trouble with facing god and this old guy stood up and started yelling at me and telling me that if I didn't turn myself over to my Higher Power I was never going to make it. But I just kept thinking—god is a man, and my whole life I have been turning myself over to men. So I said, well, my Higher Power is going to be a woman—and they all laughed and said I wasn't working the program, I wasn't taking it seriously.[42]

The insistence on visualizing the Higher Power as masculine is a feature not of AA in general but of the Protestant culture within which this particular woman (living in small-town Ontario) found AA. In Mexican-American AA groups, men as well as women are encouraged to imagine the Higher Power in the image of the Virgin Mary or of a revered patron saint, such as Our Lady of Guadalupe.[43] But insofar as AA has been largely shaped by white Protestant Americans, the Protestant image of the Higher Power as a deity whose masculine powers are unmediated by female saints has become the hegemonic definition of the Higher Power. Catholics, women who refuse to deify any male figure, aboriginal people, and others who have different religious traditions can exercise some personal control over the specific features of the Higher Power, as individuals, but they are certainly not encouraged to band together with others of similar background in order to develop a counter-spirituality.

Differences in religious and spiritual practices, then, are largely confined to the individual realm. The famous phrase in the 12 steps, "God *as we understand Him*" (underlined in the original), acknowledges differences among AA members, but the "we" is a group of individual alcoholics, not a coalition of distinct cultures.

The fact that there is no communication among the different Higher Powers, or any way of adjudicating disputes between them, may look like a schism waiting to happen; but, paradoxically, the "many guardian angels, no god" situation may contribute to AA's stability rather than undermine it. If the divine power is purely personal, and if the divinity exercises no power to judge and punish, there is nothing to fight about. "Different higher powers, same steps" is not among AA's numerous slogans, but it could be.

■ "ONE DAY AT A TIME": SLOGANS FOR DAILY LIVING

Most AA group meetings take place in rooms that are borrowed for the meeting, rather than owned or controlled by AA. Generally speaking, little is done to decorate or rearrange the room, other than moving the chairs; but an almost constant feature of the process of turning a room (most often a church basement) into an AA meeting room is the hanging up of a few hand-made, usually tattered placards with AA slogans written on them.[44] "One day at a time" is one of the most popular slogans; and those words are often repeated by members.

The old temperance movement had its own technique for sobriety, namely the temperance pledge. This was a piece of paper signed by the prospective member, a paper typically committing the signer to abstaining from alcoholic beverages *forever.* Thus, if somebody who had signed the pledge drank, even once, this represented a complete failure.

AA meetings are full of people who drank for some time, stopped for a while, went back to drinking, back to AA, and so forth. Rather than rejecting these people as backsliders, as the temperance movement would have done, AA provides them with two techniques with countervailing effects. One is the custom of celebrating months or years of sobriety with commemorative tokens, a round of applause, and sometimes even a party—a technique that rewards long-term abstention. But the other technique, embodied in the "one day at a time" slogan, counteracts the tendency of oldtimers to feel superior. Although long-term abstention is prized, AA members sometimes say that the person with the longest sobriety is "whoever woke up the earliest that morning."[45] The focus on the 24-hour cycle thus tends to equalize everyone. Short of coming to a meeting with alcohol on their breath, all alcoholics are equally sober.

The 24-hour focus is a technique for managing oneself that is used in other aspects of living. For example, people who are mourning are often told that they should focus on getting through one day at a time, a bit of homey advice that counteracts the tendency to depression caused by the prospect of a whole life without one's loved one. This effect is useful for people quitting drinking, since many report feeling that they fear that a life without alcohol will be a life without fun and without sociability. But in the specific context of drinking, the one-day-at-a-time technique has added power: the power to forgive lapses. Of course, if one goes back to drinking, then one has to recalculate the length of sobriety; but one has not become an outcast or a failure. Since failure to remain dry has historically carried powerful connotations of moral failure (especially in countries with a tradition of temperance), and since guilt feelings about going back to drinking figure very prominently in the lives and autobiographical accounts of self-diagnosed alcoholics, it is very important for the success of AA to provide its members with a relatively guilt-free way to reconnect to the organization immediately after any lapse. While rewarding members for staying sober for long periods of time, AA thus manages to simultaneously validate the efforts of those who do not quit once and for all by providing them with a technique through which they can feel good about themselves simply for having stayed sober for that day.

The moral of this story, as far as social theory is concerned, is that the admittedly inane, even vacuous slogans posted around AA meeting rooms ("Keep it simple," "Easy does it," "One day at a time") are not so vacuous. They have little semantic content, but as crystallizations of AA's homegrown collective wisdom they are full of practical meaning and power. The little slogans on the placards—repeated in self-help books and in the words of AA members—may appear to be beneath the notice of the social scientist, especially the social theorist; they are the very opposite of the serious texts favoured by academics. And yet, perhaps precisely because they have so little inherent content, they play a very important role in the practical management of people's lives. This power is not due to any feature of the text itself: their power to enable people to manage their lives has been shaped in and by the ongoing practical work of an organization, for without the practical work of AA, the slogan "one day at a time" would have little effect.

In Greco-Roman ethics, there was a theoretical term for collections of practical wisdom put together from fragments and given new life through constant re-reading and reflection: *hupomnemata*. These were guides for conduct consisting of borrowed bits of wisdom. Plutarch and his peers, as Foucault points out, sharply distinguished these collections of past wisdom from the genre that is better known to us today, "intimate journals or narratives of spiritual experience."[46] Scrapbooks rather than serious books, collectively rather than individually authored, reflecting the ethical work and wisdom of the past rather than one's personal relation of self to self, *hupomnemata* are precisely *not* constitutive of individual identity. Today, similar scrapbooks are sometimes put together by hand by individuals who scavenge through spiritual guides and self-help psy books; but they are more likely to take the form of small-format hardbacks with inspirational bits of prose and poetry. A common format is the 365-page little book with one inspiring thought for every day of the year. The popularity of the "Meditations for women who do too much" type of literature may be an indication that the discursive resources of popular North American culture are not as monopolized by narratives of victimization and/or individual heroism as critical sociologists of popular culture would have it. Attentive to the needs not fulfilled by novels, tabloids, or confessional literature, AA has been instrumental in revitalizing the *hupomnemata* genre, keeping alive the time-honoured social practices of borrowing and adapting bits of collective and/or anonymous wisdom for one's own purposes.[47]

■ BETWEEN IDENTITY AND HABIT: AA'S AMBITIOUS PRAGMATISM

One could easily study AA from the point of view of discipline and normalization, stressing the ways in which AA constitutes and reproduces the alcoholic *identity* as a master status. And this would not be inaccurate: within AA, drinking—or, rather, the drinking of those who regard themselves as alcoholics—ceases to be considered as a series of discrete acts and becomes instead a series of symptoms of an underlying identity. Indeed, one could take this analysis further to demonstrate how AA's non-expert knowledge of the alcoholic identity has served as a sort of prototype for the proliferation of identity-based forms of self-governance in the last decades of the 20th century. Twelve-step groups (Narcotics Anonymous, Sex Addicts Anonymous, Codependents Anonymous) formed themselves by extending the AA paradigm of alcoholism as a disease around which to organize an identity to other conditions. But even groups and networks that are not based on the 12 steps, such as the new identity of "people living with HIV/AIDS," use a number of techniques pioneered by AA, perhaps most significantly utilizing a disability, injury, or disease as a source of social identity. Although there have of course been some major changes, including the rejection of AA's apoliticism by groups focussed on either sexual victimization or on disability, it was nevertheless AA that historically opened up the possibility of identity-based forms of power and knowledge not controlled by established professions and bodies of expertise.[48] That lay organizations and consumer groups—not just experts—have the capability and the will to normalize their own members and constitute identities, turning disabilities, abuses, and injuries of all sorts into powerful mechanisms for acting politically and ethically, is something that we tend to take for granted today, especially in the United States, but which was a great novelty in the 1930s.[49]

While a major, if not the chief, force in the historical emergence of diseases that function as mechanisms for identity-building and even "empowerment," AA is nevertheless not the sort of organization that functions through a single mode of governance. Although it contributed in a major way to the formation of new forms to govern drinking as rooted in an alcoholic *identity* rather than as a series of discrete acts, AA was also shaped by a different sort of American cultural tradition, that represented theoretically by pragmatism.

AA's founders paid some homage to Carl Jung and to the psy sciences more generally, but they also acknowledged that the book most widely circulated among the early members was William James's *Varieties of Religious Experience*. This work elaborates the position that religion—like all other knowledges, including theology and philosophy—ought to be evaluated pragmatically, in terms of its practical effects. Focussing on religious *experience* rather than on religious belief or theological theory, this work stressed the empirical diversity of the *varieties* of such experience in ways that challenged the conventional ways of thinking about religion. James pursued the unorthodox project of putting Thomas Aquinas and Luther on exactly the same plane as Madame Blavatsky and spiritualist healers, arguing that theological controversies were meaningless unless they could be shown to have real-world consequences. In a statement foreshadowing Foucault's work, James stated in the conclusion to his lengthy documentation of various forms of religious practices that "God is real since he produces real effects."[50]

Although James's targets were philosophy, intellectual history, and theology more than medicine or psychiatry, pragmatism was profoundly opposed to the emerging psy sciences' project to posit deep identities lying underneath phenomenal appearances. James was a professional psychologist, but in his context that meant he knew about the sciences of the brain and the nervous system. Although he was persuaded by the argument that much experience is determined unconsciously, he was quite scathing toward psychoanalysis's efforts to construct itself as a general theory, arguing that the privileging of sexual experience and sexual trauma as causal factors shaping human individuality was quite arbitrary.

For both James and his compatriot John Dewey, the emerging scientific project to replace the act-based governance of traditional (liberal) law and religion by the identity-based governance of the psy sciences was fundamentally misguided, because it re-enacted rather than transcended the old philosophical battle between empiricism and rationalism. Are human beings a series of distinct acts and sensations, as Hume argued, or are we characterized by an underlying essential soul or by its scientific modern equivalent, an underlying psychic identity? John Dewey's pragmatist framework sought to displace this binary by deploying the in-between, hybrid category of habit. As mentioned in chapter 1, Dewey deployed habit to deconstruct the old theological battle between the advocates of free will and the believers in determinism, since habits are precisely those patterns of action that are neither fully willed nor utterly determined, occupying that space in between perfect autonomy and utter necessity.

If habit can be used, as it was by the pragmatist philosophers, to deconstruct the fundamental binary opposition of the whole field of alcoholism and addiction—freedom vs. determination—habit can also be used to deconstruct a related binary, that between act and identity. The deconstruction of the act vs. identity opposition that grounds Foucault's well-known views about the replacement of the act-based apparatus of sovereignty by the normalizing, identity-constituting tools of discipline was not explicitly carried out by either James or Dewey, but all the elements for such a deconstruction are present in their work, particularly Dewey's.

In an argument that validated the low-status spiritual practices of his day (such as the "mind cure" of Christian Science) and that was very agreeable to the early AA pioneers, James critiqued the assumption made by Protestant religious thought of his time that moral goodness was to be found in the deep structures of the soul. But if moral goodness is for James not identity-based, neither is it composed of isolated virtuous acts (as other religions claim). As Dewey notes, acts are never as discrete as empiricist philosophy claimed. Acts are in their vast majority not willed one at a time, but rather are rooted in and caused by habitual patterns. The testimony of AA members suggests that it is extremely difficult, if not impossible, to suddenly will ourselves into a new identity; and neither can we suddenly perform an act that has no precedent in our biography (refuse a drink, say). The pragmatist conclusion that we must, if we seek to work on the self, change our *habits*,[51] is thus in excellent agreement with the practical wisdom of AA and of many earlier projects to treat inebriety.

Unlike identity-based governance, which totalizes the self, habit-based governance decentres and fragments the self. If we think of alcoholism as an identity, we are territorializing the self. But the opposite project—the attempt to manage heavy drinking as a series of isolated acts, as if we were free to begin each day and each evening anew—has also been notoriously unsuccessful, as countless addiction-autobiographies testify. The practical failure of this intellectualist type of recovery project has a theoretical correlate: attempting to govern drinking as if each drink were an isolated decision perpetuates the fiction of an autonomous will that decides on each action from scratch. Repeatedly getting drunk, or repeatedly using alcohol to soothe emotional wounds, builds up certain grooves and patterns. In William James's work, these grooves are presented as physically existing in one's neurons; in Dewey's work, habitual patterns are presented, less somatically, as partly physical and partly ethical. It is Dewey's explicitly hybrid interpretation of habit that best reflects the experience of most recovering alcoholics.

Now, AA's *theory* of alcoholism as a disease fits the familiar Foucauldian pattern of identity-based governance. Foucault analyzed the transformation of the discrete series of acts known as sodomy into the full-fledged identity of the homosexual; similarly, AA believes that, although the drinking of normal people is indeed just a series of acts, the drinking of alcoholics is the effect or result of an underlying alcoholic identity.[52] AA's techniques for sobriety, however, are somewhat at odds with its own theory. Slogans such as "one day at a time," "easy does it," and so forth, do not make any presuppositions about identity: as argued above, they are more accurately interpreted as a modern-day version of the ancient scrapbooks for daily ethical meditation, the *hupomnemata*. And *hupomnemata* were one of a variety of ethical techniques designed to build up virtue not through cleansing the transcendental soul (neither the Greeks nor the pre-Christian Romans had such souls) or through mapping the essential identity of particularly psychic types, but rather through the slow accumulation of good habits on the purely superficial level of habit.

While AA's theory of alcoholism as an identity is rooted in the double intellectual heritage of AA's founders—religions and medicine/psy sciences—AA's techniques can without injustice be regarded as rooted in a much more ancient tradition of ethical work on the self. Pierre Hadot has pointed out, in an argument that has many parallels with American pragmatism, that in Greco-Roman culture the binary opposition of mind and body, thought and nature, freedom and necessity had not yet occurred. Ethical reflection at that time unified rather than separated thought and the body: spiritual exercises did not then involve, as they did later for Christians, a struggle *against* the body. Pre-Christian spiritual exercises were a project to simultaneously shape and govern bodily conduct and mental habits without separating the self into ontological levels (body vs. soul, symptom vs. underlying cause, acts vs. identity).[53]

AA's techniques for governing the soul use neither medical tools (objectivist observation, diagnosis, etc.) nor the tools of the psy sciences. Its practical techniques bear a strong resemblance to Hadot's spiritual exercises: they constitute a cobbled-together, low-theory, unsystematic system for habit reform. These techniques do not separate symptoms from disease, incidental or trivial acts from underlying structures: the most apparently trivial situation can be fraught with ethical significance, and it is up to the alcoholic him/herself, not to any authorized observer, to arrange the incidents and experiences of his/her life as they please and to give them meaning. Marriage, for instance, regarded by psy experts as a sign of emotional stability and maturity, appears in the narratives of AA members both as a good sign and a bad sign, sometimes as a symptom of being overly dependent and at other times—even in the same narrative—as an indication that one is finally able to achieve intimacy.[54]

If there is no standard list of symptoms, there is similarly no sacred list of treatment techniques. In AA, the point is not to generate a system of knowledge about alcoholism, but rather to provide members with an array of practical examples and suggestions among which the member will choose whatever works. This is why the techniques need to be taught primarily in group meetings and in one-to-one conversations, with books taking a definite second place. Each member will find some slogans meaningful and others not helpful, and be inspired by some of the stories heard at group meetings while being put off by others—just as James argued that it did not matter whether one gained one's spiritual wisdom from Saint Teresa of Avila or from a streetcorner astrologer, as long as it worked.

In any case, the texts, whether they be stories heard at a meeting, the 12 steps, or the meditations for every day not authorized by AA but bought and used by many members, are not so much texts as mnemonic devices. When an AA member thinks of a particular phrase, slogan, or story, he/she is meant to think not of intrinsic meaning but of the particular context in which that statement was first heard or read. When hearing a slogan being repeated, listening to an audiotape of an AA conference, or reading over one's favourite part of the Big Book, an alcoholic is reminded of the ways in which his or her soul became rearranged, as it were, on contact with that story or phrase. This is true, in the pragmatist sense of "it works," even for non-members: as I think about the meaning of "one day at a time," I do not think about theories of temporality. Rather, I call to mind the working-class, middle-aged woman in bargain-basement clothes who at one particular AA meeting stood up and, somewhat haltingly, described to the group just what sort of effects that phrase had on her conduct. She did not say, as the priests of my childhood would have said, that X or Y is the *true* meaning of the text. Instead, as if heeding the pragmatist thinkers' advice to focus on effectivity and practical effects, she simply outlined how exactly the text had helped *her* to persevere in sober conduct at a difficult moment. The people listening were thus not told what to think, or even what to do, but simply encouraged to reflect on the ways in which they could define for themselves how to appropriate and use the same text.

The discussions about habit formation that are found not only within AA, but in virtually all of the literature on alcoholism recovery written by those with practical experience are nevertheless rarely consistently pragmatist. The language of identity rarely disappears completely. AA members describing in detail how they worked to reshape the behavioural and ethical grooves of their soul, for instance by pushing themselves to attend an AA meeting every time they felt like going to the pub, will easily switch into comments that classify certain behaviours, such as working too hard, as symptoms of an underlying alcoholic identity.[55] The alcoholic identity, like all contemporary identities, tends to unify and centralize the set of habits that converge or are folded into an individual. While, if we remain strictly on the level of habits, there is no necessary link between drinking and other habits, positing an identity tends to territorialize habits and turn them into parts of a system. People both in AA and outside of it often say: I smoke because I am an alcoholic (or an addict); I work really hard to please the boss because I am an alcoholic; and so forth. This way of externally forcing a unification of the multiplicity of habits that make up one's conduct forecloses the possibility—envisaged by Dewey—of managing oneself consistently, not as a bundle of sensations (as Hume famously said) but rather as a bundle of semi-willed habitual patterns that are not necessarily unified from beneath by a single master identity. Having developed in the dual shadow of disciplinary governance and the American politics of identity, AA shrinks from considering the possibility that, if some people tend to drink when they are tired or angry, this may be a matter of habit, similar to pacing the room when one is nervous, biting one's nails when waiting for something, or pulling on one's hair while reading. While such habits are not completely automatic, in the sense that it is possible to become aware of them and change them, the habits were never deliberately chosen.

The coexistence of habit and identity within AA, therefore, is not a peaceful one. The theory of the alcoholic identity—that alcoholism is for those who are alcoholic not a matter of conduct but a matter of identity—does not do justice to AA's own practical wisdom, and prevents both AA and those who study it from developing the more novel possibility of a fully habitual ethics. Such a possibility, glimpsed several decades ago by

John Dewey, has not been consistently articulated at the level of discourse—although, as has been shown not only in this chapter but in the preceding ones, there is much evidence from the field of alcoholism treatment to suggest that this theoretical avenue is well supported by the practical experience of inebriates and alcoholics.

■ NOTES

1. See, for instance, K. Plummer, *Telling Sexual Stories: Power, Change and Social Worlds* (London, Routledge, 1995).
2. Tradition 10 states: "No AA group or member should ever, in such a way as to implicate AA, express any opinion on outside controversial issues—particularly those of politics, alcohol reform, or sectarian religion. The Alcoholics Anonymous groups oppose no one" (Alcoholics Anonymous [The Big Book], 3rd ed, 567).
3. A. Collins, "The Pathological Gambler and the Government of Gambling," *History of the Human Sciences* vol. 9, no. 3 (1996), 69–100.
4. This is not to say that either AA or alcohol science caused rising levels of alcohol consumption; the rising level of aggregate consumption that occurred in most industrialized countries in the period 1945–75 was part of a general shift in both the economics and the culture of consumption.
5. Challenging the monopoly of doctors over diagnosis does not necessarily challenge medicine as such, since, as Nikolas Rose has observed, the history of medical authority is not coterminous with the history of the profession. There are various assemblages, including AA, in which medical techniques are deployed for a number of ends. See N. Rose, "Medicine, History, and the Present" in C. Jones and R. Porter, *Reassessing Foucault: Power, Medicine and the Body* (London, Routledge, 1994).
6. Alcoholics Anonymous, 1996 Membership Survey, no pagination.
7. Interview no. 9, 1997.
8. Some AA texts prefer the term "illness" to "disease," precisely because it sounds less medical.
9. This was the definition given to me by a man chairing a small AA group (group no. 2); it is closely based on the text of the Big Book.
10. P. Antze, "Symbolic Action in Alcoholics Anonymous" in Mary Douglas, ed., *Constructive Drinking* (Cambridge University Press, 1987), 149–81.
11. For an interpretation of the clinical gaze that differentiates clinical judgment from the disciplinary logic of science, see T. Osborne, "Medicine and Epistemology: Michel Foucault and the Liberality of Clinical Reason," *History of the Human Sciences* vol. 5, no. 2 (1992), 63–93.

12. The distinction between rationalities and techniques of government is drawn from N. Rose and P. Miller, "Political Power beyond the State: Problematics of Government," *British Journal of Sociology* vol. 43, no. 2 (1992), 173–205.

13. The term "hybridity" is borrowed from Bruno Latour's work on science and modernity, *We Have Never Been Modern* (Princeton, Princeton University Press, 1993).

14. R. Smith, *Inhibition: History and Meaning in the Sciences of the Brain* (London, Transaction, 1992).

15. AA's survey findings are consistent with the group observation studies carried out by myself and my research assistant, Kimberley White-Mair. It is quite common to hear people at AA meetings declare that they have been sober for 10, 15, or even 20 years.

16. The text of the 12 steps is as follows:

    1. We admitted we were powerless over alcohol—that our lives had become unmanageable.

    2. Came to believe that a Power greater than ourselves could restore us to sanity.

    3. Made a decision to turn our will and our lives over to the care of God as we understood Him.

    4. Made a searching and fearless moral inventory of ourselves.

    5. Admitted to God, to ourselves, and to another human being the exact nature of our wrongs.

    6. Were entirely ready to have God remove all these defects of character.

    7. Humbly asked Him to remove our shortcomings.

    8. Made a list of all persons we had harmed, and became willing to make amends to them all.

    9. Made direct amends to such people wherever possible, except when to do so would injure them or others.

    10. Continued to take personal inventory and when we were wrong promptly admitted it.

    11. Sought through prayer and meditation to improve our conscious contact with God, as we understood Him, praying only for knowledge of His will for us and the power to carry that out.

    12. Having had a spiritual awakening as the result of these Steps, we tried to carry this message to alcoholics, and to practice these principles in all our affairs.

17. A long-term member of AA, married to a wine connoisseur, described at length her ultimately successful struggles to allow and even support her husband's interest in good wines (interview no. 17).

18. "Spiritual awakening" was the phrase used by AA's founder, Bill W., to refer to a

significant spiritual experience he had some time after he had stopped drinking. AA's other founder, Dr. Bob, never had such an evangelical experience.

19. M. Mann, *New Primer on Alcoholism*, 2nd ed (New York, Holt, Rinehart and Winston, 1958 [1st ed. 1950]).

20. Quoted in J.S. Rice, *A Disease of One's Own: Psychotherapy, Addiction, and the Emergence of Codependence* (New Brunswick, NJ, and London, Transaction, 1996), 149.

21. In contrast to AA's emphasis on individual responsibility for one's drinking, groups such as Adult Children of Alcoholics and Codependents Anonymous tend to encourage the blaming of parents, and sometimes of social institutions, always on the assumption that "the inner child" is corrupted from the outside.

22. A useful analysis of the bootstrap culture of self-improvement is the collection edited by R. Keat and N. Abercrombie, *Enterprise Culture* (London, Routledge, 1991). Further evidence that, in AA, ambition is not valued in the way it is in the rest of American society is found in Makela et al., *Alcoholics Anonymous: A Study of Mutual Help in Six Societies* (Madison, University of Wisconsin Press, 1996), 129.

23. Hamilton B., *Getting Started in AA* (Center City, Minn., Hazelden, 1995), 53.

24. From interview no. 14.

25. Hamilton B., *Getting Started in AA*, 96.

26. In North America, most AA self-help books today are not published by AA itself but by the commercially run Hazelden organization. AA official publications are always anonymous, although it is acknowledged that Bill Wilson, AA's founder, wrote most of the original Big Book (and received the royalties from it, an exceptional practice that was never repeated).

27. N. Robertson, *Getting Better: Inside Alcoholics Anonymous* (New York, William Morrow, 1988), 100. As Robertson and others point out, AA is highly unusual among philanthropic organizations in that, instead of fundraising, it prevents its members from giving large donations: no member may donate more than $1,000 per year, and no estate gifts of more than $1,000 are allowed.

28. Makela et al., *Alcoholics Anonymous*, 94. See also E. Kurtz, *Not-God: A History of Alcoholics Anonymous* (Center City, Minn., Hazelden, 1991).

29. The term "drunkalogues" is from interview no. 17.

30. "Oldtimers" are sometimes granted a certain privilege to make instant judgments about newcomers, but the oldtimers' cross-talk is often followed by a reminder that "we cannot take inventory for others" (a reference to steps 5–8).

31. The Makela et al. study repeats the conventional wisdom about AA being largely middle class (*Alcoholics Anonymous*, 104); but our group observation would suggest the opposite, namely that AA, at least in Toronto, is largely working class, not only numerically but also in terms of the communicative practices used in group meetings. A meeting held in

the cafeteria of a major bank head office (group no. 1) was remarkable in that less than a quarter of the men present were wearing ties, and those remained uniformly silent; the women who spoke also seemed to be blue-collar rather than white-collar workers.

32. Hamilton B., *Getting Started*, 67.

33. Group meetings do not provide any insights into the workings of sponsorship, but there is a detailed discussion of AA members' mixed feelings about becoming sponsors, in G. Hettelhack, *Second-Year Sobriety* (San Francisco, Harper, 1992).

34. Anonymous AA member, quoted in K. Davis, *Primero Dios: Alcoholics Anonymous and the Hispanic Community* (Selingsgrove, Susquehanna University Press, 1995), 24.

35. Interview no. 12.

36. Several individuals interviewed indicated that they had been victims of child sexual abuse, but the struggle for sobriety was always the main plot line—a narrative tactic completely at odds with the general perception of child sexual abuse as that which trumps all other issues.

37. *Alcoholics Anonymous*, ch. 4, "We Agnostics."

38. Group no. 1.

39. Hamilton B., *Getting Started in AA*, 29.

40. P. Antze, *"Symbolic Action in Alcoholics Anonymous,"* 162. This is confirmed by several of our interviews, in which AA members spoke of their Higher Power in maternal/loving terms.

41. Nevertheless, AA is still a Protestant organization in many respects. Many groups close each meeting with the Protestant version of the Lord's Prayer. Some group business meetings in the Toronto area have debated the question of the Lord's Prayer almost as vehemently as they have argued the most divisive question in AA today, namely whether smoking should be allowed at meetings (interview no. 17).

42. Interview no. 14, 1997.

43. Davis, *Primero Dios*, 29.

44. Indeed, AA meetings are conspicuously lacking in computer-generated images, transparencies, videos, and other paraphernalia of modernity. The only objects that circulate regularly among AA members, other than the dull-looking pamphlets produced by the organization, are audiotapes (copied from other tapes rather than commercially sold) of AA members' statements and discussions at conventions.

45. Hettelhack, *Second-Year Sobriety*, 10.

46. M. Foucault, "Writing the self" in A. Davidson, ed., *Foucault and His Interlocutors* (Chicago, University of Chicago Press, 1997), 237.

47. Sometimes these bits of wisdom are neither anonymous nor collective—the fame of Kahlil Gibran's *The Prophet* will attest to this—but AA has done a remarkable job of collecting, circulating, and distributing anonymous *hupomnemata* that generate no royalties.

48. One could also mention early homosexual activists in this context. As AA did, people like Dr. Magnus Hirschfeld built hybrid assemblages for the self-governance of deviant populations through techniques that were partly borrowed from the psy and medical sciences and partly developed in experience-based self-help contexts. But the hybrid knowledge of the homosexual identity that existed in the 1930s did not proliferate into other realms until our own times.

49. W. Brown, *States of Injury: Power and Freedom in Late Modernity* (Princeton, Princeton University Press, 1995).

50. W. James, *The Varieties of Religious Experience* (New York, Random House, 1994 [1902]), 561.

51. J. Dewey, *Human Nature and Human Conduct* (New York, Random House, 1922), part I.

52. People in AA and AA texts spend very little time analyzing the drinking of non-alcoholics, since they do not believe that alcoholics can learn from normal drinkers to drink moderately; therefore, the comments here and elsewhere on AA's perception of normal drinkers rely mostly on the implicit contrast that helps AA to define alcoholism not in terms of an amount of alcohol consumed but in terms of a specific identity.

53. P. Hadot, *Philosophy as a Way of Life: Spiritual Exercises from Socrates to Foucault* (Oxford, Blackwell, 1995).

54. A lengthy account of her own life by Angie D., a Mexican-American member active in AA for 20 years, describes one marriage as an integral part of her sobriety, but also recounts a long period of sobriety in which she made a promise to herself to "not get married, one day at a time" (Angie D., audiotape distributed by AA members, 1984).

55. See, for example, C. Knapp, *Drinking: A Love Story* (New York, Dial Press, 1996).

CHAPTER 15

WELFARE LAW, WELFARE FRAUD, AND THE MORAL REGULATION OF THE "NEVER DESERVING" POOR

Dorothy E. Chunn and Shelley A.M. Gavigan

The dismantling and restructuring of Keynesian social security programmes have impacted disproportionately on women, especially lone parent mothers, and shifted public discourse and social images from welfare fraud to welfare as fraud, thereby linking poverty, welfare, and crime. This article analyzes the current, inordinate focus on "welfare cheats." The criminalization of poverty raises theoretical and empirical questions related to regulation, control, and the relationship between them at particular historical moments. Moral regulation scholars working within post-structuralist and postmodern frameworks have developed an influential approach to these issues; however, we situate ourselves in a different stream of critical socio-legal studies that takes as its point of departure the efficacy, contradictions, and inherently social nature of law in a given social formation. With reference to the historical treatment of poor women on welfare, we develop three themes in our critical review of the moral regulation concept: the conceptualization of welfare and welfare law, as illustrated by welfare fraud; the relationship between social and moral with respect to the role of law; and changing forms of the relationship between state and non-state institutions and agencies. We conclude with comments on the utility of a "materialist" concept of moral regulation for feminist theorizing.

▪ INTRODUCTION

> The continuing offensive against welfare provides, perhaps, the single most gener-
> al threat to Western women's interests at present—at least for those many women
> who are not wealthy, and who still take the major responsibility for caring work
> in the home. (Segal, 1999: 206–7)

> ... the statistics unequivocally demonstrate that both women and single mothers
> are disproportionately adversely affected by the definition of spouse ... although
> women accounted for only 54% of those receiving social assistance and only 60%
> of single persons receiving social assistance, they accounted for nearly 90% whose
> benefits were terminated by the [new] definition of spouse ... (Falkiner v Ontario
> [2002]: 504, para. 77)

The attacks on the policies and practices of the Keynesian welfare state have resulted in
wholesale dismantling and restructuring of social security programmes for the poor.
These sweeping changes to social assistance, aptly characterized by some as a war on
the poor, have a disproportionate impact on poor women, as even Canadian courts
have begun to acknowledge (*Falkiner v Ontario*, 2002). Indeed, it has become axiomatic
to observe, as Lynne Segal does above in relation to welfare, that welfare law is principally (and ideologically) concerned with the lives and issues of poor women, especially
lone-parent mothers.

In this article, we will identify and analyze the pride of place the focus on "welfare
cheats" occupies in the current attack on the poor. It is important to emphasize that
this preoccupation with welfare "fraud" is but the most visible form of assault. The attack on welfare in the province of Ontario over the last decade, for instance, included
deep cuts to the level of welfare benefits (*Masse v Ontario*, [1996]; see also Moscovitch,
1997: 85), a broadening definition of "spouse" (*Falkiner v Ontario*, 2002), restructuring
of the legislation from "welfare" to "work,"[1] mandatory drug testing,[2] the introduction of a "quit/fire" regulation (which requires the cancellation or suspension of assistance to a recipient who resigns employment without just cause or is dismissed with
cause),[3] anonymous snitch lines, designed to encourage people to report suspected
welfare abuse by their neighbours (Morrison and Pearce, 1995; Morrison, 1998: 32),
and "zero tolerance" in the form of permanent ineligibility imposed upon anyone convicted of welfare fraud (Golding and Middleton, 1982; Evans and Swift, 2000; *Rogers
v Sudbury* (2001: 5); *Broomer v Ontario* [2002]). In this process, the restructuring of
welfare has shifted and been shifted by public discourse and social images (see Golding

and Middleton, 1982; Evans and Swift, 2000): welfare fraud became welfare *as* fraud. Thus poverty, welfare and crime were linked.[4] To be poor was to be culpable, or at least vulnerable to culpability.

Two Ontario women convicted of welfare fraud offer case studies of the culpable poor in this new era. Kimberly Rogers pleaded guilty to welfare fraud in the spring of 2001. Her fraud involved receiving a student loan and welfare assistance at the same time (previously but no longer permitted by Ontario's legislation).[5] In light of the fact that she was pregnant, and had no prior criminal record, the judge sentenced her to a six-month period of house arrest. However, as a result of the "zero tolerance" policy celebrated by the Ontario government, which then stipulated three months, and later, permanent ineligibility of people convicted of welfare fraud, Ms Rogers had no source of income (MacKinnon and Lacey, 2001; Keck, 2002). Confined to her small apartment by virtue of the "house arrest" condition of her sentence for welfare fraud, it took a court order directing that she receive interim assistance pending the hearing of her challenge to the constitutionality of the new ineligibility rules (*Rogers v Sudbury* (2001)). Even when her assistance ($468 per month) was reinstated on an interim basis, her rent ($450 per month) consumed the bulk of her monthly cheque. As a friend later observed: "No one can stretch $18 for a whole month" (MacKinnon and Lacey, 2001). Isolated, in her eighth month of pregnancy, with an uncertain future at best, and unable to leave her apartment, Ms Rogers died of a prescription drug overdose during a sweltering heat wave in mid-August 2001. The circumstances of Ms Rogers's death gave rise to a coroner's inquest in the fall of 2002. The coroner's jury made 14 recommendations for changes in government policies and practices, directed to no less than five provincial ministries; the first of which was that the zero tolerance lifetime ineligibility for social assistance as a result of welfare fraud be eliminated (Ontario, 2002).[6]

In 1994, Donna Bond, a single mother of two teenage children, had been charged with "welfare fraud" to the amount of $16,477.84 over a 16-month period—a bank account that had not been disclosed in her annual Update Report. At her trial, Ms Bond testified that she had saved all the money she had ever received from part-time employment, baby bonus, child tax credits, and income tax refunds (all of which she had disclosed in her annual reports to welfare). While she had initially planned to buy a car with this money, the serious health problems of her children made her realize that they "will require financial assistance to deal with these problems in the years ahead" (*R. v Bond* [1994]: para. 8). She decided to set the money aside as a trust fund for the children. When the account was discovered (easily it seems), she said that she had "honestly believed that she did not have to report the savings because they were for the children" (para. 13).

The trial judge admitted to a dilemma:

> ... I was very impressed by the sincerity and achievement of the accused and trou-
> bled by the paradox of criminalizing the actions of this woman who scrimped as
> a hedge against the future financial health needs of her children. If she had spent
> this money on drinking, or drugs, or in any other irresponsible way, there would
> be no basis for any criminal charge. A conviction seems to send the message it
> was wrong to be conscientious about the welfare of her children and foolish to be
> frugal. (para. 14)

Troubled as he was, convict he did, neither the first nor last "sympathetic" judge to
enter a conviction for fraud against a welfare mother (Martin, 1992; Carruthers,
1995). While critics might regard this case as affording an instance in which reasonable doubt as to guilt ought to have existed, the trial judge took a different view of her
culpability: "[H]er commendable frugality and her selfless motives for committing the
offence are matters for consideration on sentencing" (*R. v Bond* [1994]: para. 14). Were
this normatively perfect mother not convicted of welfare fraud, she might well have
been recognized by a community organization, or a women's magazine, as "Mother
and Homemaker of the Year."

In our view, the *Bond* and *Rogers* cases raise many theoretical and empirical questions
related to regulation, law, morality, and the relationship between them at particular historical moments. We rely on their cases to develop three themes in this article:

- the conceptualization of welfare and welfare law as illustrated by welfare fraud;
- the relationship between social and moral with respect to the role of law;
- changing forms (and continued relevance) of the state and its relationship with
  non-state institutions and agencies.

An increasingly prominent approach to these issues in critical socio-legal studies
through the 1980s and 1990s was evident in the proliferating literature on the arguably
related concepts of "moral regulation," "risk," "governance," and "governmentality"
generated by scholars working within post-structuralist and postmodern frameworks.
We focus here primarily on moral regulation in the Canadian context. While the concept of moral regulation initially was developed by Marxist-influenced theorists (Hall,
1980; Corrigan and Sayer, 1981; 1985), a number of Canadian scholars have employed
a (re)formed concept in their work which illustrates the decentring trend in theories of
regulation and control (Valverde and Weir, 1988: 31–4; Valverde, 1991, 1998; Loo, 1992:
125–65; Strange and Loo, 1997; Little, 1998) that also characterizes contemporary theorizing about governance and governmentality (Dean, 1994, 1999; Stenson, 1999). The
moral regulation literature in Canada is not confined within a particular discipline, but

it does tend to be connected to interdisciplinary work that often has an historical focus (see Hunt, 1997, 1999; Strange and Loo, 1997; Campbell, 1999).

The strength of this scholarship is the light it sheds on non-state forces and discourses, as well as the important insight that the state does not hold a monopoly on "social" and "moral" initiatives. The criticism of blunt, over-inclusive notions of "law and state as social control" and of the excesses of economic determinism is also well taken. However, we also find echoes of the sociological, criminological, and (some) feminist literature on "social control" in this work on moral regulation. Indeed, it seems to us that contemporary writers have used the concept of moral regulation to analyze many of the same issues that were of concern to social control scholars a century earlier (Chunn and Gavigan, 1988: 107–28): the relationship between state and civil society, public and private, formal and informal control, and the construction, control, or regulation of "moralized" subjects, objects, and projects (see Hunt, 1997: 275–301; 1999). Thus, while we share many of the same concerns as moral regulation scholars and have some sympathy for their projects and arguments, we nonetheless want to argue for a more fully social and materialized form of the concept of moral regulation. In short, we want to rematerialize the moral by situating moral regulation in relation to particular forms of social formation and within specific forms of state, law, and social policy (Stenson and Watt, 1999; Clarke, 2000).

Rather than jettison the concepts of "social" or "control" we want to argue that "moral regulation" need not be considered as an alternative or necessarily superior concept and that, therefore, sites and forms of regulation and control require different, not alternative, forms of analysis. So, while we agree that recourse to the language of "control" or "social control" too often obscures the complex and contradictory sources, contexts, and objects encompassed, we are of the view that regulation neither supplants nor captures the field. Not every state action or law is an expression of "social control"—but nor is it necessarily a form of regulation, moral or otherwise. To assume that moral regulation is inevitably more flexible or precise than social control is to replicate the theoretical error of over-inclusivity. Thus, despite the significance of non-state actors and processes, it remains important to identify the links, forms, and sites of state action and inaction. We want to distance our notion of moral regulation from one which suggests that the state is disappearing or ceasing to be relevant. In our view, the state never ceases to be a player, even when benched, ignored by some, or out-manoeuvred by others.

We are influenced here by a body of socio-legal scholarship that has undertaken and advanced this form of inquiry and analysis.[7] We will illustrate our critical engagement with the concept of moral regulation with reference to the historical treatment of poor women on welfare (see also Little, 1998). We focus in particular on the always precarious position of such women within the overarching (apparently anachronistic) category of the "deserving poor," through the example of welfare legislation and policy, and the current preoccupation with welfare fraud. In our view, state provision of social assistance to the poor was neither principally nor incidentally an expression of benign state coercion or social control, although distinguished scholars in the field have worked within this framework (Piven and Cloward, 1971). Our understanding of the regulatory nature of welfare legislation, and its moral content, has been enhanced by moral regulation scholars (e.g., Little, 1998). But, as we will illustrate later, moral regulation offers a partial, perhaps historically specific, analysis of the operation of welfare law. Recent experience of welfare law reform and preoccupation with welfare fraud—this redefinition, restructuring, harassment, and disentitlement, coupled with the ever present threat of criminal prosecution—suggests to us that the state and its coercive apparatus continue to play an important role, analysis of which is neglected at our peril.

The article is organized in five sections. We begin with a review of some of the moral regulation literature, devoting particular attention to Canadian contributions, and outline our conceptualization of the issues related to regulation. Next, we examine welfare law reform in the 1990s with an emphasis on the emergence of our specific exemplar of welfare fraud. In the following two sections, we revisit the concept of moral regulation and consider the (in)ability of recent forms of moral regulation discourse to explain the current state preoccupation with welfare fraud. We conclude with some comments on the utility of a "materialist" concept of moral regulation for feminist theorizing on socio-legal relations.

■ A GENEALOGY OF MORAL REGULATION AND ITS (SOCIO-) LEGAL FORMS

> In the last instance (as they say) it is the nature of the state which shapes the nature of crime control. A quite different theoretical agenda could also be constructed that does not give the state such a privileged position, that sees the real force of social control as lying outside the formal punitive system. (Cohen, 1985: 272)

Moral regulation has no agreed-upon meaning. Indeed, as Steve Tombs (2002) has observed recently in respect of forms of constraint of corporate behaviour, the "disarmingly simple and often used term" "regulation" covers myriad forms of actions, processes and actors, such that "it is perhaps a less than useful term" (p. 113). While we want to hold onto "regulation" as a legal form, we acknowledge that its pairing with "moral" does not render its meaning any less opaque. Alan Hunt has similarly noted that the late 20th-century turn to moral regulation in sociological and socio-legal literature "has not been accompanied by any close attention to the concept 'moral regulation' itself" (Hunt, 1997: 276; 1999: 7–8).

Nonetheless, one is hard-pressed to find any scholarship in the area that fails to acknowledge that the elaboration of a contemporary concept of moral regulation, whatever its theoretical antecedents and progenitors, owes much to the collaborative work of Philip Corrigan and Derek Sayer (1985). In *The Great Arch: English State Formation as Cultural Revolution,* they presented a close analysis of the particularity of state formation in England, and specifically, the "cultural" project of English state formation:

> ... moral regulation: a project of normalizing, rendering natural, taken for granted, in a word "obvious," what are in fact ontological and epistemological premises of a particular and historical form of social order. Moral regulation is coextensive with state formation, and state forms are always animated and legitimated by a particular moral ethos. (p. 4)

This concern with *forms* of social relations and state action or state formation may be found as well in their pioneering (if seemingly lesser known) contribution to Marxist theorizing on the rule of law and "specifically legal forms of regulation" (1981: 30). They argued that "moral topography" is integral to law—"a mapping of the social world which normalises its preferred contours—and, equally suppresses or at best marginalises other ways of seeing and being" (1981: 33). But if this moral topography is integral to law, so too is law integral to morality:

> For law is not merely the passive reflection of the moral and material framework which overarches it. There is a dialectic to be observed ...

> Law is absolutely central to this regulation ... It is, in sum, the major means through which the boundaries of preferred moral classifications can be regulated: defined, emphasised, focused, nuanced, shifted. (1981: 40)

Some critics have chided Corrigan and Sayer for "disabling" their analysis by their ongoing commitment to the relevance of the state in moral regulation (Dean, 1994: 145–68; Valverde, 1994: 212). However, as Alan Hunt (1999) points out, since Corrigan and Sayer's immediate objective "was precisely to provide an account of state-formation; it seems to be beside the point to criticise such a project for being state-centred" (p. 15).

It is also clear that their work stands as an exemplar to those who would erect a narrow or crude version of Marxist theorizing in order to illustrate its inadequacy.

While Corrigan and Sayer placed the moral regulation project squarely within state actions and legal relations, one of the promises of less "state-centred" scholars is the way in which moral regulation can render visible the fact that the state has not held a monopoly on "moral" projects. The state must be decentred (Valverde, 1991), or its relationship with non-state agencies better appreciated (Valverde, 1995), or erased as a significant player altogether (Valverde, 1998). For Mariana Valverde (1994), the heart of moral regulation, or moral reform in a "moral capitalist setting ... is not so much to change behaviour as to generate certain ethical subjectivities that appear as inherently moral" (p. 216; see also Weir, 1986). The focus is less on the (material) consequences of regulation or reform than on the (discursive) contest. However, the concept of "control" has not completely vanished, as the new interest in "self control" and "self regulation" might suggest (Valverde, 1998; Stenson, 1999). One might be forgiven for continuing to consider the "echoes" of social control when "agencies of moral regulation" are identified as "schools, welfare agencies, charities" (Valverde, 1994: 215; see also Little, 1998).

But, as others have asked: "Why moral?" (Dean, 1994: 147) (To which we may be seen to be adding: "Why regulation?") What is meant by "moral" and why is the concept "moral" employed in preference to "social"? It is not a theoretical imperative, as Lorna Weir's (1986) early important work has demonstrated. The answer may derive in part from the distance sought to be established between an older, cruder, instrumentalist concept of social control and a more finely tuned, nuanced yet precise and specific concept of moral regulation (Valverde and Weir, 1988: 31–4; Hunt, 1997; 1999; Strange and Loo, 1997; Little, 1998; Campbell, 1999). Yet much of the literature seems more able to explain why regulation is preferred to control, leaving the inference that the meaning of moral is self-evident.

For Alan Hunt (1997), moral regulation facilitates a richer, more cogent analysis of social relations than is possible with the

> more conventional category "social control" which has the disadvantage of assuming a unitary and self-conscious project of some primary agent ... that imposes itself on others ... Moral regulation in contrast is more messy; it is never unitary, its agents vary widely, it never goes uncontested and its self-consciousness is complex. (p. 277)

Margaret Little's (1998) illuminating historical study of the moral regulation of single mothers in Ontario owes an intellectual debt to moral regulation scholars who reject

the image of regulator as "powerful," in favour of "the contestation of different definitions of morality and the alliances formed" (p. xix). Little is committed to appreciat-
ing the importance of "resistance to change" as well as the "cultural activities of the
state and other social agencies" (p. xix). However, she suggests that the claims of moral
regulation are modest:

> ... [M]oral regulation provides us with another lens through which to examine
> the complexities of welfare policy. This model cannot explain the conditions ob-
> served, but it can help to highlight relationships and regulations that many take
> for granted. (p. xix, emphasis in original)

But Dean's (1994) question still looms: "Why moral?" (p. 147). Ultimately, Dean rejects
the concept—in part because "the adjective, moral, remains indeterminate ... it delineates no clear domain that is (even relatively) autonomous from forms of political regulation and state power" (p. 147)—and he argues that "governmentality" is less problematic and more useful as an analytic construct. For Hunt (1999), moral regulation is
a useful concept, but for "analytical purposes only" since there is "no place where 'the
moral' rules alone or even predominates" (p. 8). As he conceptualizes it:

> The moral dimension of regulation is not to be found in the intentions of the
> regulatory agents on the simple methodological grounds that we can have
> no sure access to intention, and no means of distinguishing motive from
> self-justification. Rather, my definition of moral regulation is a process in
> which moral discourses, techniques and practices make up the primary field
> of contestation. (Hunt, 1997: 279)

We are mindful that for some scholars who have helped to develop moral regulation
as an analytic frame, its appeal lies in the focus on non-state actors and processes it is
seen to facilitate. Thus, the state is decentred from a ubiquitous "pride of place" position in shaping and containing "civil society."[8] While sympathetic to this "decentring"
emphasis, we want to argue for a renewed focus on social and state forces, and in particular the contradictions and contributions of forms of law and state to gendered and
anti-racist class struggles in the realm of moral regulation. In other words, moral
regulation must be situated expressly within the context of capitalist class relations and
struggles; not least of which, in the current context, is capital's (globalized) attack on
the "straw house" of the Keynesian welfare state. We want to reinsert and re-articulate
the relationship between legal regulation and moral regulation without collapsing them
into each other or the state, or rendering one or other invisible.

Our concern is that despite the richness, depth, and diversity of the scholarship reviewed earlier, the concept of moral regulation that emerges from it does not deliver the contestation, the messiness, the resistance that it promises. In our view, it continues to be important to attend to the different forms of regulation, the different sites, forms and levels of state, and social policy and law. To illustrate our position, we draw on Stuart Hall's early work on law, state, and moral regulation; specifically, his analysis of the reformist 1960s' era of the "legislation of consent" in Britain when laws relating to divorce, homosexuality, abortion, prostitution were liberalized (Hall, 1980). Hall's organizing question is (p. 2): "What was it about the shifts in the modality of moral regulation which enabled this legislation, plausibly, to be described as 'permissive'?"

Hall reminds us that in "the 'legislation of consent' no single uncontradictory tendency is to be discovered" (p. 7). By way of illustration, Hall argues that the highly influential Report of the Wolfenden Committee on prostitution and homosexuality "identified and separated more sharply two areas of legal and moral practice—those of sin and crime, of immorality and illegality" (p. 11). In so doing, Wolfenden created "a firmer opposition between these two domains" and "clearly staked out a new relation between the *two modes of moral regulation— the modalities of legal compulsion and of self-regulation*" (p. 11–12, emphasis added). Wolfenden recommended decriminalization and "*privatisation* of *selective* aspects of sexual conduct" (p. 13, emphasis in original). Hall identifies the "double taxonomy" of the Wolfenden recommendations: Towards stricter penalty and control, towards greater freedom and leniency (p. 14). Here then was the core of the tendency of the 1960s' permissive legislation: "*Increased regulation* coupled with *selective privatisation* through contract or consent, both in a new disposition" (p. 21, emphasis added), a "more privatised and person-focused regulation, tacit rather than explicit, invisible rather than visible" (p. 21).

For us, Hall's questions, method of analysis, and insights continue to be cogent. In identifying the "double taxonomy" of control and penalty and freedom and leniency, or simultaneous deregulation and increased regulation, Hall reminds us of the complexity of the unity of the 1960s' reforms. The state was pulled back and re-inserted in different ways in the same pieces of legislation; its invisibility in one area was reinforced by its visibility in the other. From our perspective, his insight that "self-regulation" was inextricably related to increased "public" regulation is important. The lines between unacceptable public and permissible private conduct were ever more sharply drawn. In this way, two modalities of moral regulation, legal compulsion and self-regulation, one neither displacing nor transcending the other, co-existed in a complex unity.

Before applying this conceptualization of moral regulation to our exemplar of welfare fraud, we would first like to provide an overview of the always unstable terrain of Canadian welfare law and policy in the twilight years of the 20th century, a period marked by the teeter-tottering of the welfare state. In the next section we look at welfare law reform during the 1990s in order to consider the heightened interest, indeed legal shifts, in the area of welfare fraud in Canada.

■ WELFARE REFORM IN THE 1990s

> The new zero tolerance policy is the first of its kind in Canada, and a key step in Ontario's welfare reforms.[9]

Although governments of all political stripes (re)formed welfare policy and legislation during the 1990s (Moscovitch, 1997; Bashevkin, 2002), we use Ontario as our primary exemplar. Taking its cue from the Klein administration in Alberta (see Denis, 1995; Kline, 1997), the Harris government arguably was the most draconian among the Canadian provinces in effecting changes.[10] Welfare, and in particular a vow to "crack down" on welfare "fraud," were the centrepiece of the Ontario government's welfare policy (Ontario, 1999; 2000a). Indeed, one of the first things the Harris Tories did upon election in 1995 was to introduce a 22 percent cut to welfare rates and to redefine (i.e., broaden) the definition of spouse in welfare law in order to disentitle a broader range of previously entitled recipients (see Gavigan, 1999). Although all of Canada's welfare poor live on incomes that are thousands of dollars below the poverty line (National Council of Welfare, 2002; 2003), in post-1995 Tory Ontario, the welfare rate cut ensured that the "poverty gap" widened even further (McMullin, Davies, and Cassidy, 2002; National Council of Welfare, 2003: 66, f. 5. 2). The household income of a single employable recipient of social assistance in Ontario fell to 35 percent of the federal government's low income cut-off measure; the income of a single parent with one child dropped to 58 percent of the poverty line (Gavigan, 1999: 212–13; National Council of Welfare, 2003: 28, t. 2. 1). An Ontario couple with two children on welfare had an income ($18,400) that is 20 percent of the estimated average income of a four-person family in Ontario ($90,606) (National Council of Welfare, 2003: 31, t. 3.1).

The discourse and politics of welfare fraud have obscured the imprecision of what is considered to be fraud, and by whom. In Harris Tory discourse, it came to encompass all forms of overpayments, whether resulting from administrative errors or not, including people in jail whose welfare should have been terminated upon incarceration, as well as formal fraud convictions—numerically insignificant as these continue to be. Indeed, the government's own "Welfare Fraud Control Reports" tend to collapse categories, frequently failing to distinguish between benefit "reduction" and "termination," and the reasons therefore (Ontario, 2003). As the coroner who presided at the Kimberly Rogers's Inquest observed of the evidence that had been presented during the two months of hearings: "Overpayments ... may occur for a number of reasons, most of which are related to administrative items and the settlement of supplementary income received in previous periods; while overpayments are common, overpayments due to fraud are very uncommon" (Eden, 2003).

Crackdowns on welfare abuse during the 1970s and early 1980s (see Golding and Middleton, 1982; Rachert, 1990) were followed by the overhaul of welfare policies in most liberal democracies. In Ontario in 1988, the Social Assistance Review Committee (SARC) released *Transitions*, a 600-page report with 274 recommendations on Ontario's social assistance system (Ontario, 1988). The issues of "system integrity" and "welfare fraud" were dealt with in seven pages, and yielded but two recommendations (p. 380). These recommendations were motivated not because the Committee was convinced that the system was being "bled" by fraud, but in order to address and instil public confidence in the system (pp. 384–6):

> We have no evidence to suggest that fraud in the social assistance system is greater than it is in the tax system or the unemployment insurance system. Nevertheless, because public confidence in the social assistance system depends in a large part on the belief that the funds are being well spent and that abuse is being kept to a minimum, we accept that some of the measures adopted to control social assistance fraud may need to be more extensive that they are in other systems. (p. 384)

Significantly, however, the *Report* identified adequacy of benefits as the "*single most important weapon in the fight against fraud in the system*" (p. 384, emphasis added).

In a comprehensive response to the recommendations concerning "system integrity," Dianne Martin (1992) criticized the Committee for abandoning its own guiding principles, in particular its commitment to the creation of a welfare regime based on dignity and autonomy of social assistance recipients. Noting the dearth of reliable data on the incidence of welfare fraud in Ontario, Martin suggested that the most reliable indicator (conviction rate) placed the incidence rate at less than 1 percent (p. 93). The disproportional criminalization and punitive treatment of women on welfare figured prominently among Martin's concerns, and even when judges appeared to be sympathetic, women were convicted and incarcerated (p. 91). The guiding sentencing principles, as Martin noted (p. 66), stressed deterrence as "the paramount consideration" even where the case was "pitiful" (see also *R. v Thurrott* (1971); Wilkie, 1993; Carruthers, 1995).

The complexity of the rules and the reporting requirements facing welfare recipients has not diminished over the 15 years since the *Transitions Report* was released. On the contrary, as Jan Morrison (1995) has illustrated, the rules and reporting requirements have become more difficult and intrusive. As noted earlier, the previous legislation permitted a welfare recipient to receive social assistance as well as an income-based student loan in order to attend college or university. No longer. Now she runs the risk of a welfare fraud conviction (McKinnon and Lacey, 2001; Keck, 2002).

From a modest, almost insignificant, place in *Transitions*, the fight against welfare fraud emerged as a centrepiece of provincial welfare policy in Ontario, irrespective of governing political party (Moscovitch, 1997; Morrison, 1995; Little, 1998: 139–63). Far from being a minor residual concern triggered by a few "cheats" (McKeever, 1999: 261–70), policies of "Enhanced Verification" and the introduction of "snitch lines," "zero tolerance," and "permanent ineligibility" all illustrate the shift that has occurred. More intense measures were developed to ensure that a recipient is eligible, and the creation of the "snitch hotline" was designed to encourage the anonymous reporting of suspected fraud and abuse by neighbours. Again, despite the modest results (Morrison and Pearce, 1995; Little, 1998; Ontario, 1999; 2000a; 2003; *Rogers* v *Sudbury* (2001)), the government celebrated this form of "deputization" of its citizenry to inform on friends, neighbours, and acquaintances. Far from instilling "public confidence" in the social security system (Ontario, 1988), these initiatives ensured that a lack of public confidence is maintained and encouraged, whilst now conveying the impression that fraud was rampant, and that every person on welfare needed to be watched and reported and tested.

It is important to note as well that unlike the situation in Britain (McKeever, 1999: 261–70), this shift in the direction of increased surveillance and criminalization of welfare recipients, notably women on welfare, illustrates that the (coercive form of) criminal law and (the regulatory form of) welfare law are inseparable. The *Criminal Code* continues to be used to prosecute welfare recipients where fraud is suspected, and even "sincere, devoted mothers" like Donna Bond find themselves at risk of prosecution and conviction. For all the heightened intensity and investigation of welfare fraud, however, the convictions boasted by the Ontario government—1123 in 1997–8, 747 in 1998–9, and 547 in 1999–2000—amounted to no more than 1.36 percent of the total number of welfare recipients in the province based on Ontario welfare statistics (Ontario, 1999; 2000a, b); and less than 1 percent based on National Council of Welfare Statistics (2000).[11]

■ WOMEN, WELFARE, AND FRAUD: THE "NEVER DESERVING" POOR

In using welfare law and, in particular, welfare fraud to interrogate the efficacy of (moral) regulation, it is important to be clear about what we are and are not saying. While we share the view that law is central (Corrigan and Sayer, 1981: 40), we are not asserting that the law is necessarily determinative of the nature of the relations that it defines, governs, or regulates (Gavigan, 1986: 279–312). Nor are we denying the relevance of informal and non-legal practices, and indeed non-state practices (assuming they can be identified). We are arguing against the "expulsion of law" (Hunt, 1993) and the erasure of the state. Indeed, it is ironic that just as the regulatory state has been identified by the right as a problem because of its "pervasive" and intrusive presence in everyday life and business transactions, the state has similarly been rolled back in the critical socio-legal scholarship we discussed earlier. We concur with those who continue to argue for the interconnectedness of the material, social, and cultural and the need to look at redistribution as well as identity/self-formation (Collins, 1991; Fraser, 1997; Roberts, 1997; Boyd, 1999; Brenner, 2000; Razack, 2002).

We are influenced as well by Alan Hunt's (1993) "relational theory of law," which "does not artificially separate legal from other forms of social relations" (p. 225), and his important insight:

> [R]elational theory facilitates the recognition and exploration of the degree and forms in which legal relations penetrate other forms of social relations ... It also embraces the idea that the "presence of law" within social relations is not just to be gauged by institutional intervention but also by the presence of legal concepts and ideas within types of social relations that appear to be free of law. (p. 225)

Of particular relevance for our purposes is Hunt's comment on the pervasive theme in governmentality literature that sites of power are dispersed:

> In reorienting the focus of attention toward the plurality of power, and to the significance of local and capillary power there is an unwelcome, but avoidable tendency to expel the state. Without derogating from or evading the significance of the plurality of power it is essential to "bring the state back in." (pp. 312–13)

We are concerned that the neglect of law and state as social relations in some of the moral regulation scholarship reinforces the "artificial separation" of legal relations from other social relations and thus risks rendering invisible what Richard Kinsey (1979) once characterized as the "despotism of legality." In theorizing welfare fraud, it seems clear that there have been important shifts in welfare policy which seem not to be captured by "moral regulation" in its Foucauldian form. We want to argue that a significant ideological shift (evident in welfare-related practices) has occurred, and that it is impossible to de-centre the state and the heightened attention to welfare fraud during the 1990s.

In this discussion, we are not suggesting that the welfare reforms of the 1990s marked a complete departure from past practices. We see important historical continuities in welfare legislation and policy that need to be emphasized (Abramovitz, 1996; Little, 1998; Mosher, 2000). First, welfare policy has always been premised on the separation of the "deserving" from the "undeserving" poor. Second, the social support accorded to the deserving was, and continues to be, based on "the principle of less eligibility" or the assumption that welfare recipients should not receive more money than the worst-paid worker in the labour force. Third, the "deserving" have always been at risk of falling into the ranks of the "undeserving"; as Little (1998) well demonstrates, single mothers on social assistance have been and are subjected to intrusive and "moral" surveillance of their homes, their cleanliness, their childrearing abilities, their personal lives, and so on (see also Buchanan, 1995: 33, 40). Fourth, criminal prosecutions for welfare fraud have always occurred (Rachert, 1990; Martin, 1992: 52–97; Evans and Swift, 2000).

What then made the 1990s different from earlier times? We see an important ideological shift from welfare liberalism to neo-liberalism (see also Stenson, 1999). However, our analysis leads us to conclude that the shift is one in which a major state presence and resources are still required. On the one hand, the state is ideologically de-centred but no less present (Denis, 1995). The form of the state and its social policy has shifted; social programmes designed to ameliorate or redistribute have been eroded, laying bare a heightened state presence which condemns and punishes the poor. On the other hand, the effect of this ideological shift has been a huge expansion in the category of undeserving poor. Indeed, virtually no one is considered "deserving"; even those who do receive social assistance are viewed as temporary recipients who must demonstrate their willingness to work for welfare and who ultimately will be employed as a result of skills and experience gained through workfare and other government-subsidised programmes. Thus, sole-parent mothers who historically were more likely to be deemed "deserving" than were childless men and women are no longer so "privileged" (Buchanan, 1995; Moscovitch, 1997; Little, 1998; Mortenson, 1999; Mosher, 2000; Swift and Birmingham, 2000; Bashevkin, 2002).

This redefinition of the "undeserving poor" has required a massive redeployment but, arguably, not a reduction in the allocation of state resources to welfare. The downsizing of social assistance payments is accompanied by a concomitant increase in state-subsidised make-work and workfare programmes that ostensibly will (re)turn participants to the labour force, and a dramatic increase in the state-implemented technologies and programmes which are aimed at ferreting out and punishing the "undeserving" poor (Mortenson, 1999; Mosher, 2000; Swift and Birmingham, 2000). Indeed, the lifetime ban upon conviction for welfare fraud arguably ensures a lifetime of (secondary) punishment (without parole) and unameliorated poverty following upon such a conviction.

In sum, we want to emphasize that there are important differences between the past and the current context in which welfare and welfare fraud are being framed. We are witnessing a profound attack on the "social," indeed the erosion of social responsibility, and in this attack, the authoritarian, neo-liberal state is an important player. As we illustrate in the next section, despite the apparent transcendence of social relations and state forms (in favour of dispersed pluralities of power)—where, as Alan Hunt has argued (1997), the "social" is replaced by the moral and the moral is a realm unto itself—moral regulation, whether in its emergence or its repudiation, must be understood in relation to state and social policy.

■ MORAL REGULATION RECAST

It is imperative to recognize that the increased emphasis on welfare and welfare fraud has occurred in the context of state (re)formation in liberal democracies. We concur with (moral regulation) scholars who argue that the success of the "new right" in Ontario and elsewhere cannot be reduced to economics and globalization. Rather, restructuring and the decline of "the social" must "be understood in the context of a vast cultural offensive to transform society" in which "the ability to wield state power is essential ..." (Denis, 1995: 373; see also Hall, 1988). As Denis (1995) argues: "Far from losing its sovereignty, the state reasserts its power over the lives of citizens ... It turns itself into the 'authoritarian state,' one of whose main characteristics is to usher in a new, more intense regime of moral regulation ..." (p. 373).

In concluding our discussion of welfare fraud we want to return to Hall's (1980) argument that the "legislation of consent" was shot through with contradictory tendencies making the "unity" of the various statutes involved "a necessarily complex one" (p. 7). We can identify contradictory tendencies related to welfare reform in Ontario and elsewhere during the 1980s and 1990s that restructured the relation between the two modes of moral regulation—self-regulation and compulsion. Specifically, we can identify a "double taxonomy" (p. 14) in the welfare reforms towards both expanded privatization and increased regulation. On the one hand, we see the intensified individualization of poverty through the emphasis on personal responsibility, the imposition of self-reliance and the relegation of former welfare recipients to the market (see also Cossman, 2002). The slight and grudging acknowledgement of social responsibility for the poor that marked the Keynesian state has been rescinded. Now, as in the 19th century, poverty is a problem of individuals in civil society and the solution to poverty is an individualized one to be found principally in the labour market and/or marriage.[12]

This intensified individualization of poverty has major implications for lone-parent women. Historically, the "deserving" mother on welfare may have been "hapless" (Evans and Swift, 2000) and "pitied, but not entitled" (Gordon, 1994), but she also was a public servant of sorts so long as she was considered to be (morally) fit. During the 1990s, Ontario and other governments began divesting themselves of public servants, including "welfare moms," and placed the emphasis on creating choices to work and become self-sufficient. Now, work is strictly confined to the (private) market and mother work no longer receives even the tacit recognition that it was accorded by Keynesian states. The promotion of individual responsibility and self-reliance together with the equation of work with paid, private-sector employment is very clear in the statement of key principles underpinning Ontario's (re)formed welfare system: "Doing nothing on welfare is no longer an option ... Participation [in Ontario Works] is mandatory for all able-bodied people, including sole-support parents with school-aged children" (Ontario, 2000b: 1; see also Lalonde, 1997).

Defining work as paid employment means that women who do unpaid work can no longer be dependent on the state, but they can work for welfare or be dependent on an individually responsible, self-reliant, employed spouse or same-sex partner. The Harris government underscored this point by refining and expanding the "spouse in the house" rule on the ground that "no one deserves higher benefits just because they are not married."[13] Thus, while "welfare dependency" has become a form of personality disorder signifying inadequacy and "diagnosed more frequently in females" (Fraser and Gordon, 1994: 326), the "approved" alternative, or perhaps supplement, to the market for sole-parent women is marriage and the family (Murray, 1990). As Segal (1999) points out: "This is why single mothers can be demonized if they *don't* work, even while married women with young children can be demonized if they *do*" (p. 206, emphasis in original).

On the other hand, concomitant with the emphasis on the intensified individualization of poverty is the intensified state regulation and surveillance of dwindling numbers of public welfare recipients, now re-defined as individuals who need "temporary financial assistance ... while they satisfy obligations to becoming and staying employed" (Ontario Works Act, 1997, s. 2). Since welfare "is temporary, not permanent" (s. 2), the state must ensure that public money is not being wasted on "fraudsters." The Ontario legislation invokes the neo-liberal language of self-reliance through employment, temporary financial assistance, efficient delivery, and accountability to taxpayers.[14] However, as noted earlier, Ontario poured extensive resources into the establishment of an elaborate and constantly expanding system of surveillance aimed at detecting and preventing fraud and misuse of the social assistance system. At the same time as massive cuts to welfare rates were implemented, the government allocated considerable money for special staff with expanded powers to investigate welfare fraud: there were 300 such investigators in 1998–9 and the government was providing "additional funding for up to 100 more staff to do this work" (Ontario, 2000b). Additional government resources were used to create and maintain the Welfare Fraud Hotline and a province-wide Welfare Fraud Control Database, and to prosecute alleged "fraudsters." Clearly, the state is not reluctant to spend public money if the funding is spent on policing welfare recipients as opposed to providing for them.

Of course, if we move beyond what government authorities themselves say, it becomes clear that the moralization and criminalization of the poor in general and "welfare moms" in particular are far from being a seamless process. Contradictions are evident both among those who apply welfare law and policy and among those who are the targets of moralization. Judicial decision-making, for instance, is not all of a piece in cases involving mothers charged with welfare fraud. Some of the criminal cases where women were convicted, of welfare fraud for "spouse in the house" and hence not living as a single person, do illustrate the neo-liberal ideological shift from bad mothers to bad choices (R. v Sim (1980); R. v Jantunen [1994]; R. v Slaght [1995]; R. v Plemel [1995]). But not every woman charged with welfare fraud is convicted, or if convicted, sent to jail. Some judges go to lengths to ensure this. Donna Bond received a conditional discharge, 50 hours of community service, and six months' probation.[15] In another Ontario case, Trainor J. refused to convict a battered woman for welfare fraud (R. v Lalonde (1995); see also Carruthers, 1995). Moreover, in Lalonde, the welfare authorities had acquiesced to the man's presence in the home and only charged her when the man "self-reported" his presence. Finally, following an inquest into the house-arrest death of Kimberly Rogers, a coroner's jury in Sudbury made a number of recommendations, including that the zero tolerance lifetime ineligibility be eliminated and that the provincial government should assess the adequacy of welfare rates.[16]

Accounts of "welfare mothers" also reveal diversity in practices among financial aid and frontline workers (Mortenson, 1999). Some workers are empathetic and supportive; others are punitive and controlling of their "clients." Likewise, the poor, including "welfare mothers," are far from constituting a homogeneous category (Gavigan, 1999: 213–18; Swift and Birmingham, 2000). While welfare recipients arguably have a common class position, the ways in which they acquire that class position are diverse and mediated by other social relations of gender, race, sexual orientation, and (dis)ability, that in turn, influence the ways and extent to which mothers on welfare, for instance, are active agents in shaping these relations. Many women live in constant fear of the scrutiny that may result in the loss of welfare assistance for not reporting income, having partners stay overnight, or being reported for child abuse and losing their children (Mortenson, 1999: 122–3; Falkiner v Ontario

(2002): 515, paras 103, 104). As a result, they engage in continual "self-censorship" of their activities (Little, 1998: 180). Others resist or challenge current welfare law and policy through the establishment and participation in informal support networks of "welfare moms" and/or anti-poverty agencies and organizations (Buchanan, 1995; Little, 1998; Mortenson, 1999).

Interview studies also reveal ideological contradictions among "welfare mothers." A few espouse the social Darwinism of neo-liberal law and policy. They see themselves as short-term, "deserving" welfare recipients who through workfare programmes and/ or their own hard work will become "contributing" members of society again (Mortenson, 1999). Some also feel resentful of and more "deserving" than other mothers on welfare whom they feel are "faring better in the distribution of scarce resources, including jobs" (Swift and Birmingham, 2000: 94–5). In contrast, others strongly reject the neo-liberal thrust of current welfare legislation and policy, equating workfare programmes and the rationales for them as government propaganda:

> I went to one of these ... workfare programs, and it was unbelievably stupid ... You have to be gung ho about making nothing and not getting any benefits or security, is basically what they're telling you in so many words. And then they're doing all these self-esteem boosting exercises with you, so that you're just *really* gung ho about fucking working for nothing. It's ridiculous ... The pay is $5 a day and you have to work 40 hours a week for $5 a day ... It's a cheap labour strategy .... (Mortenson, 1999: 66, emphasis in original)

Although the scope of this article precludes detailed discussion, we want to emphasize that the regulation/deregulation contradiction in the area of welfare legislation and policy reforms aimed at the poor also should be viewed in the context of government actions related to the welfare of the affluent and the regulation of capital. Increased criminalization and punishment of welfare fraud have occurred simultaneously with the deregulation and "disappearance of corporate crime" (Snider, 1999; see also Pearce and Tombs, 1998: 567–75; Glasbeek, 2002; Tombs, 2002). Massive welfare cuts targeting poor people are implemented at the same time as huge corporate tax cuts which, together with direct fiscal subsidies, arguably are forms of social welfare for the rich (Young, 2000; Abramovitz, 2001). The deregulation and de facto decriminalization of corporate wrongdoing benefit a minority of (primarily) affluent white men while the criminalization of poverty and the intensified prosecution of welfare fraud punish the poor disproportionately (see Beckett and Western, 2001).

And, although state law has never been used effectively against corporate crime, we agree with Snider (1999) that the disappearance of corporate crime matters:

> [A]bandoning state sanctions has far-reaching symbolic and practical con-
> sequences. State laws are public statements that convey important public
> messages about the obligations of the employer classes ... The situation is
> paradoxical indeed: while crimes of the powerful were never effectively
> sanctioned by state law, such laws are nonetheless essential to the operation of
> democratic societies. (p. 205)

The concomitant deregulation of corporate crime and increased punitiveness toward
welfare fraud (and "street crime" more generally) suggest that in an authoritarian form
of liberal democratic state, government interventionism is re-directed, not eliminated
(Hall, 1988; Denis, 1995: 368). State withdrawal from Keynesian social programmes
and the economy occurs in tandem with government activism around issues such as
capital punishment and youth crime (Denis, 1995: 369; Hermer and Mosher, 2002). In
our conclusion, we consider the implications of this shift in the focus of state interventionism for the regulation of mothers on welfare.

■ CONCLUSION

In our view, there are some clear historical continuities (as well as differences)
between social control and moral regulation as analytic constructs that warrant
further study. As we argued earlier, moral regulation became an influential concept
in non-Marxist analyses of power, regulation and control in the context of the neo-
liberal state of the late 20th century when the apparent triumph of privatization,
globalization, and unfettered (indeed unregulated) transnational capital seemed
to symbolize the decline of "the social" and the nation-state itself. The more recent
literature on moral regulation tends to focus primarily on "self-control" and "self-
formation" which are thereby divorced from "a contemplation of the state" (Cohen,
1985: 5) and from a consideration of the political and economic issues of redistribution
(Fraser, 1997; Segal, 1999). In some contemporary moral regulation scholarship, "poverty" is a discursive construct which displaces the class analysis that characterized the
Marxian-informed (historical), socio-legal literature from the 1970s and early 1980s
(Hay et al., 1975; Thompson, 1977; Hall et al., 1978; Fine et al., 1979; Corrigan and
Sayer, 1981; Fine, 1984).

In the contemporary context, much moral regulation literature has argued for
a position that "privileges" non-state sites; a position which is seen to offer an antidote to both "right-wing," neo-liberal theory and an "economistic," state-focussed
neo-Marxist perspective. Frequently, however, the latter is represented as a crude

version of instrumentalist neo-Marxism that arguably owes more to the "repressive" concept of social control than to Marx. As Garland (1997) puts it, "that brand of Marxist theory was always decidedly unsociological, and it can hardly be said to exhaust the analytical range of sociological work" (p. 205). Contemporary "post-Marxist" scholars have aimed to follow another analytical path. Their writings echo Foucault on the dispersed nature of power and the productive versus repressive aspects of control/regulation. Yet, like their social control predecessors, they often end up looking at controllers/regulators, frequently in "non-state" sites. On this point, we again find one of Garland's (1997) comments on the governmentality literature to be equally applicable to some of the writing on moral regulation:

> It is precisely because the authorities' analysis can be incorrect ... that one wants to generate alternative accounts. Moreover, these alternative analytical accounts are crucial if one wants to explain not just the nature of programmes but also the impact that they have in the fields that they govern. (p. 201)

Can a "materialist" concept of moral regulation have any utility for feminist theorizing? In our view, the concept has analytic utility as long as we continue to attend to the location of moral regulation in social policy and forms of law and state, and maintain an emphasis on the contradictions, social antagonisms, and class relations in a given social formation. The hard lives of poor women and their children impel us to resist any form of analysis that is also not attentive to the jagged edges of coercive laws that condemn them to the new ranks of the never deserving poor.

■ NOTES

We acknowledge with thanks our indebtedness to Marie Fox and the anonymous reviewers of our article for their incisive comments, suggestions, and encouragement. We also wish to thank the organizers (Lorna McLean, Tamara Myers, and Joan Sangster) and participants in the "Women and the Criminal Justice System Workshop" (Trent University, Peterborough, Ontario, Canada, May 1999), for their feedback on an earlier version of this article. Edward Yanoshita and Susan Graça provided valuable research and technical assistance respectively. Responsibility for the errors and weaknesses that remain rests with us.

1.   General Welfare Assistance Act, R. S. O. 1990, c. G.6, as rep. by Social Assistance Reform Act, 1997, S. O. 1997, c. 25 enacting Ontario Works Act, 1997, S. O. 1997, c. 25, s. 1 and Ontario Disability Support Program Act, 1997, S. O. c. 25, s. 2. The purpose of the

Ontario Works legislation is to establish a programme that, as expressed in s. 1:

(a) Recognizes individual responsibility and promotes self reliance through employment;

(b) Provides temporary financial assistance to those most in need while they satisfy obligations to become and stay employed;

(c) Effectively serves people needing assistance; and

(d) Is accountable to the taxpayers of Ontario.

2. Ontario Works Act, 1997, O. Reg. 134/98 (amended to O. Reg. 197/02), Reg. 29 (1.5) and (1.6).

3. Ontario Works Act, 1997, O. Reg. 134/98, Reg. 33.

4. See Hermer and Mosher (2002) for commentary on Ontario's Safe Streets Act, 1999, S. O. 1999, c. 8. This legislation (more aptly, the Mean Streets Act) renders illegal the street activity of "squeegee kids" and panhandlers.

5. Ontario Works Act, 1997, O. Reg. 134/98, Reg. 9 (a) and (b), provide that no single person who is in full-time attendance at a post-secondary educational institution is eligible for assistance if the person is in receipt of a student loan or is ineligible for a student loan because of parental income.

6. On 2 October 2003, the Ontario Tories were defeated by the Liberal Party in the provincial election. On 17 December 2003, the Hon. Sandra Pupatello, the new Minister of Community and Social Services, characterized the Tory government as having treated people on welfare as "a typical punching bag" and she expressed the new government's commitment to a "series of reforms," so that "the system actually works for people," including an increase in welfare rates The Minister also acknowledged the Government's obligation to respond to the recommendations of the Kimberly Rogers Inquest recommendations (Ontario, Legislative Assembly of Ontario, First Session, 38th Parliament, Official Debates (*Hansard*) No. 17A Wednesday 17 December 2003 at 868). On 9 January 2004, the Minister announced that the government would repeal the lifetime ban for those convicted of welfare fraud. However, the Minister also restated the Government's commitment to "no tolerance" for welfare fraud. The permanent ineligibility sections of the Regulations were repealed by O. Reg. 456/03 made under the Ontario Works Act 1997. See also, Galloway (2004: A9). In our view, as significant as the repeal of the lifetime ban is, it is equally important to note that Kimberly Rogers would still find herself liable to a conviction for welfare fraud, and if serving a sentence of house arrest, the amount of social assistance would still leave her only $18 a month to live on after her rent was paid. It needs to be recalled that when she died whilst serving her sentence of house arrest, Ms Rogers's welfare benefits had been reinstated by court order; it simply was not enough for her to live on, and the conditions of house arrest limited her access to other resources and sources of support.

7.   For a political economy approach to these issues, see Fudge and Cossman (2002).

8.   See, however, Glasbeek (1998; 2003), whose study of the Toronto Women's Court is attentive both to the question of moral regulation and to the role of and relationship between the state and social actors.

9.   Ontario Progressive Conservative government policy statement, 18 January 2000.

10. See *Masse v Ontario* [1996]; *Rogers v Sudbury* (2001); *Broomer v Ontario* [2002]. The more recent initiatives of the Campbell provincial government in British Columbia challenge and may surpass the dubious record of the Harris Tories; see "B.C. Throne Speech outlines massive change" (Matas, 2002: A 15).

11. For instance, the most recent figures available from the provincial Ministry of Community, Family and Children's Services, indicate that criminal convictions for welfare fraud have been in steady decline since 1997–8, falling to 393 convictions in 2001–2 (Ontario, 2003: t. 1).

     With respect to the zero tolerance lifetime ban introduced on 1 April 2000, The Income Security Advocacy Centre reported that a total of 106 individuals were permanently ineligible to receive financial assistance due to welfare fraud for offences committed between 1 April 2000 and 27 November 2002.

12. This is illustrated no less clearly than by the repeal of the General Welfare Act in Ontario, and the introduction in its place of Ontario Works legislation. General Welfare Assistance Act, R. S. O. 1990, c. G.6, as rep. by Social Assistance Reform Act, 1997, S. O. 1997, c. 25 enacting Ontario Works Act, 1997, S. O. 1997, c. 25, s. 1 [OWA] and Ontario Disability Support Program Act, 1997, S. O. c. 25, s. 2 [ODSPA].

13. The Ontario Court of Appeal struck down this expanded definition of spouse for "its differential treatment of sole support mothers on the combined grounds of sex, marital status and receipt of social assistance, which discriminates against them contrary to s. 15 of the Charter" (*Falkiner v Ontario* (2002): 515 para. 105). It is significant to note that one is deemed to be a spouse after three months' cohabitation; this is a much shorter time period of cohabitation (approximately 2 years and 9 months shorter) than is required under Ontario's provincial family law legislation before spousal support obligations and entitlements are triggered.

14. See Ontario Works Act, 1997, s. 1 (a), (b), (c) and (d).

15. Sentencing took place on 19 September 1994. *R. v Bond* [1994], certificate of conviction (on file with the authors).

16. Recommendations 1 and 4 of the "Verdict of Coroner's Jury into the Death of Kimberly Ann Rogers," released on 19 December 2002. The Coroner's Inquest, which lasted two months, involved eight parties with Standing, all represented by counsel. The Jury heard from 41 witnesses, and returned its Verdict and Recommendations on 19 December 2002. The Jury heard that of the 5000 or so welfare recipients in

Kimberly Rogers's home community of Sudbury, there were at most one or two convictions for welfare fraud annually. Evidence before the jury showed that "the Crown and the Courts were unaware that upon conviction the accused would be subject to a suspension of benefits." Recommendation 14 called for ongoing professional training of criminal justice personnel in this regard. The 14 recommendations form part of a letter dated 17 January 2003 sent by the presiding Coroner, Dr. David S. Eden to the Chief Coroner of Ontario (on file with the authors).

■ CASES CITED

Broomer v *Ontario* [2002] (Attorney General) O. J. No. 2196 (Ont. Sup. Ct. J.), online QL (OJ)

Falkiner v *Ontario* [2002] (Ministry of Community and Social Services, Income Maintenance Branch), 59 O. R. (3d) 481; O. J. No. 1771 (Ont. C. A.), online QL (OJ)

Masse v *Ontario* [1996] (Ministry of Community and Social Services, Income Maintenance Branch) O. J. No. 363 (Ont. Ct. J. – Div. Ct.), online QL (OJ), leave to appeal denied, O. J. No. 1526 (Ont. C. A.), online (QL (OJ)

R. v *Bond* [1994] O. J. No. 2185. (Ont. Ct. Gen. Div.), online QL (OJ)

R. v *Jantunen* [1994] O. J. No. 889 (Ont. Ct. Gen. Div.), online QL (OJ)

R. v *Lalonde* (1995) 22 O. R. (3d) 275; O. J. (Ont. Ct. Gen. Div.)

R. v *Plemel*, [1995] O. J. No. 4155 (Ont. Ct. Gen. Div.), online QL (OJ)

R. v *Sim* (1980) 63 C. C. C. (2d) 376 (Ont. Co. Ct. J. Cr. Ct.)

R. v *Slaght* [1995] O. J. No. 4192 (Ont. Ct. Gen. Div.), online QL (OJ)

R. v *Thurrott* (1971) 5 C. C. C. (2d) 129 (Ont. C. A.)

Rogers v *Sudbury* (2001) 57 O. R. (3d) 460 (Ont. Sup. Ct. J.)

■ REFERENCES

Abramovitz, Mimi. *Regulating the Lives of Women: Social Policy from Colonial Times to the Present.* Boston: South End Press, 1996.

Abramovitz, Mimi. "Everyone Is Still on Welfare: The Role of Distribution in Social Policy." *Social Work* 46(4) (2001): 297–308.

Bashevkin, Sylvia. *Welfare Hot Buttons: Women, Work and Social Policy Reform.* Toronto: University of Toronto Press, 2002.

Beckett, Katherine and Bruce Western. "Governing Social Marginality: Welfare, Incarceration, and the Transformation of State Policy." *Punishment and Society* 3(1) (2001): 43–59.

Boyd, Susan B. "Family, Law and Sexuality: Feminist Engagements." *Social & Legal Studies.* 8(3) (1999): 369–90.

Brenner, Johanna. *Women and the Politics of Class.* New York: Monthly Review Press, 2000.

Buchanan, Monica. "The Unworthy Poor: Experiences of Single Mothers on Welfare in Chilliwack." British Columbia, M.A. thesis. Burnaby, B. C.: Simon Fraser University, 1995.

Campbell, Robert. "Managing the Marginal: Regulating and Negotiating Decency in Vancouver's Beer Parlours, 1925–1954." *Labour/Le Travail* 44 (1999): 109–27.

Carruthers, E. "Prosecuting Women for Welfare Fraud in Ontario: Implications for Equality." *Journal of Law & Social Policy* 11 (1995): 241–62.

Chunn, Dorothy E. and Shelley A. M. Gavigan. "Social Control: Analytical Tool or Analytical Quagmire?" *Contemporary Crises* 12 (1988): 107–28.

Clarke, John. "Unfinished Business? Struggles over the Social in Social Welfare." In *Without Guarantees: In Honour of Stuart Hall,* edited by Paul Gilroy, Lawrence Grossberg, and Angela McRobbie, 84–93. London: Verso, 2000.

Cohen, Stanley. *Visions of Social Control: Crime, Punishment and Classification.* Cambridge: Polity Press, 1985.

Collins, Patricia H. *Black Feminist Thought.* New York: Routledge, 1991.

Corrigan, Philip and Derek Sayer. "How the Law Rules: Variations on Some Themes in Karl Marx." In *Law, State, and Society,* edited by Bob Fryer et al., 21–53. London: Croom Helm, 1981.

Corrigan, Philip and Derek Sayer. *The Great Arch: English State Formation as Cultural Revolution.* London: Basil Blackwell, 1985.

Cossman, Brenda. "Family Feuds: Neo-Liberal and Neo-Conservative Visions of the Re-privatization Project." In *Privatization, Law, and the Challenge to Feminism,* edited by Brenda Cossman and Judy Fudge, 169–217. Toronto: University of Toronto Press, 2002.

Dean, Mitchell. "'A Social Structure of Many Souls': Moral Regulation, Government and Self-Formation." *Canadian Journal of Sociology* 19(2) (1994): 145–68.

Dean, Mitchell. *Governmentality: Power and Rule in Modern Society.* London: Sage Publications, 1999.

Denis, Claude. "'Government Can Do Whatever It Wants': Moral Regulation in Ralph Klein's Alberta." *Canadian Review of Sociology and Anthropology* 32(3) (1995): 365–83.

Eden, David S. "Letter to Chief Coroner of Ontario re: Inquest into the Death of Kimberly Rogers" (on file with the authors), 2003.

Evans, Patricia M. and Karen J. Swift. "Single Mothers and the Press: Rising Tides, Moral Panic, and Restructuring Discourses." In *Restructuring Caring Labour,* edited by Sheila M. Neysmith, 73–92. Toronto: Oxford University Press, 2000.

Fine, Bob. *Democracy and the Rule of Law.* London: Pluto, 1984.

Fine, Bob et al., eds. *Capitalism and the Rule of Law.* London: Hutchinson, 1979.

Fraser, Nancy. *Justice Interruptus: Critical Reflections on the "Postsocialist" Condition.* New York: Routledge, 1997.

Fraser, Nancy and Linda Gordon. "A Genealogy of Dependency: Tracing a Keyword of the U.S. Welfare State." *Signs* 19(2) (1994): 309–26.

Fudge, Judy and Brenda Cossman. "Introduction: Privatization, Law and the Challenge to Feminism." In *Privatization, Law and the Challenge to Feminism,* edited by B. Cossman and J. Fudge, 3–37. Toronto: University of Toronto Press, 2002.

Galloway, G. "Liberals Scrap Lifetime Ban for Those Who Cheat Welfare System," *Globe and Mail,* 10 January, 2004.

Garland, David. "'Governmentality' and the Problem of Crime: Foucault, Criminology, Sociology." *Theoretical Criminology* 1(2) (1997): 173–214.

Gavigan, Shelley A. M. "On 'Bringing on the Menses': The Criminal Liability and the Therapeutic Exception in Ontario Abortion Law." *Canadian Journal of Women and Law* 1 (1986): 279–312.

Gavigan, Shelley A. M. "Poverty Law, Theory and Practice: The Place of Class and Gender in Access to Justice." In *Locating Law: Race/Class/Gender Connections,* edited by E. Comack, 213–18. Halifax, NS: Fernwood, 1999.

Glasbeek, Amanda. "Maternalism Meets the Criminal Law: The Case of the Toronto Women's Court." *Canadian Journal of Women and Law* 10 (1998): 480–502.

Glasbeek, Amanda. "A Justice of Their Own: The Toronto Women's Court, 1913–1934." Ph.D. dissertation. Toronto: York University, 2003.

Glasbeek, Harry. *Wealth by Stealth: Corporate Crime, Corporate Law, and the Perversion of Democracy.* Toronto: Between the Lines, 2002.

Golding, Peter and Sue Middleton. *Images of Welfare: Press and Public Attitudes to Poverty.* Oxford: Martin Robertson, 1982.

Gordon, Linda. *Pitied But Not Entitled: Single Mothers and the History of Welfare.* Cambridge, MA: Harvard University Press, 1994.

Hall, Stuart. "Reformism and the Legislation of Consent." *Permissiveness and Control: The Fate of the Sixties Legislation,* edited by National Deviancy Conference, 1–43. London: Macmillan, 1980.

Hall, Stuart. "The Toad in the Garden: Thatcherism among the Theorists." In *Marxism and the Interpretation of Culture,* edited by C. Nelson and L. Grossberg, 35–73. Champaign: University of Illinois Press, 1988.

Hall, Stuart et al. *Policing the Crisis: Mugging, the State, and Law and Order.* London: Macmillan, 1978.

Hay, Douglas, et al. *Albion's Fatal Tree.* London: Pantheon, 1975.

Hermer, Joe and Janet Mosher, eds. *Disorderly People*. Halifax, NS: Fernwood, 2002.

Hunt, Alan. *Explorations in Law and Society: Toward a Constitutive Theory of Law*. London: Routledge, 1993.

Hunt, Alan. "Moral Regulation and Making-up the New Person: Putting Gramsci to Work." *Theoretical Criminology* 1(3) (1997): 275–301.

Hunt, Alan. *Governing Morals: A Social History of Moral Regulation*. Cambridge: Cambridge University Press, 1999.

Keck, Jennifer. "Remembering Kimberly Rogers." *Perception* 25(3/4) (2002): 10–11. http://www.ccsd.ca/perception/2354/kimberly.html.

Kinsey, Richard. "Despotism and Legality." In *Capitalism and the Rule of Law*, edited by Bob Fine et al., pp. 46–64. London: Hutchinson, 1979.

Kline, Marlee. "Blue Meanies in Alberta: Tory Tactics and the Privatization of Child Welfare." In *Challenging the Public/Private Divide: Feminism, Law and Public Policy*, edited by S. B. Boyd, 330–59. Toronto: University of Toronto Press, 1997.

Lalonde, Linda. "Tory Welfare Policies: A View from the Inside." In *Open for Business, Closed for People: Mike Harris's Ontario*, edited by Diana Ralph et al., 92–102. Halifax, NS: Fernwood, 1997.

Little, Margaret Jane Hillyard. *No Car, No Radio, No Liquor Permit: The Moral Regulation of Single Mothers in Ontario, 1920–1997*. Toronto: Oxford University Press, 1998.

Loo, Tina. "Don Cramner's Potlatch: Law as Coercion, Symbol, and Rhetoric in British Columbia, 1884–1951." *Canadian Historical Review* 73(1992): 125–65.

MacKinnon, Mark and Keith Lacey. "Bleak House." *Globe and Mail*, 18 August, 2001.

Martin, Dianne. "Passing the Buck: Prosecution of Welfare Fraud; Preservation of Stereotypes." *Windsor Yearbook of Access to Justice* 12 (1992): 52–97.

Matas, Robert. "B. C. Throne Speech Outlines Massive Change." *Globe and Mail*, 13 February, 2002.

McKeever, Grainne. "Detecting, Prosecuting, and Punishing Benefit Fraud: The Social Security Administration (Fraud) Act 1997." *Modern Law Review* 62(2) (1999): 261–70.

McMullin, Julie, Lorraine Davies, and Gale Cassidy. "Welfare Reform in Ontario: Tough Times in Mothers' Lives." *Canadian Public Policy* 28(2) (2002): 297–314.

Morrison, Ian. "Facts About the Administration of Social Assistance/UI that Criminal Lawyers Need to Know." In *Charged with Fraud on Social Assistance: What Criminal Lawyers Need to Know*, A-12–A-14, Department of Continuing Legal Education, Law Society of Upper Canada, Toronto [unpublished], 1995.

Morrison, Ian. "Ontario Works: A Preliminary Assessment." *Journal of Law and Social Policy* 13 (1998): 1–32.

Morrison, Ian and Gwyneth Pearce. "Under the Axe: Social Assistance in Ontario in 1995." *Journal of Law and Social Policy* 11 (1995): 1–18.

Mortenson, Melanie. "B.C. Benefits Whom? Motherhood, Poverty, and Social Assistance Legislation in British Columbia." M.A. thesis. Burnaby, B. C.: Simon Fraser University, 1999.

Moscovitch, Allan. "Social Assistance in the New Ontario." In *Mike Harris's Ontario: Open for Business, Closed to People*, edited by Diana Ralph, André Régimbald, and Néréé St-Amand, 80–91. Halifax, NS: Fernwood Publishing, 1997.

Mosher, Janet E. "Managing the Disentitlement of Women: Glorified Markets, the Idealized Family, and the Undeserving Other." In *Restructuring Caring Labour*, edited by Sheila M. Neysmith, 30–51. Toronto: Oxford University Press, 2000.

Murray, Charles. *The Emerging Underclass.* London: Institute of Economic Affairs, 1990.

National Council of Welfare. *Poverty Profile 1998.* Ottawa: Minister of Public Works and Government Services Canada, 2000. http://www.gov.on.ca/css/page/brochure/fraud-nov98.html.

National Council of Welfare. *Poverty Profile 1999.* Ottawa: Minister of Public Works and Government Services Canada, 2002.

National Council of Welfare. *Welfare Incomes 2002.* Ottawa: Minister of Public Works and Government Services Canada, 2003.

Ontario. *Transitions: Report of the Social Assistance Review Committee (SARC Report).* Toronto: Queen's Printer, 1988.

Ontario. *Ministry of Community and Social Services: Welfare Fraud Control Report 1997–8.* Toronto: M.C.S.S., 1999.

http://www.gov.on.ca/css/page.brochure/fraudnov98.html.

Ontario. *Ministry of Community and Social Services: Welfare Fraud Control Report, 1998–9.* Toronto: M.C.S.S., 2000a.

http://www.gov.on.ca/css/page/brochure/fraudnov99.html.

Ontario. *Ministry of Community and Social Services: Making Welfare Work: Report to Taxpayers on Welfare Reform.* Toronto: M.C.S.S., 2000b. http://www.gov.on.ca/css/page/brochure/makingwelfarework.html.

Ontario. *Office of the Chief Coroner: Verdict of the Coroner's Jury into the Death of Kimberly Ann Rogers, Held at Sudbury, Ontario* (on file with the authors), 2002.

Ontario. *Ministry of Community, Family and Children's Services: Welfare Fraud Control Report 2001–2.* Toronto: M.F.C.S., 2003.

http://www.gov.on.ca/CFCS/en/programs/IES/OntarioWorks/Publications/FraudReport.

Pearce, Frank, and Steve Tombs. *Toxic Capitalism: Corporate Crime and the Chemical Industry.* Aldershot: Ashgate Dartmouth, 1998.

Piven, Frances Fox and Richard A. Cloward. *Regulating the Poor: The Functions of Public Welfare.* New York: Pantheon Books, 1971.

Rachert, John A. "Welfare Fraud and the State: British Columbia 1970–7." M.A. thesis. Burnaby, B.C.: Simon Fraser University, 1990.

Razack, Sherene, ed. *Race, Space and the Law: The Making of Canada as a White Settler Society.* Toronto: Between the Lines, 2002.

Roberts, Dorothy. *Killing the Black Body: Race, Reproduction, and the Meaning of Liberty.* New York: Pantheon, 1997.

Segal, Lynne. *Why Feminism? Gender, Psychology, Politics.* New York: Columbia University Press, 1999.

Snider, Laureen. "Relocating Law: Making Corporate Crime Disappear." In *Locating Law: Race/Class/Gender Connections,* edited by E. Comack, pp. 183–206. Halifax, NS: Fernwood, 1999.

Stenson, Kevin. "Crime Control, Governmentality and Sovereignty." In *Governable Places: Readings on Governmentality and Crime Control,* edited by R. Smandych, 45–73. Aldershot: Ashgate Dartmouth, 1999.

Stenson, Kevin and Paul Watt. "Governmentality and 'the Death of the Social'?: A Discourse Analysis of Local Government Texts in South-East England." *Urban Studies* 36(l) (1999): 189–201.

Strange, Carolyn and Tina Loo. *Making Good: Law and Moral Regulation in Canada.* Toronto: University of Toronto Press, 1997.

Swift, Karen J. and Michael Birmingham. "Location, Location, Location: Restructing and the Everyday Lives of 'Welfare Moms.'" In *Restructuring Caring Labour,* edited by Sheila M. Neysmith, 93–115. Toronto: Oxford University Press, 2000.

Thompson, E. P. *Whigs and Hunters.* London: Penguin, 1977.

Tombs, Steve. "Understanding Regulation?" *Social & Legal Studies* 11 (2002): 113–31.

Valverde, Mariana. *The Age of Soap, Light, and Water: Moral Reform in English Canada, 1885–1925.* Toronto: McClelland & Stewart, 1991.

Valverde, Mariana. "Moral Capital." *Canadian Journal of Law and Society* 9 (1994): 212–32.

Valverde, Mariana. "The Mixed Social Economy as a Canadian Tradition." *Studies in Political Economy* 47 (1995): 33–60.

Valverde, Mariana. *Diseases of the Will: Alcohol and the Dilemmas of Freedom.* Cambridge: Cambridge University Press, 1998.

Valverde, Mariana and Lorna Weir. "The Struggles of the Immoral: Preliminary Remarks on Moral Regulation." *Resources for Feminist Research* 17 (1988): 31–4.

Weir, Lorna. "Studies in the Medicalization of Sexual Danger: Sexual Rule, Sexual Politics, 1830–1930." Ph.D. dissertation. Toronto: York University, 1986.

Wilkie, Meredith. *Women Social Security Offenders: Experiences of the Criminal Justice System in Western Australia.* Perth, WA: University of Western Australia, Crime Research Centre, 1993.

Young, Claire. *Women, Tax and the Gendered Impact of Funding Social Programs through the Tax System.* Ottawa: Status of Women Canada, 2000.

CHAPTER 16

"GOVERNMENTALITY" AND THE PROBLEM OF CRIME:

FOUCAULT, CRIMINOLOGY, SOCIOLOGY

David Garland

Michel Foucault's *Discipline and Punish* (1977) made a huge impression on criminology, providing it with a theoretical language with which to analyze the practices of punishment, and with a heightened sense of criminology's own status as a power/knowledge apparatus, linked into these very practices.

Now, a dozen years after his death, Foucault has begun to exert a theoretical influence of a quite different kind. From 1978 until his death in 1984, Foucault's work developed around a new theme: "the government of others and the government of one's self." It focused particularly upon the relations between two poles of governance: the forms of rule by which various authorities govern populations, and the technologies of the self through which individuals work on themselves to shape their own subjectivity. These analyses of Foucault—broadly described as studies of "governmentality"—have inaugurated a vigorous research programme and an impressive scholarly literature, anatomizing practices of government across a range of social and economic fields (see Burchell et al., 1991; Rose and Miller, 1992; Barry et al., 1993, 1996; Dean, 1994; Hunt and Wickham, 1994). Analyses of this kind have recently begun to consider the field of crime control and criminal justice (Stenson, 1993: O'Malley, 1996), suggesting that a second and rather different "Foucault effect" might be about to be felt within theoretical criminology.

At a time when criminologists are trying to come to terms with a reconfigured criminological field (see Feeley and Simon, 1992; Garland, 1996), the governmentality literature offers a powerful framework for analyzing how crime is problematized and controlled. It is focused upon the present, and particularly upon the shift from "welfarist" to "neo-liberal" politics. It avoids reductionist or totalizing analyses, encouraging instead an open-ended, positive account of practices of governance in specific fields. It aims to anatomize contemporary practices, revealing the ways in which their modes of exercising power depend upon specific ways of thinking (rationalities) and specific ways of acting (technologies), as well as upon specific ways of "subjectifying" individuals and governing populations. It also problematizes these practices by subjecting them to a "genealogical" analysis—a tracing of their historical lineages that aims to undermine their "naturalness" and open up a space for alternative possibilities.

Part One of this article will summarize the key themes of this "governmentality" literature, dealing first with Foucault's own analyses and then with the work of others who have developed and applied his ideas. In Part Two, I illustrate the productivity of this governmentality approach in opening up new ways of understanding the discourses, problems and practices of contemporary crime control. Finally, in Part Three, I consider some of the limitations and problems of this framework, and argue, against some of its proponents, that an engagement with (certain forms of) sociological analysis would allow governmentality studies to overcome some of these limitations.[1]

■ PART ONE: "GOVERNMENTALITY"

Foucault on "the Free Subject" and "the State"

Foucault's analyses of discipline (Foucault, 1977, 1980) tended to attract criticism for their "neglect" of the state, and for their supposed tendency to characterize human individuals as "docile bodies" rather than active subjects. Whether as a response to these criticisms, or else as the fulfilment of a research agenda that, in the mid-1970s, had been only partially developed, Foucault's later work on governmentality addressed both of these problems.

The 1982 essay "The Subject and Power" presented a revised[2] concept of power that stressed the importance of *the active subject* as the entity through which, and by means of which, power is exercised. In this conception, governmental power is not "objectifying" but "subjectifying." It constructs individuals who are capable of choice and action, shapes them as active subjects, and seeks to align their choices with the objectives of governing authorities. This kind of power does not seize hold of the individual's body in a disciplinary grip or regiment individuals into conformity. Instead, it holds out technologies of the self, to be adopted by willing individuals who take an active part in their own "subjectification." Far from abolishing the individual's capacity for choice and action, this kind of power presupposes it.

Government is not, then, the suppression of individual subjectivity, but rather the cultivation of that subjectivity in specific forms, aligned to specific governmental aims. From the sinning, confessing subject of the Christian faith, to the self-interested, enterprising subject of liberalism, the subjects of government are to be conceived of as active in the process of their own government, rather than the passive effects of powers over which they exert no control. "Power is exercised only over free subjects, and only insofar as they are free" (Foucault, 1982: 221).

Foucault's analyses of government steer clear of any institutional or substantive account of "the state" and instead focus upon particular practices of governing, located in a variety of different sites. This foregrounding of *practices*, together with an extended conception of "governmental authorities"—embracing families, churches, experts, professions, and all the various powers that engage in "the conduct of conduct"—dissolves any rigid line of demarcation between the "public" and the "private" or between "state" and "civil society." So while the state is undoubtedly a nodal point from which emerge all sorts of projects of government, and a locale from which many "private" powers derive support for their authority, it is by no means the *fons et origo* of all governmental activity.

In considering the practices of government adopted by state and other agencies, Foucault asks a series of questions: How do practices of governing others link up with the practices by which individuals govern themselves? How have governing authorities understood their powers and the problems they address? What rationalities of governing are implicit in their practices? How did they come to produce a knowledge of the fields which they sought to programme? Through what technologies and *dispositifs* (specific assemblages of actors, knowledges, practices and techniques) are programmes and rationalities translated into realized effects?

The first of these questions is taken up in Foucault (1979), where he discusses how, from the 18th century onwards, factors relating to the life of the human species—such as birth rates, longevity, demography, public health and migration—came to be subjects of governmental knowledge and control. Later, as his investigations shifted to a more ethical register, and to "the technologies of the self," Foucault continued to stress the link between the various ways of freely becoming one's self, and the governing practices of authorities who promote these forms of selfhood as means to political ends.

[...]

Governmentality after Foucault

Foucault's analyses form the starting point for a whole new research literature dealing with a range of substantive topics (see Barry et al., 1993, 1996; Burchell et al., 1991). My aim in this section is not to summarize this work, but merely to highlight the themes that are of most relevance to scholars working in the field of crime control and criminal justice policy.

(i) "The Social" as a Realm of Government

Jacques Donzelot's history of "the policing of families" (1979) and his account of the modern welfare state (1991a, 1991b) have shown in detail how different forms of expert authority come to operate in the space between the state and the individual. *The Policing of Families* shows how philanthropists, doctors, social workers, psychiatrists, feminists and birth control campaigners each developed schemes for transforming the family. The success of these programmes depended upon the extent to which they could be aligned with the objectives of state authorities (national efficiency, the health of the population, control of the birth rate, control of crime) *and* with the desires and aspirations of individual family members (the wish to achieve social promotion and respectability, to be a good mother, to educate one's children, to manage the household budget, etc.).

Donzelot's account[3] demonstrates that governmental power is not concentrated exclusively in the state, but is instead dispersed throughout the social field in hospitals, schools, social work offices, juvenile courts and clinics, each of which concentrates professional powers and acts as a centre of governance. Governmental power flows through—and acquires its effectiveness from—this network of professional enclosures and agencies. Fanning out from these settings it cultivates alliances between the doctor and the mother, the teacher and the schoolchild, the social worker and the neighbour, etc., and seeks to adjust the behaviours and self-image of individuals, bringing them into line with socially approved aspirations and identities.

Donzelot's claim is that there has been a proliferation of such governmental authorities seeking to normalize the family and to improve its functioning. The result has been the emergence of a complex skein of governmental practices that operate in the space between the state and the family. These governmental practices draw upon a variety of new knowledges of the individual and of the population. They set and respond to new notions of what the individual can aspire to be. They exercise a light and unobtrusive form of monitoring and exhortation that shifts to compulsion only where individuals make claims upon the state or else exhibit conduct that has been legally proscribed.

This dense, interlocking network of governance, which Donzelot calls "the social," is instantly recognizable as a feature of contemporary welfare states. This style of social regulation promotes the ends of good government not by means of a coercive totalitarian state, but instead by relying upon a series of "private" powers and "voluntary" alliances. It thus preserves the liberal values of freedom and autonomy—at least for those who comply with the prevailing norms and function in ways that are deemed by experts to be adequate (see Hirst, 1980)—while simultaneously "governing" how these freedoms are typically exercised.

This method of governing does not rely upon sovereign force, nor even upon discipline. Instead it rests upon a multiplicity of expert authorities and upon the willingness of individuals—whether as family members, or workers, or citizens—to exercise a "responsibilized" autonomy, and to pursue their interests and desires in ways which are socially approved and legally sanctioned.

(ii) Statistics and Bio-power

Ian Hacking's histories of statistics (1990, 1991) have shown how censuses and statistical enumerations helped create a conception of the population as an entity with its own regularities, and how ideas such as probability, the law of large numbers, normal distributions, and deviation from the mean developed as ways of understanding the social dynamics and aggregate patterns that characterized this new entity.

Statistical knowledge fuels bio-political technologies—and is produced by them—in the same way that a knowledge of individuals spirals in and out of disciplinary practices. Budgetary calculations, economic forecasts, demographic projections, actuarial tables, scientific surveys, market research and epidemiological studies all function as technologies of government in the modern state. Statistical information forms the basis for political problematizations, such as the 19th-century worries about "national decline," "racial degeneracy" and "national efficiency" (to which eugenics and social security were opposed, but equally "statistical," responses) or the contemporary concerns about our "ageing population" and its fiscal and social consequences.

[...]

Statistical processes classify and regroup the population, moving people into categories that had no significance prior to the act of counting and sorting. (High-rate offenders, career criminals, or repeat victims are criminological examples of this kind of process.) In doing so, they link individual self-governance to large-scale processes of rule.

(iii) Technologies of insurance and risk-based reasoning

[...]

Insurance arrangements illustrate very clearly what Foucault means when he talks about "an apparatus of security." Insurance underpins the free play of autonomous and self-directed transactions within the economic and social spheres by constructing a safety net beneath them. Risk-taking, including individual decisions about work, marriage, child-bearing, investment, etc., is thus facilitated by its existence. The security offered by insurance thus enhances freedom and choice by removing some of the anxiety associated with the normal events of the life course and this, in turn, tends to enhance the economic performance of the nation.

[...]

Insurance also generates a new form of knowledge. Actuarial decisions (such as assessing risk, setting a price on premiums, or fixing the limits of compensation) depend upon detailed statistical enumerations and calculations of the rates at which events happen—storms at sea, accidents in the workplace, unemployment, ill-health, death. Over time, the accumulation of large databases, and a predictive knowledge of risk probabilities, has produced a new way of reasoning that has significant social implications and possibilities.[4]

Conventional moral and judicial reasoning is individualistic and backward-looking. It assumes that harms and accidents occur in an otherwise orderly world because some individual has acted in a negligent or wrongful way, and it proceeds to make post hoc decisions about who is to blame and who should bear the costs. In contrast, actuarial reasoning focuses its attention upon the population, and assumes that accidents are regular and predictable, not at the level of the individual, but at the level of the population.[5] [...]

Actuarial reasoning about risk gives rise to distinctive techniques for managing risk. Risk-management is forward-looking, predictive, oriented to aggregate entities and concerned with the minimization of harms and costs, rather than with the attribution of blame or the dispensation of individual justice. [...]

(iv) Rose and Miller and the Analysis of Neo-liberalism

In a series of influential essays, Nikolas Rose and Peter Miller (Miller and Rose, 1990; Rose, 1996; Rose and Miller 1992) have restated and developed some of Foucault's ideas and set out a new problematic for the analysis of "power beyond the state." This framework argues that power should be viewed as a matter of networks and alliances through which "centres of calculation" exercise "government-at-a-distance." Power is not a matter of imposing a sovereign will, but instead a process of enlisting the cooperation of chains of actors who "translate" power from one locale to another. This process always entails activity on the part of the "subjects of power" and it therefore has built into it the probability that outcomes will be shaped by the resistance or private objectives of those acting "down the line."

[...]

Like Donzelot, Rose and Miller describe how professional groups and reform campaigns problematize aspects of economic or social life, then seek to align their specific aims with the political objectives of the state and the subjective choices of individuals. They argue that governmental practices of this kind confound the logic of sociological concepts which oppose state to civil society, the public to the private, the coercive to the consensual and so on. Similarly, they suggest that standard sociological accounts which talk of "the expanding net of social control," the increasing powers of the state or the "social grounding" of political power, fail to catch the point about modern forms of power. Against what they see as sociology's inherent reductionism and essentialism, they insist that the objectives of governmental power are various, its techniques multiple and differentiated, and its locale(s) dispersed and largely beyond the state. Moreover, individuals relate to it not as coerced objects or as ideological dupes but as autonomous subjects whose subjectivity is shaped by their active engagement with the powers that govern them and by which they govern themselves.

[...]

Rose and Miller's research, and that of many of the "history of the present" researchers, takes as its major topic the contemporary phenomenon of neo-liberalism. The shift away from "welfarism" with its state-based forms of social provision to the more marketized, entrepreneurial, consumerist forms of social organization is a major fact of our time, and the point of Foucault's genealogical approach was to make it possible to view such facts in a critical, historical perspective. It also so happens that concepts such as "action-at-a-distance," "governing through freedom" and "the active subject of power" are particularly apposite for the analysis of neo-liberal policies which are explicitly designed to maximize entrepreneurial activity, to empower the consumer and to replace state or professional governance with market mechanisms.

■ PART TWO: GOVERNMENTALITY AND THE PROBLEM OF CRIME

The governmentality literature does not offer a general thesis that can be "applied" to the field of crime control. Nor does it provide a unified account of the present—such as "postmodernity" or "risk society"—under which can be subsumed the facts of criminal policy or the developmental tendencies of the criminal justice system. It does, however, isolate a series of objects of analysis, and suggest certain lines of enquiry that strike me as having great potential for researching and interpreting current developments in this field.

[...]

Rationalities of Crime Control

[...]

It seems plausible to suggest that in recent decades the governance of crime has come to be problematized in new ways, partly in reaction to chronically high crime rates and the failure of criminal justice controls (Garland, 1996), and partly under the influence of broader shifts away from welfarist styles of government towards neo-liberal ones.

It also seems plausible to argue that, in response to this emergent field of problems and political forces, a new rationality for the governance of crime is coming into existence, together with a new rationality for the governance of criminal justice. Described in very broad terms, this is a governmental style that is organized around *economic* forms of reasoning, in contrast to the social and legal forms that have predominated for most of the 20th century.

By an "economic" rationality, I don't mean simply that value-for-money considerations and fiscal restraint have nowadays become prominent and explicit aspects of crime control discourse and practice—though this is certainly a feature of the contemporary scene. I mean to point to (i) the increasing reliance upon an *analytical language* of risks and rewards, rationality, choice, probability, targeting and the demand and supply of opportunities—a language that translates "economic" forms of reasoning and calculation into the criminological field; (ii) the increasing importance of *objectives* such as compensation, cost-control, harm-reduction, economy, efficiency and effectiveness; and (iii) the increasing resort to *technologies* such as audit, fiscal control, market competition and devolved management to control penal decision-making.

[...]

This kind of thinking developed first in the private sector—in the practices of insurance companies, private security firms and commercial enterprises, concerned to reduce those costs of crime that fall on them. Commercial and insurance-based thinking about crime control focuses upon reducing or displacing the costs of crime, upon prevention rather than punishment and upon minimizing risk rather than ensuring justice. [...]

This way of thinking also draws upon other sources. One such source is the work of Gary Becker (1968) and other economic analysts of crime, whose ideas have recently been imported into the language of criminal policy (Cook, 1986; van Dijk, 1994). Another is the cluster of criminological theories—rational choice theory, routine activity theory, and the various approaches that view crime as a matter of opportunity—which I have described elsewhere as "the new criminologies of everyday life" (Garland, 1996). In contrast to older criminologies, which assumed that the individual offender could be differentiated and corrected, these theoretical frameworks view crime as a normal, mundane event, requiring no special disposition or abnormality on the part of the offender. [...]

Since their emergence, these theories have received considerable critical scrutiny, usually from the point of view of rival criminological traditions whose proponents complain that the new theories fail to get to the root causes of crime, or else that they take too superficial a view of human nature and of criminal conduct. In contrast to that kind of critique, the aim of the Foucauldian approach is to address the substance of these discourses and the practical programmes that they support. It aims to pay careful attention to what they say, how they say it, and to the complex of preconditions that make these statements sayable, and which govern their emergence, functioning and transformation. It aims to describe how agents, knowledges, powers and techniques are assembled into specific apparatuses for the exercise of these new ways of governing crime, thus making these ways of thinking into practical ways of acting. And though this approach will tend to imply a critical stance—insofar as it is describing modes of exercising power and of projecting forms of subjectivity that are otherwise hidden—it seeks to maintain the neutral gaze of an analyst rather than the hostile glare of a rival with competing claims to truth. This strikes me as a valuable way of coming to terms with the new configuration of crime control that is currently emerging, the very newness of which tends to undercut our conventional stock of "critical" and "progressive" positions, most of which derive from an earlier period of the history of the field.

The Criminogenic Situation

[...]

Criminogenic situations are commonplace in modern society. They take a variety of forms and come in all shapes and sizes: unsupervised car-parks, town squares late at night, deserted neighbourhoods, poorly lit streets, shopping malls, football games, bus stops, subway stations, etc. Their status as more or less "criminogenic"—as hot spots of crime or low-rate, secure areas—are established by reference to local police statistics, victim surveys and crime pattern analysis. [..]

"The criminogenic situation" poses difficulties for government because it generally has a commercial or social value of its own which sets limits upon crime control. Precisely because crime occurs in the course of routine social and economic transactions, any crime-reducing intervention must seek to preserve "normal life" and "business as usual." The characteristic modes of intervening involve the implantation of non-intrusive controls in the situation itself, or else attempts to modify the interests and the incentives of the actors involved (see Shearing and Stenning, 1985). The situation can be "governed," but it cannot be completely or coercively controlled. Practices of situational governance must operate lightly and unobtrusively, working with and through the actors involved. The aim is to align the actors' objectives with those of the authorities, to make them active partners in the business of security and crime control. In this way the situation is allowed to retain its "natural" character, but is made more secure against the occurrence of criminal events. The parallels with the problems of "securing" economic processes through "liberal" government suggest themselves forcefully.

This analysis also calls to mind Foucault's suggestion that the forms of modern power might be viewed as a "triangle of sovereignty-discipline-government." Thus we find, coexisting on the terrain of crime control, three practicable objects and three forms of exercising power in respect of them: (i) the *legal subject*, governed by sovereign command and obliged to obey or be punished; (ii) the *criminal delinquent*, governed by discipline and required to conform or be corrected; and now (iii) the *criminogenic situation*, governed by the manipulation of interests and the promotion of mechanisms of self-regulation. Each of these stands for a particular way of acting upon the problem of crime, supported by a complex of laws, institutional practices and forms of expertise, and each way of acting commands the support of particular groups (the judiciary, the social work establishment, the new crime prevention agencies, etc.). The interweaving of these different modes of "governing crime" produces an intricate web of policies and practices that cannot be reduced to a single formula. There is no phased historical progression from "sovereign punishment" to "discipline" to "government at a distance," nor is there an easy or coherent relationship between these different conceptions and practices of crime control. In any concrete conjuncture the field of crime control will manifest an uneven (and often incoherent) combination of these modes of action, the specific "mix" depending upon the balance of power between the different groups involved, as well as the residues of past practices and institutional arrangements. The value of Foucault's analysis (which is both genealogical and typological) is that it allows us to analyze the crime control field as a *field of power relations and subjectifications* and draws attention to the impact of new knowledges and technologies upon the power relations between governmental actors as well as between the rulers and the ruled.

The attempt to govern criminogenic situations has led to a set of new objectives—the reduction of crime and the fear of crime, the promotion of a culture of security consciousness, the enhancement of public safety, etc.—which are seen to be best achieved by acting through (rather than acting upon) the actors involved. This gives rise to a "responsibilization strategy" whereby state authorities (typically the police or the Home Office) seek to enlist other agencies and individuals to form a chain of coordinated action that reaches into criminogenic situations, prompting crime-control conduct on the part of "responsibilized" actors (see Garland, 1996). Central to this strategy is the attempt to ensure that all the agencies and individuals who are in a position to contribute to these crime-reducing ends come to see it as being in their interests to do so. "Government" is thus extended and enhanced by the creation of "governors" and "guardians" in the space between the state and the offender.

[...]

The Criminal Justice System as an Entity to Be Governed

A striking feature of the present period is the degree to which official attention has become focused not just upon the government of crime, but also upon the problem of governing criminal justice. Rises in the flow of cases through the criminal justice system, resulting in crowded court calendars and overcrowded prisons, prompted government concern about new problems such as costs, efficiency and coordination in criminal justice. This, in turn, led to the development of techniques for representing and controlling these problems. Over time, there was a transformation in the way that "criminal justice" was understood. What was previously viewed as a loosely coupled series of independent agencies—police, prosecution, courts, prison, probation, each with its own objectives and working ideologies, each with its own sphere of autonomous action—came to be seen instead as a "system." This "system" is an entity which can be known and governed. It has become a practicable object of government. [...]

Active Subjects

Crime control practices embody a conception of the subjects they seek to govern. For most of the 20th century, the subjects of crime control have been the "individual delinquent" and the "legal subject." The new economic rationality attempts to make up new kinds of individuals, or rather, to create and impart new forms of subjectivity, which individuals and organizations will adopt for themselves.

One new form of "subjectification" is the responsibilized, security-conscious, crime-preventing subject—*homo prudens*—analyzed by O'Malley (1992) and Adams (1995). A related, though opposed, figure is what has been called "situational man" (see Clarke and Cornish, 1986). Situational man is criminology's version of the economic subject of interest. He (or less often, she) is a moderately rational, self-interested individual, unfettered by any moral compass or superego controls; a consumer who is alert to criminal opportunities and responsive to situational inducements.

[...]

In assuming the reality of situational man, the authorities begin to give substance to it, projecting it on to live men and women, and "making people up" in this form. Thus research is conducted into the reasoning processes of burglars or robbers, offenders are officially identified as career criminals, sentencers shape their sentences on the basis of these perceptions, and convicted offenders are treated as entrepreneurial actors rather than as subjects of need or candidates for rehabilitative treatment.

Penal Technologies of the Self

In contemporary prison and probation regimes one sees a similar characterization of the criminal subject, and a determined effort to assimilate individual offenders to its terms by means of new "technologies of the self." Techniques of correction stress the offender's responsibility for his or her criminal actions and insist that he or she must "address" and "take responsibility" for them. This is not merely a reversion to an older punitive mode which assumes that the offender has the attributes of a free-willed legal subject. On the contrary. Instead of assuming that all adult individuals are "naturally" capable of responsible, self-directed action and moral agency, contemporary penal regimes treat this as a problem to be remedied by procedures that actively seek to "subjectify" and to "responsibilize" individuals.[6]

[...]

The new stress upon the offender's "autonomy" and "responsibility" can also be seen in recent policy on community penalties and the idea of "punishment in the community." Part of the appeal of probation and community service and monetary penalties is that they avoid the "objectifying" tendencies of imprisonment and organize a form of penal control in which the offender is enlisted in the process of his or her own control. Instead of removing the individual into the near-total control of a custodial enclosure, these community measures seek to insert regulatory devices into the offender's natural habitat and daily routines, producing a light framework of supervision but leaving plenty of opportunity for the offender to practise self-control. Techniques such as intermittent supervision and reporting, electronic monitoring, tracking, drug-testing and attendance for work are used, as are alliances with other sources of social control (such as the family, landladies, employers, bail hostel workers, etc.), to try to build an environment conducive to self-control and the practice of a responsibilized freedom.[7]

No doubt there are other lines of research which a governmentality analytic would help to open up for criminologists. [...] But I hope I have said enough to suggest that the field of crime control is certainly one in which "governmental" analyses can be effectively and productively employed.

The present article is written in the hope of encouraging such work, and suggesting lines of enquiry. However, and in anticipation of such work being done, it might be useful to point to some of the limitations of this analytical scheme, and some of the problems that inhere in the governmentality literature. Analytical frameworks are most effectively deployed with a degree of self-consciousness about their boundaries and blind-spots. The governmentality approach has been developed to address particular kinds of questions in a particular kind of way. Some of its objects of analysis—such as the rationalities of rule, and the self-problematizing activities of rulers—were simply not visible prior to the development of Foucault's approach. Other theoretical objects, as I will argue, are rather less distinctive, and may be compatible with other, more developed, traditions of research. Some of its methodological protocols—such as the requirement to study programmes in their own terms—strike me as well founded. Others—such as its apparent hostility to causal analysis and explanation—seem to me much less convincing. Some of its key concepts—such as the idea of "governing through freedom"—are illuminating when properly deployed, but are easily misused and misunderstood. Finally, the idea of a "history of the present" is attractive but also ambiguous. My own preferred usage would be to think of this as an approach concerned to produce a critical, historical and sociological account of contemporary practices but it can also be regarded as a rather more philosophical (or "archaeological") enterprise concerned less with contemporary practices, than with the "absent conditions" or "historical *a prioris*" that make these practices possible. This suggests something of a tension between the reconstruction of governmental rationalities and the construction of a history of the present. Writers in the governmentality literature usually claim to be doing both, but the latter task requires a broader, more sociological agenda than the former. To understand the present, one must establish not just the rationalities that structure practices of government, but also the ways in which these practices sometimes diverge from the pattern implicit in these rationalities.

■ PART THREE: THE LIMITS OF "GOVERNMENTALITY" ANALYSIS

If the governmentality literature is to become a resource for thinking about contemporary patterns of crime control, it will be necessary to elaborate and more precisely define some of its key concepts, and to build upon the genealogical analyses that Foucault developed.

Some of the governmentality concepts are neologisms ("bio-power," "pastoral power," "governmentality"); others are historical terms ("police," "raison d'etat") and others are conventional terms of analysis to which Foucault imparts a slightly unconventional meaning (e.g., his use of the terms "liberalism" and "security"). This can lead to some confusion. It is not clear, for example, how "pastoral power," "bio-power" and "security" relate to one another; are they distinct kinds of practices, or different names for the same kind of thing? Nor is it clear how these relate to the notion of "governmentality." Is bio-power an earlier term for the "governmental" form of power, or merely a specific instance of it? Is the contrast between the "anatomo-political" and the "bio-political" (Foucault, 1979) the same as the contrast between "discipline" and "government" (Foucault, 1991)?

[...]

The idea of a "governmentalized state" is also somewhat problematic. Which state is not "governmentalized" to some degree? [...] Alternatively, if the defining feature of "governmentality" is the adoption of a specific set of objectives towards which the "conduct" of the population is to be "conducted" (such as health, welfare, prosperity and so on) or of specific techniques and methods of so doing (e.g., the "liberal" style of rule-at-a-distance), then it would seem more appropriate to use terms that evoke these definitive features.

Another potential source of confusion is the use of the term "governmental" to describe the conduct (and sometimes the status) of a range of authorities who are not part of what conventional political discourse would term the "state" or "the government."

The purpose of this Foucauldian usage is clear enough—it serves to emphasize the idea that power is exercised, and conduct shaped, by agencies which are often thought of as "private" or "non-political." [...] Nevertheless, the conventional political discourse of the modern period has come to reflect the fact of a "governmentalized state"—and the concentration of governmental powers and resources that this represents—by using the term "the government" to refer to the legally constituted rulers of the nation-state. To generalize the idea of "governmental" to refer to all sources and locales that exercise social power inevitably invites confusion.

Governmentality writers have, for similar reasons, rejected what they see as the confounding distinction between state and civil society, arguing that modern forms of government "combine action by political and non-political authorities" (Barry et al., 1993: 2) or link together "public and private security" (Rose, 1996: 37). But against this one might observe that the conventional distinction between state and civil society, or between "public" and "private" is not intended to mean that any particular practice or policy will operate exclusively in one or other of these realms. Most sociological analyses stress the interaction and mutual dependency of state and non-state practices, just as most policy analysis depicts the relays that must run between public and private action if government policy is to be effective in bringing about its intended effects.

Nor is the distinction between "state" and "non-state" merely an analytical one that can be jettisoned at will. To be demarcated in public law as a state agency is to be afforded special access to legal, economic and military resources, as well as to a special form of authority and a network of supporting organizations. In a stable, constitutional democracy, where the rule of law operates, such resources make a large difference to the capacity of an agency to exercise power and to govern effectively. [...]

An Incomplete Genealogy

Foucault's genealogies of the mentalities of government that arose in the 17th or 18th centuries were not attempts to establish their historical meaning or to understand how they functioned in the early modern period. His concern was to identify rationalities and technologies that were instrumental in forming our present, either because they still function in the contemporary period, or else because they gave rise to problems and solutions which do. But unlike his work on the prison, the asylum, or on sexuality, Foucault never completed his genealogical account of governmental reason, nor published a major book on the topic. His analyses are suggestive rather than substantive. The genealogical threads trail off before they reach the present. There is no detailed account of how particular ways of governing today are dependent upon these lines of descent and structured by them. So whereas his genealogical studies of the prison or of sexuality were quite specific in their focus, and undeniably relevant to our understanding of present practices, the studies of governmentality do not grasp hold of present-day practices with the same precision or revelatory clarity.

[...]

Governing through Freedom

One of the recurring motifs of the governmentality literature is the idea that we are "governed" through and by means of our "freedom." This is a typically Foucauldian paradox, and sounds at once critical and revelatory, particularly in entrepreneurial, consumerist societies in which choice and individuality are dominant cultural themes. The conventional idea of freedom contrasts sharply with the notion of being dominated, or being ruled. To suggest that we are ruled "through our freedom"—that what we cherish as our autonomy, our individuality, our independence of power relations, is precisely the basis for our being governed by others—sounds analytically audacious and devastating in its political implications. If the governmentality literature has a central *critical* claim, then this is undoubtedly it.

However, on closer inspection, this claim turns out to be less interesting than it at first seems. When used in respect of "neo-liberal" practices of government, the idea of "governing through freedom" is a misleading characterization of the phenomenon. When used in respect of the formation of free persons, it turns out to be very close to certain sociological accounts of individual socialization.

Underlying the claims about "governing through freedom" and the notion that "power presupposes freedom" is a punning conflation between two ideas which are actually quite distinct: the concept of *agency*, and the concept of *freedom*.[8] These two concepts are being run together here as if they were the same thing, when in fact they are importantly different.

The idea of agency refers to the capacity of an agent for action, its possession of the "power to act," which is the capacity to originate such actions on the basis of calculations and decisions. Agency is a universal attribute of (socialized) human beings, as well as of human organizations and corporate entities. The exercise of directive power in the social sphere is, as Foucault suggests, dependent upon this human capacity for action, as are the various techniques of rule-at-a-distance, which depend upon the calculative actions of dispersed decision-makers.

Freedom, on the other hand, generally refers to a capacity to choose one's actions without external constraint.[9] Freedom (unlike agency) is necessarily a matter of degree—it is the configured range of unconstrained choice in which agency can operate. The truth is that the exercise of governmental power, and particularly neo-liberal techniques of government, rely upon, and stimulate, *agency* while simultaneously reconfiguring (rather than removing) the *constraints* upon the freedom of choice of the agent.

[...]

The neo-liberal strategy is to require all the actors in an organization to become "responsible decision-makers"—which is to say agents who are subjected to the penalties for failure or error, and who must carry out calculative work which would previously have been done by others on a more centralized basis. Allowing "agency"—in the sense of specific powers of decision—is sometimes liberating, sometimes not. It depends upon contexts and constraints. Devolving budgetary allocation powers while cutting budgets—a typical neo-liberal practice—often means that subordinates in organizations have to take on the unwelcome task of imposing cuts. Allowing agency in other circumstances can extend decision-making powers in ways that are experienced as empowering. It all depends. The analysis of these arrangements and the modes of governing that they entail is of great importance for contemporary criminology because the field of crime control is nowadays traversed by practices of this kind. The governmentality literature has been developed specifically to anatomize these arrangements and offers a powerful tool for this task, provided one steers clear of its rhetorical slips and conflations.

Making up Free Subjects

The phrase "govern through freedom" is also used to refer to the "making up" of persons, whose preferences and durable dispositions are oriented towards a set of objectives that coincide with those promoted by governing authorities. (Examples would include the active citizen, the consumer, the enterprising subject, the psychiatric outpatient, etc.) Precisely because these preferences and objectives have been internalized, they have the experiential quality of being "freely chosen" by the individual. But, as the governmentality literature points out, authorities and experts and powers of various kinds play a large part in "making up" the persons in these ways, as do the technologies of the self and conceptions of personhood that these authorities promote.

I find no fault with this analysis, though it must be said that there is nothing particularly original in it. The socialization processes whereby cultural practices interact with developing individuals (who possess the evolved potentialities of the human organism) to produce individuated social agents, capable of intentional, meaningful action, is one that is very familiar to readers of sociological textbooks. So too is the paradox, pointed out by Nietzsche (1956) (but better analyzed by Durkheim [1973] or Mead [1934]), that to become "free" (by which he means capable of willing and directing our own conscious action) we must first be subjected to the controls and disciplines and learning experiences of socialization.[10]

Moreover, the Foucauldian approach tends to focus upon the identification and analysis of "technologies of the self" and their relation to broader governmental strategies, and it has little to say about the question of how particular personal styles come to be adopted by particular social groups, or the psychological processes involved in embracing an individual self-conception. The governmentality literature doesn't tell us much about who "chooses" particular identities, and why, or about the process of "choosing" and the limits of choice. Nor does it have anything to say about the durability of these internalized dispositions in the absence of the external rituals and processes that sanction and reinforce them. It thus leaves off from these questions at a point where sociological and criminological research might want to begin.

Rationalities and Technologies as Ideal Types
The anatomization of rationalities and technologies is one of the strengths of the governmentality approach. But it would be a mistake to focus upon the structure of conceptual and technological assemblages at the expense of an analysis of the pragmatics of use. There is a need to study the way that these knowledges and techniques are put to use, and the meanings they acquire in context. We need to examine the extent to which they are implemented, their corruption in practice, the unforeseen consequences that they produce, and the relation they establish with the field that they seek to govern.

[...]

Despite Foucault's explicit concern with power and practices and the history of the present, there remains in his work—and in the work of his followers—the traces of his previous incarnation as a "historian of systems of thought" and an archaeologist whose concern is to uncover and differentiate *epistemes*. In other words, there is a tendency to use historical materials *philosophically* to demonstrate that there are different ways of knowing, rather than asking, as a sociologist or historian might, "how did these things function?" and "what did these things mean?" The result is the analytical reconstruction of what are, in effect, historically grounded ideal types. The rationalities and technologies are presented in an abstracted, perfected, fully formed way. They are compared one to the other, and their contrasts are taken to suggest the contrasts between different historical periods or social arrangements. But as Weber (1985) makes clear in *his* methodology of ideal types, the creation of such abstractions is not an end in itself but rather a heuristic step in the process of empirical analysis. The abstracted entities ("the spirit of capitalism," "formal-rational law," "neo-liberal rationality") allow the analyst to investigate the messy realm of practices and relations and the compromised, corrupted, partial ways in which these entities inhabit the real world. Ideal types—or reconstructed rationalities—are a basis for empirical analysis, not a substitute for it.

[...]

Programmes and Problems

The governmentality literature takes it as axiomatic that government is a problem-solving activity—a way of programming the social world to correct problems that emerge there. Indeed the chief concern of this approach is to specify how authorities come to understand and manage their relations to the problematized field, and the forms of power, knowledge and technology necessary to these activities. However, the literature tends to conceptualize these problems and fields *through* the perceptual grid of the programmes and rationalities that the authorities generate to deal with them. There is no concern to establish an independent analysis of its own. Consequently, there is no attempt to measure the authorities' analysis against an alternative, avowedly more realistic account, different from that of the programmers. This seems to me to be a weakness, particularly in relation to the analysis of crime control.

[...]

My view is not that state discourses and programmes disguise their true meaning and have to be read obliquely or contextually to uncover their concealed purposes and objectives—although this is sometimes the case (see Garland, 1985). Most of the time one can take at face value the claim that the authorities would like to reduce crime, protect citizens, do justice, uphold the rule of law and so on. I agree with the Foucauldians that programmatic social policy objectives are usually just what they say and not some devious cover for capitalist class interests, the reproduction of patriarchy, or some other system-function. But because programmers are usually candid in their concerns doesn't mean that they are correct in their analysis. It is precisely because the authorities' analysis can be incorrect—based on false assumptions about how the world works, how "the crime problem" is created, how punishments have their effects, etc.—that one wants to generate alternative accounts. Moreover, these alternative analytical accounts are crucial if one wants to explain not just the nature of programmes but also the impact that they have in the fields that they govern.[11] A history of the present should do more than anatomize the governmental programmes that are brought to bear. It should also seek to explain the pattern of their effects, including their failures and unanticipated consequences.

[...]

Non-instrumental Rationalities of Government

The governmentality analysis is carefully attuned to technical and knowledge-based rationalities, but it tends to neglect the expressive, emotionally driven and morally toned currents that play such a large part in the shaping of penal policy. Foucault's work tended to avoid what other theorists refer to as the "ideological" aspects of government (see Cousins and Hussain, 1986). It focused upon the techniques and practices that directly shape subjectivity and action, rather than upon the symbols and values which, if they influence action at all, do so through the medium of representations and actors' consciousness. In a similar vein, the governmentality literature also focuses upon instrumental rationalities to the neglect of what Weber would term "value-rational" frameworks of action.

Value-rational conduct tends to be poorly theorized but strongly emotive and expressive. Its logic is absolutist not strategic. Its heavily symbolic discourse is grounded in values rather than knowledge, and its dynamic force is collective emotion rather than instrumental calculation. As I have argued elsewhere (Garland, 1990), penal policy is partly shaped by forces of this kind, and it is a failing of the Foucauldian approach that it tends to neglect these, or else to translate them into forms of instrumentality, such as the "sovereign" mode of exercising power.[12]

[...]

Nor is this expressive populism merely a matter of empty political gestures or symbols without substance. As Bottoms (1995) and Garland (1996) argue, it is a political force that has shaped recent penal practice in the UK, the USA and elsewhere. Indeed, it seems plausible to suggest that populist and "governmentalized" politics are actually twinned, antithetical phenomena—the first provoking the second as a kind of backlash against the rule of experts and the dominance of professional elites. The facility with which politicians in the 1990s are able to sideline expert opinion by appealing directly to (their representations of) "what the people want" strongly suggests a level of popular antagonism to a professionalized system that is experienced as failing. It also indicates a decline in the organized power of professional groups such as social workers, psychologists and criminologists who staff that system. Contemporary populism expresses the discontents of a governmentalized state. It invokes a set of political forces hostile to the professional establishment that until recently dominated penal policy making.

Governmentality and Sociological Analysis

The criticism that an approach "doesn't deal with everything" is not a particularly damaging one. All analytical frameworks are partial, and there is much to be gained by specificity and the targeting of enquiry. My argument has been that an effective history of the present must go beyond the reconstruction of abstracted rationalities and enquire about the ways in which the rationalities and technologies of government are instantiated in the actual practices and discourses that make up a field. My discussion—of ideal types, programmes and problems, and non-instrumental rationalities—has tried to show that governmentality research inevitably raises a series of sociological questions as soon as it moves away from an archaeological stance towards an attempt to make sense of the present. Governmentality studies do pose a distinctive set of research questions. But in pursuing these questions, they inevitably begs a series of more familiar sociological problems, the resolution of which is important to the results of the enquiry. Rather than viewing governmentality research as an autonomous mode of enquiry, it should be developed in conjunction with the sociological tools necessary to it.

The methodological arguments of some governmentality writers give the impression that "sociology" as such is somehow incompatible with their style of analysis. But it would be more accurate to say that *some forms* of sociological analysis are incompatible with governmentality research, while others are not. Foucault's own analyses make no attempt to locate his own positions vis-à-vis contemporary sociology. His is the voice of a strong author who has set aside "the anxiety of influence" (Bloom, 1973). The work of other governmentality writers—notably Rose and Miller (1992), Mitchell Dean (1994) and Colin Gordon (1991)—does discuss their relation to sociology, but the overall impression these discussions create is that governmentality studies raise quite different questions than do sociological enquiries, and are conceptually and epistemologically incompatible with sociological approaches. There is also a rejection of systematic generalization and theory-building, which reinforces the tendency to distinguish governmentality studies quite sharply from all forms of sociological analysis.[13]

It is of course true that there are many forms of sociological theory, and that some of them—notably the state-centred, Marxism-influenced social control theories of the

1970s (to which the governmentality writers frequently refer)—are indeed at odds with the assumptions, methods and analytical claims of the governmentality work. But to many sociologists, that brand of Marxist theory was always decidedly unsociological, and it can hardly be said to exhaust the analytical range of sociological work. Indeed, the inordinate stress which that approach gave to the powers of the state, and its recasting of the idea of "social control" to mean state control, were actually at odds with the original and abiding mainstream concerns of sociology, which generally focused upon the effects of power structures and spontaneous social controls in non-state organizations, such as closed institutions, communities, families, workplaces and professional settings.

Many sociologists will have little trouble accepting the Foucauldian claim that power is dispersed throughout society as well as being concentrated in the state, and that power operates through networks of action that traverse the legal-constitutional divisions that supposedly separate the state from civil society. Nor will this view upset the standard assumptions of historical sociology, which have generated many studies of the reformation of morals, of religious movements, of the mass mobilization, and of the social history of total war. In that sociology, many of the positions developed by the late Foucault have long been the orienting premises of research. Similarly, the Foucauldian rejection of the idea of a unified, totalized conception of "society" in favour of a more open-ended, pluralist account of social relations and institutions is actually well established in parts of the sociological literature— not least the tradition that stems from the work of Max Weber (see also Hirst and Woolley, 1982; Mann, 1986).

In the light of this, it would seem unhelpful to regard governmentality studies and sociological analysis as mutually exclusive undertakings.[14] The idea of "rationalities of rule"—and the analysis of the ways of thinking and acting that they entail—is a major contribution of the Foucauldian approach, and has already produced a corpus of substantive research. There is no reason why studies of governmentality cannot be extended and enhanced by drawing upon sociological analysis, or at least upon those forms of sociology which, like Foucault, reject the idea of a unified category of "society" and adopt a pluralist conception of social relations and forms of power. As I have tried to demonstrate here, recourse to more conventional historical and sociological scholarship will be necessary if the aim of the analysis is to understand a field of practices such as crime control. This does not mean that those working on governmentality must give up what they do and retrain as historians or empirical sociologists. But it does mean that a more fruitful dialogue might be encouraged between these forms of work. Theoretical criminology has much to gain from, and perhaps something to offer to, a dialogue of this kind.

■ NOTES

I wish to thank Peter Goodrich, Alan Hunt, James B. Jacobs, Pat O'Malley, Alan Pottage, Nikolas Rose, Clifford Shearing, Richard Sparks, Neil Walker, Gary Wickham, Peter Young and the participants in the Workshop on New Forms of Governance, Toronto, 25–26 October 1996 for their helpful comments on this article.

1. This article aims to engage two rather different audiences. Its first concern is to address theoretically inclined criminologists who are not familiar with the governmentality literature and for whom this can serve as an introduction. The other imagined readership (with whom it seeks to open a critical dialogue) is already familiar with the governmentality literature and might be advised to proceed directly to Part Two.

2. Perhaps "clarified" would be more accurate than "revised" here. Foucault's later discussions of power differ from those of *Discipline and Punish* in their analytical emphasis and analytical context rather than in their conceptual structure.

3. Although it did not use the language of governmentality, and was in fact produced around the same time as Foucault's first lectures on the theme, Donzelot's work is very clearly about the practices of government and the way that these link up with state politics and technologies of the self.

4. For a rather different analysis of the sociological implications of "risk" in modern society, see Beck (1992).

5. Or more precisely, at the level of the risk-category in which groups of individuals can be located because they share characteristics with others who have, in the past, been victims of similar harms.

6. This points up an important contradiction in contemporary criminal justice. The legal framework, which dominates current sentencing practice, assumes the truth of the fiction that individuals who are not mentally ill are therefore "responsible" and proceeds to deal with them on this basis. The prison authorities, on the other hand, recognize that many offenders lack the learned capacity for responsible action and put into place a machinery for creating and reinforcing this absent capacity—a machinery which no doubt fails much of the time. The responsible offender is thus conjured in and out of existence by the different working ideologies of criminal justice agencies.

7. Simon (1993) provides an excellent analysis of how U.S. parole officers try to introduce a measure of structure and routine into the "disorganized" lives of their (workless) clients.

8. What makes this pun possible is the 19th-century idea of "free-will," which characterized human beings as "free agents" as opposed to "causally determined" non-agents. Neither Foucault nor subsequent writers on governmentality subscribe to this crude conception, but its familiarity allows the agency–freedom conflation.

9. It would be a true paradox to claim that a person can be governed through free-dom if "freedom" is defined in this conventional way. It would amount to saying that the realm of the unconstrained is constrained. Any such freedom would be an illusion. Dahl and Lindblom long ago discussed the ability of "manipulative" forms of power (such as advertising) to create this illusion by their ability to "simulate feelings of 'free choice' and evoke enthusiasm and initiative" (quoted in Wrong, 1988: 28).

10. See Hunter (1996) and Hindess (1996) for lucid analyses of this paradox in the context of research on governmentality.

11. There is, of course, no innocent or privileged extra-theoretical access to "how things really are." The alternative analytical account proposed here will depend upon socio-logical and historical positions that may themselves be challenged. But this alterna-tive account has the benefit of being free of the particular political and institutional commitments that anchor the analyses of programmers and officials, and its own commitments (to the disciplines of sociology, to the field of academic discourse, to its institutions and politics) and its own methods may provide it with a better claim to social understanding and explanation.

12. Politicians and others may, of course, engage in the politics of expressive justice for instrumental reasons. See Anderson (1995) for a case study.

13. The rejection of theory-building seems to flow from the anti-essentialist and anti-totalizing pluralism of Foucauldian analysis (and has echoes of old battles against the-oretical Marxism). But the wish to avoid dogma in its reductionist or universalizing forms need not mean that analytical conclusions must be limited to local studies and instant cases. Generalization and theory-building (which are fundamental aspects of scientific enquiry) should be limited only by the characteristics of the field under study and the scope it offers for legitimate generalization across different cases, not by *a priori* considerations. Theoretical work need not aim to produce "grand theory" or totalized accounts of "society" and its (singular) "history."

14. Note that Foucault's own work—which often drew heavily upon the historical sociology of the Annales school (see Foucault, 1977: 75–6)—neither proposed nor ad-hered to a rigid demarcation of this kind. It is also worth bearing in mind that some of the questions and problems developed in the Foucauldian literature have also been addressed—albeit from different theoretical starting points and assumptions—by sociological scholars. Durkheim (1973), Mead (1934), Cooley (1920) and Elias (1978, 1982) analyze the social moulding of subjects capable of self-directed, intentional con-duct. Each of these writers argues that social controls ("government") operate in and through the individual, rather than against individuality. Like Foucault, they view individuality, in its various forms, as an expression of social and cultural routines,

not an escape from them. The link between strategies of governing others and technologies for governing selves is, of course, addressed by Weber (1985) and, rather differently, by Elias (1978, 1982). Philip Selznick (1969, 1992; Nonet and Selznick, 1978) analyzes the potential and problems of what Foucauldians call "governing-at-a-distance." His work has influenced that of Teubner and Luhmann, whose systems theory research addresses related problems of regulation and self-regulation from a rather different theoretical starting point.

■ REFERENCES

Adams, J. *Risk*. London: UCL Press, 1995.

Anderson, D.C. *Crime and the Politics of Hysteria*. New York: Times Books, 1995.

Audit Commission. *Going Straight: Developing Good Practice in the Probation Service*. London: Audit Commission, 1991.

Audit Commission. *Helping with Enquiries: Tackling Crime Effectively*. London: Audit Commission, 1993.

Audit Commission. *Misspent Youth: Young People and Crime*. London: Audit Commission, 1996.

Barry, A., T. Osborne and N. Rose. *Economy and Society Special Issue on Liberalism and Governmentality*. London: Routledge, 1993.

Barry, A., T. Osborne and N. Rose, eds. *Foucault and Political Reason. Liberalism, Neo-liberalism and Rationalities of Government*. Chicago: Chicago University Press, 1996.

Bayley, D. *Police for the Future*. New York: Oxford University Press, 1994.

Beck, U. *The Risk Society: Towards a New Modernity*. London: Sage, 1992.

Becker, G. "Crime and Punishment: An Economic Approach," *Journal of Political Economy* 76 (1968): 128–47.

Bloom, H. *The Anxiety of Influence*. New York: Free Press, 1973.

Bottoms, A.E. "The Philosophy and Politics of Sentencing and Punishment." In *The Politics of Sentencing*, edited by C. Clarkson and R. Morgan. Oxford: Clarendon Press, 1995.

Burchell, G. "Peculiar Interests: Civil Society and Governing the System of Natural Liberty." In *The Foucault Effect. Studies in Governmentality*, edited by G. Burchell, C. Gordon and P. Miller, 119–50. London: Harvester Wheatsheaf, 1991.

Burchell, G. "Liberal Government and Techniques of the Self." In *Foucault and Political Reason*, edited by A. Barry, T. Osborne and N. Rose. Chicago: Chicago University Press, 1996.

Burchell, G., C. Gordon and P. Miller, eds. *The Foucault Effect: Studies in Governmentality*.

London: Harvester Wheatsheaf, 1991.

Castel, R. "From Dangerousness to Risk." In *The Foucault Effect*, edited by G. Burchell, C. Gordon and P. Miller. London: Harvester Wheatsheaf, 1991.

Castel, R. "'Problematization' as a Mode of Reading History." In *Foucault and the Writing of History*, edited by J. Goldstein. Oxford: Blackwell, 1994.

Clarke, R. and D. Cornish. "Introduction." In *The Reasoning Criminal: Rational Choice Perspectives on Offending* , edited by R. Clarke and D. Cornish. New York: Springer-Verlag, 1986.

Cook, P.J. "The Demand and Supply of Criminal Opportunities." *Crime and Justice* 9 (1986): 1–27.

Cooley, C.H. *Social Process*. New York: Scribner, 1920.

Coser, L.A. "The Notion of Control in Sociological Theory." In *Social Control: Views from the Social Sciences*, edited by J.P. Gibbs. Beverly Hills: Sage, 1982.

Cousins, M. and A. Hussain. "The Question of Ideology: Althusser, Pecheux and Foucault." In *Power, Action and Belief: A New Sociology of Knowledge*, edited by J. Law. London: Routledge, 1986.

Dean, M. *The Constitution of Poverty: Towards a Genealogy of Liberal Governance*. London: Routledge, 1991.

Dean, M. *Critical and Effective Histories: Foucault's Methods and Historical Sociology*. London: Routledge, 1994.

Dean, M. "Foucault, Government and the Enfolding of Authority." In *Foucault and Political Reason*, edited by A. Barry, T. Osborne and N. Rose. Chicago: Chicago University Press, 1996.

Donzelot, J. *The Policing of Families*. London: Hutchinson, 1979.

Donzelot, J. "The Mobilization of Society." In *The Foucault Effect*, edited by G. Burchell, C. Gordon and P. Miller. London: Harvester Wheatsheaf, 1991a.

Donzelot, J. "Pleasure in Work." In *The Foucault Effect*, edited by G. Burchell, C. Gordon and P. Miller. London: Harvester Wheatsheaf, 1991b.

Durkheim, E. *Moral Education*. New York: Free Press, 1973.

Elias, N. *The Civilizing Process: The History of Manners*. Volume 1. Oxford: Basil Blackwell, 1978.

Elias, N. *The Civilizing Process: State Formation and Civilization*. Volume 2. Oxford: Basil Blackwell, 1982.

Ewald, F. "Insurance and Risk." In *The Foucault Effect* , edited by G. Burchell, C. Gordon and P. Miller. London: Harvester Wheatsheaf, 1991.

Feeley, M. and J. Simon. "The New Penology: Notes on the Emerging Strategy of Corrections and Its Implication." *Criminology* 30 (1992): 449–74.

Feeley, M. and J. Simon. "Actuarial Justice: The Emerging New Criminal Law." In *The*

Futures of Criminology, edited by D. Nelkin. London: Sage, 1994.

Ferrant, A. "Containing the Crisis: Spatial Strategies and the Scottish Prison System." Ph.D. dissertation. Geography Department, University of Edinburgh, 1997.

Foucault, M. *Discipline and Punish*. London: Allen Lane, 1977.

Foucault, M. *The History of Sexuality: An Introduction*. Volume I. London: Penguin, 1979.

Foucault, M. *Power/Knowledge: Selected Interviews and Other Writings 1972–1977*, edited by Colin Gordon. New York: Pantheon, 1980.

Foucault, M. "Omnes et Singulatim: Towards a Criticism of 'Political Reason.'" In *The Tanner Lectures on Human Values II*, edited by S. McMurrin, 223–54. Salt Lake City: University of Utah Press, 1981.

Foucault, M. "The Subject and Power." In *Michel Foucault*, 2nd Edition, edited by H.L. Dreyfus and P. Rabinow. Chicago: Chicago University Press, 1982.

Foucault, M. *The Use of Pleasure: The History of Sexuality*. Volume 2. London: Penguin, 1987a.

Foucault, M. *The Care of the Self: The History of Sexuality*. Volume 3. London: Penguin, 1987b.

Foucault, M. "Governmentality." In *The Foucault Effect*, edited by G. Burchell, C. Gordon and P. Miller. London: Harvester Wheatsheaf, 1991.

Garland, D. *Punishment and Welfare*. Aldershot: Gower, 1985.

Garland, D. *Punishment and Modern Society*. Oxford: Clarendon Press, 1990.

Garland, D. "Social Control." In *The Social Science Encyclopedia*, edited by A. and J. Kuper. London: Routledge, 1995.

Garland, D. "The Limits of the Sovereign State: Strategies of Crime Control in Contemporary Society." *British Journal of Criminology* 36(4) (1996): 445–71.

Garland, D. "The Punitive Society: Penology, Criminology, and the History of the Present." *Edinburgh Law Review* 1(2) (1997): 1–20.

Gemmell, M. *The Monitoring and Evaluation of the Sentence Planning Initiative: Interim Report*. Edinburgh: Scottish Prison Service, 1993.

Giddens, A. *The Constitution of Society*. Cambridge: Polity, 1984.

Giddens, A. The Consequences of Modernity. Cambridge: Polity, 1990.

Gordon, C. "Governmental Rationality: An Introduction." In *The Foucault Effect* , edited by G. Burchell, C. Gordon and P. Miller. London: Harvester Wheatsheaf, 1991.

Hacking, I. "Making Up People." In *Reconstructing Individualism*, edited by T. Heller, M. Sosna and D. Wellbery. Stanford: Stanford University Press, 1986.

Hacking, I. *The Taming of Chance*. Cambridge: Cambridge University Press, 1990.

Hacking, I. "How Should We Do the History of Statistics?" In *The Foucault Effect*, edited by G. Burchell, C. Gordon and P. Miller. London: Harvester Wheatsheaf, 1991.

Heimer, C. *Reactive Risk and Rational Action: Managing Moral Hazard in Insurance Contracts*. Berkeley: University of California Press, 1985.

Heydebrand, W. and C. Seron. *Rationalizing Justice*. Albany: SUNY Press, 1990.

Hindess, B. "Liberalism, Socialism and Democracy: Variations on a Governmental Theme." In *Foucault and Political Reason*, edited by A. Barry, T. Osborne and N. Rose. Chicago: Chicago University Press, 1996.

Hirst, P. "The Genesis of the Social." *Power and Politics* 3 (1980): 67–83.

Hirst, P. and P. Woolley. *Social Relations and Human Attributes*. London: Tavistock, 1982.

Hunt, A. "Governing the City: Liberalism and Early Modern Forms of Governance." In *Foucault and Political Reason*, edited by A. Barry, T. Osborne and N. Rose. Chicago: Chicago University Press, 1996.

Hunt, A. and G. Wickham. *Foucault and Law*. London: Pluto Press, 1994.

Hunter, I. "Assembling the School." In *Foucault and Political Reason*, edited by A. Barry, T. Osborne and N. Rose. Chicago: Chicago University Press, 1996.

Janowitz, M. "Social Control and Sociological Theory." *American Journal of Sociology* 81(1) (1975): 82–108.

Latour, B. "The Powers of Association." In *Power, Action and Belief*, edited by J. Law. London: Routledge, 1986.

Latour, B. *Science in Action*. Milton Keynes: Open University Press, 1987.

Litton, R.A. *Crime and Crime Prevention for Insurance Practice*. Aldershot: Avebury, 1990.

Mann, M. *The Sources of Social Power*. Cambridge: Cambridge University Press, 1986.

Mead, G.H. *Mind, Self and Society*. Volume 1. Chicago: University of Chicago Press, 1934.

Miller, P. and N. Rose. "Governing Economic Life." *Economy and Society* 19 (1990): 1–19.

Nietzsche, F. *The Genealogy of Morals*. New York: Anchor Books, 1956.

Nonet, P. and P. Selznick. *Law and Society in Transition: Towards Responsive Law*. New York: Harper and Row, 1978.

O'Malley, P. "Risk, Power and Crime Prevention." *Economy and Society* 21(3) (1992): 252–75.

O'Malley, P. "Risk and Responsibility." In *Foucault and Political Reason*, edited by A. Barry, T. Osborne and N. Rose. Chicago: Chicago University Press, 1996.

Pasquino, P. "Theatrum Politicum: The Genealogy of Capital—Police and the State of Prosperity." In *The Foucault Effect*, edited by G. Burchell, C. Gordon and P. Miller. London: Harvester Wheatsheaf, 1991.

Peters, A.A.G. "Main Currents in Criminal Law Theory." In *Criminal Law in Action*, edited by J.J. van Dijk et al. Arnhem: Gouda Quint,1986.

Radzinowicz, L. *The History of the English Criminal Law and Its Administration*. Volume 3. London: Stevens, 1956.

Rose, N. "Governing 'Advanced' Liberal Democracies." In *Foucault and Political Reason*, edited by A. Barry, T. Osborne and N. Rose. Chicago: Chicago University Press, 1996.

Rose, N. and P. Miller. "Political Power beyond the State: Problematics of Government." *The*

British Journal of Sociology 43(2) (1992): 172–205.

Ross, E.A. *Social Control.* Boston, MA: Bacon, 1901.

Selznick, P. *Law, Society and Industrial Justice.* New York: Russell Sage Foundation, 1969.

Selznick, P. *The Moral Commonwealth.* Berkeley: University of California Press, 1992.

Shearing, C. and P. Stenning. "From the Panopticon to Disneyworld: The Development of Discipline." In *Perspectives in Criminal Law,* edited by A. Doob and E. Greenspan. Aurora: Canada Law Book Co., 1985.

Simon, J. "The Rise of Risk: Insurance, Law and the State." *Socialist Review* 95 (1987): 61–89.

Simon, J. "The Ideological Effects of Actuarial Practices." *Law and Society Review* 22 (1988): 772–800.

Simon, J. *Poor Discipline: Parole and the Social Control of the Underclass, 1890–1990.* Chicago: University of Chicago Press, 1993.

Simon, J. and M. Feeley. "True Crime: The New Penology and Public Discourse on Crime." In *Punishment and Social Control,* edited by T. Blomberg and S. Cohen. New York: Walter de Gruyter, 1995.

Skinner, Q. "Meaning and Understanding in the History of Ideas." *History and Theory* 8 (1969): 3–53.

Stenson, K. "Community Policing as a Governmental Technology." In *Economy and Society Special Issue on Liberalism and Governmentality,* edited by A. Barry, T. Osborne and N. Rose. London: Routledge, 1993.

Tuck, M. "Community and the Criminal Justice System." *Policy Studies* 12(3) (1991): 22–37.

van Dijk, J.J.M. "Understanding Crime Rates: On the Interactions between the Rational Choices of Victims and Offenders." *British Journal of Criminology* 34 (2) (1994): 105–21.

Walker, S. *Taming the System: The Control of Discretion in Criminal Justice, 1950–1990.* New York: Oxford University Press, 1993.

Weber, M. *The Protestant Ethic and the Spirit of Capitalism.* London: Unwin Paperbacks, 1985.

Wrong, D. *Power.* Oxford: Basil Blackwell, 1988.

■ CRITICAL THINKING QUESTIONS

1. What is Dean's critique of Corrigan's approach to moral regulation? Why does he see Foucault's theory of governmentality as a more useful approach to regulation? Why does he emphasize ethical self-formation over cultural moral regulation?

2. Valverde writes that Alcoholics Anonymous employs an "innovative approach to ethical governance, an approach relying primarily on self-governance rather than advice or exhortation" (p. 120). How does AA do this, and why is this significant? How is Valverde's study of Alcoholics Anonymous an articulation of Dean's theoretical formulations?

3. Both Dean and Valverde move the analysis away from the state and generate an approach to moral regulation that focuses on the ways that individuals are encouraged to conform their innermost selves through working on their own ethical self-formation. How does this more Foucauldian approach differ from other moral regulation studies examined in this text? With which approach are you more sympathetic, and why?

4. What is Chunn and Gavigan's critique of moral regulation as a concept and as a methodology? How does this link to their earlier critiques of social control? Why do they now argue for a return to theories of social control alongside a theory of moral regulation? Do you think these are compatible approaches? Why or why not?

5. What is Garland's critique of Foucault and governmentality? Why does Garland argue that the Foucauldian project is not always adequate to understanding crime and crime control? What does he mean when he says that a more "sociological" analysis is necessary to supplement Foucault's contributions? What role should power, the state, and agency play as we build our analyses of crime, "normality," and deviance?

■ FURTHER READINGS

Graham Burchell, Colin Gordon, Peter Miller, eds. *The Foucault Effect: Studies in Governmentality.* London: Harvester Wheatsheaf, 1991.

    This collection of essays, including by Foucault, has established the groundwork for governmentality studies. This is essential reading for those interested in pursuing the idea of governmentality.

Kelly Hannah-Moffat. *Punishment in Disguise: Penal Governance and Federal Imprisonment of Women in Canada.* Toronto: University of Toronto Press, 2001.

Hannah-Moffat's study of the federal Prison for Women is an excellent application of a feminist and Foucauldian governmentality analysis. Tracing the genealogy of women's imprisonment in Canada, Hannah-Moffat demonstrates the combined effects of both state and non-state actors on the character and meanings of the incarceration of federally sentenced women.

Richard Ericson and Aaron Doyle, eds. *Risk and Morality.* Toronto: University of Toronto Press, 2003.

While risk discourses have come to characterize criminological research, this collection of essays demonstrates how "these discourses and practices are always imbued with moral language and ethical clauses" (p. 1). Alan Hunt's essay, in particular, directly links risk studies with moral regulation. Together, these diverse and interdisciplinary contributions indicate one important direction that those interested in regulation, crime, and morality have taken up.

COPYRIGHT ACKNOWLEDGEMENTS